The
BFI Companion
to Eastern European
and Russian Cinema

Edited by

Richard Taylor, Nancy Wood,
Julian Graffy and Dina Iordanova

Series Editor: Ginette Vincendeau

bfi Publishing

First published in 2000 by the
British Film Institute
21 Stephen St, London W1P 2LN

The British Film Institute is the UK national agency with responsibility for
encouraging the arts of film and television and conserving them in the national
interest.

Set in 9.5/11pt Times Ten by Fakenham Photosetting Limited, Fakenham, Norfolk
Printed in Great Britain by St Edmundsbury Press, Bury St Edmunds

Cover designed by Megan Smith
Cover images: (front) *Burnt by the Sun* (Mikhalkov, 1994); (back) *Blind Chance*
(Kieślowski, 1981).

British Library Cataloguing-in-Publication Data
A catalogue record for this book is available from the British Library
ISBN 0–85170–752–1 (hbk)
ISBN 0–85170–753–X (pbk)

CONTENTS

ACKNOWLEDGMENTS

All credit for the East European Cinema section is due to the contributors whose expertise and dedication made viable a potentially unwieldy project: Peter Hames, Ronald Holloway, Dina Iordanova, András Bálint Kovács, Matthew May, Stojan Pelko, Ania Witkowska. NW

I would like to acknowledge the prompt and efficient help of John M. Bates, Eva Bernath, Jan Culik, Ludmila Cvikova, Nevena Dakovic and Marko Zivkovic. If it was not for their responsiveness, the entries which I contributed would have been incomplete. DI

CONTRIBUTORS

Editors

Richard Taylor is Professor of Politics and Russian Studies at the University of Wales, Swansea. General editor of Eisenstein's *Selected Works* and author and editor of numerous books on Russian and Soviet cinema, including *The Politics of Soviet Cinema 1917–1929*, *Inside the Film Factory* (with Ian Christie), and *The Battleship Potemkin*.

Nancy Wood is Senior Lecturer in media studies at the University of Sussex (UK), co-editor of *In Search of Central Europe* and former managing editor of *East European Reporter*; currently researching the role of memory in postwar European political culture.

Julian Graffy is Senior Lecturer in Russian at the School of Slavonic and East European Studies, University College London where he teaches courses in Russian cinema.

Dina Iordanova is a lecturer in communication at the Centre for Mass Communication Research at the University of Leicester (UK) and the author of *Film, Mass Mediation and the Balkan Crisis* (forthcoming) and of numerous articles on Eastern European cinema in, among others, *Journal of Film and Video*, *Film Criticism*, *Historical Journal of Film, Radio and TV*, and *Slavic Review*.

KEY TO CONTRIBUTORS

AW – Ania Witkowska
BB – Birgit Beumers
DI – Dina Iordanova
JC – John Caughie
JG – Julian Graffy
KAB – András Bálint Kovács
MM – Matthew May
MW – Michael Wedel
PH – Peter Hames
RH – Ron Holloway
RT – Richard Taylor
SP – Stojan Pelko

GENERAL INTRODUCTION

This book aims to bring together under one volume the breadth and variety of East European and Russian cinema in a concise, accessible and informative form. Written entirely by specialists (see **Contributors**), it is meant equally for professionals – teachers, students – and for film enthusiasts. The desire to include a considerable amount of information in a manageable and affordable single volume dictated drastic choices. A general principle has been to increase coverage, including of recent material, with a large number of short entries. The entries contain key factual points about a person, institution or critical concept, as well as areas of interest and debate, in other words not just what a person or institution did and when, but why they are interesting, famous or controversial.

The *Companion* does not claim to be exhaustive or 'impartial'; all entries express, to some extent, the opinion of their writers (who are identified by their initials – see under **Key to Contributors**). At the same time, it tries to be as inclusive and accurate as possible, given all the difficulties that such an enterprise presents. Extreme care has been taken to check all sources, in the hope of reducing errors to a minimum. All historical works have more or less hidden agendas and have to operate choices further to those dictated by constraints of space. Choices in the *Companion* have been made according to the following principles:

– the necessity to acknowledge the important figures and landmarks of East European and Russian Cinema, as sanctioned by reputable historians and by the expertise of the writers;
– the desire, at the same time, to redress the balance of established film history:

    a) towards the cinema of 'small' countries,
    b) towards popular traditions (the entertainment cinema, the despised, supposedly mediocre, genres, and the stars and directors of popular cinema often unknown outside their own countries),
    c) towards 'other voices': women, gays and lesbians, post-colonial communities;

– as far as possible, the desire to provide a perspective from *within* the cinema itself.

There are four major types of entries:

1. Historical overviews of the cinemas of the former Czechoslovakia, the former Yugoslavia, Hungary, Poland, Bulgaria, Romania and Albania. Readers unfamiliar with these national cinemas are encouraged to read these first, before 'browsing' or looking up entries.

2. *Entries on personnel*: directors, actors, cinematographers, musicians, writers and others are classified under their surname or most common name. This is followed by their date and place of birth and, as the case may be, death, as well as their real name, if relevant. The first words of the entry briefly characterise the person. To save space, the country in which a person was born and/or died is indicated next to their birth/death place only if situated outside this person's country, e.g.:

WAJDA, Andrzej   Swalki 1926

Polish director ...

but

VERTOV, Dziga   Denis A. Kaufman; Bialystok, Poland [Russian Empire] 1896 – Moscow 1954

Soviet director and theorist ...

As a rule, biographical details such as marriage and children are indicated only if considered relevant to the work or achievements of the person.

3. *Critical entries* on well-established genres or movements such as **Czech New Wave** or **Bulgarian 'poetic realism'**.

4. *Entries on institutions*, ranging from film schools (**FAMU**) and festivals to production companies, archives and other institutions.

Cross-referencing
• Within entries: an asterisk at the end of a name denotes a separate entry – for instance, 'shaped in the films directed by * ...'.
• At the end of entries (or within the text) attention may be drawn to other related entries [> CZECH NEW WAVE].

Bibliography
• At the end of entries, a single short bibliographical reference may be indicated (under **Bib**) in an abbreviated form, to direct the reader to further reading.
• At the end of the *Companion*, a general bibliography contains full references to books on East European and Russian cinema. Preference has been given to works in English, though authoritative works in other languages are included.

INTRODUCTION TO EASTERN EUROPEAN CINEMA

It would be misleading to conceive of the cinemas of Eastern Europe in monolithic terms. The fact that they appear together in a volume like this is more indicative of the geo-political order they inhabited for more than four decades of this century, than of any innately common characteristics. And even here, there are exceptions: most notably in the case of former Yugoslavia where, since Tito's break with Stalin in 1948, the country claimed the status of a non-aligned socialist state pursuing its own political, economic and cultural agenda.

If the cinemas of Eastern Europe tended to be perceived by western audiences as emanating from a common stable of themes, aesthetics and genres, this is no doubt in part due to the post-Yalta political constraints which they shared and which, however differently applied by their respective regimes, nonetheless had as their common denominator the ultimate subordination of cinema to the authority of state institutions and dictates. Cinema was not a mere reflection of the primacy of politics over art and popular culture – the Czech New Wave of the 1960s, to take just one example, would not have been possible if this were so – but film industries and cultures did develop in intimate tandem with this implacable power relation.

In the 1990s, this relation of power was dismantled as the civil societies of Eastern Europe in their turn cast off the yoke of Soviet domination (the Cold-war line dividing Europe into two was abolished and the East European countries re-emerged on their own from the shadow of the Soviet Empire. The changing international balance meant that they had to reposition themselves within the wider context of a new Europe). But this reconfiguration of geo-politics did not automatically abolish the prevailing mental division of Europe: while a 'return to Europe' became a major priority of East European countries, such ambitions encountered a Western Europe still entrenched in attitudes which confirmed an enduring separation of 'the West from the Rest'. Moreover, at the very moment when a rapprochement of Eastern Europe with Europe proper finally seemed to be gaining ground, nationalist-inspired wars in 'The Balkans' drove a new wedge into the project of European reconstruction. If, by the beginning of the new millennium, the concept of Eastern Europe as a dreary, unpredictable outpost of the Soviet Empire had become obsolete, new divisions were nonetheless in place which severed the dynamically-developing states of Central Europe from the volatile and retrogressive condition of their Balkan counterparts.

While Central Eastern Europe came nearer Europe 'proper,' the shift in the Balkans seemed to move in the opposite direction, and from a dreary unpredictable outpost of the old Soviet Empire they gravitated toward a gloomy orientalist fringe of the new Europe. The discourse on what used to be Eastern Europe during Cold-war times was more and more often replaced with the juxtaposition of Ottoman and Austro-Hungarian legacies. By the beginning of the new Millennium, the concept of Eastern Europe as an entity had grown obsolete. Developments in the economic, social, and political

1

spheres, furthered the dissolution of what used to be called Eastern Europe into Central East European and Balkan parts.

How might we summarise the transformation undergone by cinema during this stormy decade of transition? The end of the communist period brought state interference in film-making to an end, but it also initially meant massive cuts and the withdrawal of centralised government funding. The shift to a market economy affected every level of the film industry from its basic infrastructure to its mode of financing and administration. The pattern of changes in the media economy and film industries was similar throughout all East European countries: a sharp decrease in state funding, empty studios looking to attract foreign film crews, the disappearance of domestic films from the circuits, armies of idle film professionals, and the redefinition of concepts like 'copyrights', 'entertainment', and 'audience'. Freedom of expression and the end of state censorship had finally been achieved, but an emerging new constraint – let's call it 'market censorship' – now seemed to pose the greatest threat to indigenous film cultures. As the national entries show, with state budgets for culture cut to the bone, and the rapid privatisation of many cultural institutions previously supported by state subsidies, film studios* foremost among these, film production was to undergo a drastic transformation.

The funding crisis led to shrinking production, particularly in features and animation. Financing for film production changed profoundly, moving from the unit-based studio system to producer-driven undertakings. State subsidies, competitive in some countries or automatic in others, became a hotly contested territory, underlining the historical irony that the state interventionist measures once so despised) were in some cases the only hope of safeguarding and reviving the failing film industries. The involvement of national television networks in film production became of crucial importance, alongside international co-production funding and the expanding sector of private financing. Film industries grew increasingly dependent on cross-border 'runaway' productions, which could take advantage of the cheaper facilities and locations but did not allow for serious artistic input, thereby fostering a new form of Western cultural colonialism. Most studios became partially or fully privatised, and today compete in attracting foreign film crews to shoot on location.

The concurrent crisis in distribution and exhibition led to a sharp drop in box-office indicators for all productions carrying an East European label. The abolition of centralised cultural management divorced domestic film production from exhibition and distribution, and earlier distribution networks, domestically and internationally, were ruined before new ones had come into being. In some places new multiplexes were built, while elsewhere, after privatisation, film theatres were turned into bingo halls. Most of the new private distributors who emerged subsequently chose to abide strictly by market rules and to opt for Hollywood box-office winners rather than play the losing card of domestic productions. As ticket prices rose sharply, the total number of admissions declined – a decline further exacerbated by changing patterns of cultural consumption which favoured video distribution (and much to the ire of Hollywood's market moguls, the rampant growth of video piracy). Although well received at festivals, at film markets East European films were considered hard sells and performed poorly.

Between 1991 and 1994, the drop in the number of movies produced was

2

significant. More recently, however, a greater number of features are being released. After the initial disarray, and as we reach the turn of the new century, the production cycle is in the process of stabilisation, legislation is being clarified, funding mechanisms are being created and the exhibition and distribution sectors have been much improved. In some countries, the output reached former levels fairly quickly (the Czech Republic, Hungary) while in others the crisis persists (Bulgaria). The break-up of Yugoslavia has spawned separate, non-interacting mini-industries in the successor states.

Recently, critical attention has turned to the category of 'popular' European cinema in order to shift the emphasis away from a more *auteur*-dominated approach to film culture. Because of the relative absence of an independent 'civil society' in the countries of the former Soviet Empire, where popular tastes and preferences could be freely registered and expressed in non-state spheres and institutions, the *auteur*-tradition not only preserved its dominance, but functioned as a site of individual moral resistance to an ideology which eulogised the putative collective interest and will. Moreover, it is again not coincidental that the best-known cinematic *auteurs* – Wajda*, Szabó*, Jancsó*, Meszaros*, Menzel*, Makavejev*, Kusturica*, Pintilie*, Vulchanov*, to name but a few – often took as their subjects individuals whose moral trajectory was inextricably linked to the historical and political dramas undergone by their nation.

How has this specific type of auteurism fared with the transition? For a while in the 1990s, East European film-makers seemed to be losing their domestic audience. The years when people would go to the cinemas simply to see national film productions seemed to be beyond retrieval. *Auteurs* had trouble identifying to whom they were addressing their works: if they tried to appeal to the volatile mass taste they faced the overwhelming competition of imported mass culture. If they decided to address a more sophisticated audience they were doomed to failure by an underdeveloped market economy of distributors and exhibitors who were not interested in targeting scattered pockets of potential viewers.

Toward the end of the 1990s, however, some national productions came near the top of domestic box office charts. The most successful directors, like the young Czech Svěrák'* or the young Macedonian Manchevski*, are those who energetically manage to raise funds, most often from a combination of domestic and foreign sources, and who realise that securing international distribution for a film is of equal importance to obtaining production financing. For political or economic reasons, many have chosen the international path. The number of East European film-makers working in the diaspora – Poland's Agnieszka Holland* and Ryszard Bugajski*, Serbian Goran Paskaljević* and Srdjan Dragojević*, Croatian Lordan Zafranović*, Bosnian Emir Kusturica* – is growing.

Common trends and experiences characterised the great range of nationally-inflected forms of cinematic expression under state socialism. Each national cinema had its storehouse of Socialist Realist* epics dating from the late 1940s and early 1950s; most of the countries could point to films which reflected the 'thaw' of the late 1950s in their bolder investigation of social issues; Bulgaria, Czechoslovakia, Hungary and Poland all experienced virtually simultaneously a 'new wave of film-making in the 1960s, inspired by reformist political initiatives at home on the one hand, and the whiff of for-

3

mal experimentation emanating from elsewhere in Europe on the other. Meanwhile, mindful of these developments but reflecting the country's distinctive liberalisation process, Yugoslavia's socially-conscious film directors launched a 'Black Wave'* which challenged political, moral and aesthetic orthodoxies.

Looking at post-communist cinema, we would refrain from hurriedly declaring that a new, profoundly different profile of Eastern European cinema is emerging. The trend is, rather, one of continuity in topics and style. The state-financed historical super-productions are now replaced by privately financed 'heritage' super-productions. The partisan action-adventures and the socialist comedies of communist times are now replaced by Mafia action-adventures and post-socialist comedies that flagrantly target the box-office. Films focusing on the ethical concerns of everyday life, the so-called cinema of moral anxiety, have been replaced by films focusing on the drab everyday life and moral despair of post-communism. In spite of commercialisation, all East European countries continue making the same type of art films they were making before, and continue releasing films dealing with traditional thematic spheres such as history and heritage*, Stalinism*, the Holocaust*, and the experience of war. One can also pinpoint a common preoccupation with the moral life of the nation when democratic changes bring in their wake the vices and virtues of advanced capitalist economies. There is a proliferation of films focusing on the issues of ethnic minorities and the politics of ethnicity, reflected in the great interest shown in the Gypsy* genre, or the films made in response to the Yugoslav break-up* – a theme that has achieved international resonance. The traditions of lyric cinema, surrealism, magical realism, and experimental avant-garde animation are kept alive. The cinematic image of the deconstruction of the Berlin Wall was widely used by film-makers as the central metaphor of a new era. And not only at home, but also internationally, many films enjoyed a significant critical acclaim (*Kolya, Underground, Before the Rain*). In fact, if one looks at the number of festival prizes awarded to films from Eastern Europe, it will not be difficult to show that the 1990s was one of the most successful decades for East European film-making.

These successes clearly counter-balance the widely-held belief that East European cinema is undergoing a major crisis. If there is a crisis, it is one that is characteristic of European cinema in general, affecting its Western and Eastern counterparts alike, a crisis of identity in an era that marks the end of national cinemas. The volatility in East European cinema coincided with a clearly articulated period of insecurity in European cultural policies, driven by stalled trade negotiations and a growing anti-American sentiment. The establishment of pan-European funding bodies came partly as a reaction to the overwhelming triumph of commercialism in cinema. The share of international subsidies for film-making in poverty-stricken East European studios quickly increased as the concept of 'national cinema' gave way to a 'new European' one. This increasing dynamism is seen in collaborative artistic projects which cross traditional boundaries and bring together previously isolated spheres. In this respect, East European film-making has undoubtedly become an intrinsic part of European cinema, and of its culture more broadly, contributing in its own distinctive way to the eradication of lingering Cold-war divisions and tending to those war wounds more recently inflicted.

Nancy Wood and Dina Iordanova

4

INTRODUCTION TO RUSSIAN CINEMA

Russian Cinema in the 1990s

At the time the late 1980s seemed to herald a period of renewal for Soviet cinema, just as they did for all of Soviet society. With the weakening of both ideological and economic constraints the number of films produced, which had hovered around 150 per year for decades, suddenly underwent an enormous increase, reaching 300 in 1990, and the ambition and daring of the subjects of these films was breathtaking to Soviet audiences used to rigorous Party control of the industry. But just as the fabled *perestroika* turned out to be a false dawn, an end rather than a beginning, so the dangers this heady growth presented to the cinema were apparent to those who chose to look closely. Changes to the laws by which the cinema was governed meant that new independent producers could now function outside the state system, but many of those who moved into cinema production for financial motives would soon find surer ways to turn a profit. The state industry itself was moved to a system of economic self-financing, but a loosening of the distribution and exhibition system led to a huge inrush of (often third-rate) American films, which proved extremely popular with audiences who had hitherto been deprived of them. Buyers from regional and republican distribution chains at the new 'alternative' film markets increasingly declined to purchase the majority of new Soviet films. Instead, cults grew around popular American stars, such as Sylvester Stallone and Arnold Schwarzenegger, and, for more refined tastes, around directors such as Derek Jarman, Peter Greenaway and Pedro Almodovar. So called 'video salons' grew up all over the country, often showing pirated copies of films that would not get official distribution, and there was a huge growth in video piracy. Unlicensed copies of new Hollywood films could now be bought in Moscow before their British release. Private cable television channels opened up relying overwhelmingly on building up audiences by showing feature films. Most crucially of all, rampant inflation and other social crises – crises faithfully recorded in the new documentary and feature films of the time – undermined cinema-going as a mass, regular habit, a habit that had survived to a far greater extent in the Soviet Union than in the rest of Europe. Between 1986 and 1991 total attendances fell from 4,000,000,000 to 2,500,000,000, and it was estimated that there were 14,000,000 unsold seats every day. This led to increasing cinema closures, to cinemas being leased out or sold off for more lucrative uses – cinema foyers becoming video and compact disc stores, or showrooms for expensive foreign cars. Thus the fact that the Sixth Congress of the Union of Filmmakers of the USSR*, held in June 1990, presided over the reorganisation of the Union into a so-called 'Federation of Sovereign National and Territorial Organisations of Film Makers', each of them further split into guilds for the various cinematic professions, could only be seen as symbolic of larger fissures.

One year later, a far more symbolic event occurred: in August 1991 a group of political hard-liners effected a coup against Gorbachev, and for three days Moscow was in turmoil. The defeat of this coup meant the end of the system that Gorbachev had been attempting to 'rebuild' through his fabled *perestroika*. By the end of the year the Soviet Union had dissolved itself and Gorbachev was out of power.

The country was entering a new world in which everything, even its name, had changed. In these altered conditions Soviet film-makers had to learn fast – particularly about the role of the producer, a function previously carried out by state functionaries, and about marketing. Because of poor distribution and almost non-existent marketing, scarcely any of the vast numbers of Russian films being made were bringing their investors a return on their money. The number of films made each year began a vertiginous decline. From 300 in 1990 it fell to 213 in 1991, 172 in 1992, 152 in 1993, and, as economic crises recurred with sickening predictability, to sixty-eight in 1994, forty-six in 1995 and twenty-eight in 1996. In the last years of the century it would not rise far above this level.

Much was written about the 'normalisation' of post-Soviet society, and this had a profound effect upon cinema audiences. Now that they had access to an unrestricted range of cinematic product, not to mention a vastly increased range of leisure activities, the previously stable audience atomised into a number of small groups with contradictory tastes, and it would take a number of years for film-makers to identify those tastes and to produce again the genuine popular hits that were such a feature of the Brezhnev years.

Attempts were made to internationalise the Russian film industry. A number of films were made on Russian subjects with American and British money. But the artistic compromises that this involved – making films largely in English, using Western stars, and simplifying plots to make them accessible to Western audiences ill versed in Soviet history (by this very token making them laughably simplistic for Russian audiences) meant that these films satisfied neither East nor West and the experiment soon foundered. Russian directors had greater success with European, particularly French, co-productions, where there was a greater tradition of allowing directors the licence to follow their own vision, but even here some degree of compromise was inevitable, and relations between French production companies and Russian directors were rarely harmonious. One way in which the internationalisation of the industry was, indeed, successful was in the increasing tendency of Russian actors, directors and other film workers to work, and some-

6

times to base themselves, abroad. Thus the expenditure of the Russian cinema industry, on equipment and people, was increasingly in hard currency, while the income generated continued to be in the increasingly unstable rouble, a recipe for further financial disaster. For a while Russian studios tried to lease their studio space and get their technicians work on Western films made in Russia, such as Sally Potter's *Orlando* (1992), but increasing inflation put paid to this and recently Russian film-makers have found it financially viable to film abroad – much of Nikita Mikhalkov's* recent film *The Barber of Siberia*, for example, was shot at the Barrandov Studios* outside Prague.

As the decade went on, the Western interest that had been acute in the late 1980s, both in the rediscovered masterpieces that had for so long been shelved [*Glasnost* and the Cinema*], and in the new cinema of social engagement, declined. Russian films were no longer winning prizes at Western festivals, and were often not even being invited to participate in them. In Russia many of the stalwarts of the late Soviet period were finding it difficult to adapt to new conditions.

A new generation was coming to the fore, formed in the Gorbachev period and more able to adapt to conditions of independence and artistic and financial risk-taking. But the indifference shown to their films by Russian distributors and Western festival programmers alike meant that their films were failing to reach audiences. In response to this, the 1990s have witnessed a large growth both in the number and in the importance of Russian film festivals and prizes. Most important among the festivals is the so-called *Kinotavr*, officially the Open Russian, and latterly the Open International Film Festival, first held in the town of Podolsk in 1990 and held each June since 1991 in Sochi on the Black Sea. In recent years it has been able to show virtually every new feature film produced in Russia in the prior twelve months, and many of those produced in the former Soviet republics, as well as becoming a well-reported social event. The leading Russian film prizes are the Nikes, distributed each year since 1988 by the Russian Film Academy and now broadcast live on the main television channel, in a ceremony which very obviously attempts to emulate the Oscars. That these festivals and prizes are in general more attuned to the endeavours of the post-Soviet generation of film-makers is amply illustrated by events at the Yalta *Kinoforum* of 1994 when Ivan Dykhovichny*, Vladimir Khotinenko*, Alexander Khvan*, Sergei Selyanov* and Valeri Todorovsky*, all of whom have come to cinematic prominence as directors, but also, significantly, as producers, in the 1990s, were nominated as 'Directors of the Twenty-First Century'.

Increasingly, the place to see the most important and adventurous new Russian films has been on television, with a number of channels finding space for ambitious and intelligent programming strands that would be the envy of young film-makers in Britain, or on video. Simultaneous cinematic and video release is now commonplace as the new production companies, notably NTV-Profit, and STV, which is headed by the directors Sergei Selyanov and Alexei Balabanov*, aim to cope both with the non-functioning distribution system and with video piracy by setting up their own video distribution outlets.

Support also comes, once again, from the Russian state, particularly since the new law 'On State Support of Cinematography' of 1996, which in theory arranged annual state subventions of $10–15,000,000 dollars to finance production. Thus the state, which at the beginning of the decade, with the privatisation of the studios, was almost entirely removed from production funding, is once more of fundamental importance. Whereas only nineteen of almost 400 films being made in the Soviet Union at the beginning of the decade attracted state funding, by 1995 out of fifty-one films being made in Russia fifteen were fully funded and a further twenty partially funded by Roskomkino, the Russian State Cinema Committee. But the country's continuing financial crisis means that only a small percentage of these funds are actually distributed on time, and rampant inflation substantially devalues funds disbursed late. Some funds are not paid at all. The draft 1999 budget allocated 264 million roubles to the film industry, but it was expected that only 30 per cent of this figure would actually be distributed.

The Union of Filmmakers of the Russian Federation* has also attempted, in recent years, to revitalise the industry. The film director Nikita Mikhalkov* was swept into the chairmanship of the union at its Third Congress in December 1997 on a programme of renewal, planning the building and refurbishment of a chain of fully equipped modern cinemas across the country and taxes both on videos and sales to television (television channels in the Russian Federation show over three hundred hours of films over the three days of the weekend) to finance production.

The old state studios have been split up or privatised. Increasingly they are run not by the old cinema bureaucrats but by directors who have developed an acute sense of popular taste by assessing the box-office fates of their own films. Both the big studios and the many independent production companies that have developed over the decade have attempted in recent years to produce a number of low-budget films that have at least a chance, through combined theatrical release, video sales and television rights, of recouping the money spent on them.

At the century's end the Russian cinema industry is in a position with which it has grown familiar – in a prolonged crisis in which, despite all the odds, it continues to survive and in some respects to prosper. It celebrated the centenary of cinema with intelligence and resourcefulness, with specially commissioned films, with television programmes, and with book and magazine publications, on a scale that was not matched in many cinematically wealthier countries. At last, in the work of such directors as Dmitri Astrakhan*, Alexander Rogozhkin* and Alla Surikova*, it is turning out popular comedies whose mixture of nostalgia and self-mockery has found major success with audiences. At the other end of the scale it is making serious at-

8

tempts to analyse the disastrous wars the country has been recently involved in, particularly in the Caucasus, in Sergei Bodrov's* *Prisoner of the Mountains*, Vadim Abdrashitov's* *Time of the Dancer* and Rogozhkin's *Checkpoint*. It is endeavouring to depict the lives and values of a new generation of alienated young people, most notably in Alexei Balabanov's* *Brother*. It looks back without prejudice at the recent past, in Sergei Ursuliak's* *Russian Ragtime* and Dmitri Meskhiev's* *The American Bet*. It is beginning to win prizes again at international festivals, notably for the work of Alexander Sokurov, whose *Mother and Son* was one of the most internationally praised films of 1997, but also for Petr Lutsik's *Outskirts*, for Todorovsky's *The Land of the Deaf*, for Balabanov's *Of Freaks and Men*. It has won the Oscar for Best Foreign Language Film, with Mikhalkov's *Burnt by the Sun*, and been shortlisted both for Bodrov's *Prisoner of the Mountains* and for Pavel Chukhrai's* *The Thief*. It has also, in a way the Soviet industry was never entirely at home with, produced a new group of genuine stars, including Vladimir Mashkov*, Oleg Menshikov* and Sergei Makovetsky*, capable of carrying any film they play in, their reputations burnished by a number of popular TV programmes about cinema and a vibrant cinematic press [Russian and Soviet Film Press*] which makes up in enthusiasm for what it lacks in circulation figures compared with the Soviet years. It has begun the refurbishment of its cinemas, and major cities now boast some excellent cinemas with up-to-date equipment which has led to a new fashion for cinema-going (which though usually, so far, for big-budget American films is also beginning to include domestic product). It has even just produced, in Nikita Mikhalkov's *The Barber of Siberia*, one of the most expensive epics ever made outside the Hollywood system, complete with international stars, and launched it at the Kremlin Palace of Congresses. This does not look like a cinema in terminal decline.

Julian Graffy

PLATE 1: Kusturica's *Bila jedom jedna zemlja/Underground* (1995)

PLATE 2: Askoldov's *Komissar/The Commissar* (1967)

PLATE 3: Pudovkin's *Potomok Chingis-khana/Storm Over Asia* (1928)

PLATE 4: Protazanov's *Aelita* (1924)

PLATE 5: Makavejev's *W.R. – Misterije Organizma/W.R. – Mysteries of the Organism* (1971)

PLATE 6: Jancsó's *Szegénylegények/The Round-up* (1965)

PLATE 7: Forman's *Lásky jedné plavovlásky/A Blonde in Love* (1965)

PLATE 8: Krzysztof Kieślowski

PLATE 9: Švankmajer's *Lekce Faust/Faust* (1994)

PLATE 10: Sergei Eisenstein

PLATE 11: Wajda's *Popiół i Diament/Ashes and Diamonds* (1958)

A

ABDRASHITOV, Vadim Yu.

Russian director. In 1974 Abdrashitov graduated from VGIK*, where he had studied in the workshop of Mikhail Romm* and Lev Kulidzhanov*. In constant collaboration with the scriptwriter Alexander Mindadze, he made a series of films analysing the official institutions and the moral ambiguities of the late Soviet era. In *Slovo dlya zashchity/Submission for the Defence* (1977), *Povorot/ The Turning Point* (1978), *Okhota na lis/Fox Hunting* (1980), and *Ostanovilsya poezd/A Train Stopped* (1982) personal crisis forces the hitherto conformist protagonist into moral reassessment. In the allegorical *Parad planet/Parade of the Planets* (1984) a group of army reservists enters a mysterious 'other' world. *Plyumbum, ili opasnaya igra/Plumbum, or A Dangerous Game* (1986) is another parable of the dangers of blind conformism, this time in a teenage boy. In *Sluga/The Servant* (1988), a conductor picks up a hitchhiker and, as their roles are reversed, layers of Soviet corruption are revealed. After two less successful films, *Armavir* (1991), in which the sinking of a Soviet liner forces the passengers to reassess their lives, and *P'esa dlia passazhira/Piece for Passenger* (1994), Abdrashitov and Mindadze returned triumphantly to form with *Vremya tantsora/Time of the Dancer* (1997), their contribution to a recent cycle of films meditating on the Chechen and other Caucasian wars. Three friends settle on land won in a war in which two of them fought but despite the idyllic southern setting, a mounting sense of omen assails them and their families, and the film ends in anguish and tragedy, offering a bleak diagnosis of the possibilities available in contemporary Russia. The film was nominated for five Nikes, the Russian Oscars, winning two, and won the Grand Prix at the leading Russian film festival, the Sochi *Kinotavr*, in 1998. JG

ABULADZE, Tengiz E.

Georgian director. Abuladze studied at the Rustaveli Theatrical Institute in Tbilisi (1943–6) and then at VGIK*, in the workshop of Sergei Yutkevich*. In 1947, under the influence of *Ivan Groznyi/Ivan the Terrible*, he and a fellow student, Revaz Chkheidze, wrote to Eisenstein* asking for work: he told them to complete their studies first. Abuladze graduated in 1953 and returned to Tbilisi, where he joined the Gruziafilm studios. His first films were documentaries, co-directed in 1954 with Chkheidze. In 1955 they co-directed *Lurdzha Magdany/Magdana's Donkey*, which won the Best Short Film award at

Cannes in 1956. Abuladze's later films include *Chuzhie deti/Other People's Children* (1958), set in contemporary Tbilisi; *Ya, babushka, Iliko i Illarion/I, Grandmother, Iliko and Illarion* (1963), a tragi-comedy set in a mountain village; and *Ozherel'e dlya moyei lyubimoi/A Necklace for my Beloved* (1973). But his reputation rests on a trilogy of philosophical films concerned with questions of good and evil, life and death. *Vedreba/The Prayer* (Russian title *Mol'ba*) (1968), based on the poems of Vazha Pshavela, is an epic tale of love, hatred and revenge, shot in black-and-white in the harsh Georgian landscape. *Natris Khe/The Wishing Tree* ((Russian title *Drevo zhelaniya*) (1977) is set in a Georgian village before the Revolution and concerns the dreams and aspirations of a beautiful young girl and a man's search for the legendary tree that can make dreams come true. The third film of the trilogy, *Monanieba/Repentance* (Russian title *Pokayanie*) (1984) is one of the most important films of the *perestroika* period. It tells the story of the death of an old man of power, Varlam Aravidze, and the refusal of a woman, Ketevan Barateli, to let his corpse rest in peace. At the woman's trial the evil past is revealed and confusion is sown among Aravidze's surviving family, especially his son Abel (played by the same actor Avtandil Makharadze) and his grandson. Varlam Aravidze is given the physical features of Hitler, Mussolini, Beria and Stalin to turn him into a composite dictator, and Abuladze uses anachronism (blending medieval knights and Rubik cubes) to point to the universality of his parable, but the film is also decked with the realities of the Soviet 1930s. *Repentance* was written for Georgian television in 1981–2, and shot in late 1983 and early 1984. It was finally released in Tbilisi in October 1986, after support from Eduard Shevardnadze, then the Soviet Foreign Minister, later President of Georgia. It was also the first film to benefit from the intervention of the Conflict Commission established by the Union of Filmmakers* after their Fifth Congress in May 1986. It was released in Moscow in January 1987, and then shown widely throughout the Soviet Union and the rest of the world. *Repentance* is over-long and its stylistic confusion links it to the contradictory moods of the mid-1980s but it is a brilliantly acted and sometimes deeply moving evocation of the seductions of power. JG

AGIT-FILMS

Soviet short films, also known as 'agitki'. Produced during the Civil War of 1917–21, these films were simple in form and straightforward in content and dealt with topical matters of politics, production, health and hygiene. They were primarily intended for exhibition through the network of agit-trains touring the frontlines and areas recently recaptured from the White forces.

Agit-films were a temporary solution to an emergency problem: they were a short cut to resolving communication difficulties between rulers and ruled and provided valuable experience in film-making

11

– especially in montage* as a method of using scant resources economically – for a new generation of directors such as Lev Kuleshov* and Dziga Vertov*, who worked together on the 'October Revolution' agit-train. RT

ALBANIA

Until World War II, isolated and largely illiterate Albania possessed about twenty cinemas in the main towns, showing exclusively imported material. The only cinematic evidence of prewar Albania is in a few foreign newsreels and travelogues. The communist regime of Enver Hoxha (1944–85) nationalised the cinema in 1947, and immediately began using it for propaganda by making two newsreels with Soviet assistance. Moscow was largely responsible for the building of the Shqiperia e re/New Albania film studio in Tirana, and was virtually the only source of equipment and technical skills. Its construction, begun in 1952, allowed a steady production of newsreels, and documentaries such as *Rruga e lavdishme/The Glorious Road* (1952). Soviet director Sergei Yutkevich's* *Skanderbeg* (1954), about Albania's medieval national hero, was partly put together in the Albanian studio, and presented for political reasons as a Soviet-Albanian co-production. It helped confirm film as a mass medium, and by the mid-1950s there was an annual audience of five million for the hundred or so cinemas (from a population of *c.* three million), including mobile units for rural areas.

Until 1958, features were almost entirely from the Soviet Union and Eastern Europe. The first Albanian feature, *Tana* (1958), directed by Kristaq Dhamo and starring Tinka Kurti, relied on the modest documentary tradition in its handling of the collectivisation of the countryside. Hysen Hakani's *Debatik/Communist Youth* (1961), on the resistance of children during the Italian occupation of 1938–43, set a pattern for storylines based on this period and subject. The break with Moscow in 1960, and growing political and cultural isolationism, made it necessary to increase domestic production. This was hampered by the loss of most foreign assistance, though there were enough Moscow-trained technicians and directors to begin to develop an autonomous film industry and provide some training at the Tirana Higher Institute of Arts. Only one film a year was made until the late 1960s, but then production rose steadily to about twelve features annually in the early 1980s.

Hoxha's insistence on sticking to a Stalinist line of ideological struggle, and his refusal to follow Soviet revisionism, turned Albania into a bastion of Socialist Realist* film production. Every film was obliged to perform some political task, though in the special context of Albanian history. With slow television development, film had a key role, along with schools and various state institutions, in promulgating not merely the propaganda of class struggle but a 'socialist morality'. In particular this meant the central role of the 'positive hero' – the 'new man' edu-

12

cated by the Party. This pattern is firmly established in Dhimitër Anagnosti and Viktor Gjika's *Komisari i dritës/Commissar of the Light* (1966), in which a man returns to his home village after the liberation in 1944 to fight against the local priest and landowner, and a counter-revolutionary brigade, but whose greatest achievement is to set up the first school in the village and to inspire pupils. Anagnosti's other main films include *Cuca e maleve/The Mountain Girl* (1974), a ballet showing the strong influence of Chinese 'heroic' opera; *Lulëkuqet mbi mure/Red Poppies on Walls* (1976), starring Kadri Rashi and dynamically describing a children's rebellion against a fascist schoolmaster; the satirical comedy *Perralle nga e kaluara/A Tale from the Past* (1988); and *Kthimi i ushtisë së vdekur/Return of the Dead Army* (1989).

Ibrahim Mucaj and Kristaq Mitro portray collective heroism in *Dimeri i fundit/The Last Winter* (1976), where a group of village women put up resistance to occupation during World War II. Viktor Gjika achieves a subtler political approach with strong performances in *Rrugë të bardha/White Roads* (1974), where the 'new man' is a sympathetic contemporary figure struggling for love and against snow-drifts. Gjika's sensitivity for images, music and dramatic development can also be seen in *Gjeneral gramafoni/The General Gramophone* (1977), which shows the struggle to preserve Albanian folk music during the Italian occupation. *Yje mbi Drin/Stars above the Drin* (1977, dir. I. Zhabjaku) shows the final phase of almost complete ideological isolationism, the enemies now the Chinese 'revisionists' conspiring to destroy a hydro-electric plant. Kujtim Çashku and Piro Milkani's *Ballë për ballë/Face to Face* (1979), starring Sulejman Pitarka, has a conspiracy theme set around the departure of the Russians in 1960. With a significant annual production, a wider range of subjects could now be covered. In the record year of 1984, seven of the fourteen features dealt with contemporary subjects, while most of the rest were set in or around World War II. Productions included comedies, children's films and films based on ancient history and folklore. But as an Albanian delegate said at a Balkan film festival, whatever the subject matter every effort had to be made to omit 'sentimentality, physiological and moral anomalies, pornography, sadism, psychological and Freudian dimensions, naturalism and individualism'.

Cinema screens increased to 450 in 1975, and attendances reportedly reached twenty million, with a carefully chosen selection of heavily censored and selectively subtitled French, Italian and other European films. In 1978 a modernisation of the film studio began, but lack of access to the latest technology made it a limited project. The first colour feature, made with East German assistance, appeared in 1974. By the 1980s, most films were in colour and processing quality improved, though remaining relatively poor. Production of short documentaries increased to about thirty annually by the mid-1980s, mostly devoted to propaganda, scientific and educational subjects, and the activities of Hoxha. Occasional full-length documentaries, like *Kujtime te vegjëlisë/ Memories of Childhood* (1985), were usually homages to Hoxha.

13

Leading woman director Xhanfize Keko made a series of features about and for children, notably *Beni ecen vete/Beni's First Steps* (1978). Cartoon and puppet films were first made in the 1970s, and production reached about twelve films annually in the 1980s; worthy of note are *Zogu pushbardhe/The Fluffy White Chick* (1984–5), a popular children's series, and *Plumb ballit/Bullet in the Head* (1985), a grotesque satire on traitors. Television began in 1969, producing the only films shown at the biennial national film festival in Tirana. Most notable is Vladimir Prifti's *Udha e shkronjave/The Path of Letters* (1982), starring Sander Proci. Attempts to export Albanian films have been very limited, though a few foreign festival prizes were won by children's and documentary films. The national film archive contains 5,000 titles. The literary monthly *Nentori* and the weekly *Drita* publish film reviews and other film news.

The collapse of Hoxha's successor Ramiz Alia's regime (1990–2), and economic paralysis, reduced feature production to five films in 1990, and almost nothing since. Saimir Kumbaro's *Vdekja e kalit/ Death of the Horse* (1992) is the major exception, an intense evocation of the fate of the individual under totalitarianism. The younger generation of talented film actors, as well as many others in the industry, are scattered outside Albania. Cinemas currently remain open, despite their difficulties in obtaining international releases (which are nonetheless often shown in pirated form on Albanian television), offering a mix of genres never before seen in Albania, including Greek soft-porn comedies and Japanese action films. The Minister of Culture in the post-1992 government is director Dhimitër Anagnosti, reflecting the important role of film personnel during and after the fall of the regime. The national film studio is seriously run down, and hopes for foreign investment have yet to be fulfilled. Kujtim Çashku's historical saga *Balada e Kurbinit/Ballad of Kurbini* (1990) and his psychological drama *Colonel Bunker* (1996) which explores in a critical light the legacy of the Hoxha regime, were acclaimed at international festivals in the 1990s. MM

ALEXANDROV [ALEKSANDROV], Grigori V.
Grigori Mormonenko; Sverdlovsk [now Yekaterinburg], Russian Empire 1903 – Moscow 1983

Soviet director and scriptwriter, who began his career as a stage assistant at the Yekaterinburg Opera and first appeared on stage at the Proletkult Theatre in Moscow in 1921, the beginning of his creative association with Sergei Eisenstein*. Alexandrov moved with Eisenstein from theatre to cinema in 1924, helping with *Stachka/The Strike* (1925) as both actor and assistant director. He acted in and co-directed *Bronenosets Potëmkin/The Battleship Potemkin* (1926) and, with Eisenstein, scripted and directed both *Oktyabr'/October* (1928) and *Staroe i novoe/The Old and the New* (1929). He spent the years

1929–32 travelling with Eisenstein and Eduard Tisse* in Western Europe, the US and Mexico, assisting on the unfinished project for *¡Que viva México!* (1930–2). Alexandrov returned to the USSR before his associates and made the film that was to found the Soviet genre of musical comedies, *Vesëlye rebyata/The Happy Guys* (1934), starring his wife Lyubov Orlova*. His films reflected the ideological preoccupations of the age, but with their lavish choreography they were hugely popular with Soviet audiences. *Tsirk/The Circus*, with its anti-fascist message, followed in 1936, and *Volga-Volga*, with Igor Ilyinsky's* unforgettable parody of the bureaucrat Byvalov, in 1938. In the following decade Alexandrov made two more musical comedies, *Svetlyi put'/The Radiant Path* (1940), extolling the virtues of shock labour, and *Vesna/Springtime* (1947). In 1949 he made the war film *Vstrecha na El'be/Meeting on the Elbe*, and in 1952 the biographical *Kompozitor Glinka/The Composer Glinka*. His last film, *Lyubov' Orlova* (1983), was a study of his wife. In the 1950s Alexandrov taught at VGIK*. His films were influential in creating a Soviet popular cinema, combining the constraints of the political correctness associated with Socialist Realism* and a genuine feel for the emotions of mass audiences. RT

ANDONOV, Metodi   Kališče 1932 – Sofia 1974

Bulgarian director. A master of the psychological drama, Andonov is primarily known as the director of the biggest box-office hit in Bulgarian film history. After graduating from the Sofia Academy of Dramatic Art (VITIS), he directed stage productions at the Satirical Theatre for a decade before making *Bjalata staja/The White Room* (1968), based on a novel by Bogomil Rainov. This uncompromising confrontation with dogmatism in the Stalinist period won him instant recognition at home and abroad. And it was, surprisingly, approved for release in the post-'thaw' period. Andonov next directed *Njama ništo po-hubavo ot lošoto vreme/There's Nothing Finer than Bad Weather* (1971), another detective story from a screenplay by Rainov, and then the box-office hit *Kozijat rog/The Goat's Horn* (1972). Seen by more than three million people during its original release, it established writer-screenwriter Nikolai Haitov* as the country's leading movie storyteller. Andonov's last film, *Goljamata skuka/The Great Boredom* (1973), was another thriller scripted by Rainov. His premature death in 1974 at the age of forty-two was a major loss to Bulgarian cinema. RH

ANIMAFILM

Romanian animation studio, established in 1964 in Bucharest. The earliest animation was in the 1920s, but regular production began in

1950 as part of the new Bucharest studio, with Matty Aslan, Constantin Popescu and his son Ion Popescu-Gopo*. Following the international success of Popescu-Gopo's 'little man with the flower' in 1956, a School of Animation was created, and eventually the specialist AnimaFilm studio. Other pioneers were Olimp Varasteanu, Nell Color, Florin Angelescu and inventive puppeteer Bob Calinescu. Annual production increased from fifteen films to over sixty in the 1980s. International awards in the 1970s, for technical creativity, were won by Isabella Petrasincu's *Parada fiurilor/The Figures' Parade* (1973) and Laurentiu Sirbu's *Puiul/The Chick* (1973). Since 1966 the important biennial Mamaia Animation Festival has shown the genre's best. Internationally successful science-fiction animation, and the 'little man with the flower' style, have continued to flourish. Techniques include cut-up paper, puppetry, pixilation and computerised drawing. Animation series, mostly for television, were developed from the mid-1970s. Zoltan Szilagyi won many prizes in the 1980s, the first for *Nodul Gordian/The Gordian Knot* (1980). From 1985 there has been more concentration on feature-length films, about two a year, and popular series. Since the 1989 revolution, AnimaFilm, dominating hard currency earnings from foreign sales, has been the only relatively viable part of the industry in Romania. Its break from the bureaucratic state monopoly and entry into joint ventures with Spanish-based Dale Multibrook (1991) have resulted in the importation of much-needed modern technology. MM

Bib: *Romanian Animation Films* (1966–84).

ANIMATION IN EASTERN EUROPE

Eastern Europe's contribution to the development of animation art is a significant one. It is characterised by the coexistence of multiple original artistic visions. Until 1989, animation in Eastern Europe was almost exclusively financed, produced, and distributed within an elaborate state-run studio system – AnimaFilm* in Romania, Krátky Film in the Czech Republic, Pannónia Film Studios in Hungary, the Experimental Cartoon Film Studio and SeMaFor in Poland, Sofia studios in Bulgaria, and Zagreb in Yugoslavia. Centrally subsidised, animation was one of the costlier film arts to flourish here. The studios produced numerous award-winning animations, and turned Eastern Europe into a worldwide leader in the area. After 1989, state funding was reduced to a minimum; the new box-office-oriented approaches in production and distribution led to a drop in the output numbers in animation. In the 1990s, many East European animators migrated to the West. The Zagreb World Festival of Animated Films is still one of the two most important animation venues in the world, alternating every other year with the Annecy Film Festival. The festival in Mamaia, Romania, was another important venue for the region's animators.

Throughout the 1980s, an international animation festival also took place in Varna, Bulgaria. Animated cartoons from Czechoslovakia* and Poland* enjoyed most international exposure. Best known for their unique style were Czech puppeteers Jiří Trnka* and Karel Zeman*, and surrealist Jan Švankmajer*. The most popular animators from Poland were Walerian Borowczyk*, Jan Lenica*, Daniel Szczechura, Piotr Dumala, and émigré Zbig Rybcziński*. The first Hungarian cartoonist, István Kató Kiszly, made his first animation in 1914. Throughout the 1930s and 1940s, the leading figure in Hungarian animation was Gyula Macskássy who assembled a team of animators in his studio, mostly making promotional cartoons and children's shorts using various techniques. Many Hungarian animators of this first generation emigrated and established themselves in the West. János Halász became a co-founder of a cartoon studio in London in 1936. György Marczincsák (aka George Pal) worked first in the Netherlands in the 1930s and contributed substantially to Dutch animation culture, and then in Hollywood where he became an Oscar-winning member of Paramount's team. The first colour animation, *Little Rooster's Diamond Farthing* (1951) directed by Macskássy and Edit Fekete, marked the beginning of the second phase in the history of animated cartoons in Hungary. Starting with József Nepp's *Passion* (1964), throughout the 1960s, Hungarian animators became increasingly preoccupied with intellectual and philosophical explorations and created many cartoons for adults. The new generation of film-makers included also József Gémes, Marcel Jankovics, Béla Vajda, Ferenc Cakó, and many more, winning worldwide recognition for Hungarian animation. Besides Pannónia Film Studios in Budapest, experimental workshops developed in Kecskemét and Pécs. The 1980s, beginning with Ferenc Rofusz's Oscar for *The Fly* (1981), were the best years for Hungarian animation. During this decade the members of the third generation of animators – Forenc Cakô, Csaba Vargo, Mária Horváth – enjoyed international acclaim. In post-communist times, the restructuring of the animation industry led to the creation in 1992 of Hungarian Cartoon, an umbrella organisation which includes ten smaller studios for animated cartoons and two for puppet animation operations and employs about 500 animators. Gábor Csupo, co-founder of the Los Angeles-based animation production company Klasky-Csupo, came into prominence in the 1990s with his work on the American cartoon series *Rugrats*. The Yugoslav Zagreb School of Animation* is well known for its 'reduced animation' style with animators Vatroslav Mimica*, Dusan Vukotić*, Vladimir Kristl, Nedeljko Dragić, and Borivoj Dovniković–Bordo. The best-known animator from Romania is Ion Popescu-Gopo*, and from Bulgaria – Todor Dinov, author of award-winning cartoons *Margaritkata/The Daisy* (1963) and *Prometej/Prometheus* (1969). Donyo Donev created the most popular series *Trimata Glupatsi/The Three Fools* in the 1980s, a satire on traditional mores. DI

ANIMATION: CZECHOSLOVAKIA

Czechoslovak animation dates back to the 1920s but first attracted international attention when Karel Dodal's work was shown at the 1937 Paris Exhibition. His best-known film was *Hra bublinek/The Bubble Game* (1936), a colour animation advertising Sapona soap, which featured abstract design and recalls Len Lye's* work for the GPO Film Unit. Dodal's assistant, Hermína Týrlová, made her debut as a puppet film-maker with *Ferda mravenec/Ferda and the Ants* (1942), beginning a long career in which she worked exclusively on children's films. Týrlová, and others working at the Baťa film studios at Zlín (later Gottwaldov, now Zlín again), were to provide the basis of the postwar development of Czech animation. It was, however, the nationalisation of the industry in August 1945 that laid the foundations for major developments. The leading figures were Jiří Trnka* and Karel Zeman*, both of whom made cartoon and puppet films, and carried off the main prizes for these categories at the first Cannes festival in 1946. Already well established before the communist takeover of 1948, animation continued to flourish in the 1950s when mainstream cinema was subject to the restrictions of Socialist Realism*. The success of Trnka's *Císařův slavík/The Emperor's Nightingale* (1948) and *Staré pověsti české/Old Czech Legends* (1953), and of Zeman's *Cesta do pravěku/A Journey to Primeval Times* (1955) and *Vynález skázy/An Invention for Destruction* (1958), established Czech animated features as the principal alternative to the Disney tradition. While its public image was overshadowed by the Czech New Wave* in the 1960s, animation continued to make a striking impact, with Zeman making features through to the 1970s. Trnka's former assistants, Břetislav Pojar and Stanislav Látal, also established themselves in the area of puppet film. Among many other outstanding film-makers to emerge from the Czech studios were Jiří Brdečka, Václav Bedřich, Zdeněk Miler (best known for his delightful 'Mole' series) and the trio of Jaroslav Doubrava, Adolf Born and Miloš Macourek, who produced some of the most acute and acerbic short films of the 1980s. The pioneer of Slovak animation, Viktor Kubal, made the first two Slovak animated features, *Zbojník Jurko/Jurko the Outlaw* (1976) and *Krvavá paní/Bloody Lady* (1980).

   The outstanding figure of the past twenty years has been Jan Švankmajer*, although official disapproval ensured only limited exhibition of his films in Czechoslovakia. His disturbing visions won acclaim at festivals from the late 1970s and his films have become a major international influence. A new generation of animators began to emerge in the 1980s, including Jiří Barta, Pavel Koutský and Igor Ševčík. Barta's work in puppet film has gained him an international following, especially with *Zaniklý svět rukavic/The Extinct World of Gloves* (1982), an elaborate satire on film genres, and his feature *Krysař/The Pied Piper* (1986), which uses carved walnut puppets. PH

18

ANIMATION: POLAND

Poland boasts one of the great pioneers of animation, Władysław Starewicz*, whose work, made in Russia, Lithuania and France and using a mixture of model animation, live action and drawing, is bizarre, witty and inventive. In Poland itself animation work dates from the establishment of the Experimental Cartoon Film Studio in Katowice in 1947, which moved to Bielsko Biała in 1956.

Until the mid-1950s most Polish animation was geared to the children's market. With the political changes in 1956, animators such as Witold Giersz began to make the satirical, surreal and politically coded animated films associated with Eastern Europe. Giersz's *Mały Western/Little Western* (1960) and *Czerwone i Czarne/Red and Black* (1963) gained several international awards. In the late 1950s, Jan Lenica* and Walerian Borowczyk* worked together on several shorts, using collage and photo-montage techniques. Borowczyk later moved to live-action films but Lenica, known also for his poster designs, continued to animate. His *Labirynt/Labyrinth* (1963) is a post-modern vision of the Icarus myth set in an eerie city inhabited by monstrous beings.

In the late 1970s and 1980s the work of Jerzy Kucia from the Krakow unit and Zbigniew Rybczyński* from SeMaFor Studios was especially noted. The surreal films of Piotr Dumała, such as *Wolność Nogi/The Freedom of the Leg* (1990) and *Franz Kafka* (1991), have attracted international attention. Dumała works as an independent, financing his own films and studio by working for the expanding commercial market. With large and well-staffed animation studios, Poland, like other East European countries, is increasingly used as a cheap production partner for Western animation productions. Although many studios are closing down with the advent of the free market, others are forming partnerships with larger, foreign companies. AW

ASANOVA, Dinara K.　　Frunze, Kirgizia [USSR] 1942 – Murmansk 1985

Russian director Asanova entered VGIK* in 1962, and studied in the workshop of Mikhail Romm* and Alexander Stolper, making her diploma film *Rudolfio* from a story by Valentin Rasputin in 1969. She worked as an assistant to Larisa Shepitko* on the latter's film *Znoi/Heat*, made for Kirgizfilm in 1973. In 1974 she began work as a director at the Lenfilm studios. Asanova's key films are all concerned with the emotional and moral development of young people and she used improvisational methods with her young actors. Her first feature, *Ne bolit golova u dyatla/The Woodpecker Doesn't Get a Headache* (1974) is the story of the first love of a jazz-crazed schoolboy, Fly. It was followed by *Klyuch bez prava peredachi/Private Key* (1976), another teenage school drama. *Patsany/Tough Kids* (1983) is set in a correctional summer camp for difficult youngsters and follows the efforts of the camp organiser to redeem them by gaining their respect. *'Milyi, dorogoi, lyubimyi, edinstvennyi ...'/'My Sweet, My Dear, My Love, My Only One ...'* (1984) is the story of nineteen-year-old Anna, who steals a child in order to test the feelings of her boyfriend. After Asanova's premature death Igor Alimpiev directed the montage film *Ochen' vas vsekh lyublyu/I Love You All Very Much* (1987) about her career. JG

ASKOLDOV, Alexander Moscow 1932

Russian director. Askoldov's parents were arrested in 1937 and his father shot. After studying in the Philological Faculty of Moscow University, Askoldov studied direction and scriptwriting in 1964–5. His only feature film is *Komissar/The Commissar* (1967), a film that was shelved until 1987. Work on the script, based on Vasili Grossman's 1934 short story 'In the Town of Berdichev', began in 1965, and *The Commissar* was planned as one of a number of films that would look back at the revolutionary period in time for its half-century. But with its pregnant female commissar, the film could never have been a conventional paean to the new era, and Askoldov's treatment, which stressed the joys and humanity of the Jewish family at the centre of the film, caused repeated interventions from the censor. After the victory of Israel in the 1967 Six-Day War, the film's fate was sealed. Askoldov's intransigence over attempts to get him to alter his film led to the end of his work in cinema and his dismissal from the Communist Party. During the late 1970s and early 1980s he directed experimental musical theatre. The film was finally shown after Askoldov's own intervention at a press conference during the 1987 Moscow Film Festival. With a remarkable central performance by Nonna Mordyukova, and stunning black-and-white photography that evokes comparisons with Eisenstein* and Dovzhenko*, *The Commissar* has at last achieved the recognition it merits. JG

ASTRAKHAN, Dmitri Kh. Leningrad 1957

Russian director. Astrakhan graduated from the Leningrad State Institute for Theatre, Music and Cinema in 1982 and began work as a theatrical director. He was artistic director of the Sverdlovsk Young People's Theatre from 1981 to 1987, and in 1987–90 he directed at the Bolshoi Drama Theatre and other Leningrad theatres, and abroad. From 1991 to 1995 he was artistic director of the N. Akimov Comedy Theatre in St Petersburg. He has directed over thirty plays. Though he made a film for television in 1987, his cinematic career began in the early 1990s, and he has so far made seven feature films as well as a television series, *Zal ozhidaniya/Waiting Room* (1998). Unlike the majority of his director contemporaries who have made their reputations during the 1990s, he spurns *auteur* cinema in favour of catering to popular taste. The plot of an Astrakhan film first establishes the identity and values of a community, a family or other group, and then brings them to a point of crisis in which they are required to make a choice. His first feature *Izydi/Get Thee Hence* (1991) is a pre-Revolutionary tale of a Jewish family threatened by a pogrom, while the second, *Ty u menya odna/You Are My Only One* (1993) shows a post-Soviet St Petersburger deciding whether to take the chance of American emigration or remain in penury with his wife and daughter. His greatest popular success has been with *Vse budet khorosho/Everything Will Be O.K.* (1995), where again the post-Soviet seduction of emigration is weighed against the less obvious charms of the Russian present in a film that captures with painful accuracy the snatched joys and major humiliations familiar to contemporary audiences in their own day-to-day existence. Nostalgia for a time remembered as secure and reliable is another ingredient in the contemporary Russian mental mix. It is always a potent factor for Astrakhan's characters and it weighs heavily in his space-travelling *Chetvertaya planeta/The Fourth Planet* (1995). Additionally appealing for audiences is the way Astrakhan's early films use a repertory of his theatrical actors, who reappear in variations of their basic character from film to film. But his next film marked something of a departure. The Jewish wartime drama, *Iz ada v ad/From Hell to Hell* (1997) was an altogether darker affair, culminating in a pogrom in the Polish city of Kielce. He followed it with a dull and anonymous television thriller, *Kontrakt so smert'yu/Contract with Death* (1998) and then made the romantic comedy, *Perekrestok/Crossroads* (1998). JG

B

BAAROVÁ, Lida   Prague [then Austria-Hungary] 1914

Czech actress. Lida Baarová made her film debut in Miroslav J. Krňanský's comedy *Kariéra Pavla Čamrdy/The Career of Pavel Čamrda* (1931), following this with two films opposite Vlasta Burian*. She was soon signed up by Ufa and appeared in a number of German films, including the successful romantic comedy *Barcarole*, 1935. In Germany she became Joseph Goebbels' mistress, rejecting an offer from MGM in order to stay with him. When Hitler refused Goebbels' request to divorce his wife and marry Baarová, all her films were banned in Germany. Despite the scandal, she maintained her Czech career and reputedly became involved in anti-Nazi espionage. She was expelled from the Czech studios by the Nazis in 1941 and continued her career in Italy, making her final appearances in Federico Fellini's *I Vitelloni* (1953) and the Spanish film *Rapsodia de sangre* (1957). Her best films, however, were those made in Czechoslovakia between 1937 and 1941, where she appeared in *Ohnivé léto/Fiery Summer* (1939), directed by Václav Krška and František Čáp*, and in four films for Otakar Vávra, including *Panenství/Virginity* (1937) and *Dívka v modrém/The Girl in Blue* (1940). She retired to Austria, where she continued to act in the theatre, appearing on stage in R. W. Fassbinder's *The Bitter Tears of Petra von Kant* in the 1970s. In 1995 Baarová appeared in a biographical documentary, *Sladke horkosti Lidy Baarove/Lida Baarová's Bittersweet Memories* (d. Helena Trestikova). PH

Other Films Include: *Funebrák, Leliček ve službách Sherlocka Holmese/Lelíček in the Service of Sherlock Holmes* (1932). **In Germany**: *Verräter/The Traitor* (1936); *Die Fledermaus, Patrioten* (1937); *Preussische Liebesgeschichte/Prussian Love Story* (1938, released 1950). **In Czechoslovakia**: *Maskovaná milenka/The Masked Lover* (1940); *Turbina/The Turbine* (1941). **In Italy**: *La Fornarina* (1942).

BACSÓ, Péter   Kosice, Czechoslovakia 1928

Hungarian director. Bacsó is one of the most distinguished, original, and prolific Hungarian film *auteurs*. His trademark is a clearly articulated, sarcastic take on the reality of state socialism. Bacsó studied directing in Budapest and collaborated on Géza Radványi's *Valahol Európában/Somewhere in Europe* (1947). He started his film career as a writer for Makk's* *Simon Menyhért születése* (1954) with Tibor Déry and *Liliomphy* (1954) with Yvette Biró as well as for *Macskajáték/Cat's Play* (1972) and *Szerelem/Love* (1971); for Fábri's* *Édes Anna/Anna* (1958), *Ház a sziklák alatt/House under the Rocks* (1958), and *Két félidö a pokolban/Eleven Men* (1962). Bacsó also wrote the scripts for most of his own films. He first came to international acclaim at Locarno with his *Jelenidö/Present Indicative* (1971). Bacsó's best-known film is *A Tanú/The Witness* (1969), a biting satire on the absurdities of the socialist system of the 1950s and a mockery of totalitarianism in Hungary. The protagonist, Jószef Pelikán (Ferenc Kállai) has since become a synonym for a naïve victim of the Kafkaesque bureaucratic machine. A quarter of a century later Bacsó revisited the simple-minded Pelikán (again played by Kállai), and offered a sarcastic exploration of the social mores in post-communist times in *Megint tanú/Witness Again* (1994). Here he exposed the *nouveau riche* culture of profiteering which took over from state socialism. An uncompromising criticism of Stalinist Hungary is found in Bacsó's *Te rongyos élet/O, Bloody Life!* (1983) exploring the fate of a group of 'untrustworthy' subjects deported from Budapest by the regime in the spring of 1951. DI

Other Films Include: *Zongora a levegöben/A Piano in Mid-Air* (1975); *Ereszd el a szakállamat!/Let Me Go!* (1975); *Riasztólövés/Alarm Shot* (1977); *Áramütés/Electric Shock* (1978); *Ki beszél itt szerelemröl/Who is Speaking about Love?* (1979); *A Svéd, akinek nyoma veszett /The Man Who Went up in Smoke* (1980); *Tegnapelött/The Day Before Yesterday* (1981); *Sértés/Offence* (1982); *Hány az óra, Vekkerúr?/ What Is the Time, Mr Vekker?* (1985); *Banánhéjkeringö/Banana Skin Waltz* (1986); *Titánia, Titánia, avagy a dublörök éjszakája/Titania, Titania or the Night of the Stuntmen* (1988); *Sztálin menyasszonya/ Stalin's Girlfriend* (1991); *Live Show* (1992); *Balekok és Banditák/ Gulls and Gangsters* (1997).

BAKY, Josef von Bacska, Hungary 1902 – Munich 1966

Hungarian-born director working at Ufa* in the 1930s and 1940s, with a sure hand for navigating the propagandist ends to which his films could be put. In 1928 Baky became assistant director to Geza von Bolvary*. From 1936 he directed for Ufa, specialising in popular comedies (*Intermezzo*, 1936; *Menschen vom Varieté/People from the Variety*, 1939) and women's pictures (*Die kleine und die große Liebe/ Minor Love and the Real Thing*, 1938). The enormous success of *Annelie* (1941), a combination of both genres, prompted Goebbels to assign him to *Münchhausen* (1943), the hugely successful twenty-fifth anniversary Ufa colour production. However, Baky's 1944 *Via Mala*, an alpine story of patricide, was banned and not shown until after the war. In 1947 Baky founded Objektiv-Film which, among other films, produced *Der Ruf/The Last Illusion* (1949), starring Fritz Kortner as an émigré academic returning to a professorial chair in Germany. Today counted among the few '*Trümmerfilme*' ('ruin films') which have retained their unsettling potential beyond their historical moment, it was not a commercial success, and Baky's company folded. Other more profitable films, across a range of genres, followed in the 1950s, before he retired in 1961. MW

Other Films Include: *Ihr erstes Erlebnis/Her First Experience* (1939); *Der Kleinstadtpoet/Small Town Poet* (1940); *Und über uns der Himmel/ And the Sky Above Us* (1947); *Der träumende Mund/Dreaming Lips* (1953); *Tagebuch einer Verliebten/Diary of a Married Woman* (1953); *Hotel Adlon* (1955); *Robinson soll nicht sterben/The Girl and the Legend* (1957); *Die seltsame Gräfin/The Mysterious Countess* (1961).

BALABANOV, Alexei O. Sverdlovsk [USSR] 1959

Russian director and scriptwriter. Balabanov studied to be a translator at the State Pedagogical Institute in Gorky (Nizhny Novgorod), graduating in 1981, and served in the Soviet Army. From 1983 to 1987 he worked as an assistant director at the Sverdlovsk Film Studios. In 1990 he graduated from the Higher Courses for Scriptwriters and Directors in Moscow, where he had studied on an experimental course in *cinéma d'auteur* with Boris Galanter. Since 1990 he has lived and worked in St Petersburg. His first two features were based on Beckett and Kafka: *Schastlivye dni/Happy Days* (1991) and *Zamok/The Castle* (1994). He contributed 'Trofim' to the film almanac made to celebrate the centenary of cinema, *Pribytie poezda/The Arrival of a Train* (1995), weaving a narrative of peasant life around a story about a contemporary film-maker filming the arrival of a Russian train. With *Brat/Brother* (1997) he stirred up critical debate with a new type of hero: the killer, who is at the same time a knight. Danila executes people, but he never stops helping the poor. The film is both within the mainstream of Russian cinema, in its concern with the cruelty of everyday life, and outside it, in the absence of an authorial moral stance. Balabanov provides no answers to the question of what will become of the moral values of Russia's young generation hardened by the Chechen war. His *Pro urodov i lyudei/Of Freaks and Men* (1998) again confirms the absence of a moral position. The film, set at the turn of the century, shows the subversion of social structures: servants dominate the bourgeoisie, the educated classes are replaced by the perverted and debased proletariat, freaks take over from people. Yet the film does not function as a social critique. Shot in black-and-white (with silver halide) in the style of early twentieth-century photographs, its aesthetic perfection contrasts with the sadomasochistic motives chosen by the photographer in the film for his work: the pleasure he gets from women's beaten, naked buttocks as the object of photos. Balabanov comments on cinema as a medium which, from its beginning, was not merely a means of propaganda and education offering moral guidance, but also catered for the masses, and the sick taste of those rejoicing in the humiliation of others. Balabanov has been termed the Russian Tarantino for the absence of a moral stance and the parodic treatment of the subject matter in his films. In 1999 he made *Brat 2/Brother 2*, which follows his hero's further adventures in Moscow and the US. BB

BALAYAN, Roman G. Nerkin Oratag, Nagorno-Karabakh Region of Azerbaijan [USSR] 1941

Russian director. From 1959 to 1961 Balayan worked as an actor in the theatre in Stepanakert, the capital of Nagorno-Karabakh. From 1961 to 1964 he studied at the directorial faculty of the Erevan Theatrical Institute in Armenia. In 1969 he graduated from the directorial faculty of the Kiev Theatrical Institute. He began to work at the Dovzhenko Film Studios in Kiev in 1970. Many of the films he has directed have been adaptations from nineteenth-century Russian literature. *Kashtanka/Chestnut* (1975) and *Potselui/The Kiss* (1983), both made for TV, are taken from Chekhov, while *Biryuk/The Lone Wolf* (1977) is from Turgenev, to whom he returned for ... *Pervaya lyubov'/ ... First Love* in 1995. *Khrani menya, moi talisman/Protect Me, My Talisman* (1986) is a contemporary tale but is set in Boldino, a place where Pushkin once lived, and is played out in Pushkin's long shadow. In 1989 Balayan made a faithful adaptation of Nikolai Leskov's tale of provincial passion *Ledi Makbet mtsenskogo uezda/A Lady Macbeth of the Mtsensk District*, a story that would later be updated to the present day by Valeri Todorovsky*. But for all this concentration on the classics, Balayan's most memorable film is *Polety vo sne i nayavu/Dream Flights* (1982), in which Oleg Yankovsky plays a forty-year-old engineer whose aspirations from life had been dictated by the Khrushchevian Thaw and who finds it hard to come to terms with banal and depressing reality. The film was found to speak for an entire disappointed generation. In 1998 Balayan made the thriller *Dve luny, tri solntsa/Two Moons, Three Suns*, in which Vladimir Mashkov* plays a Moscow archaeologist whose younger brother is mysteriously killed in one of the post-Soviet Caucasian wars and whose desire to avenge his brother draws him into a murky world of contract killers. JG

BALÁZS BÉLA STÚDIÓ (BBS)

Hungarian film studio. BBS is a unique film studio of its kind. It was founded – informally in 1959, then officially in 1961 – as an experimental studio by the second postwar Hungarian generation of film directors to which István Szabó*, Zoltán Huszárik*, István Gaál, Pál Gábor, Sándor Sára*, Zsolt Kézdy-Kovács, Ferenc Kardos, Judit Elek, János Rózsa and others belonged. BBS has enjoyed a special status in the Hungarian state-owned and politically controlled film production sector. It was subsidised (by an annual sum equal to the budget of an average Hungarian feature film), and was run entirely by young filmmakers, whose decisions did not need the approval of higher authorities. BBS had no obligation to release publicly the films it produced; hence, these films were free of both dependence on the market and political censorship. Such conditions allowed BBS to become an important centre for independent short, documentary and experimental film-making.

In the early 1970s, when a new generation took over the management, the studio became more involved politically, as evidenced by a new trend in social issues documentaries. More and more films were denied authorisation for public release, though the authorities could not stop a film being made. In 1976 a special section was created by director Gábor Bódy* for experimental and avant-garde cinema. The studio became increasingly open, allowing virtually anyone to make films if their proposal was accepted by the leadership. In the early 1980s it became a key centre of experimental and avant-garde art in Hungary, as painters, sculptors, musicians and writers tried their hand at film-making. In 1985 the studio was awarded a special prize, in Milan, for its activities. Since 1989 it has been a non-profit foundation. KAB

BALÁZS, Béla

Herbert Bauer; Szeged 1884 – Budapest 1949

Hungarian film theoretician, scriptwriter, poet and film critic. Balázs was one of the first important theorists of the cinema, proclaiming its independence as an art form. His first theoretical work, *Der sichtbare Mensch* (*The Visible Man*, 1924), is widely considered the foundation of silent film aesthetics. Here he emphasises the importance of the 'physiognomy of the visible world' as the basis of cinematic expression. In his other key theoretical work, *Der Geist des Films* (*The Spirit of the Film*, 1930), Balázs treats in a detailed manner the dynamics of montage, taking a position opposed to the intellectual montage theory of Sergei Eisenstein*. In this book he also begins to analyse sound film.

Balázs had to leave Hungary because of his participation in the 1919 communist revolution. He lived in Vienna and later in Berlin, working both as a scriptwriter and film critic. He wrote the scripts of more than two dozen films and also tried his hand at directing. The films made from his scripts were not significant for the most part, though two are worth mentioning: an expressionist film from 1926, *Die Abenteuer eines Zehnmarkscheines* (dir. Berthold Viertel), and *Das blaue Licht/The Blue Light* (1932) by Leni Riefenstahl. Balázs wrote a number of poems, short stories and dramas, two of which were made world-famous by Hungarian composer Béla Bartók: *Fából faragott királyfi* (*The Wooden Prince*) and *A kékszakállú herceg vára* (*Bluebeard's Castle*). From the 1930s until the end of the war he lived in Moscow, teaching at the Academy of Film Art (VGIK*). He returned to Hungary in 1945, founded the Hungarian Film Research Institute (now the Hungarian Film Institute), taught at the Academy of Theatre and Film Arts and was guest lecturer at a number of film schools all over Europe. He died in 1949, right at the beginning of the communist dictatorship. Ironically, given his earlier communist allegiances, he was viewed by the communists as a 'bourgeois' theorist and author, which is why they began to marginalise him shortly before his death. KAB

Bib: Joseph Zsuffa, *Béla Balázs: the Man and the Artist* (1987).

BARNET, Boris V.

Moscow 1902 – Riga, Latvia
[USSR] 1965

Soviet director, actor and scriptwriter. Barnet, who came from an English family, trained as a boxer in the army, then studied in Lev Kuleshov's* workshop and acted in the latter's *Neobychainye priklyucheniya Mistera Vesta v strane Bol'shevikov/The Extraordinary Adventures of Mr West in the Land of the Bolsheviks* (1924), and in Fyodor Otsep's* *Miss Mend* (1926), which he also co-scripted and co-directed, before directing a series of light-hearted comedies beginning with *Devushka s korobkoi/The Girl with a Hatbox* (1927) and *Dom na Trubnoi/The House on Trubnaya* (1928). His first sound film was *Okraina/The Outskirts* (1933), a study of the effects of the Revolution on a small provincial town and a comment on the relationship between the individual and history. In 1936 he made a comedy about a collective fish farm, *U samogo sinego morya/By the Bluest of Seas*. His three World War II films, including *Staryi naezdnik/The Old Jockey* (1940, released 1959), were banned. As a reaction perhaps, Barnet, usually a most unpolitical man, directed and acted in one of the earliest Cold War films, *Podvig razvedchika/The Exploits of a Scout* (1947), awarded a Stalin Prize in 1948. In his later films he returned to comedy, as in *Shchedroe leto/Bounteous Summer* (1950), *Liana* (1955), and his last film, *Polustanok/Whistle-Stop* (1963), which foreshadows the work of Vasili Shukshin*. He also made a number of film dramas dealing with the history of the revolutionary movement and socialist construction, such as *Stranitsy zhizni/Pages from a Life* (1948), *Poet/The Poet* (1956), *Borets i kloun/The Wrestler and the Clown* (1957), *Annushka* (1959, about the suffering endured by Soviet women during World War II) and *Alyonka* (1961). Barnet committed suicide while making *Sūtŋu sazvērestība/The Ambassadors' Plot* in Riga. RT

BARRANDOV FILM STUDIOS

The main studios in Czechoslavakia were designed by Max Urban, architect and film pioneer, and built in 1932–3. The studios stand on a small plateau to the west of Prague, named after Joachim Barrande, a French geologist. Planned as a centre for international production, in the 1930s Barrandov saw the filming of Julien Duvivier's French-language version of *Le Golem/Golem* (1936) and multi-language versions of Victor Tourjansky's *Volga en flammes/Volha v plamenech/Volga in Flames* (1933) and Nicolas Farkas' *Port Arthur* (1936). However, the studios developed mainly as a centre for national production, catering for an increased domestic audience until they were expanded again during the Nazi occupation as an alternative centre for German production (G. W. Pabst made *Paracelsus* there in 1942). After the war, along with the newly built Koliba Film Studios in Bratislava, Barrandov became a centre for the nationalised industry.

The studios again showed interest in attracting foreign companies during the 1970s and 1980s, usually with politically correct subjects. Among the films made there were *Operation: Daybreak* (1975), *Yentl* (1983), *Amadeus* (1984), and *Rosa Luxemburg* (1986). Since 1989, facilities have been provided for films responding to the city's more obvious exotic attractions (for example, Steven Soderbergh's *Kafka* [1991], Ian Sellar's *Prague* [1991], George Sluizer's *Utz* [1992], Harold Pinter's adaptation of *The Trial* [1992]). In 1991 a controversial decision was made to cut back the large permanent staff at Barrandov, with the loss of many skills and trades and over 1,700 jobs. In 1993 a new holding company was established with an advisory board that included Miloš Forman*.

The plan to fully privatise Barrandov Studios by selling facilities and property was opposed by many, including veteran New Wave directors Věra Chytilová* and Jiří Menzel.* Believing it unprofitable in a market economy the opponents of privatisation feared that the commercialisation of the studio would lead to the end of the Czech film industry. The Czech government retained a golden share in the studio, mandating that Barrandov continue primarily in film production, and that government approval would be needed for long-term rent or sale of studio land. In 1999 Barrandov's majority shareholder since 1995, Moravia Steel, indefinitely postponed the long-expected sale of the facilities after the studio's economic performance was said to be more than satisfactory. **Web-site:** http://www.barrandov.cz. PH

BATALOV, Nikolai P.   Moscow 1899–1937

Soviet actor, who began his career on stage at the Moscow Art Theatre and first appeared in film as a Red Army soldier in Yakov Protazanov's* *Aelita* (1924). Subsequently he often played heroic workers, as in Vsevolod Pudovkin's* *Mat'/The Mother* (1926; as Pavel), Fyodor Otsep's* *Zemlya v plenu/Earth in Captivity* (1928), Nikolai Ekk's* *Putёvka v zhizn'/The Path to Life* (1931) and Lev Kuleshov's* *Gorizont* (1933). His acting was marked by depth and warmth of characterisation and he was always popular with Soviet audiences. RT

BAUER, Branko   Dubrovnik, Croatia 1921

Croatian director and scriptwriter. What Hitchcock and Hawks were for the French *politique des auteurs*, Bauer was for the young film critics in 1970s Yugoslavia. By discovering him, they rediscovered the notion of *auteur* and genre: from teen adventures (*Sinji galeb/Blue Seagull*, 1953) to war psycho-thrillers (*Ne okreći se, sine/Don't Turn Back, Son*, 1956), Bauer knew how to play with emotions, and children. He would repeat this game twenty years later with a television series (and the movie) *Zimovanje u Jakobsfeldu/Wintering in*

Jakobsfeld (1975), the story of a young boy finding shelter and work in a small Pannonic village during World War II. One of the most successful television series ever in former Yugoslavia, it turned the young actor Slavko Štimac into a national hero. As a film-maker with high social awareness, Bauer found an original way of putting a tough political message into a genre form and occasionally diluting it with a touch of humour. Back in 1957, he directed the highly acclaimed *Samo ljudi/Traces*, a melodramatic love story about a war invalid and a blind girl, full of half-hidden dark undertones. His most successful socially critical film was *Licem u lice/Face to Face* (1963), which demonstrated how the idea of socialist self-management could degenerate into local nepotism and corruption. SP

Other Films Include: *Milioni na otoku/Millions on the Island* (1954); *Tri Ane/The Three Annes* (1959); *Martin u oblacima/Martin in the Clouds* (1961); *Prekobrojna/Superfluous* (1962); *Nikoletina Bursać* (1964); *Doći i ostati/To Come and to Stay* (1965); *Četvrti suputnik/ Fourth Companion* (1967); *Salaš u Malom Ritu* (1976); *Boško Buha* (1979).

BAUER, Yevgeni F.　　Moscow 1865 – Crimea [Russian Empire] 1917

Russian director. After a brief career as a newspaper caricaturist, actor and stage designer for popular winter garden theatres, Bauer became, even more briefly, the leading figure in Russian pre-Revolutionary cinema. He began by designing the sets for *Trëkhsotletie tsarstvovaniya doma Romanovykh/The Tercentenary of the Rule of the House of Romanov* (1913), and directed more than eighty films in the ensuing four years. Heavily influenced by Russian literary Symbolism and the national version of *art nouveau* known as *style moderne*, Bauer's films were characterised by their sense of architecture and volume, their distinctively spacious sets, the sparing use of furniture and furnishings and subtle use of light and shade. He was the first to create a new sense of screen reality, as opposed to straightforward naturalism. Ivan Perestiani* remarked: 'Bauer had a gift for using light. His scenery was alive, mixing the monumental with the intimate. ... A beam of light in his hands was an artist's brush.' Bauer's best-known films dealt with the extremes of human experience, the borderlines between life, art and death, as in *Ditya bol'shogo goroda/A Child of the Big City* (1914), *Grëzy/Daydreams* and *Posle smerti/After Death* (both 1915) and *Zhizn' za zhizn'/A Life for a Life* (1916). He produced, designed, scripted and photographed most of his films, which were very popular with Russian audiences. He made Vera Kholodnaya* a star and became, from 1913, the principal money-earner for Alexander Khanzhonkov's* studio, which paid him the largest salary in Russian cinema at the time and in which he became a principal shareholder. But he never achieved his ambition to become a screen actor: while practising in the Crimea to play the part of a lame artist, he fell and broke his leg, caught pneumonia and died. RT

BEK-NAZAROV, Amo

Yerevan, Armenia [Russian Empire] 1892 – Moscow 1965

Armenian Soviet director, actor and scriptwriter. Bek-Nazarov began his career as a screen actor during World War I in the films of Yevgeni Bauer*, Ivan Perestiani* and Vladimir Gardin*, and directed his first features in the Georgian studio in the 1920s. His best-known works were the silent *Namus* (1926), generally regarded as the first Armenian feature film, the historical drama *Zore* (1927) and the comedy *Shor i Shorshor/Shor and Shorshor* (1927). His career continued throughout the sound period and his *Zangezur* (1938) was awarded the Stalin Prize in 1941. After his death the Armenian film studio was named after him. RT

BLACK WAVE – see YUGOSLAV 'BLACK WAVE'

BOBROVA, Lidia A.

Zabaikalsk, Siberia [USSR] 1952

Russian director and scriptwriter. Bobrova graduated in history from Leningrad State University in 1975. In 1983 she graduated from the Scriptwriting Faculty at VGIK*, where she had studied with Evgenii Gabrilovich, and in 1991 she finished the Higher Courses for Directors in the workshop of Vladimir Grammatikov. Her concern is with life in the countryside. In *Oi, vy, Gusi/Hey, You Geese* (1991) she explores the degradation of a Russian family which, in the course of the film, turns into a metaphor for life in Russia at large. *V toi strane/In That Land* (1997) is filmed with non-professionals in the countryside. Bobrova here investigates the alcoholism which casts its shadow over the male population, leaving the women to run the family. A sick farmer is offered a voucher to spend a month in a sanatorium on the Black Sea, but never actually manages to get there. Other places represent a threat to life as lived by the village community, and even when this fear is overcome they still remain tantalisingly out of reach. As with her contemporary Sergei Selyanov*, the rural settings of Bobrova's films reflect a return to the traditions, roots and simple values of country life, while the city represents the intrusion of harmful influences. Bobrova was awarded the State Prize in 1999 for her contribution to film-making. BB

30

BODROV, Sergei

Russian director and scriptwriter. Bodrov graduated from the scriptwriting faculty of VGIK* in 1974, and worked as special correspondent for the satirical weekly *Krokodil* [Crocodile] from 1975 to 1980. He has written the screenplays for over twenty films, and is the author of stories and satirical sketches. Since 1984 he has filmed both in Russia and abroad, living most of the time in Los Angeles. His directorial debut came with *Neprofessionaly/Non-professionals* (1985), the story of a travelling rock band made in Kazakhstan, while *SER/Freedom is Paradise* (1989) established his reputation internationally. Like many of Bodrov's films, it is concerned with the poverty-stricken criminal classes: an orphan boy searches for his father, whom he finds in prison. *Katala/The Swindler* (1989) also deals with the collapse of a relationship against a backdrop of corruption and crime, as does *Belyi korol', krasnaya koroleva/White King, Red Queen* (1992). In *Ya khotela uvidet' angelov/I Wanted to See Angels* (1992) Bodrov returns to the young generation and its degradation into the criminal underground, where personal happiness remains a dream. *Kavkazskii plennik/The Prisoner of the Mountains* (1996) can be seen as the major Russian anti-war film of the 1990s. Based on Tolstoy's story, it offers a perspective on war in terms of individual human loss rather than the clash of ideas or ideals. In a belligerent region in the Caucasus Zhilin and Kostylin are taken prisoner by the Muslim, Abdul, who wants to exchange them for his son, who is held captive by the Russian military. The exchange fails since the Russians cheat. The prisoners try to escape: Kostylin is killed, while Zhilin is taken back to Abdul. Abdul's son is shot by accident, but the grieving Abdul nevertheless lets Zhilin go. As Zhilin returns to freedom, Russian helicopters arrive to destroy the village in an act of revenge. Bodrov does not discriminate against any culture: the history of the two captives is told with the same compassion as the history of Abdul's family. The Muslims are both victims and aggressors, and so are the Russians. This film investigates the response of men who are reduced to objects of the state and deprived of political ideals. BB

BÓDY, Gábor

Hungarian film director. Bódy was the only internationally renowned Hungarian experimental director, and he was by far the most controversial figure of the third postwar generation of film-makers. He studied philosophy and later graduated from the Academy of Theatre and Film Arts in Budapest. In the mid-1970s he created an experimental section in the Balázs Béla Stúdió* and complemented his experimental film-making with intensive theoretical research and teaching. In the 1980s his interest turned to other visual media, and during a stay in Germany he created an international video-periodical for distribution of video art called 'Infermental'. He used extended video and Super-8 footage in his last feature film, *Kutya éji dala/The Dog's Night Song* (1983), in which he took on the main role. Bódy made three feature films and a number of experimental films and videotapes, and all his work is characterised by the systematic dissection of the surface of visual forms and the conventions of representation. Although he did not face problems of political censorship – his interest in cinema was of a different nature – his kind of film-making activity became increasingly difficult to sustain in the mid-1980s. His last film, representing different contemporaneous avant-garde and underground sub-cultures, was viewed by studio officials as an anarchistic and destructive work and funds were not forthcoming for further video-art experiments. Bódy committed suicide on 24 October 1985. KAB

Other Films Include: *Amerikai anzix/American Postcard* (1975); *Nárcisz és Psyché/Narcissus and Psyche I-II-III* (1980).

BOLVARY, Geza von   Budapest 1897 – Rosenheim, Germany 1961

Hungarian director of musical comedies in the prosperous German and Austrian cinemas of the 1930s and 1940s. Already known for his silent melodramas and comedies, Bolvary became hot property after his first sound film, the Willy Forst vehicle *Zwei Herzen im 3/4 Takt/Two Hearts in Waltz Time* (1930), which made him the specialist of a new musical sub-genre, the Viennese film operetta. The film's huge international success led to a number of follow-ups centred on popular German actors – Forst again (*Ein Tango für Dich/A Tango for You*, 1930; *Die lustigen Weiber von Wien/Merry Wives of Vienna*, 1931), Zarah Leander (*Premiere*, 1937), and Willy Fritsch (*Die Fledermaus*, 1945). Most notable among his postwar films, apart from other musicals, were a number of entertaining but historically and politically intriguing portraits of musicians, including the classic *Ein Lied geht um die Welt/Joseph Schmidt Story* (1958). MW

Other Films Include: *Champagner/Champagne, The Vagabond Queen* [UK], *The Wrecker* [UK] (1929); *Der Herr auf Bestellung* (1930); *Der Raub der Mona Lisa/The Theft of the Mona Lisa* (1931); *Wiener G'schichten/Vienna Tales* (1940); *Schicksal/Fate* (1942); *Schrammeln* (1944); *Fritz und Friederike* (1952); *Mein Leopold* (1955); *Schwarzwaldmelodie/Melody from the Black Forest* (1956); *Was die Schwalbe sang/What the Swallow Sang* (1956); *Zwei Herzen im Mai/Two Hearts in May* (1958).

BONDARCHUK, Sergei F. Belotserka, Ukraine 1920 – Moscow 1994

Soviet director and actor. Graduate of VGIK*, who first appeared in Sergei Gerasimov's* *Molodaya gvardiya/The Young Guard* in 1948. He subsequently became one of the leading actors in Soviet cinema but is best known in the West for directing a four-part version of Tolstoy's *Voina i mir/War and Peace* (1966–7), which won an Oscar, and *Waterloo* (1970, a Soviet–Italian co-production), both notable for their large-scale battle scenes and the quality of their acting. Vasili Shukshin*, Orson Welles and Rod Steiger have appeared in his films, as has Bondarchuk himself, from his directorial debut, a film version of Sholokhov's *Sud'ba cheloveka/The Fate of a Man* (1959). Bondarchuk also filmed Sholokhov's *Oni srazhalis' za rodinu/They Fought for Their Country* (1977). RT

BOROWCZYK, Walerian Kwilcz 1923

Polish director. Borowczyk studied fine art and worked in lithography and poster design before turning to animation. His first films, made with Jan Lenica*, revealed a bizarre and dark vision with a satirical edge influenced by surrealism. The success of *Dom/House* (1958) launched his European career and in 1959 Borowczyk moved to France. Here his macabre wit came to the fore in films like *Renaissance* (1963). Switching to live action, Borowczyk made impressively original features, especially *Goto, l'île d'amour/Goto, Isle of Love* (1969) and *Blanche* (1971). Films such as *Contes immoraux/Immoral Tales* (1974) and *La Bête/The Beast* (1975) established Borowczyk as something of an 'eroticist', but subsequent features moved to sexploitation, using material largely unworthy of his talents. AW

Other Films Include: *Les Jeux des anges* (1964, anim.); *Le Théâtre de Monsieur et Madame Kabal* (1967, anim.); *Dzieje Grzechu/Story of a Sin* (1975); *La Marge* (1976); *Les héroïnes du mal/Three Immoral Women* (1979); *L'armoire/The Wardrobe* (1979); *Lulu* (1980); *Docteur Jekyll et les femmes/The Blood of Doctor Jekyll* (1981); *Ars amandi/The Art of Love* (1983); *Emmanuelle 5* (1987); *Cérémonie d'amour/Rites of Love* (1988).

BOSNIA and HERZEGOVINA – see (former) YUGOSLAVIA

BOSTAN, Elisabeta   Buhuşi 1931

Romanian director and scriptwriter, specialising in children's and youth films. One of the earliest graduates of the Bucharest Theatre and Film School, she made innovatory shorts, and achieved prominence with her sensitive evocation of childhood in a series about a boy called *Naica* (1963–7). Her first feature, *Puştiul/The Kid* (1961), was followed by a skilful effort to adapt and film for a wide audience the highly literary work of Ion Creanga – *Amintiri din copilărie/Childhood Memories* (1965). *Veronica* (1972) and *Mama/Rock'n'Roll Wolf* (1977) provide flights of intelligent fantasy in which music plays a key role. The latter film initiated a number of features and series for children co-produced with the USSR, notably *Salţimbanci/Clowns* (1981). *Unde eşti copilărie?/Where Did You Go, My Childhood?* (1988) is an eloquent rites of passage film. As the most resilient Romanian woman film-maker, Bostan continues to work at home and abroad, and lectures at the Institute of Theatre and Film. MM

Other Films as Director Include: *Tinerete fara batrînete/Kingdom in the Clouds* (1968); *Veronica* (1972); *Veronica se întoarce/Veronica Comes Back* (1973); *Promi-siuni/Promises* (1985); *Zîmbet de soare/ Sunny Smile* (1987); *Desene pe asfalt/Drawings on Asphalt* (1989); *Campioana/The Champion* (1990); *Telefonul/A Telephone Call* (1991).

BOYANA STUDIOS

Bulgarian film studios. When one considers that back in 1953 only one feature film was produced in Bulgaria, the growth of Bulgarian cinema since then is nothing short of sensational. The quality of film production rose with the increased sophistication of the home audience. Before World War II, there were only 165 movie theatres scattered across the entire country; by the end of the 1960s there were more than 3,000. Boyana Studios, constructed in the 1950s at the foot of Mount Vitoša overlooking Sofia, and expanded in the 1960s into 'Film City Boyana', include five separate and independent sections: Boyana Feature Film Studio, the Sofia Animation Studio, the paired Vreme Popular Science and Documentary Film Studios, and Boyana Film Laboratory.

Until 1983, Boyana Feature Film Studio was composed of four creative groups, each with its own artistic director. Beginning in 1983, however, when an ill-fated reform was introduced by the newly appointed general director Nikolai Nennov, the four creative groups were disbanded and feature film production placed under the double

34

management of Zako Heskija and Ljudmil Kirkov*. However, as the quality of feature film production noticeably decreased during the 1980s, the worldwide reputation of the Sofia Animation Studio correspondingly increased. Todor Dinov (*Jabolkata/The Apple*, 1963; *Margaritkata/The Daisy*, 1965), the father of Bulgarian animation, inspired a 'school' of highly talented film cartoonists who quickly won world recognition: Donju Donev (*Trimata glupazi/The Three Fools*, 1970; *De Facto*, 1973), Stojan Dukov (*En Passant*, 1975), Ivan Vesselinov (*Naslednici/The Heirs*, 1970), Henri Kulev, Slav Bakalov, Ivan Andonov, Rumen Petkov, Radka Bačvarova, Hristo Topuzanov, Zdenka Dojčeva, Genčo Simeonov, Georgi Čavdarov, Asparukh Panov, Nikola Todorov, Proiko Proikov, Penčo Bogdanov, Velislav Kazakov and Vlado Šomov. The philosophical parables of Dinov, Donev and Dukov became the trademark of Bulgarian animation during the 1970s, supported to a great extent by the biennial Varna World Animation Film Festival.

On the documentary and popular science side, it was Zahari Žandov* who first signalled a new Bulgarian cinematography when his documentary *Hora sred oblacite/Men amid the Clouds* (1946) won a prize at the Venice festival. Hristo Kovačev, whose *Ot edno do osem/ From One to Eight* (1966) also won a prize at Venice, chronicled the history of the Bulgarian working class at the Documentary Film Studio from 1950 onwards. And Januš Vazov, whose career at the Popular Science Studio began in 1951, made more than forty films on art and folklore (*Narodno vajatelstvo/Folk Sculpture*, 1956), history and biology, and occasionally feature films with documentary elements, such as *Stepni hora/Steppe People* (1985). In 1988 director Ljudmil Stajkov* worked here on the super production *Vreme na nasilie/Time of Violence*, shot by cameraman Radoslav Spassov*.

The studios at Boyana possess an extensive stock of wardrobe and props, but the land of the studios has been reclaimed by its former owners and its future is problematic. Since 1989 there have been substantial cuts in personnel. Under the current legislation, the studios are an independent state-run unit, Boyana Film, which develops film production and distribution activities and heavily relies on runaway Western productions. Boyana Film is directed by film-maker Evgeni Mikhailov, under whose artistic supervision a series of documentaries on Bulgarian cinema was produced and broadcast on national television in 1998. **Web-site:** http://www.boyanafilm.bg. RH

BREGOVIĆ, Goran
Sarajevo 1953

Yugoslav composer (Bosnia), working in France. Nickname Brega. A Sarajevan of Serbo-Croatian origin, Bregović's intensive and explosive music is a fusion of Balkan folklore and electronic poliphony. In the world of cinema he is best known for his collaboration with 'the Balkan Fellini', Emir Kusturica*. Bregović wrote the musical score for the acclaimed *Dom za vešanje/Time of the Gypsies* (1989), *Arizona Dream* (1993), and the multiple award-winning *Underground* (1995). Bregović is a connoisseur of the elaborate folk tradition of Gypsy music, as well as of other genres of the 'world beat' category. In the 1990s he was invited to work on French co-productions which relied on his sensitivity to the world's musical traditions – like the Morocco-set *La nuit sacrée/Sacred Night* (1993, Nicolas Klotz), the Tunisia-set *Le nombril du monde/The Navel of the World* (1993, Ariel Zeitoun), and the Georgia-set *Les mille et une recettes du cuisinier amoureux/A Chef in Love* (1996, Nana Dzhordzadze). A prolific composer working in a variety of genres, from folk to jazz, throughout the 1980s Bregović was the leader of the most popular Yugoslav rock group, the Sarajevo-based Bijelo dugme/White button. During his Sarajevo years Bregović also worked with Bosnian directors Ademir Kenović on *Kuduz* (1989) and Bato Cengić on *Gluvi barut/Silent Gunpowder* (1990). Since the early 1990s Bregović lives in Paris and besides writing film music he tours Europe as an actively performing musician of his own highly original works. In France he came to be appreciated for the music in Patrice Chéreau's *La Reine Margot/Queen Margot* (1994). DI

BREJCHOVÁ, Jana   Prague 1940

Czech actress. Jana Brejchová was the leading female star of Czech cinema in the postwar period. Although she lacked formal training, her physical beauty and grace were soon noticed in her early films, *Štěňata/Puppies* (1957), co-scripted by Miloš Forman*, and Jiří Weiss's* *Vlčí jáma/The Wolf Trap* (1957). Parts in key films such as Vojtěch Jasný's *Touha/Desire* (1958) and Jiří Krejčik's *Vyšší princip/A Higher Principle* (1960) led to major acting roles in Evald Schorm's* *Každý den odvahu/Everyday Courage* (1964) and *Návrat ztraceného syna/Return of the Prodigal Son* (1966). Equally at home in comedy and drama, she continued to lend distinction to Czech films in the 1970s and 1980s, notably in Vladimír Drha's study of mother–daughter relations, *Citlivá místa/Sensitive Spots* (1988). Her sister, Hana Brejchová, was cast in the leading roles of Forman's *Lásky jedné plavovlásky/A Blonde in Love* (1965) and Jaroslav Papoušek's *Nejkrásnější věk/The Best Age* (1968). PH

Other Films Include: *Žižkovská romance/A Local Romance* (1958); *Baron Prášil/Baron Münchhausen* (1961); *Bloudění/Wandering* (1965); *Ženu ani květinou neuhodíš/Never Strike a Woman – Even with a Flower* (1966); *Noc nevěsty/Night of the Bride* (1967); *Farařův konec/End of a Priest* (1968); *Zabil jsem Einsteina pánové/Gentlemen, I Have Killed Einstein* (1969); *Luk královny Dorotky/The Bow of Queen Dorothy* (1970); *Slečna Golem/Miss Golem* (1972); *Mladý muž a bílá velryba/Young Man and the White Whale* (1978); *Útěky domů/Escapes Home* (1979); *Schůzka se stíny/A Meeting with Shadows* (1982); *Zánik* *samoty Berhof/The End of the Lonely Farm Berghof* (1983); *Vlastně se nic nestalo/Killing with Kindness* (1988); *Ma ja pomsta/Vengeance is Mine* (1994); *Hrad z pisku/The Sandcastle* (1994, dir. Zuzana Zemanova); *Poceti mého mladsiho bratra/The Conception of My Younger Brother* (2000, dir. Vladimír Drha).

BUFTEA (BUCUREŞTI/Bucharest) STUDIO

Romanian feature film studio at Buftea, a 'film city' sixteen kilometres outside Bucharest. Mostly built between 1952 and 1958 on a thirty-hectare lakeside, Buftea represents a highly centralised film industry started almost from scratch. Nationalisation of production in 1948 led directly to plans for Buftea, with workshops, labs, housing, a power plant, etc. The four original sound stages extended to 1,000 sqm – among the largest in Eastern Europe – and by the 1970s there were five stages with a total area of 3,000 sqm. There are impressive permanent sets, including a castle, and forty trained thorough-bred horses on site. The original equipment, from all over Europe, was of good quality, and Buftea is still reasonably equipped. In 1968 Orson Welles, while working at Buftea, flattered the studio with the compliment that 'there are very few in the world that can compete'. Responsible for all except documentary and animation films, Buftea has produced nearly 500 features and many television series. In addition to regular contacts with East European countries, there have been co-productions with the West – primarily France and West Germany – at their highest in the 1970s. Many, like Sergiu Nicolaescu's French–Romanian series 'William the Conqueror', were epics, and a massive French television series was finished in 1987. Before the 1989 revolution the management had already decided that viability lay in providing facilities for foreign producers, but the economic crisis facing feature production and the ending of political commitment to cinema threaten the very existence of Buftea. In 1998 the Romanian government sold the studio to a private company, Media Pro. It is expected that after a facelift and fresh investment boost, Buftea will be reoriented to specialise in television production. MM

BUGAJSKI, Ryszard   Warsaw 1943

Polish director. Bugajski studied philosophy at Warsaw University and graduated from Łódź* in 1973. He translated and produced plays for television before co-directing his debut feature, *Kobieta i Kobieta/A Woman and a Woman* (1980) with Janusz Dymek. In 1980 he joined Andrzej Wajda's* prestigious Film Unit 'X' and in 1981 made *Przesłuchanie/The Interrogation* (released 1989). This harrowing tale of the political arrest of a young woman and her subsequent torture by the authorities was set in the Stalinist era. Even so, the film was considered too inflammatory by the cultural *apparatchiks* of Jaruzelski's Poland and was banned. Although a pirate video circulated widely in Poland, the film was only seen internationally in 1990, winning the Best Actress award at Cannes for Krystyna Janda* as well as international distribution and acclaim. With no work prospects in Poland, Bugajski emigrated to Canada in 1985, where he is currently directing for the cinema and television (as Richard Bugajski). In Canada he made a feature film about the problems of the natives in British Columbia, *Clearcut* (1992). His 1995 film, *Gracze/Players*, was a Polish production but its release there was delayed by new allegations of censorship. AW

BULAJIĆ, Veljko Nikšič, Montenegro 1928

Montenegran director whose debut film in 1959, *Vlak bez voznog reda/Train without a Timetable* (about the mass migrations after World War II), won two Golden Arenas at the annual national film festival in Pula*. The 'good guy' of Yugoslav cinema, privileged by the authorities and hated by colleagues, he directed two of the biggest spectacular epics of the 1960s dealing with the partisan struggle during World War II: *Kozara* (1962) and *Bitka na Neretvi/Battle on the River Neretva* (1969) [> YUGOSLAV 'PARTISAN FILMS']. For the latter he acquired an international cast (including Franco Nero, Sergei Bondarchuk, Orson Welles and Yul Brynner) and won Oscar nominations. In 1980 he directed a television series of interviews with Tito, *Tito's Memoirs*. He was deeply involved in another huge project, *Veliki transport/Great Transport/The Courageous* (1983). Although thematically close to his successful debut, the film was a disaster, both artistically and financially, drawing Bulajić into a series of court cases, newspaper polemics and scandals. Bulajić's latest project is a superproduction on the siege of Sarajevo 1992–5. SP

Other Films Include: *Rat/War* (1960); *Uzavreli grad/When the Fires Started/Smouldering City* (1961); *Skopje 1963* [doc] (1964); *Pogled u zjenicu sunca/A Glance at the Pupil of the Sun* (1966); *Atentat u Sarajevu/Assassination in Sarajevo/The Day that Shook the World* (1975); *Čov-jek koga treba ubiti/A Man to Kill* (1979); *Visoki napon/High Voltage* (1981); *Obecana zemlja/Promised Land* (1986); *Donator* (1989); *Sarajevo* (in production).

BULGARIA

River traffic on the Danube brought the Lumière Cinematographe to Bulgaria. The first presentations took place in February 1897 in the port town of Ruse, and a few months later in Sofia. When Vasil Gendov, a pioneer of Bulgarian cinema, opened his modern theatre in

Sofia in 1908, he could depend on a regular flow of movies from France and Germany by way of Vienna and the Danube. To save his enterprise when World War I broke out, he turned to film production and starred himself in a self-directed Max Linder copy: *Balgaran e galant/The Bulgarian is Gallant* (1915). Its immediate box-office success launched a primitive Bulgarian national cinema. Between 1915 and 1948, when the film industry was nationalised, fifty-five feature films were made, eleven of them produced by Gendov-Film and many starring the director himself and his wife Žanna Gendova.

One minor silent masterpiece, Boris Grežov's *Sled požara u Rusija/ After the Fire over Russia* (1929), the story of White Russians who emigrated to Bulgaria to work in the mines, is recognised as the high point of the pioneer days of Bulgarian cinema. Grežov also directed the first Bulgarian sound film, *Beskrăstni grobove/Graves without Crosses* (1931), a production all the more remarkable for lamenting the victims of the military 'White Terror' of 1923. The first 'art film' – featuring actors from the National Theatre – was Nikola Larin's *Pod staroto nebe/Under the Old Sky* (1922), based on Tsanko Tserkovski's drama. During the interregnum period, Bulgarian productions by private companies – Gendov-Film, Rila-Film, Balkan-Film, Kubrat-Film and Rex-Film – had to contend with more attractive imported fare: by the mid-1920s, German films had cornered an estimated 45 per cent of the home market, followed by American films with 29 and French with 18 per cent. Against these commercial giants, the Bulgarian film industry survived mostly by filming popular folk legends and well-known literary classics: Gendov's *Bay Ganjo* (1922), Grežov's *Momina skala/ Maiden Rock* (1923), Peter K. Stojčev's adaptation of Elin Pelin's novel *Zemya/Land* (1930) and his *Planinska pesen/Song of the Mountains* (1934), Aleksandar Vazov's *Gramada/Cairn* (1936), and Yossip Novak's *Strahil Vojvoda/Strahil the Voyvoda* (1938). Unfortunately, most of these films were lost in an air raid on Sofia during World War II.

Following the liberation of Sofia in September 1944, private companies produced eight more films – until 5 April 1948, when the film industry was nationalised. Boris Borozanov, himself a film pioneer, wedded Bulgarian patriotism to the schematic formula of Socialist Realism* in *Kalin orelăt/Kalin the Eagle* (1950), a heroic tale about a nationalist rebel set at the end of Ottoman rule. But the real beginning of modern Bulgarian cinema is marked by documentarist Zahari Žandov's* first venture into fiction film, *Trevoga/Alarm* (1951), aided by screenwriter Angel Wagenstein*, who was able to inject some flesh-and-blood passion into Orlin Vassiliev's schematic drama. Until the death of Stalin* in 1953, and the subsequent end of the harshly restrictive, Moscow-dictated 'Žandov Years' in 1955, Bulgarian cinema was noteworthy only for the shooting-between-the-lines segments in historical epics and contemporary social films: Dako Dakovski's *Pod igoto/Under the Yoke* (1952) and *Nespokoen păt/The Troubled Road* (1955), Borislav Šaraliev's *Pesen za čoveka/Song of Man* (1954),

Žandov's *Septemvrijci/Septembrists* (1954) and his remake of Elin Pelin's *Zemya/Land* (1957), and Nikola Korabov's *Dimitrovgradci/People of Dimitrovgrad* (1956).

With the coming of the 'thaw' following the Twentieth Party Conference in the Soviet Union and the April Plenum of 1956, Bulgarian cinematography came into its own as a prominent national movement in Eastern Europe. Rangel Vălčanov* collaborated with screenwriter Valeri Petrov* on *Na malkija ostrov/On a Small Island* (1958), Binka Željazkova* with Hristo Ganev on the politically-oriented and subsequently banned *Partizani (Životăt si teče tiho...)/Partisans (Life Flows Quietly by)* (1958), and East German director Konrad Wolf with Wagenstein on *Zvezdi/Sterne/Stars* (1958), a Bulgarian–East German co-production. Despite the evident 'revolutionary' messages in all three films, their [Bulgarian] 'poetic realism'* and the psychological analysis of the leading characters made them stylistically distinctive. A third Bulgarian director was added to the 'poetic cinema' group when cameraman–documentarist Vălo Radev*, a VGIK* graduate, made his first feature film, *Kradecăt na praskovi/The Peach Thief* (1964), a Bulgarian–Yugoslav co-production. Radev was also instrumental in launching major technical innovations at Boyana* Studios, notably widescreen production and colour.

With the downfall of Nikita Khrushchev in October 1964, the screenplay for Vălčanov's *Lachenite obuvki na neznajnija voin/The Unknown Soldier's Patent Leather Shoes* was put on hold indefinitely, and it wasn't until fifteen years later that the film could be made. Vălčanov left Bulgaria to work in Czechoslovakia (*Ezop/Aesop*, 1970), while screenwriters Ganev and Petrov chose 'spiritual exile'. Over the next few years Bulgarian cinema faced a nearly ruinous crisis under four successive dictatorial general directors, until 1971 when Pavel Pissarev was appointed to the post to win back the confidence of exiled and alienated film-makers. Three important films on contemporary social themes were immediately banned upon completion: Hristo Piskov and Irina Aktaševa's *Ponedelnik sutrin/Monday Morning* (1966), Binka Željazkova's* *Privărzanijat balon/The Attached Balloon* (1967), and Ljubomir Šarlandjiev's *Prokurorat/The Prosecutor* (1968). In addition, several other screenplays were doctored, while even completed films were re-edited to conform with nebulous production formulas. Despite the severe restrictions, however, promising directorial talent continued to surface at Boyana Studios: Zako Heskija (*Gorešto pladne/Torrid Noon*, 1966), the team of stage director Griša Ostrovski and cameraman Todor Stoyanov (*Otklonenie/Sidetrack*, 1967), documentarist turned fiction film-maker Eduard Zahariev* (*Nebeto na Veleka/The Sky over Veleka*, 1968), Ljudmil Kirkov* (*Švedski krale/Swedish Kings*, 1968), Metodi Andonov* (*Bjalata staja/The White Room*, 1968), the team of stage director Hristo Hristov* and animation film-maker Todor Dinov (*Ikonostasăt/Iconostasis*, 1969), and Georgi Stojanov (*Ptici i hrătki/Birds and Greyhounds*, 1969).

The turning point came in 1972 with the release back-to-back of

Andonov's *Kozijat rog/The Goat's Horn*, the biggest box-office success in Bulgarian film history, and Ljudmil Staikov's* *Obič/Affection*, winner of the Gold Prize at the 1973 Moscow festival. Aided again by novelists, scriptwriters and playwrights – Jordan Radičkov*, Nikolai Haitov* and Georgi Mišev* – a Bulgarian 'new wave' of socially conscious films by talented directorial newcomers became the talk of international festivals: Zahariev and Mišev's *Prebrojavane na divite zajci/The Hare Census* (1973) and *Vilna zona/Villa Zone* (1975), Ivan Terziev and Nikolai Nikiforov's *Măže bez rabota/Men without Work* (1973), Hristov and Radičkov's *Posledno ljato/The Last Summer* (1972–4), Georgi Djulgerov's* *Avantaž/Advantage* (1977), and the reunited Vălčanov and Petrov's *S ljubov i nežnost/With Love and Tenderness* (1978).

The movement was curtailed somewhat by the state's enormous financial investment in a series of epic spectacles produced on the occasion of the 1,300th anniversary of the founding of Bulgaria in 681: Žandov's *Bojanskijat majstor/Master of Boyana* (1981), Djulgerov's *Mera spored mera/Measure for Measure* (1981), Staikov's *Khan Asparuh* (1981), Šaraliev's *Boris părvi/Boris I* (1985) and Stojanov's *Konstantin Filosof/Constantine the Philosopher* (1986). In the mid-1980s, the Bulgarian government started an assimilation campaign against the Muslim minorities in the country. One of the best-known works of Bulgarian cinema, Ljudmil Staikov's historical epic, *Vreme na nasilie/Time of Violence* (1988), was commissioned as part of this campaign. A lavish, impressive and compelling adaptation of the 1966 novel *Time of Parting* by Anton Donchev, it deals with the forced conversion of Bulgarian Slavs to Islam during the years of the Ottoman Empire. The clash between Turks and Bulgarians is presented as a manifestation of an eternal conflict between Islamic and Christian civilisations. The release of the film coincided with the peak of the campaign for ethnic assimilation. Thus, it indirectly endorsed the human rights' abuses committed at the time. *Time of Violence* is impressively produced, shot beautifully in the Rhodopi region, and could easily be considered a masterpiece of Bulgarian cinema if it was not for the unfortunate socio-political context in which it was made. Towards the end of the 1980s the political reforms that swept across Eastern Europe inspired some veteran directors to re-examine the Stalinist past (Djulgerov's *Lagerăt/The Camp*, 1989), while young graduates of the Sofia Film and Theatre School (VITIS) probed failings in the socialist system: Ljudmil Todorov's *Bjagašti kučeta/Running Dogs* (1988), Krassimir Krumov's *Exitus* (1988), Čaim Cohen's *Zasčitete drebnite životni/Protect the Small Animals* (1988), and Peter Popzlatev's *Az, grafinjata/I, the Countess* (1989).

Today, following the downfall of Todor Živkov and subsequent democratic elections in 1990, state funding for national film productions has been cut to the bone. From an average of twenty or so feature films annually in Bulgaria a decade ago, and approximately the same number of television films, only half a dozen domestic film and television productions were scheduled in Boyana for the 1993–4 season. Without co-production input from the West, contemporary Bulgarian cine-matography is for all practical purposes non-existent. A stark contrast with the heyday of the 1970s under Pavel Pissarev, when Boyana Studios turned out nearly one feature film a week for cinemas and tele-vision. Film remains mainly a state concern, with a new body, the National Film Centre, set up to oversee funding allocation and to assist with production and distribution. Private, co-operative and state film production companies exist, but are plagued by financial limitations, and as in other parts of the region, international co-productions are fre-quent. Some of the most successful Bulgarian films of recent years were Nikolai Volev's remake of the classic *Kozijat Rog/The Goat's Horn* (1995), George Djulgerov's *Chernata Liastovica/The Black Swallow* (1996), and Eduard Zahariev's *Zakasnialo palnolunie/Belated Full Moon* (1997). Only a handful of new directors managed to make feature films. These included Evgeni Mihailov, Lyudmil Todorov, Ivan Cherkelov, Krassimir Krumov, Docho Bodzhakov, Marius Kurkinski, Ilian Simeonov and Khristian Nochev, Mikhail Pandurski, Nidal Algafari, Milena Andonova and Andrei Slabakov. RH

Bib: Ronald Holloway, *The Bulgarian Cinema,* 1986; Ronald Holloway, 'Bulgaria: The Cinema of Poetics', in Daniel J. Goulding (ed.), *Post New Wave Cinema in the Soviet Union and Eastern Europe,* 1989; Dina Iordanova, 'Canaries and Birds of Prey: The New Season of Bulgarian Cinema', in John Bell (ed.), *Bulgaria in Transition* 1998.

BULGARIAN 'POETIC REALISM'

Bulgarian stylistic trend of the 1950s and 1960s, particularly evident in the work of cinematographers but also due to the vision of scriptwrit-ers and directors. The primary influence came from Soviet cinema in the wake of the Twentieth Party Congress in 1956, when new guide-lines for film production were laid down by Khrushchev. Bulgarian 'new wave' directors Rangel Vălčanov* (*Na malkija ostrov/On a Small Island*, 1958), Binka Željazkova* (*A bjahme mladi/We Were Young,* 1961) and Vălo Radev* (*Kradecăt na praskovi/The Peach Thief*, 1964) were heavily influenced by Soviet cameraman Sergei Urusevsky's work on Mikhail K. Kalatozov's* *Letyat zhuravli/The Cranes Are Flying* (1957), winner of the Palme d'Or at the 1958 Cannes festival. Other influences came from Italian neo-realism (Vittorio De Sica, Luchino Visconti, Roberto Rossellini) and from the poetic short films of French experimentalist Albert Lamorisse (*Le Ballon rouge/The Red Balloon,* 1956), rather than the prewar French Poetic Realism. The movement subsided significantly after Khrushchev's fall from power in 1964, although 'poetic realism' was to remain an essential trait in the best of Bulgarian cinema for some time after. RH

42

BURIAN, Vlasta

Liberec [then Austria-Hungary] 1891 – Prague 1962

Czech comedian. Regarded as the genius of Czech cabaret, Burian lived for the theatre and appeared on stage regularly, making films during the day. As with music hall and vaudeville performers elsewhere, his films were closely linked to theatrically inspired routines, with visual comedy allied to verbal humour and an inspired mimicry. He was often compared to Groucho Marx, but his thin, angular body and mournful moustache produced quite a different resonance. Between 1923 and 1956 he appeared in thirty-seven features, many directed by Karel Lamač* and Martin Frič*, opposite leading stars such as Anny Ondra*, Josef Rovenský and Theodor Pištek. Two typical films of the 1930s were *Funebrák* (1932), in which he played an undertaker's assistant, and *Lelíček ve službách Sherlocka Holmese/Lelíček in the Service of Sherlock Holmes* (1932), both directed by Lamač. For Frič, he starred in an adaptation of Gogol's *The Inspector-General* (*Revizor*, 1933) and as the Baron in *Baron Prášil/Baron Münchhausen* (1940). Tricked into parodying the exiled foreign minister, Jan Masaryk, during World War II, he was subsequently tried and forbidden to act, but returned to the screen in the early 1950s. PH

Other Films Include: *Tu ten kámen/Tutankhamun/This is the Stone* (1923); *C. a K. polní maršálek/C. and K. Field Marshal, On a jeho sestra/He and his Sister* (1931); *Anton Špelec, ostrostřelec/Anton Špelec, Sharpshooter* (1932); *Pobočník Jeho Výsosti/His Majesty's Adjutant, U snědeného krámu/The Ruined Shopkeeper* (1933); *Hrdina jedné noci/Hero of a Single Night* (1935); *Tři vejce do skla/Three Eggs, Soft-boiled* (1937); *Katakomby/The Catacombs* (1940); *Zaostřit, prosím!/Close Up, Please!* (1956).

C

ČAP, František

Čachovice [then Austria-Hungary] 1913 – Piran, Slovenia 1972

Czech/Slovene director and scriptwriter. After his debut in 1939, it took Čap only a year to become 'the most appreciated and the best paid director in Czechoslovakia', when he made *Babička/Grandmother* (1940), his adaptation of a famous Czech novel by Božena Němcová. Čap's international reputation was confirmed by awards in Venice (*Noční motýl/Night Butterfly*, 1941) and Cannes

43

(*Mužy bez kridel/Men Without Wings*, 1946). He rejected several offers from Italy and Germany during World War II; but, his films being judged 'too patriotic' by the Czech authorities in 1948, he escaped with his mother – to Munich. After two films in Germany, he was offered work in Yugoslavia in 1952, and brought some life to the heavy, literature-based Slovene cinema of the time. His teen-comedy *Vesna* (1953) and its sequel *Ne čakaj na maj/Don't Wait for May* (1957) are still among the most popular films ever made in Slovenia, while *Trenutki odločitve/Moments of Decision* (1955) touched upon the sensitive subject of the attribution of guilt between collaborators and partisans. Too different for the small Slovene setting, he died a solitary figure in Piran. SP

Bib: Zdenko Vrdlovec and Jože Dolmark, *František Čap* (1981).

Other Films Include: *Ohnive leto/Fiery Summer* (1939); *Devčica z Bezkyd/Girl from Bezkyd* (1944); *Bila tma/White Darkness* (1948); *Die Spur fuhrt nach Berlin/Adventure in Berlin* (1952); *Am Anfang war es Sünde/The Sin* (1954); *Harte Männer – Starke Liebe/Salt and Bread* (1957); *Vrata ostaju otvorena/The Door Remains Open* (1959); *X-25 javlja/X-25 Reports* (1960); *Srešćemo se večeras/We'll Meet Tonight, Naš avto/Our Car* (1962).

CENSORSHIP IN EASTERN EUROPE

The irony of censorship in Eastern Europe was that rather than prevent films from being made, the communist state would often commit production funds that could have easily been withheld, but then shelve a completed film. Under the economic logic of capitalism such waste of funds would not be allowable and the shelved films would never be made in the first place, let alone be censored. This paradoxical situation was due to a big extent to the semi-autonomous standing of the so-called film units within the film studios* where most production decisions were taken, and where mechanisms to evade direct surveillance and interference were developed. Within the units, ideological supervision was fairly relaxed and sometimes even intentionally non-existent. The organisations committed to carrying out censorship control differed from country to country. While Hungary was the only one that did not have a dedicated censorship body, it was still believed to have had the most sophisticated and elusive censorship mechanisms. Poland, on the other hand, had a special body in charge of media censorship, The Main Office for Control of the Press, Publications and Public Performances (Glowny Urzad Kontroli Prasy, Publikacji i Widowisk). In other countries, like Bulgaria, the studios had artistic commissions which approved the completed films and which worked under the close supervision of the Communist Party's ideological department. The mechanisms of censorship differed, and while a film like

Jan Nemec's* absurdist *O slavnosti a hostech/Report on the Party and the Guests* (1966) was 'banned forever' in Czechoslovakia, many other films were never officially condemned but were only given a limited release, thus effectively ensuring they were only seen by a handful of spectators. Censorship also operated through a mechanism of forbidden and permitted subject matters. Another dimension of socialist control was the subtle artistic conformism, sometimes defined as 'self-censorship', a direct result of the state's treatment of the intelligentsia as a highly prestigious social group. Thus, the totalitarian omnipresence of the state was expressed through a complex system of censorship mechanisms. State socialist censorship, however, was often exaggerated within the ideologically tense atmosphere of the Cold War. The Golden Palm awarded at Cannes to *Czlowiek z Zelaza/Man of Iron* (1981), for example, revealed overtly ideological considerations in celebrating censored art from Eastern Europe. According to Hungarian Miklós Harászty who explored the phenomenon of censorship under state socialism, here one observed a relative permissiveness – direct glorification of the state was not expected, even criticism was permitted, only one should not express doubt of the good intentions of the socialist enterprise. The state acted as a co-author in the artistic creation, audiences knew who was 'a permitted author with a permitted message' and dissent was co-opted. Harászty compared the limitations of working under state socialism to the ones of working within corporate culture, the only difference being that while in state socialism there was nothing beyond the state, in the consumerist society film-makers at least had the choice not to become corporate artists and to remain free in obscure independence. There are a number of well-known embarrassing examples of censorship from all the countries in Eastern Europe. In Poland, Aleksander Ford's* *Osmy Dzien Tygodnia/The Eighth Day of the Week* (1958, released 1983) was not distributed for twenty-five years. Many of Andrzej Wajda's* works also suffered censorship, as well as films such as Janusz Zaorski's* *Matka królów/Mother of Kings* (1982, released 1987) and Andrzej Lipicki's *Wzawieszeniu/Suspended* (1987). At least in two instances – in the cases of Jerzy Skolimowski* and Ryszard Bugajski* censorship intervention forced the film-makers to emigrate. In Hungary, films like Bacsó's* *A Tanú/The Witness* (1969) and *Te rongyos élet/Oh, Bloody Life!* (1983) were withheld from distribution due to the critical stance they took on the communist regime. In Czechoslovakia, many directors suffered from censorship and were not given the chance to work for years, particularly after 1968. Jiří Menzel's* *Skrivanci na niti/Larks on a string* (1969), for example, which was started during the period of the Prague Spring and completed after the Soviet invasion, was only released in 1990. Ironically, Yugoslavia, the country which enjoyed a relatively relaxed ideological climate, was the one where instances of harshest censorship took place. Lazar Stojanović, a pupil of Alexandar Petrović* and Dusan Makavejev*, experienced serious problems with his diploma film, the non-conventional historical treatise *Plasticni*

Jsus/The Plastic Jesus (1971) for which he had to serve a jail term. The film was only released in a cut version in 1990, long after Stojanović had emigrated to the US. Makavejev's own *W.R. – Misterije Organizma/ W.R. – Mysteries of the Organism* (1971), a work of avant-garde quality which uses a wide array of cinematic techniques and a unique narrative structure to make non-conformist statements on social and sexual liberation, was considered outrageous and shelved, which in turn led to Makavejev's emigration. The experience of Zelimir Zilnik* was a similar one, only in this case the director returned to Yugoslavia after growing disillusioned with the seemingly liberal-minded West where his work had also been censored. Sarajevan director Bato Cengić suffered serious repercussions for two satires he made in the 1970s and was deprived of the opportunity to make a feature film until 1990. It is important to note that not all film-makers who had their films censored were automatically prevented from making more. Bulgarian Binka Zeljazkova* enjoyed the reputation of a quasi-dissident and simultaneously had a high profile career. In spite of this her first film, *Zivotat si tece tiho/Life Flows Quietly by* (1958) which questioned the moral standards of nomenclature members, was disapproved by the board of Boyana Studios in Sofia and was not released for thirty years, and her 1967 *Privarzanijat balon/The Attached Balloon* was deemed too cryptic and was shelved shortly after its limited release, Zeljazkova was able to make many other films and was even awarded the title of People's Artist. Andrzej Wajda's experiences in Poland were similar – he both suffered from censorship and enjoyed a wide public recognition. Putting up with the censors bothered film-makers, and they subtly tackled the issues of censorship in many films – from Jiří Trnka's* classic animation *Ruka/The Hand* (1965), through Wajda's *Czlowiek z Marmuru/Man of Marble* (1976), Kieślowski's* *Przypadek/ Blind Chance* (1981), and Károly Makk's* *Egymásra nézve/ Another Way* (1982), to Wojciech Marczewski's* *Ucieczka z Kina Wolnosc/Escape from Liberty Cinema* (1991).

Bib: Miklós Harászty, *The Velvet Prison*, 1987.

CHERKASOV, Nikolai K.

St Petersburg 1903 – Leningrad 1966

Russian Soviet actor. After a career on stage in Leningrad, Cherkasov began playing small comic roles in films, such as Vladimir Gardin's* *Poet i tsar'/The Poet and the Tsar* (1927). His first major dramatic roles were the leading part in Iosif Kheifits's* and Natan Zarkhi's *Deputat Baltiki/Baltic Deputy*, and that of the tsarevich Alexei in Vladimir Petrov's* *Pëtr I/Peter the Great* (both 1937). He has played Gorky, Pavlov, Rimsky-Korsakov and Mayakovsky, but shot to international prominence with his title roles in Sergei Eisenstein's* *Aleksandr Nevskii/Alexander Nevsky* (1938) and *Ivan Groznyi/Ivan the Terrible*

(1944–5, Part Two released 1958). Cherkasov accompanied Eisenstein when he was summoned to see Stalin*, Molotov and Zhdanov in 1946 to discuss the 'errors' of Part Two of the latter film. After Stalin's death, Cherkasov made his last major film appearance in Grigori Kozintsev's* *Don Quixote* (1957). He was also a deputy to the USSR Supreme Soviet. RT

Bib: Nikolai Cherkasov, *Notes of a Soviet Actor* (n.d.).

CHIAURELI, Mikhail E.
Tbilisi, Georgia [Russian Empire] 1894 – USSR 1974

Georgian Soviet director and actor. Chiaureli graduated from art school in Tbilisi and made his first screen appearance in the title role in the first Georgian feature film, Ivan Perestiani's* *Arsen Dzhordzhiashvili/The Murder of General Gryaznov* (1921). He appeared in several Georgian features during the 1920s and made his directorial debut with *V poslednii chas/At the Last Moment* (1928), set in the Civil War. He made an experimental satire, *Khabarda* (1931), co-scripted with Sergei Tretyakov, and the first Georgian sound feature, *Poslednii maskarad/The Last Masquerade* (1934), followed by two works devoted to Georgian history, *Arsen* (1937) and *Georgii Saakadze* (1942–3). Chiaureli is best known, however, for the three films that constituted the kernel of Stalin's* 'personality cult': *Velikoe zarevo/ The Great Dawn* (1938), *Klyatva/The Vow* (1946) and *Padenie Berlina/The Fall of Berlin* (1949), Mosfilm studio's seventieth birthday present to Stalin. The last of these, made on Agfacolor stock taken from Nazi Germany as war booty, constitutes the apotheosis of the Stalin cult and defines the postwar 'Empire style' of Soviet propaganda. Unsurprisingly, Stalin awarded all three films the Stalin Prize. RT

CHUKHRAI, Grigori N.
Melitopol, Ukraine 1921

Soviet director. Chukhrai graduated from the workshop run by Mikhail Romm* and Sergei Yutkevich* at VGIK* in 1953 and began making films for Mosfilm in 1955. His first film, *Sorok pervyi/The Forty-first* (1956), won a Special Prize at Cannes in 1957, but he is best known for two war films: *Ballada o soldate/Ballad of a Soldier* (1959, prizes at Cannes and Venice, and Lenin Prize in 1961), and *Chistoe nebo/Clear Sky* (1961), a prize-winner at the Moscow Film Festival. He continued making films into the 1980s and taught at VGIK from 1966 to 1971. His films reflect a concern for individuals caught up in the tide of historical events. RT

CHUKHRAI, Pavel G.   Bykovo, Russia [USSR] 1946

Russian director and scriptwriter. The son of the film director Grigori Chukhrai*, he acted in Mark Donskoi's* film set in a Young Pioneer Camp, *Zdravstvuite, deti!/Hallo, Children!* (1962). After graduating from the cinematography faculty of VGIK*, where he had studied with Boris Volchek, in 1969, he worked as a cinematographer on a number of films. In 1974 he graduated as an external student from the directorial faculty of VGIK, studying with Igor Talankin. His first feature film, *Ty inogda vspominai/Remember Sometimes* (1977) is the story of a retired surgeon. It was followed by the story of adolescence *Kletka dlya kanareek/The Canary Cage* (1983) and by the social drama *Zina-Zinulya* (1986). The TV film *Zapomnite menya takoi/Remember Me This Way* (1987) a tense family drama taken from a stage play, brought Chukhrai a measure of international recognition, but with *Vor/The Thief* (1997), made from his own script, Chukhrai enjoyed worldwide success. After sweeping the board at the Nikes, the Russian Oscars, where it was nominated in ten out of eleven possible categories and won five awards, including best film, it was nominated for the Oscar for Best Foreign Language Film. *The Thief* is one of a number of recent Russian films to be set in the Stalin period, this time in the years after World War II. But unlike the majority of such dramas, it is not driven by a desire to expose the moral and political horrors the Russian people had to endure in those years, giving a densely imagined and more nuanced picture of the texture of the times. It is a tensely dramatic, sometimes melodramatic, personal and social drama which boasts excellent acting performances, in particular from Vladimir Mashkov* as the unscrupulous but attractive hero and from the child actor, Misha Filipchuk as the young son of the woman he takes up with. JG

CHURIKOVA, Inna   Belibei, Bashkir Autonomous Republic [USSR] 1943

Russian actress. In 1965 Churikova graduated from the Shchepkin Theatrical Institute and began work at the Theatre of the Young Viewer in Moscow. In 1975 she started to work at the Lenin Komsomol Theatre in Moscow. She is the winner of innumerable prizes for her work on stage and in the cinema and in 1991 was made a People's Artist of the USSR. Her first cinematic roles date from the early 1960s, but her cinematic career has been inextricably linked with that of her husband, the director Gleb Panfilov*, for whom she has played a number of sometimes unworldly, sometimes practical, but always driven, heroines. Her first such role was that of the naive and honourable young revolutionary Tania Tetkina in his first feature *V ogne broda net/No Crossing under Fire* (1967). The couple then spent a number of years trying to make a film about Joan of Arc, but permission for this was constantly refused. So instead they made *Nachalo/The Debut* (1970), in which Churikova plays Pasha Stroganova, an ordinary girl chosen to play Joan of Arc in a film. In 1975 in *Proshu slova/I Wish to Speak* she was Elizaveta Uvarova, the head of the Soviet of a provincial town, whose belief in the party and its slogans blinds her to the tragedy around her. She then played a provincial woman in Panfilov's *Tema/The Theme* (1979), and a barmaid in his *Valentina* (1981), from a play by Alexander Vampilov. In the 1980s she also played two grandly possessed heroines in her husband's adaptations of plays by Maxim Gorky, Vassa in *Vassa* (1983), from the play *Vassa Zheleznova*, a pre-Revolutionary family melodrama, and then Nilovna in his epic version of the political novel *Mat'/Mother* (1989) Churikova's singular intensity and rigour as an actress are at their most compelling in her husband's films, but she has also produced remarkable work for a number of other directors. Most notably she played the heroine, Asya Klyachina, in Mikhalkov-Konchalovsky's* depressing saga of the post-Soviet village *Kurochka riaba/Riaba My Chicken* (1994). JG

CHYTILOVÁ, Věra   Ostrava 1929

Czech director. Věra Chytilová worked as a draughtswoman, fashion model and continuity person before studying at FAMU* (1957–62). Her commitment to experiment was already apparent in her student films, and her graduation film, *Strop/Ceiling* (1962), the study of a fashion model, was a defiant mixture of cinéma vérité and formalism. There were echoes of this in her first feature, *O něčem jiném/Something Different* (1963), which told the parallel stories of a woman gymnast and a housewife, the first as documentary, the second as fiction. Working with her husband, the cinematographer Jaroslav Kučera, and writer/designer Ester Krumbachová, Chytilová directed the two most inventive films of the Czech New Wave*, *Sedmikrásky/Daisies* (1966) and *Ovoce stromů rajských jíme/The Fruit of Paradise/We Eat the Fruit of the Trees of Paradise* (1969). The first was a non-narrative montage of the destructive antics of two female teenagers which demonstrated that an avant-garde film could also be funny, while the second was an allegorical portrait of male/female relations presented in images of remarkable formal beauty. After the Soviet invasion of 1968, such excesses were not encouraged and Chytilová found herself unable to work. In 1976, she wrote an open letter to President Husák and was surprisingly reinstated, returning with a lively parable of sexual relations, *Hra o jablko/The Apple Game* (1976), and the unusually abrasive moral tale *Panelstory/Prefab Story* (1981). She renewed her collaboration with Krumbachová for a comic portrayal of a middle-aged Don Juan, *Faunovo velmi pozdní odpo-ledne/The Very Late Afternoon of a Faun* (1983). In recent years she has derived much of her inspiration from theatre, directing a film version of the mime play *Šašek a královna/The Jester and the Queen* (1987), and working with the avant-garde theatre group Sklep (The Cellar) on *Kopytem sem, kopytem tam/Tainted Horseplay/Snowball Reaction/A Hoof Here, A Hoof There (1988)*. A retrospective of her films was shown on French television in 1989, but she has still to receive similar recognition from the English-speaking world. PH

Other Films Include: *Pytel blech/A Bagful of Fleas* [short, released together with *Strop* as *U stropu je pytel blech/There's a Bagful of Fleas at the Ceiling*] (1962); *Perličky na dně/Pearls of the Deep* [episode *Automat 'Svět'/At the World Cafeteria*] (1965); *Čas je neúprosný/Inexorable Time* [short] (1978); *Kalamita/Calamity* (1980); *Chytilová versus Forman* [short] (1981, Belgium); *Praha, neklidné srdce Evropy/Prague, Restless Heart of Europe* [short] (1984); *Vlčí bouda/Wolf's Cabin* (1986); *T.G.M. – osvoboditel/Tomáš G. Masaryk – The Liberator* [short] (1990); *Mí Pražané mi rozumějí/My Inhabitants of Prague Understand Me* (1991); *Dědictví aneb Kurvahošigutntag/Inheritance or Shit-Boys-Gutntag* (1992); *T.G.M. – osvoboditel/Tomas Garrigue Masaryk – the Liberator* (1990); *Mí Pražané mi rozumeji/My Prague People Under-stand Me* (1991); *Dedictvi Aneb Kurvahosigutntag/The Inheritance or Fuckoffguysgoodbye* (1993); *Pasti, pasti, pasticky/Trap, Trap, Little Trap* (1998).

CIULEI, Liviu   Bucharest 1923

Romanian director, now in the US. Liviu Ciulei emigrated from Romania* in the early 1970s, and has pursued a successful career as a director and designer for various stage productions in the US. During his Romanian period which lasted nearly two decades, Ciulei first worked in cinema as a set designer for Dinu Negreanu, for whose *Nepotii gornistului/The Bugler's Grandsons* (1953) he designed costumes and sets, as well as acted in the film. Ciulei's actors' credits include roles in a number of 1950s films, like *In sat la noi/In Our Village* (1951), *Alarma in munti/Alarm in the Mountains* (1955), and later in his own *Valurile Dunarii/The Danube Waves* (1959) and *Padurea spînzuratilor/The Forest of the Hanged* (1964). Set against the backdrop of the anti-fascist takeover on 23 August 1944, *The Danube Waves*, a film about personal discovery and moral choices focuses on three archetypal characters: a bargee and his wife travel up the Danube where they get entangled in a confrontation between the fascists and a member of the communist underground. The film received the 1960 Grand Prize at Karlovy Vary*. In 1965, Ciulei won best director at Cannes for his anti-war *Forest of the Hanged*. Based on the novel by Liviu Rebreanu and starring Victor Rebengiuc*, the film tells the story of a Romanian drafted into the Austro-Hungarian army who has to face the death penalty for his refusal to fight against his kinsmen. DI

Other Films Include: *Eruptia/Eruption* (1957).

COMEDY: POLAND

Polish film has a reputation for being tragic, philosophical, romantic, intellectual, political – everything, it seems, except funny. Despite the popularity of Hollywood comedies, and strong comic theatre and cabaret traditions, Polish film comedies and directors are hard to find. It seems that the strictures of Socialist Realism* and script censorship have worked to the detriment of the genre.

Comedy did flourish, though, in the silent and prewar sound years, with the popular actor Adolf Dymsza in the Chaplinesque persona of 'Dodek', and the antics of Eugeniusz Bodo. The most popular film was Michal Waszyński and Jan Nowina-Przybylski's *Cham/Roughneck* (1931), sold to thirteen countries. The major directors who worked consistently in the genre in the postwar period were Tadeusz Chmielewski, whose 1958 hit *Ewa chce Spać/Eve Wants to Sleep* combined light farce with serious reflection on teenage delinquency, and Stanisław Bajera, who made the cross-dressing *Poszukiwany-Poszukiwana/On the Run* (1973).

Some of the best comedies were of course those that annoyed the authorities – Marek Piwowski's *Rejs/Trip Down the River* (1970) was limited to one release print and Antoni Krauze's* *Prognoza Pogody/ Weather Forecast* (1983) was banned outright. One success story was the futuristic *Seksmisja/Sexmission* (1984) by Juliusz Machulski*, starring one of the best contemporary comic actors, Jerzy Stuhr*. In the 1990s, with the censor gone and society ripe for ridicule, the material is there for the kind of black humour and political satire that Polish audiences enjoy. *Kraj Świata/Edge of the World* (1993) by Maria Zmarz-Koczanowicz, based on Janusz Anderman's short stories, has the rare courage to laugh heartily at the late 1980s. AW

CSERHALMI, György   Budapest 1948

Hungarian actor. György Cserhalmi's intelligent and charismatic presence is a major asset for Hungarian cinema. Cserhalmi started as a theatre actor and continued his commitment to the stage throughout his career. One of his earliest successful roles was in Miklós Jancsó's* *Szerelmem, Elektra/Elektreia* (1974) where he played Oresztész opposite Mari Töröcsik* as Electra. Cserhalmi then became one of Jancsó's permanent actors and appeared in a number of his films, most notably *Magyar rapszódia/Hungarian Rhapsody* (1979), *Allegro barbaro* (1979), *Zsarnok szíve, avagy Boccaccio Magyarországon/The Heart of the Tyrant or Boccaccio in Hungary* (1981), and *Kék Duna keringő/ Blue Danube Waltz* (1992). Cserhalmi's thoughtful appearance makes him particularly suitable for historical roles. His most remarkable one is in László Lugossy's 1848-set treatise on individual freedom colliding with historical coercion, *Szirmok, virágok, koszorúk/Flowers of Reverie* (1984). He has appeared in leading roles in the films of most

51

major Hungarian directors. He was cast by Károly Makk*, Péter Bacsó*, Gábor Bódy*, Zoltán Fábri*, András Kovács*, Sándor Sára*, István Szabó*, Béla Tarr* and Ferenc András. DI

CROATIA – see YUGOSLAVIA (former)

CYBULSKI, Zbigniew
Zbyszek Cybulski; Kniaze, Ukraine 1927 – Wrocław 1967

Polish actor. Cybulski trained in the Stanislavsky method at the Cracow Theatre School and on graduating formed the satirical theatre company Bim Bom, with fellow actor Bogumił Kobieła. Although an accomplished actor and theatre director, Cybulski is best remembered for his film role as Maciek, the increasingly disillusioned nationalist militant hired to kill a local communist leader, in Andrzej Wajda's* *Popiół i Diament/Ashes and Diamonds* (1958). The film was an international success and Cybulski heralded as the 'Polish James Dean' for his portrayal of tough yet vulnerable youth. Indeed, his expressive and handsome face, half hidden by thick dark glasses, came to symbolise a whole generation of Polish youth to international audiences. Unlike James Dean, Cybulski aged in front of his fans, continuing to work in theatre and film. His comic talent is preserved in Wojciech Has'* *Rękopis Znaleziony w Saragossie/The Saragossa Manuscript* (1965). Cybulski's death at the age of 40 remains a mystery; it was never clear whether he committed suicide or whether alcohol or fatigue made him fall under a departing train. Wajda's tribute to Cybulski, *Wszystko na Sprzedaż/Everything for Sale* (1969), with its disconcerting mixture of fact and fiction, was widely acclaimed. AW

CZECH NEW WAVE

Czech film movement. The term is used to describe the group of Czech directors who emerged in the early 1960s and spearheaded an extremely varied group of films that regularly won awards at international festivals (as well as two Oscars), marking the first significant inroads of Czech and Slovak cinema into international markets. Technically, it refers to those directors who graduated and/or made their debuts in the early 1960s, including Miloš Forman*, Věra Chytilová*, Jiří Menzel*, Jan Němec*, Evald Schorm*, Jaromil Jireš* and Ivan Passer*. The only time they banded together for a group photograph was to defend Chytilová's *Sedmikrásky/Daisies* against charges of formalism in 1967. The photograph also includes fellow New Wave directors Pavel Juráček, Hynek Bočan and Antonín Máša.

The importance of the new directors was considerable but the innovations of the 1960s were more crucially linked to structural changes within the industry and a progressive liberalisation in most areas of culture (the theatre saw productions of Beckett, Ionesco, Albee and Havel; Kafka and Hašek were reassessed and republished). All generations of film-makers participated in the changes, including Otakar Vávra*, Karel Kachyňa*, Ján Kadár* and Elmar Klos*, Vojtěch Jasný* and František Vláčil*, as well as Slovak contemporaries such as Štefan Uher* and Juraj Jakubisko*. While the directors themselves point to the simplifications implicit in the term, which did not reflect a single theoretical position, they constituted a closely-knit group and frequently collaborated. Their production of innovative and critical work between 1963 and 1969 made it longer-lived than most comparable movements, including the French New Wave. The styles of the 'wave' range from realism to surrealism, from improvisation to classical narrative, but there are many stylistic and thematic connections. The problems faced by youth in a hostile environment were touched on by virtually all the directors in the early 1960s and the influence of cinéma vérité is noticeable in a wide range of films (most obviously those by Forman, Passer and Chytilová). While there were nods in the direction of Jean-Luc Godard, Michelangelo Antonioni, Federico Fellini and the British New Wave, the importance of Czech literature should also be noted: the comic tradition deriving from Hašek, the return to avant-garde writers such as Vančura* and Nezval. Novelists Bohumil Hrabal, Josef Škvorecký, Milan Kundera and Arnošt Lustig collaborated on adaptations of their work, while writers such as Ester Krumbachová (who worked with Němec, Chytilová and Jireš) and Jan Procházka wrote important original screenplays.

The term Czech New Wave is used to include the work of Slovak directors such as Uher and Jakubisko. There was frequent interaction and their films were no less radical. At the end of the 1960s, the focus seemed to shift to Slovakia with the appearance of directors such as Dušan Hanák* and Elo Havetta. They joined Jakubisko in films that drew on Slovak inspiration and literature (Ladislav Ťažký, Ján Johanides) as well as the (West) 'European art film'* (two Alain Robbe-Grillet films were co-productions with Slovakia).

The New Wave was effectively ended by the Soviet invasion of 1968, when cultural freedoms were identified with the forces that led to the 'Prague Spring' and the threat to the Soviet model of communism. Forman, Passer, Kadár, Jasný, Weiss* and Němec were among those who left the country. Others such as Juráček and Schorm were unable to work in the cinema, and many did not resume their careers until the middle or late 1970s. The film-makers' cohesion was broken, increased vetting of scripts ensured the absence of significant social criticism, and all formal experiment was stifled. PH

Bib: Peter Hames, *The Czechoslovak New Wave* (1985).

CZECHOSLOVAKIA

Czechoslovakia has an important place in the prehistory of the cinema by virtue of the work of the physiologist J. E. Purkyně (1787–1869), who wrote on persistence of vision as early as 1818 and in 1850, with the optician Ferdinand Durst, created the Kinesiscope, with which he used animated images to demonstrate the beating of the heart and the flight of butterflies. The first Czech films were made in 1898 by the photographer Jan Kříženecký, who was the first motion picture producer in Austria-Hungary.

A permanent film theatre was opened in Prague in 1907 by the conjuror Ponrepo, and regular film production began in 1910. Fiction films were centred on the Asum company (1912–17), founded by the architect Max Urban and his wife, the popular stage actress Andula Sedláčková; the first venture was a prestigious production based on Smetana's *Prodaná nevěsta/The Bartered Bride* (1913). At the outbreak of World War I, more than a third of the 700 cinemas in the Austro-Hungarian Empire were on Czech territory. Despite wartime difficulties, the Prague building contractor Václav Havel, grandfather of President Havel, established Lucernafilm in 1914, with other companies following at the end of the war, including Weteb, Praga, Excelsior and Poja. In 1919, Czechoslovakia scored its first foreign success with Karel Degl's *Stavitel chrámu/The Builder of the Cathedral*, released in France as *La Cathédrale*. The first Slovak film, *Jánošik*, was made by Jaroslav Siakel and František Horlivý in 1921 with American financing.

The formation of the independent Czechoslovak republic in 1918 furthered attempts to develop film as part of a national culture and, despite strong competition from German and American films, feature production averaged over twenty-six films a year in the silent period. One of the most popular films of the late 1920s was Karel Lamač's* adaptation of Jaroslav Hašek's anti-war novel *Dobrý voják Švejk/The Good Soldier Švejk* (1926), which was rapidly followed by three sequels. Films of social commitment included Přemysl Pražský's *Battalion* (1927) and Karl Junghans' *Takový je život/Such is Life* (1929), while Gustav Machatý* attracted attention with the artistically ambitious *Kreutzerova sonáta/The Kreutzer Sonata* (1926) and *Erotikon* (1929).

The introduction of sound brought inevitable problems of language, but a demand for Czech-language films on the domestic market ensured a rise from only eight features in 1930 to an average of over forty in the late 1930s. The studios at Barrandov*, built in 1932–3, were originally designed as a centre for international production and were the most advanced in central Europe. The first significant international interest in Czech cinema followed the success of three films at the 1934 Venice festival: Josef Rovenský's *Řeka/The River/Young Love* (1933); the Karel Plicka/Alexander Hammid* feature documentary on Slovak folklore, *Zem spieva/The Earth Sings* (1933); and Machatý's *Extase/*

54

Ecstasy (1932), starring Hedy Kiesler (later Lamarr). All three films had a pastoral context and privileged the image as a primary component, giving birth to the notion of 'Czech lyricism'. The importance of cinematography in Czech and Slovak films was established by cinematographers such as Jan Stallich (*Řeka*, *Extase*), Václav Vich (*Erotikon*) and Otto Heller (*Před maturitou/Before the Finals*, both 1932), an influence still evident in the 1960s work of Jaroslav Kučera (*Všichni dobří rodáci/All My Good Countrymen*, 1968) and Jan Čuřík (*Holubice/The White Dove*, 1960).

Attempts to establish an art cinema were centred, in particular, on the novelist Vladislav Vančura*, who made an impressive debut with *Před maturitou*, co-directed by Svatopluk Innemann. However, the more radical forms of *Na sluneční straně/On the Sunnyside* (1933) and *Marijka nevěrnice/Faithless Marijka* (1934) failed to meet with commercial success. The 1930s also saw the debuts of the popular stage comedians Jiří Voskovec* and Jan Werich*. Two of their films were directed by the prolific Martin Frič*, who made a series of films starring comic actors such as Vlasta Burian*, Hugo Haas* and Oldřich Nový. Attacks on the rise of fascism were apparent in the Voskovec and Werich film *Svět patří nám/The World Belongs to Us* (1937) and in Hugo Haas's film of Karel Čapek's play *Bílá nemoc/The White Sickness* (1937).

The period of the Nazi occupation had its effect on film-making, with the number of films dropping from forty in 1939 to nine in 1944. Nonetheless, there were films of note from Frič and from Otakar Vávra*. The National Film Archive was formed in 1943, and a group that included Vančura, Vávra and Elmar Klos* planned the future nationalisation of the film industry. The film school, FAMU*, was founded in 1947, and in the same year a separate Slovak cinema, with its own studios at Koliba in Bratislava, was established. Nationalisation also paved the way for the international success of Czech and Slovak animation with the establishment of studios in Prague and Zlín (Gottwaldov) [> ANIMATION (CZECHOSLOVAKIA)]. Czech films again attracted attention when Karel Stekly's *Siréna/The Siren/The Strike* (1947) and Jiří Trnka's* *Špalíček/The Czech Year* (1947) won major awards at Venice in 1947 and 1948.

Following the communist takeover in 1948, there was a fairly swift adherence to the moribund formulae of Stalinist cinema, and another plunge in production combined, somewhat paradoxically, with international recognition in the field of animation. In addition to Jiří Trnka, the work of Karel Zeman*, Hermína Týrlová, Břetislav Pojar, Jiří Brdečka and others soon acquired a world following. There was a real sense in which animated film kept alive visual traditions at a time when 'formalism' was officially condemned. Following Khrushchev's 'de-Stalinisation' speech of 1956, a limited 'thaw' set in, reflecting similar developments in Poland and the Soviet Union. Older directors such as Jiří Weiss*, Ján Kadár* and Elmar Klos were able to tackle more ambitious topics, while the first FAMU graduates, such as Vojtěch Jasný* and Karel Kachyňa*, made their debuts. Together, the new films became the focus for the 1959 conference at Banská Bystrica attacking 'remnants of bourgeois thought'. However, the new repression was short-lived and soon challenged by a second generation of FAMU graduates, now described as the Czech New Wave*. Miloš Forman*, Věra Chytilová* and Jaromil Jireš* all made their debuts in 1963 and combined with older and younger colleagues in the period 1963–9 to promote a period of extraordinary creative diversity in which film-makers sometimes appeared to escape the demands of both the market and ideology. Of course, films were banned (Chytilová's *Sedmikrásky/Daisies*, 1966, Jan Němec's* *O slavnosti a hostech/The Party and the Guests*, 1966), and innovative films were only made by pushing against the system, but the achievements were considerable. Other directors of note to make their debuts included Jiří Menzel*, Ivan Passer*, Evald Schorm*, Pavel Juráček and Jan Schmidt, and, in Slovakia, Štefan Uher* and Juraj Jakubisko*.

The development of creative ideas in the film industry was but one aspect of a wider phenomenon – the growth of ideas in economics, politics, literature and the arts that made up the Czechoslovak reform movement. It was a movement that led directly to the 'Prague Spring' of 1968 and plans to introduce 'socialist democracy'. It was this threat to the Soviet model of centralised power ('the leading role of the Communist Party') that led to the Warsaw Pact invasion of August 1968. The policies of 'normalisation' that followed were designed to liquidate the reforms of the late 1960s and led to exile, silence or accommodation in all walks of life. Kadár, Forman, Passer, Jasný and Němec were among those who went into exile, while other directors such as Ladislav Helge, Schorm and Juráček were unable to work. Well over a hundred films from the 1960s were banned and directors, after appropriate acknowledgment of the correctness of the 1968 invasion, were forced to make films that were either naive or conformed to a bland and officially sanctioned image of popular entertainment. In 1973, four films were banned 'for ever' – Forman's *Hoří, má panenko!/The Firemen's Ball* (1967), Němec's *O slavnosti a hostech*, Jasný's *Všichni dobří rodáci/All My Good Countrymen* (1968), and Schorm's *Farářův konec/End of a Priest* (1968). In these circumstances, the search for minor elements of criticism or formal dissent became a precise art. Menzel, Chytilová and Jireš continued to make films, although most film-makers were kept unemployed until 1976. Some of their achievements are still notable. Menzel made *Na samotě u lesa/Seclusion near a Forest* (1976), continued his collaboration with the country's leading novelist, Bohumil Hrabal, with *Postřižiny/Cutting It Short* (1980) and *Slavnosti sněženek/The Snowdrop Festival* (1983), and gained an Oscar nomination for *Vesničko má, středisková/My Sweet Little Village* (1985). Chytilová made the critically abrasive *Panelstory/Prefab Story* (1979), while in Slovakia directors such as Uher, Dušan Hanák* and Martin Hollý frequently transcended the norms of the time.

In the post-1969 situation, animated film again permitted a freedom denied to features. The work of Adolf Born, Jaroslav Doubrava and Miloš Macourek provided a critical edge, while the 'militant surrealism' of Jan Švankmajer* followed a path totally at variance with official ideology. The tradition of puppet film found new expression in the work of Jiří Barta (*Krysař/The Pied Piper*, 1986).

Czechoslovakia is a pioneer of children's films and in the mid-1980s they made up as much as 15 per cent of the annual production of around forty features. Based principally in the Zlín (Gottwaldov) studios, many directors worked in the genre, and children's films have been a major element in film exports. The most notable specialist directors have included Věra Plívová-Šimková and Ota Koval.

In the late 1980s, there was evidence of a new generation of directors coming to the fore with feature films that presented a more direct challenge to current orthodoxies, notably Irena Pavlásková (*Čas sluhů/Time of the Servants*, 1989), Petr Koliha (*Něžný barbar/Tender Barbarian*, 1989), Miloš Zábranský (*Dům pro dva/A House for Two*, 1988), and Zdeněk Tyc (*Vojtěch, řečený sirotek/An Orphan Called Vojtěch*, 1989). These signs of a system noticeably fraying were confirmed by the 'Velvet Revolution' of November 1989. External forces like the Gorbachev reforms and the general crisis of Eastern Europe were matched by an internal situation where resistance to change had made collapse virtually inevitable.

Many of the post-Revolutionary films have been disappointing, showing a crudity and tastelessness that is partly a settling of past accounts and partly commercial necessity in a market now open to Hollywood penetration. After a drop in production from 1990, the number of features rose again in 1993 to twenty-two, with several Czech titles outperforming their US rivals on the home market. International co-productions supported projects ranging from the commercial (Menzel's *Život a neobyčejna dobrodružství vojáka Ivana Čonkina/The Life and Extraordinary Adventures of Private Ivan Chonkin* [released 1994 in US]) to the art cinema (Švankmajer's *Lekce Faust/Faust*, Drahomíra Vihanová's *Pevnost/The Fortress*). Czech television replaced Barrandov as the major producer, supporting ambitious projects such as the award-winning adaptation of Eva Kantůrková's novel *Přítelkyně z domů smutku/My Companions in the House of Anguish* (1993), directed by Hynek Bočan, and *Maje pomsta/Vengeance is Mine* (1995) by the exiled Yugoslav director Lordan Zafronović*. Approximately twenty films are now produced in the Czech Republic every year, which is consistent with Western European averages. Young Jan Svěrák* proved to be the most successful Czech director of the 1990s, with his Oscar-nominated *Obecna skola/Elementary School* (1991) and especially with his Oscar-winning *Kolja/Kolya* (1996), co-scripted by the director's father, Zdeněk Svěrák*, who also starred in the film. Other internationally acclaimed Czech films include Vladimir Michalek's *Zapomenuté svetlo/Forgotten Light* (1996) and Petr Zelenka's *Knoflíkári/The Buttoners* (1997). PH

CZINNER, Paul
Budapest 1890 – London 1972

Hungarian-born director, who began his career with expressionist films (*Homo immanis*, 1919; *Inferno*, 1919). From 1924 he worked regularly with his future wife Elisabeth Bergner and with Carl Mayer, making popular variations of the *Kammerspielfilm* (*Nju*, 1924; *Fräulein Else*, 1929; *Der träumende Mund/Dreaming Lips*, 1932), as well as the occasional historical costume drama (*Liebe*, 1926), cross-dressing comedy (*Der Geiger von Florenz/Impetuous Youth/The Violinist of Florence*, 1926), or a mixture of both (*Dona Juana*, 1927). All his German films contained exceptional star casts, including Bergner, Emil Jannings, Conrad Veidt, Rudolf Forster, Max Schreck and Alfred Bassermann, around each of whom Czinner knew how to create an appropriate cinematic frame, notable for its exceptional mobility.

In 1933, Czinner and Bergner emigrated to Britain, where they tried to adapt their brand of bitter-sweet melodrama to English tastes, with limited success. In 1939 they went to Hollywood, but were unable to work on further co-productions. In 1949 Czinner returned to Europe, directing ballet and opera films (*Don Giovanni*, 1955) and documentaries on European music and dance theatres. MW

Other Films Include: *The Woman He Scorned* (1929, UK); *Ariane* (1931); *As You Like It* (1936, UK).

D

DANELIA, Georgi N.
Tbilisi, Georgia [USSR] 1930

Georgian Russian director and scriptwriter, who studied at the Moscow Archi-tectural Institute and the Higher Courses for Directors, which he completed in 1959. Danelia's first film was *Tozhe lyudi/People Too* (1959), a short taken from an episode in *War and Peace*. His first feature was *Seryozha* (1960), co-directed with Igor Talankin, from a popular story by Vera Panova. In *Ya shagayu po Moskve/I Walk around Moscow* (1963), Danelia used humour, the charm of his actors and a popular song to describe the adventures of a group of young people centred on Kolya, played by the young Nikita Mikhalkov*. Among Danelia's other films are *Sovsem propashchii/Quite Lost* (1973), a version of Mark Twain's *The Adventures of Huckleberry Finn*, and *Osennii marafon/Autumn Marathon* (1979), a 'sad comedy' in which the hero, an academic, can never quite catch up with all his obligations (the title alludes to his enforced jogging sessions with a Danish professor). *Osenii marafon* won the main prize at the 1979 San Sebastian Film Festival. In Danelia's 1986 science-fiction comedy *Kin-Dza-Dza*, two Soviet citizens are transported to a distant planet. His next film, *Pasport/Passport* (1990), is a comedy of errors about a Georgian nationalist and his Jewish half-brother who wants to emigrate. *Orel i reshka/ Heads and Tails* (1995), a tale of young Muscovites' problems with love, life and authority, is immediately reminiscent in its wit and charm of *I Walk around Moscow*. Danelia proves yet again what a splendid director of young actors he is. The film, like its predecessors, shows Moscow at a time of change and reconstruction, and though, of course, these are darker, more uncertain times, an atmosphere of good humour, of youthful optimism, prevails. JG

DANELIUC, Mircea   Hotin 1943

Romanian director, scriptwriter and actor, often considered the strongest of the younger Romanian film-makers. A student of French literature, he graduated from film school in 1972, and worked as assistant director to Mircea Dragan. His first feature, *Cursă/The Long Drive* (1975), about the unfulfilled dreams of two truck drivers and a young woman they pick up, achieved both box-office success and critical acclaim, thereby helping to create space for contemporary movies by young directors. *Editie specială/Special Issue* (1978) used the stereotypical form of the anti-fascist war thriller to create a tightly edited psychological art movie. The highly original *Probă de microfon/Microphone Test* (1979) analysed relationships between the media and society through the stilted world of Romanian television journalism, with Daneliuc starring as a cameraman. Equally politically complex, *Croazieră/The Cruise* (1981) is a parable about a boat journey organised as a reward for good conduct. *Glissando* (1984), the first feature in which Daneliuc did not star, is an ambitious and disturbing parable of human decay set in the gambling house of a Dante-esque asylum. At the Venice festival it was compared to the films of Federico Fellini and Ingmar Bergman. *Jacob* (1988), a powerful social drama, won similar international acclaim. *Patul conjugal/Conjugal Bed* (1993) hilariously and sarcastically conveys the emotional deprivation of post-Ceauşescu Romania. In 1994 he produced *Neinvinsa – 1 Dragostea/ Unvanquished Love* and his *Senatorul melcilor/The Senator's Snails* (1995), presented at the official selection at Cannes, was a critical dissection of Romania's post-communist local politics. MM

DAPKUNAITE, Ingeborga   Lithuania [USSR] 1963

Lithuanian actress. In 1985 Dapkunaite graduated from the State Conservatory in Lithuania, where she had studied in the Theatre

Department under Jonas Vaitkus. She has worked in theatres in Kaunas and Vilnius. Her film debut came in the year of her graduation. She gained an international reputation with roles in Russian films and then began to take parts in foreign productions. She has mainly played modern, independent women, such as the prostitute Kisulia in Petr Todorovsky's* *Interdevochka/Intergirl* (1989), the bourgeoise Olga in Dmitri Meskhiev's* *Tsiniki/The Cynics* (1991), the sexually obsessed Katya in Valeri Todorovsky's* *Podmoskovnye vechera/Katia Ismailova* (1994), and Marusya in Mikhalkov's* *Utomlennye solntsem/Burnt by the Sun* (1994), a part for which she was given the Russian Film Academy's 1994 Nike award. Since moving to London, Dapkunaite has appeared as Harrer's wife in Jean-Jacques Annaud's *Seven Years in Tibet* and in Brian de Palma's *Mission: Impossible*. BB

DJULGEROV, Georgi   Burgas 1943

Bulgarian director and writer. Widely recognised as the most talented director of the middle generation of Bulgarian film-makers. After winning a prize at the Oberhausen festival for his diploma film at the Moscow Film School (VGIK*), *Bondar/The Cooper* (1969), based on a story by Nikolai Haitov* and filmed in Armenia, Georgi Djulgerov returned home and shot the same short feature again in the author's native Rhodope mountains. The remake, *Izpit/The Test*, appeared as an episode in the two-part *Šaren cvjat/Colourful World* (1971). He followed this with a widely praised feature film on the resistance movement, *I dojde denjat.../And the Day Came...* (1973), based on the personal experiences of scriptwriter Vassil Akyov. Djulgerov's breakthrough on the international scene occurred when his next feature, *Avantaž/Advantage* (1977), won the Best Director award at the 1978 Berlin film festival; it is the story of a petty conman living on the edge of society during the Stalinist years. Although less successful, his next film, *Trampa/Swap* (1978), continued the director's socio-political probing into the troubled era of the personality cult.

Djulgerov then spent three years working on *Mera spored mera/ Measure for Measure* (1981), a three-part spectacle produced for the 1,300th anniversary of the founding of Bulgaria and dealing with the Ilinden uprising of 1903 in Greek Macedonia, a project that won him praise abroad but displeasure among the authorities at home because of his unbiased approach to the sensitive political issue of Macedonia. Prevented from directing feature films at Boyana* Studios, Djulgerov soon made his mark as a director of fiction-like documentaries on sports, while at the same time teaching a new generation of film-makers at the Sofia Academy of Dramatic Art (VITIS). Upon Mikhail Gorbachev's rise to power, Djulgerov was allowed to work again in the feature film department at Boyana Studios; he responded with another statement on the Stalinist period: *Lagerăt/The Camp* (1989), an autobiographical account of his own youth in a pioneer camp of the 1950s. His latest *Tchernata lyastovitsa/The Black Swallow* (1997, Bulg./Fr.) is an exploration of the fate of a teenage Gypsy girl in the complex situation of post-communist Bulgaria. RH

DOCUMENTARY IN EASTERN EUROPE

Documentary film-making was an important part of the cinemas of all East European countries during the years of communism, and proved to be one of the most popular genres after 1989. Documentaries were produced either by dedicated studios (Kratky Film in Czechoslovakia, Ekran in Bulgaria, Dunav Film in Yugoslavia), or by units attached to the respective national television companies. Documentaries were regularly awarded prizes at the specialised festivals in Oberhausen, Mannheim, Amsterdam, Leipzig and Cracow. There was also a well-developed network of amateur film clubs where many interesting grassroots documentaries were produced and then showcased at special national meetings. Film-makers like Dusan Makavejev* and Zelilmir Zilnik* started their careers at such clubs. Many of the leading feature film directors from Eastern Europe started by making documentaries, like Czech Milos Forman*, Polish Krzysztof Kieślowski*, or Hungarian Marta Mészáros*. Others have turned occasionally to the documentary format to make important films, like Czech Jan Nemec* in his chronicle of the Prague Spring, *Oratorio for Prague* (1968), Romanian Mircea Daneliuc* in his analysis of post-Ceausescu's society in *Piata Universitatii – Romania/ University Square: Romania* (1991), and Croatian Lordan Zafranovic* in a number of works exploring the legacy of the Ustasa regime. Documentary film-making in Poland* played an important role in undermining the communist regime. Although there were instances of glorification of socialist construction, many documentaries were actually offering rather subversive commentaries on the affairs in countries of state socialism. Documentary film-makers did not hesitate to explore the sores of their societies wherever possible. Most important documentary film-makers from Yugoslavia include Hajrudin Krvavac, Vlatko Gilić, Kokan Rakonjać, Bostjan Hladnik and Lazar Stojanović* (who served a jail sentence for his 1971 diploma documentary, *Plasticni Jsus/Plastic Jesus*). Best-known Bulgarian documentarians were Hristo Kovacev, Nevena Tosheva and Oskar Kristanov. In post-communist times, against the background of financial crisis, the genre of documentary has managed more than any other to yield serious and meaningful works chronicling all aspects of the transition. Subjects favoured by documentary film-makers are the difficult process of political transformation, economic turmoil, and complex ethnic relations. In the 1990s many documentary film-makers have also taken the chance to revisit moments from the past and to critically re-evaluate the official history. DI

DOCUMENTARY: HUNGARY: THE 'DOCUMENTARY-FICTION' FILM

Hungarian film genre of the 1970s and early 1980s. The Hungarian *documentary-fiction* is close to the Jean Rouch kind of cinéma vérité. Parts are played by non-professional actors, often from the same profession as the characters they portray. The storyboard is more or less written in advance, but dialogue is improvised by the actors. Directors mostly work with two or more hand-held cameras. The first appearance of the genre was István Dárday's *Jutalomutazás/Holiday in Britain* in 1974. The narratives usually have some basis in Hungarian social reality, though two themes have predominated: the representation of everyday life and petty conflicts among lower middle-class people – Dárday-Szalay-Vitézy's *Filmregény/Film Novel* (1976) and Béla Tarr's* *Családi tűzfészek/Family Nest* (1977) – or conflicts between people of that social class and the political leadership – Dárday-Szalay's *Harcmodor/Stratagem* (1980), Vitézy's *Békeidő/Time of Peace* (1980). Film-makers within this genre had no particular artistic ambitions, considering their films primarily as political acts. The genre had a considerable impact on the representation of everyday life in mainstream Hungarian film, though it lost its momentum in the early 1980s as a consequence of a general disillusionment with the political impact of such films. KAB

DOCUMENTARY: POLAND

Poland enjoys a world-class reputation for documentary film-making. Despite – or perhaps because of – political restrictions, the documentary genre has been important to both film-makers and the cinema-going public at various points in the history of Polish cinema.

In the mid-1950s a group of documentaries known as the 'black series' looked at social problems officially considered non-existent. In the films of Jerzy Hoffman*, Jerzy Bossak and W. I. Borowik, prostitution, alcoholism and homelessness were brought to light through a mixture of staged and real situations. Many of Poland's finest directors began their careers making documentaries. Andrzej Munk's* first medium-length films, *Gwiazdy Muszą Płonąć/The Stars Must Shine* (1954) and *Błękitny Krzyż/Men of the Blue Cross* (1955), are 'docudramas', and he used his documentary experience to create a style reminiscent of Italian neo-realism in his later features. In the 1970s the documentary form was explored anew by young film-makers like Antoni Krauze*, Marcel Łoziński, Krzysztof Kieślowski* and Marek Piwowski. A manifesto published by the Cracow Group of documentary film-makers – Kieślowski, Tomasz Żygadło, Krzysztof Wojciechowski, Grzegorz Królikiewicz – declared that documentary should inform fictional work, and this concept prevailed in the 'cinema of moral unrest' of the 1970s and 1980s. Some film-makers, like Piwowski in *Rejs/Trip Down the River* (1970), mixed documentary and fiction, while in other cases the documentary ethos imbued fictional accounts of contemporary issues with a sense of integrity and authenticity. Not all film-makers, however, saw documentary merely as a schooling for feature films. Marcel Łozinski, Irena Kamieńska and Andrzej Titkow have continued to work exclusively in this form. Indeed the popularity of documentaries in Poland at the end of the 1980s can be attributed to their exposure of previously hidden historical and political events. With the economic crisis of the 1980s, many young film-makers who were unable to make features turned to documentary and short films. Among these, the amusing and well regarded films of Maria Zmarz-Koczanowicz, dealing with Polish youth sub-cultures, stand out. As Polish cinemas are now dominated by Hollywood, documentaries claim a strong following in art-house cinemas, unlike in western Europe where they are largely confined to festivals and television. With Polish society ripe for observation and comment, documentaries may well retain their popularity. AW

DONSKOI, Mark S.   Odessa, Ukraine [Russian Empire] 1901 – Moscow 1981

Soviet director and scriptwriter, who graduated in law and practised as a defence lawyer in the Ukraine before starting in film in 1926. His first two films, *V bol'shom gorode/In the Big City* (1928) and *Tsena cheloveka/The Price of a Man* (1929), were attacks on the 'bourgeois influences' of the 1920s New Economic Policy and paeans to the new Soviet morality. Donskoi achieved prominence through his 'Gorky trilogy' – *Detstvo Gor'kogo/The Childhood of Maxim Gorky* (1938), *V lyudyakh/Into the World* (1939) and *Moi universitety/My Universities* (1940), in which the life of the writer was offset against the backdrop of stultifying pre-Revolutionary Russian provincial life. *Raduga/The Rainbow* (1944) was an epic tale of the heroic exploits of a Ukrainian woman partisan against the German occupiers, for which Donskoi won both an Oscar and a USSR State Prize. He made two further Gorky adaptations – *Mat'/The Mother* (1956) and *Foma Gordeyev* (1959) – but his career declined into predictable hagiography with two films about Lenin's mother: *Serdtse materi/The Heart of a Mother* (1966) and *Vernost' materi/A Mother's Devotion* (1968). RT

DOVZHENKO, Alexander [Oleksandr] P.
Sosnitsa, Ukraine [Russian Empire] 1894 – Moscow 1956

Ukrainian Soviet director and writer. Trained as a teacher, Dovzhenko worked as a civil servant and diplomat, then studied painting in Munich and became a newspaper cartoonist. He began film work in Odessa in 1926, directing the comedies *Vasya-reformator/Vasya the*

Reformer (his first feature film) and *Yagodka lyubvi/The Fruit of Love*, and the thriller *Sumka dipkur'era/The Diplomatic Bag*. His major films, beginning with *Zvenigora* (1928), are characterised by a unique combination of lyricism, social commentary, gentle satire and powerful echoes of Ukrainian folklore. *Arsenal* (1929) was his first film to achieve widespread recognition outside the Ukraine. His next film, *Zemlya/The Earth* (1930), a highly poeticised version of collectivisation and a powerful evocation of nature and landscape, made his international reputation. His first sound film, *Ivan* (1932), traced the transformation of the hero from an unenlightened peasant to a committed communist shock worker against the background of the construction of the Dnieper dam, one of the key projects of the first Five Year Plan. After this Dovzhenko's career went downhill, as he became little more than a loyal 'servant of the state'. *Aerograd* (1935) affirmed his faith in the future of the Soviet Far East; *Shchors* (1939), set in the Civil War, was made at Stalin's* suggestion as a 'Ukrainian *Chapayev'* and won a State Prize in 1941. *Osvobozhdenie/Liberation* (1940) celebrated the reunification of western Ukraine with Ukraine proper following the Nazi–Soviet pact, while *Bitva za nashu sovetskuyu Ukrainu/ The Battle for Our Soviet Ukraine* (1943) and *Pobeda na pravoberezhnoi Ukraine/Victory on the Ukrainian Right Bank* (1945) dealt with World War II. A number of Dovzhenko's unfilmed scripts were later made by his widow Yulia Solntseva. Dovzhenko also taught at VGIK* and wrote articles on film. RT

DRACULA – see TRANSYLVANIA

DRAVIĆ, Milena   Belgrade, Serbia 1940

Yugoslav actress of Serbian origin, probably the only real star of Yugoslav cinema, discovered as a teenage girl by František Čap* for his film *Vrata ostaju otvorena/The Door Remains Open* (1959). This successful start led her to enter the Film Academy in Belgrade. By 1962 she had already gained her first Golden Arena at the national film festival in Pula*, for Branko Bauer's* *Prekobrojna/Superfluous* (1962). Since then she has appeared in over seventy films by more than thirty directors, among whom Puriša Djordjević and Dušan Makavejev* were the most important for her career. International audiences will remember her as the radical activist proclaiming the sexual revolution in Makavejev's *W. R. – Misterije organizma/W. R. – Mysteries of the Organism* (1971), while Yugoslav television viewers recall her as the host of one of the best nightclub shows (together with her husband Dragan Nikolič), *Licem u lice/Face to Face*. SP

Other Films Include: *Tri letni dri/Three Summer Days* (1994); *Urnebesna tragedija/Burlesque Tragedy* (1995, Fr.); *Bure baruta/Powder Keg* (1998, Fr.).

DRAGOJEVIĆ, Srdjan　　　　　　　　　　Belgrade 1963

Yugoslav director of Serbian origin. Dragojević's debut feature, *Mi nismo andjeli/We Are Not Angels* (1992) represented an utopian punk-rock vision of life in Yugoslavia toward the end of the century. The film enjoyed tremendous success at the box-office at home. In 1996 Dragojević made the internationally acclaimed *Lepa sela lepo gore/Pretty Villages, Pretty Flame* (1996), an earnest and disturbing take on the Bosnian war. The film won the main award at the Sao Paulo international festival and was appreciated by critics worldwide as one of the most insightful psychological film studies on the break-up of Yugoslavia. Despite declaring that he would not make any more movies dealing with the crisis in the Balkans, in 1998 Dragojević released a third feature, *Rane/Wounds*, the story of two boys coming of age in the depressed and crime-ridden reality of Milosević's Belgrade. The film enjoyed a significant success both at home and abroad. Dragojević co-wrote the scripts for all of his films. Between 1995 and 1999 he taught directing at the film department of the University of Belgrade. He left Yugoslavia in early 1999 and moved to the US. DI

DUDOW, Slatan　　Tsaribrod, Bulgaria 1903 – East Berlin, GDR 1963

Bulgarian–East German director. Dudow's name is a synonym for socially committed film-making concerned with the problems of the working classes. He was one of the leading figures of East German cinema, having made all his films at the DEFA studio. Dudow emigrated from his native Bulgaria after the pro-fascist coup of 1923. He graduated in drama at Humboldt University in Berlin and got involved with socialist intellectual circles. He worked on stage productions of Soviet plays and on the crew of film productions directed by Fritz Lang and G. W. Pabst, making his directing debut with *Zeitprobleme: wie der Arbeiter wohnt/Problems of the Time: How Does the Worker Live* (1930). In 1932, Dudow directed one of the classical works of socialist cinema, *Kühle Wampe oder: Wem gehört die Welt?/To Whom Does the World Belong?* co-written by Bertolt Brecht with whom Dudow had collaborated on a number of theatrical projects. *Kühle Wampe* tells the story of a working-class family, forced to move to a slum, when overwhelmed by the results of unemployment and depression. The film contained a clear anti-fascist message in times when Nazism was gathering strength. Under the Nazi regime Dudow went into exile and spent most part of the 1930s and the war time in Switzerland. After

World War II he made one of the first GDR films, *Unser täglich Brot/Our Daily Bread* (1949), a schematic socialist-realist workers' drama which loosely continued the tale of the worker's family from *Kühle Wampe*, with a musical score by Hans Eisler. Dudow wrote or co-wrote the scripts for most of the films he directed. DI

Other Films Include: *Seifenblasen/Soap Bubbles* (1934); *Familie Benthin/The Benthin Family* (1950); *Frauenschicksale/Women's Fates* (1952); *Stärker als die Nacht/Stronger Than the Night* (1954); *Der Hauptmann von Köln/The Captain from Cologne* (1956); *Verwirrung der Liebe/Love Confusion* (1959); *Christine* (1963).

DUNAYEVSKY, Isaak O.   Lokhvitsa, Ukraine [Russian Empire] 1900 – Moscow 1955

Russian composer. Dunayevsky composed the music for Grigori Alexandrov's* popular musical comedy films *Vesëlye rebyata/The Happy Guys* (1934), *Tsirk/The Circus* (1936), *Volga-Volga* (1938), *Svetlyi put'/The Radiant Path* (1940) and *Vesna/Springtime* (1947). He also scored Ivan Pyriev's* *Bogataya nevesta/The Rich Bride* (1938) and *Kubanskie kazaki/The Kuban Cossacks* (1950). His catchy tunes combined elements of folk and popular music, marches and dances, and were very popular. RT

DYKHOVICHNY, Ivan V.   Moscow 1947

Russian director, actor and scriptwriter. In 1979, after ten years' work as a theatrical actor, Dykhovichny entered the Higher Courses for Directors, where he was taught by Eldar Ryazanov* and, briefly but influentially, by Andrey Tarkovsky*, graduating in 1982. Tarkovsky's influence is apparent in Dykhovichny's early shorts, including *Elia Isaakovich i Margarita Prokof'evna/Elia Isaakovich and Margarita Prokofevna* (1981), from a story by Isaak Babel. Dykhovichny found international success with his 1988 version of Chekhov's story *Chernyi monakh/The Black Monk*, which he co-scripted with Sergei Solovyov*. Dykhovichny's most important film is *Prorva/Moscow Parade* (1992), a Franco-Russian co-production starring the German singer Ute Lemper. *Moscow Parade*'s achievement, among the number of historically based films of the late 1980s and early 1990s, is to capture the glamour of the façade of 1930s' Stalinist Moscow as well as the decay and corruption beneath. In 1995 he made *Muzyka dlya dekabrya/Music for December*, the story of an artist who returns to Russia from American emigration with tragic consequences for those he left behind, and *Zhenskaia rol'/A Woman's Role*, a short documentary looking at the symbolic, often tragic roles into which pre-Revolutionary and Soviet Russian cinema cast its women characters. In a surprising departure, Dykhovichny has just made *Neznakomoe oruzhie ili Krestonosets-2/Unfamiliar Weapon*, or *Crusader 2* (1999). The original *Crusader* film starred the king of Russian stuntmen, Alexander Inshakov, who reappears here in an unfunny comedy about a group of New Russians shooting a historical film in Greece and syphoning off their sponsors' money. The film has not advanced Dykhovichny's reputation. JG

E

EGGERT, Konstantin V. 1883–1955

Russian director, actor and entrepreneur. Eggert worked on the stage, including the Moscow Art Theatre, from 1912 and in cinema from 1924, when he appeared in Yakov Protazanov's* *Aelita*. His career is closely associated with the Mezhrabpom studio*, in which he became a major shareholder and for which (with Vladimir Gardin*) he directed his first film *Medvezh'ya svad'ba/The Bear's Wedding* (1926), an adaptation by Anatoli Lunacharsky* of a gothic horror story by Prosper Mérimée, which starred Eggert and Lunacharsky's wife Natalya Rozenel and proved to be far more popular at the Soviet box-office than Eisenstein's* *Bronenosets Potëmkin/The Battleship Potemkin*. He directed four more features, culminating in a Balzac adaptation in 1937. He was arrested, and ended his artistic career as an actor in the Gulag. RT

EISENSTEIN [EIZENSHTEIN], Sergei M. Riga, Latvia [Russian Empire] 1898 – Moscow 1948

Soviet director and film theorist. Eisenstein trained as a civil engineer but abandoned his courses and joined the Red Army after the Revolution. Assigned to a theatrical troupe during the Civil War, he gained valuable experience designing and painting sets and producing plays. In 1921, with his childhood friend Maxim Strauch*, he joined the Proletkult Theatre and staged a series of experimental agitational plays, using the techniques of circus, music hall and cabaret in what he termed a 'montage of attractions' [> SOVIET MONTAGE], which was intended to galvanise audiences into an ideologically motivated reaction. One of his productions included a short film, *Dnevnik Glumova/Glumov's Diary* (1923), a spoof of an American thriller. But he was slowly becoming aware of the limitations of theatrical realism, especially when he staged *Protivogazy/Gas Masks* (1924) in a gas works. The experiment failed and Eisenstein, as he put it, 'fell into cinema'. He had already worked with Esfir Shub* re-editing imported films for Soviet audiences and in his first full-length film, *Stachka/The Strike* (1925), he applied the montage of attractions to cinema for the first time. Unlike Lev Kuleshov*, Eisenstein thought that the essence of montage lay in the *conflict* between different elements, chosen for their effectiveness, and that from this conflict a new synthesis would arise. The actors' role was diminished to that of representing 'types', while the director became supreme. Although he used professional actors in all his films, he chose people for their physical type rather than their acting ability, at least in his silent films. Hence an unknown worker played Lenin* in *Oktyabr'/October* (1928). Eisenstein achieved international recognition with his second feature, *Bronenosets Potëmkin/The Battleship Potemkin* (1926). The fictitious sequence of the massacre on the Odessa steps proved so powerful that it became embedded in the popular consciousness as an actual historical event, as did the storming of the Winter Palace in *Oktyabr'*. This film had to be re-edited because of Trotsky's fall from grace, and all Eisenstein's subsequent work was dogged by political difficulties. His film about collectivisation, begun as *General'naya liniya/The General Line*, was re-cut and eventually finished as *Staroe i novoe/The Old and the New* in 1929. Eisenstein did not even wait for its Moscow premiere: he had already left with Grigori Alexandrov* and Eduard Tisse* for the West, ostensibly to learn about the new medium of sound. Eisenstein had already theoretically investigated the possibility of incorporating sound into montage, devising the notion of orchestral counterpoint, proclaimed in the 1928 'Statement on Sound' signed with Alexandrov and Vsevolod Pudovkin*. The idea of 'attractions' gave way to that of 'stimulants', which would provoke a complex series of associations in the audience, setting them thinking along a line predetermined by the director. He called this 'intellectual cinema', and *Oktyabr'* represents his first experiment in this direction. Critics accused him of making films that were 'unintelligible to the millions'.

Eisenstein eventually went to Hollywood: the projects he put forward were rejected and he ended up in Mexico, shooting his first sound film, *¡Que viva México!* However the money ran out and he returned to Moscow in 1932. Boris Shumyatsky* rejected a number of Eisenstein's projects but in 1935 allowed him to start working on a new film about collectivisation, *Bezhin lug/Bezhin Meadow*. After two years this was stopped for financial and political reasons, and it was only after Shumyatsky's own fall from grace in 1938 that Eisenstein was able to complete his next, and most accessible, film *Aleksandr Nevskii/Alexander Nevsky*, starring Nikolai Cherkasov*. In this film he was also, for the first time, able to realise his ideas on audiovisual montage and orchestral counterpoint in a remarkable collaboration with Sergei Prokofiev*, especially in the famous 'Battle on the Ice' sequence. The film marked his rehabilitation and he was awarded the

Order of Lenin in 1939. Eisenstein's last film, *Ivan Groznyi/Ivan the Terrible* (1943–6) was never completed. The first part, released in 1945, was an instant critical success and it earned the Stalin Prize for Eisenstein and Cherkasov. In the second part, however, the deliberate historical parallels between Ivan and Stalin* became all too apparent and, although completed, the film was not shown, its existence not officially acknowledged until 1958. In it Eisenstein extended his exploration of montage into the use of colour. The third part of *Ivan* was never finished.

Eisenstein's work in film theory and practice made him the towering figure in Soviet cinema history, referred to by all others simply as 'The Master'. His major theoretical works have been translated into English as *The Film Sense* (1942); *Film Form* (1949); *Film Essays and a Lecture* and *Notes of a Film Director* (both 1970); *Writings, 1922–34* (1988); *Towards a Theory of Montage* (1991); *Beyond the Stars* (1995), *Writings, 1935–48* (1996) and *The Eisenstein Reader* (1998). RT

EKK, Nikolai V.

Nikolai Ivakin; Riga, Latvia [Russian Empire] 1902 – Moscow 1976

Soviet director, actor and scriptwriter. Ekk graduated from Vsevolod Meyerhold's Directing Workshop and worked in his theatre until 1927 when he graduated from the GTK film school, where he had worked under Pavel Tager, one of the pioneers of sound in the USSR. Ekk directed the first Soviet sound film, *Putëvka v zhizn'/The Path to Life* (1931), which dealt with the communal re-education of the homeless orphans left after the 1917–21 Civil War. The film was highly regarded at the first Venice film festival in 1932. He also directed, and starred in, the first Soviet colour film, *Grunya Kornakova* (1936), and made another colour feature, *Sorochinskaya yarmarka/Sorochintsy Fair*, based on the Gogol story, in 1939. He was then sent into internal exile in Tashkent and left unemployed and unemployable for nearly two decades. Among subsequent works was a stereoscopic (3-D) film, *Chelovek v zelënoi perchatke/The Man in the Green Gloves* (1968). He also worked as a stage director and scripted all his films. RT

EKRAN

Slovene monthly film magazine, established in 1962 in Ljubljana with the intention of providing a critical evaluation of modern cinema. Initially relying on translations from French, Italian and American authors, *Ekran* reached its first peak at the end of the 1960s with original contributions centred on the Yugoslav 'Black Wave'*. In the 1980s, the magazine was closely linked with a strong local school of Lacanian psychoanalysis and it opened its pages to French film theory (Raymond Bellour, Pascal Bonitzer, Michel Chion), creating an inter-disciplinary field of humanist and cultural studies. This theoretical focus prompted the organisation of an annual autumn film school and the creation of a book series, Imago. Recent circulation was 2,000. SP

ERMLER, Fridrikh M.
Rechitsa, Latvia [Russian Empire] 1898 – Moscow 1967

Soviet director. A member of the Communist Party from 1919, Ermler served in the Civil War in both the Red Army and the secret police. After training as an actor and working as a scriptwriter, he directed his first film, the short comedy *Skarlatina/Scarlet Fever* (1924). His subsequent silent films depicted problems of everyday life, rather than heroics: *Kat'ka – bumazhnyi ranet/Katka's Reinette Apples* (1926), *Dom v sugrobakh/The House in the Snowdrifts* and *Parizshkii sapozhnik/The Parisian Cobbler* (both 1928). Ermler's last silent film was also his best: *Oblomok imperii/A Fragment of Empire* (1929) contrasted the old world with the new through the story of an amnesiac Civil War soldier returning to the new Soviet Union. His first sound film, made with Sergei Yutkevich*, *Vstrechnyi/Counterplan* (1932), was a psychologically well-judged account of the problems of the first Five Year Plan period, while *Krest'yane/Peasants* (1935) represented a defence of collectivisation. He then made the two-part *Velikii grazhdanin/A Great Citizen* (1938–9), devoted to the life of Stalin's* murdered rival Sergei Kirov, and, among other works, a film version of the Battle of Stalingrad, *Velikii perelom/The Great Turning Point* (1946), which won a prize at Cannes. His films demonstrated a strong sense of realism and a measure of creative independence that their subject matter often belied. RT

F

FÁBRI, Zoltán
Budapest 1917–94

Hungarian director. A preoccupation with the deepest moral dilemmas and with the ethical foundations of everyday-life behaviour are the main features of Fábri's work. He studied fine arts and drama and initially pursued a career in theatre, a background accountable for the theatrical feel of many of his films. During his versatile career he worked on stage productions, illustrated books, co-wrote the scripts for most of his films, and for some acted as a production designer. Fábri debuted in cinema with the collectivisation story *Vihar/The Storm* (1951), but his first internationally renowned film was another village life drama, *Körhinta/Merry-go-round* (1955), a debut for actress Mari Töröcsik*. The political-moral treatise *Hannibál tanár úr/Professor Hannibal* (1956) explored the shaky moral grounds of fascism by looking at the harassment of an innocuous schoolteacher in Budapest between the wars. Based on Ferenc Molnár's novel, the Oscar-nominated *A Pál utcai fiúk/The Boys of Paul Street* (1967) is another allegory of war concerned with the clashes of some boys over a contested vacant lot in Budapest. Fábri's best-known film is the shattering *Az Ötödik pecsét/The Fifth Seal* (1976), set during the time of Nazi occupation. The events of the film take place over a single night in which the five protagonists are faced with the most challenging moral choices they may ever need to make. Moral choices again are the topic of *Fábián Bálint találkozása Istennel/Balint Fabian Meets God* (1979), about a peasant whose personal story of violence, torment and remorse follows the historical swings of the Hungarian Soviet republic. DI

Other Films Include: *Életjel/Fourteen Lives* (1954); *Édes Anna/Anna* (1958); *Nappali sötétség/Darkness in Daytime* (1963); *Utószezon/Late Season* (1966); *Isten hozta örnagy úr/Welcome Sir Major* (1969); *Hangyaboly/Ant-Hill* (1971); *Plusz-mínusz egy nap/One Day More, One Day Less* (1973); *Requiem* (1981); *Gyertek el a névnapomra/The House-Warming* (1983).

FAINZIMMER, Alexander M.   Yekaterinoslav [now Dnepropetrovsk], Ukraine [Russian Empire] 1906 – USSR 1982

Soviet director. Graduated from Pudovkin's* workshop at the GTK (later VGIK*) film school in 1928 and made films from 1930 to 1980, but is best known for his first sound film, the satirical grotesque *Poruchik Kizhe/Lieutenant Kijé* (1934), for which Sergei Prokofiev* wrote the score. The Belorussian studio which produced the film, Belgoskino, was closed down shortly afterwards for politically suspect activities. Fainzimmer also directed *Ovod/The Gadfly* (1955) from a script by Viktor Shklovsky* and with a score by Dmitri Shostakovich*. RT

FALK, Feliks   Stanisławów, Ukraine 1941

Polish director and scriptwriter. Falk graduated from Łódź in 1974, after which he joined Andrzej Wajda's* 'X' Production Unit and became part of the 'cinema of moral unrest', rising to prominence with *Wodzirej/Top Dog* (1978). Set in a small town, the film follows Danielak, portrayed by the brilliant comic actor Jerzy Stuhr*, as he ruthlessly plays the system to get a coveted job. The popular sequel, *Bohater Roku/Hero of the Year* (1987), expressed a more general disenchantment, showing Danielak in the early 1980s trying to make a comeback but finding a new official mentality resilient to his manipulations. AW

Other Films Include: *Był Jazz/And There Was Jazz* (made 1981, rel. 1984); *Kapitał, Czyli Jak Robic Pieniądze w Polsce/Capital, or How to Make Money in Poland* (1989); *Koniec Gry/The End of the Game* (1991); *Samowolka/A.W.O.L.* (1993); *Lato milosci/Summer of Love* (1995); *Daleko od siebie/Far from Oneself* (1996).

FAMU

Prague film school (FAMU: the Film Faculty of the Academy of Music and Dramatic Arts) formed in 1947, and one of the first of the national film schools. It initially comprised seven departments: dramaturgy, direction, photography, documentaries, reportage, techniques, production and theory. Starting with less than half a dozen teachers, the staff was considerably expanded in the 1960s. The first graduates appeared in 1949–50, and virtually all subsequent Czech and Slovak film-makers trained there.

The FAMU system of education was closely identified with the figure of Otakar Vávra*, who characterised its approach as a balance between theory and practice. The importance of literature was recognised and the novelist Milan Kundera lectured there in the 1960s (before the publication of *The Joke*). The dearth of good scripts in the 1980s has been linked to a diminished role for literature in training rather than to ideology as such, although the two were linked. A high proportion of students come from abroad and some of the best-known graduates have included Aleksandar Petrović*, Frank Beyer, Agnieszka Holland* and Emir Kusturica*. The former Dean, František (Frank) Daniel, took the FAMU 'system' to the US in the 1970s. The appointment of film theorist Jan Bernard as Dean in 1993 signalled a desire to maintain the school's founding principles. PH

FEST

International film festival. Established in Belgrade in 1970 as a 'festival of festivals', FEST soon became an important gathering point for film-makers from around the world. A special attraction of the early years was a midnight programme called 'Brave New World', organised by Dušan Makavejev*. Some of the rebellious mood of the early 1970s was captured in the film *Nedostaje mi Sonia Heine/I Miss Sonja Henie*, for which each of FEST's famous guests (Miloš Forman*, Tinto Brass, Sergio Leone, Paul Morrissey) directed one episode with the same cast and the same text – based only on the words of the title. In the 1980s, the audience was still coming (over 200,000 visitors in the best years) but the guests were not. FEST became a kind of distributors' fair and was near collapse under the economic and cultural embargo on Serbia in 1993. In 1995 Emir Kusturica* acted as a general manager to the festival alongside critic, Nenad Dukic. In spite of the difficult conditions of international isolation, the festival still takes place annually. SP

FILM FESTIVALS IN EASTERN EUROPE

National film festivals have taken place in all East European countries since the 1950s. The most important international fora for film-makers were Karlovy Vary* in Czechoslovakia and the Moscow International Film Festival*. A system of active cinematic exchange among the East European countries existed. Since 1989 the festival scene has undergone a substantial transformation. Some older festivals became defunct and new ones came into being. The Karlovy Vary International Film Festival which started in 1950 established itself not only as the most important venue for Czech film, but for East European cinema in general. Throughout the 1980s and the 1990s it was programmed by Eva Zaoralova. Other Czech festivals are the international festival of television programmes, Golden Prague as well as the Golden Golem (Prague) a commercial undertaking of post-communist times which in the 1990s made a short-lived attempt to outweigh Karlovy Vary. Two festivals started in Slovakia in the early 1990s – the fórum Bratislava festival of first feature films, and the Art Film Festival in Trencanske Teplice. The Polish national film festival traditionally takes place in Gdansk. In the late 1970s and early 1980s it provided the venue for important political activities of Solildarnosz and KOR. Smaller-scale festivals take place in various cities, like Warsaw, Katowice, Posnan, Gdynia and Lagow. Cracow is the site of an International Short Film Festival. There is an annual film festival for the Polish diaspora in the US in Chicago. Hungarian film production is showcased annually every February during the Hungarian Film Week in Budapest. Other festivals in Hungary include the Gysr Media Wave and Titanic (Budapest). A number of festivals take place across former Yugoslavia. The festival in Pula* which showcased the entire Yugoslav production before the break-up is now focusing on new Croatian cinema. It takes place around the end of July and awards the Golden Arena to the best Croatian production. A secondary venue is the Days of Croatian Film in Zagreb which showcases the country's production in documentaries, video and experimental genres. The Slovenian Film Art Fest in Ljubljana takes place in November. Within Serbia, besides the most significant Belgrade Film Fest* in February, there is the

Belgrade Festival of Yugoslav Documentary and Short Film in March and the Festival of Auteur Films. Other festivals take place in Subotica (on Lake Palic), Sopot, Vrnjacka Banja, Nis and Herzeg-Novi. Besides the International Film Festival in Skopje in March, Macedonia organises the internationally respected Brothers Manaki Festival in Bitolja in October which focuses exclusively on the art of cinematography. The Sarajevo Film Festival came to existence during the last year of the Bosnian war and has since become one of the most important venues for film-makers from the region. The Bulgarian national film festival, Golden Rose, takes place in Varna on the Black Sea coast. In the 1990s it became a biennial. For nearly two decades Varna also hosted an annual international Red Cross Film Festival. Sofia hosts three new small-scale festivals – of European co-productions, of musicals, and *Kinomania*. The festival in Costinesti on the Black Sea coast started in the late 1970s as a national festival but has been changing its profile since. Several festivals which take place outside Eastern Europe have established themselves as important fora for East European cinema. One such is the Thessaloniki International Film Festival in Greece which has been in existence since the early 1950s and takes place in late November. Since the 1980s the festival has maintained a constant *Balkan Survey* feature which regularly showcases the best and most recent work from the Balkan countries. The film festival in Cottbus in the Lausitz region of former East Germany near the Polish border is entitled Young East European Cinema. It started in the early 1990s and quickly came to be dubbed the Mecca of East European film. The Alpe-Adria Meetings with Central and East European Cinema in Trieste, Italy (Jan.–Feb.) were established in 1988 for the purpose of promoting the best and most recent film productions from the Central and East European countries. After the break-up of Yugoslavia, Trieste became the primary meeting place for film-makers from the Central European and South-East European regions. Other festivals which regularly feature special sections devoted to Eastern Europe are the Rotterdam International Film Festival in January, the Berlin International Film Festival in February, the Istanbul International Film Festival in March, and the Créteil International Festival of Women's Films in March/April. The Russian-centred Festival of Slavonic and Orthodox Peoples *Zolotoy Vityaz* (*Golden Knight*) takes place in different countries in May. There are specialised festivals for animated films in Zagreb* and the Ukraine. DI

FILM POLSKI

Polish film institution. Film Polski was established in 1945 with Aleksander Ford* as chief. Administered by film-makers, it was responsible for every area of the industry, from film stock manufacture to production, distribution and exhibition. The political relaxation of the mid-1950s allowed the formation of the '*zespoły*' or film units, de-

74

volving the production function from the institutional centre and to groups of film-makers. With a leading director heading each unit, comprised of like-minded colleagues, a large degree of autonomy could be achieved. The best example is the famous 'X' unit, under Andrzej Wajda's* direction, which produced some of the finest and most politically challenging films of the 1970s. Although scripts were vetted, there was relatively little interference during filming, and it was left to Film Polski and its control of distribution and exhibition to determine the fate of completed films. It was common practice to delay distribution, or print only a limited number of politically 'unpopular' films. By failing to exploit films to their full commercial potential, Film Polski contributed to the economic malaise of the industry. In matters of international promotion, film-makers were at its mercy since all submissions to foreign festivals were made through Film Polski.

Film Polski entered the post-communist era with a reputation tainted by corruption and inefficiency. Its staff, however, had experience of, and good contacts in, the international film community. Film Polski is now a government-sponsored co-operative and functions in two distinct areas. Firstly, it continues to deal with the international promotion of Polish film as a whole and of Poland as a co-producer/location for filming. Its second (privately financed) function is to make international film sales for the independent film producers and film units now operating in Poland. AW

FILMSKE SVESKE

Yugoslav film magazine, established at the Belgrade Film Institute in 1968. The fact that the French translation of the title would be 'Cahiers du cinéma' is not the only link between the two magazines: from the beginning, *Filmske sveske* was concerned with Marxism, semiotics and structuralism. It managed to widen its views and to maintain a high level of film theory through translations of French and American authors and original contributions. Although it gradually changed from a monthly magazine to a yearbook of film theory, it had a great impact on theoretical film studies in the former Yugoslavia. SP

FILM STUDIOS IN EASTERN EUROPE

Film production and distribution under state socialism worked within a specific administration framework. Each country had a government body in charge of film-making (i.e. Ministry of Culture; Film Commission), the film financing was centralised and came exclusively from the state. The national television companies were also involved in film production and often ran their own studios. The films were picked up by state-run distribution organisations and were exhibited within a chain of state-owned theatres. A system of exchange of feature films between the Eastern bloc countries was in place, thus most films were getting at least some exposure abroad. A state-appointed commission was deciding which film would be sent to which international festival. The unions of film-makers worked under close observation and guidance from the state and represented a strong trade organisation, membership in which was by election and was considered quite prestigious. Most state production companies were structured after the model of the Polish film units (*zespol filmovy*). Under this system, introduced in the early 1960s, the film units within the studios of the Eastern bloc functioned as the basic film production entity and had relative creative autonomy within the system. The units, usually led by a well-established director, comprised of several other directors, as well as screenwriters, cameramen, set and costume designers, and sometimes even actors sharing similar artistic visions. These were all salaried employees who only received bonuses upon the completion and release of a new film. Sometimes the film units were more prominent than the studios themselves, e.g. the film units run by Wajda (X) and Zanussi (TOR). In post-communist times, the East European cinema industries suffered massive cuts and withdrawal of secure funding early in the 1990s. Profound changes in production financing included the substitution of film units with independent producers, the introduction of new strategies in state subsidies which are now awarded on a per project basis and only cover a percentage of the production costs, the growing role of television as co-producer in feature film-making, the increased number of international co-productions, as well as the emerging presence of private domestic and international investment in film-making. A number of smaller production companies are working on a contractual basis with the bigger studios. Under the new conditions production levels stabilised relatively fast and the balance in output numbers, disturbed originally by the drastic cuts in centralised financing, was restored in many of the East European countries.

The studios across Eastern Europe had capacity and size compatible with those in Western Europe. This allowed the East European countries to have film output numbers comparable to Western Europe. The studios were meant to serve mostly the needs of the national film industries. Studio executives of the communist era, however, maintained contacts within the international film community, and a number of international co-productions were still made in Eastern Europe during the Cold War. These East European studios were especially sought after when one needed to shoot historical epics as large numbers of extras and cavalry were easy to secure. Most studios were built in the 1950s: Shqiperia e re (New Albania) in Albania (Alba film since 1992), Boyana* in Bulgaria, Jadran Film* in Croatia, Avala in Serbia, Buftea* in Romania. The Polish state cinematography committee, Film Polski*, maintained four main studio spaces: WDFiF in Warsaw, Leg Studios in Cracow, Łódź in Central Poland, and Wroclaw in Silesia. Hungary operated three state-owned studios under the umbrella film agency Mafilm, as well as the experimental Balász Béla Studio*. The thriving East German film production evolved exclusively around one of the largest studios, DEFA near Berlin in the GDR. It had been in existence since the 1930s and had advanced production facilities for its time. The largest film studio was Barrandov*, built initially in the early 1930s. The studios' facilities had been further improved during the German occupation of the country by the Nazis who had plans to make Barrandov a film-making centre equal to the other studios in Babelsberg and Munich. The studio was nationalised in the late 1940s, and continuous state investments made it possible to build a special effects stage, a projection tunnel, and a water tank which made shooting under water possible. Barrandov was the site where most of the celebrated films of the Czech New Wave* were shot. It also attracted international co-productions, like Milos Forman's* *Amadeus* (1984, US) and Barbra Streisand's *Yentl* (1984, US). It has eleven sound stages with total stage space of 7,000 sqm (seven stages at Barrandov and four stages at the satellite studios at Hostivar). Barrandov also has post-production facilities, large makeup and dressing rooms, laboratories, special effects, sound mix, dubbing, multi-media, and music studio units. Secondary production facilities for the Czech Republic were located at the Bata film studios in Gotwaldov (Zlin), with four large sound stages, and a territory of 150,000 sqm. Gotwaldov is also the home of an extensive collection of children's films. Kratky Film in Prague has been an animation and documentary studio and archive since the 1940s. The Slovak studio, Koliba in Bratislava, was built after World War II. In the 1990s, with maintenance budgets reduced to the bare minimum and equipment becoming out-of-date, but still with much lower production costs than the West, the studios throughout Eastern Europe are in increasing competition with each other, struggling to attract Western co-productions to secure the use of local technicians and actors for supporting roles. Various degrees of privatisation have been instituted in all the studios. As Barrandov has been a highly sought-after filming and post-production location, its privatisation in the 1990s has been the subject of numerous volatile moves. The Czech government, however, has issued a decree stipulating that Barrandov is to continue to function as a film production site. DI

FILMVILÁG

Hungarian film magazine. The most important Hungarian magazine of film theory and criticism, founded in 1958. In the 1980s *Filmvilág* provided an important forum for intellectuals from many diverse fields, allowing them to debate issues (under the 'cover' of film) which would otherwise be censored. This role was inherited from another monthly, *Filmkultúra*, a magazine which had the same critical function in the 1960s and early 1970s until its editor, Yvette Bíró, was dismissed for political reasons. While remaining primarily a film magazine, *Filmvilág* has always placed cinema within a wider cultural context; more recently, it has expanded to include general media issues. KAB

FORD, Aleksander

Łódź 1908 – Florida, US
[Copenhagen, Denmark?] 1980

Polish director. Ford's career began in the silent era, with several shorts and a feature, *Mascotte/Mascot* (1930). One of the founding members of START (Society of Devotees of Artistic Film) in 1930 and of the film-makers' cooperative SAF in 1935, he became a leading figure in the development of the postwar film industry; he was head of Film Polski* between 1945 and 1947 and artistic director of the Studio Film Unit from 1955 to 1968. He directed the first Polish epic, *Krzyżacy/Knights of the Teutonic Order* (1960), based on the classic novel by Nobel laureate Henryk Sienkiewicz, which celebrated Poland's victory at the battle of Grunwald (1410). A blockbuster, later considered essential patriotic and educational viewing, the film still tops the Polish box-office charts. Ford was one of the victims of the communist anti-Semitic drive of 1968. He lost his administrative job and emigrated shortly afterwards, working in Scandinavia, Germany and the US until his death. AW

Other Films Include: *Ulica Graniczna/Border Street/So That Others May Live* (1949); *Piątka z Ulicy Barskiej/Five from Barska Street* (1954); *Ósmy Dzień Tygodnia/The Eighth Day of the Week* (1958, rel. 1983); *Sie sind frei, Doktor Korczak/Dr Korczak, the Martyr* (1973, Ger./Israel).

FORMAN, Miloš

Čáslav 1932

Czech director and scriptwriter educated at FAMU* (1951–6), where he studied scriptwriting. Forman worked as an assistant to Alfred Radok on *Dědeček automobil/Old Man Motor Car* (1956) and directed productions for Radok's Laterna Magika theatre. He co-scripted *Nechte to na mně/Leave it to Me*, directed by Martin Frič* (1955), and *Štěňata/Puppies* (1958), directed by Ivo Novák, before making his debut as writer/director with *Konkurs/Talent Competition/Competition* and *Černý Petr/Black Peter/Peter and Pavla* in 1963. Together with his colleagues Ivan Passer* and Jaroslav Papoušek, he worked with non-professional actors and semi-improvised dialogue to present a view of working-class life free from the stereotypes of Socialist Realism*. *Černý Petr* and *Lásky jedné plavovlásky/A Blonde in Love/Loves of a Blonde* (1965) had obvious links with late neo-realism and cinéma vérité, as well as with classic comedy. Focusing on the impermanence of young love, the confusion of middle age and the gulf between generations, they also provide a profound social analysis. When Passer and Papoušek made their own directing debuts with *Intimní osvětlení/Intimate Lightning* (1965) and *Nejkrásnější věk/The Best Age* (1968), they produced works in very much the same style. Forman's satire on bureaucracy, *Hoří, má panenko/The Firemen's Ball* (1967), was interpreted as a direct assault on the Communist Party and banned 'for ever' in 1973, only to be re-released a few months before the collapse of the Jakeš government in 1989.

Forman was already abroad, working on the script for his first American film, when Czechoslovakia was invaded by the Warsaw Pact countries in 1968. *Taking Off* (1971, US) continued the improvised, group-centred approach of his Czech films, but he has subsequently opted for literary subjects and a conventional approach to narrative. His Oscar-winning *One Flew Over the Cuckoo's Nest* (1975, US), clearly a comment on totalitarianism, gained much from his emphasis on ambiguous characterisation and ensemble playing, while *Amadeus* (1984, US), filmed in Prague with a mainly Czech team under conditions of press blackout, had much to say on the relationship of the artist to patronage and bureaucracy. In 1975, he became a US citizen and co-director of the Film Department at Columbia University, New York, and now works mainly in North America although, he became, in 1993, a board member of the newly privatised Barrandov* studios. His most well-known film in recent years is *The People vs Larry Flint* (1996) and his influence was recognised in March 1997 when he was the subject of an *Omnibus* documentary. PH

Bib: Miloš Forman and Jan Novák, *Turnaround* (1994).

Other Films Include: *Laterna magika II/Magic Lantern II* [co-d] (1960); *Dobře placená procházka/A Well-Paid Stroll* [TV] (1966). **In the US**: *Visions of Eight* [episode *The Decathlon*] (1972); *Hair* (1979); *Ragtime* (1981); *The Little Black Book* (1999); *Man on the Moon* (1999). **In France**: *Valmont* (1989).

FORMER SOVIET UNION – see SOVIET UNION

FRANK, Herz   Latvia 1926

Latvian documentary director and scriptwriter. After work as a photographer and journalist, Frank began to write the scripts for documentary films. Since 1965 he has scripted and directed over twenty films. Among the most important are *Zapretnaya zona/Forbidden Zone* (1975) and *Vysshii sud/Supreme Court [Last Judgement]* (1987), which traces the life of a young man from his trial and conviction for murder until his execution. In 1989, together with Vladimir Eisner, he directed *Zhili-byli-sem' Simeonov/Once There Lived Seven Simeons*, the story of a doomed attempt by a Siberian family jazz ensemble to hijack a plane and escape from the Soviet Union. JG

FREINDLIKH, Alisa B.   Leningrad 1934

Russian actress. Freindlikh graduated from the Leningrad Theatre Institute in 1957 and joined the ensemble of the Komissarzhevsky Theatre; later she moved to the Lensovet Theatre, and since 1983 she has worked at the St Petersburg Bolshoi Drama Theatre. She received the Stanislavsky Prize for her theatrical work in 1976, and was made People's Artist of the USSR in 1981. She has played numerous roles for film and television, and is well-known for her portrayal of the refined manners characteristic of the old intelligentsia. Her most important film roles include Vyrubova in Elem Klimov's *Agoniya/Agony* (1975), Kalugina in Eldar Ryazanov's* *Sluzhebnyi roman/An Office Romance* (1977), Ogudalova in his *Zhestokii romans/A Cruel Romance* (1984), the stalker's wife in Andrei Tarkovsky's* *Stalker* (1979), and most recently the writer, Irina Dmitrievna in Valeri Todorovsky's* *Podmoskovnye vechera/Katya Ismailova* (1994). BB

FRIČ, Martin   Mac Frič; Prague [then Austria-Hungary] 1902 – Prague 1968

Czech director. Czechoslovakia's most prolific film-maker, Martin Frič directed eighty-five films, working in most genres but specialising in comedy. After leaving school, he was an actor, screenwriter and cameraman before beginning a collaboration with Karel Lamač* in 1924. He made a series of comedies with leading comic actors of the 1930s and 1940s, including Vlasta Burian*, Hugo Haas*, Jiří Voskovec* and Jan Werich*, and Oldřich Nový. Apart from his films with Voskovec and Werich, his outstanding comedies were probably *Kristián* (1939) and *Pytlákova schovanka/The Poacher's Ward* (1949), respectively a delightful comedy about fake identity and a satire on kitsch. Frič also directed *Jánošík* (1936), an international success and the second film about the legendary Slovak folk hero. During the 1950s, at the height of the Stalinist repression, he renewed his association with Werich for *Císařův pekař – Pekařův císař/The Emperor's Baker – The Baker's Emperor* (1951). Never an *auteur* in the accepted sense, Frič deserves credit for producing films of quality and as a mediator between stage, cabaret and screen. The role of his films in the preservation of popular culture is confirmed by their success in times of political adversity and again after his death. PH

Other Films Include: *Páter Vojtěch/Father Vojtěch* (1928); *Varhaník u sv. Víta/The Organist at St Vitus' Cathedral* (1929); *Dobrý voják Švejk/*

The Good Soldier Švejk (1931); *Anton Špelec, ostrostřelec/Anton Špelec, Sharpshooter* (1932); *Život je pes/A Dog's Life, Revizor/The Inspector-General* (1933); *Hej rup!/Heave Ho!* (1934); *Ulička v ráji/A Street in Paradise* (1936); *Svět patří nám/The World Belongs to Us* (1937); *Baron Prášil/Baron Münchhausen, Katakomby/Catacombs* (1940); *Valentin Dobrotivý/Valentine the Kind-hearted* (1942); *Návrat domů/The Return Home* (1948); *Medvěd/The Bear* [TV] (1961); *Král Králů/King of Kings* (1963); *Hvězda zvaná Pelyněk/A Star Called Wormwood* (1964).

G

GAIDAI, Leonid I.

Svodbodnyi, Amur Region, Russia [USSR] 1923–Moscow 1993

Russian director, actor and scriptwriter. Gaidai graduated from the Theatre Studio of the Irkutsk Regional Drama Theatre in 1947, and worked as a stage actor. In 1955 he graduated from VGIK*, where he had studied film direction in the workshop of Grigori Alexandrov*. He was an assistant on Boris Barnet's* film *Liana* (1955) and in 1956 he co-directed *Dolgii put'/The Long Path*, based on stories by Korolenko, with Valentin Nevzorov. His first solo film was *Zhenikh s togo sveta/The Fiancé from the Other World* (1958) a satire on bureaucracy set in a resort town. Gaidai went on to direct several of the most popular comedies of the Khrushchev and Brezhnev years. *Pes Barbos i neobychnyi kross/The Dog Barbos and the Unusual Cross-Country Run* (1961), a contribution to the portmanteau film *Sovershenno sekretno/Top Secret*, is the tale of three poachers and their dog. It was followed by *Delovye liudi/Businessmen* (1962), taken from three O. Henry stories. With the eccentric comedy about the student Shurik, *Operatsiya 'Y' i drugie priklyucheniya Shurika/Operation 'Y' and Other Adventures of Shurik* (1965) Gaidai embarked upon the series of phenomenally successful films which would cement his popularity with Soviet viewers. It was seen by seventy million viewers in the first year, making it the most popular film of 1965. It was followed by *Kavkazskaya plennitsa. Ili novye priklyucheniya Shurika/The Woman Prisoner of the Caucasus. Or The New Adventures of Shurik* (1966), in which Shurik saves a Caucasian girl from a forced marriage to a *nomenklatura* worker, which also topped the charts, and was seen by seventy-six million viewers. *Brilliantovaya ruka/The Diamond Hand* (1968), a tale of the machinations of Western contrabandists, which also attracted seventy-six million viewers, was the most popular film of

1969. With *Dvenadtsat' stul'ev/The Twelve Chairs* (1971), Gaidai turned to the work of the great Soviet satirists Il'f and Petrov, following it with *Ivan Vasil'evich menyaet professiyu/Ivan Vasil'evich Changes Profession* (1973) taken from a play by Mikhail Bulgakov, which was seen by sixty million viewers.

Though Gaidai would never again reach such dizzy heights, he continued to make popular films, including a dozen contributions to the comic *Fitil'* [Fuse] series. In the year before his death he had another popular success with the adventures of the Russian mafia in the US in *Na Deribasovskoi khoroshaya pogoda, ili Na Braiton-Bich opyat' idut dozhdi/It's Fine on Deribasovskaia, or It's Raining Again on Brighton Beach* (1992). He was made People's Artist of the Russian Federation in 1974, and People's Artist of the USSR in 1989. JG

GARDIN, Vladimir R.   Moscow 1877 – Leningrad 1965

Russian director, actor and teacher. Gardin started a film career in 1913, directing with Yakov Protazanov* the popular romantic melodrama *Klyuchi schast'ya/The Keys to Happiness*. In the pre-Revolutionary period he was best known for adaptations of Russian literary classics, including Tolstoy's *Anna Karenina, Kreitserova sonata/The Kreutzer Sonata* (both 1914) and *Voina i mir/War and Peace* (co-directed with Protazanov), and Turgenev's *Nakanune/On the Eve* (both 1915). In 1919 Gardin helped found the State Film School (later VGIK*), where he taught for many years and which he later also headed. He continued directing after the Revolution but his films, made in the tradition of melodrama and popular with audiences, were criticised by the avant-garde for their artistic conservatism and the woodenness of their acting. Works such as *Slesar' i kantsler/The Locksmith and the Chancellor* (1924), *Krest i mauzer/The Cross and the Mauser* (1925), *Medvezh'ya svad'ba/The Bear's Wedding* (1926, co-dir. Konstantin Eggert*) and, above all, his version of the life of Pushkin, *Poet i tsar'/The Poet and the Tsar*, became synonymous with all that was supposedly wrong with the traditions of pre-Revolutionary Russian cinema. Nevertheless he continued teaching and appeared in several major films, including Fridrikh Ermler's* and Sergei Yutkevich's* *Vstrechnyi/Counterplan* (1932), Vladimir Petrov's* *Pëtr I/Peter the Great* (1937–9) and Mikhail Romm's* *Sekretnaya missiya/Secret Mission* (1950). RT

GELOVANI, Mikhail G.   Lasuria, Georgia [Russian Empire] 1893 – Moscow 1956

Georgian Soviet actor who began his stage career at the Rustaveli Theatre in Tiflis (Tbilisi) in 1913 and later moved to the Moscow Art Theatre. He started acting in films in 1924 but is remembered for his virtual monopoly of the portrayal of Stalin in such central films of the personality cult as Sergei Yutkevich's* *Chelovek s ruzh'ëm/The Man with a Gun*, Mikhail Chiaureli's* *Velikoe zarevo/The Great Dawn* (both 1938), *Klyatva/The Vow* (1946) and *Padenie Berlina/The Fall of Berlin* (1949), Grigori Kozintsev's* and Leonid Trauberg's* *Vyborgskaya storona/The Vyborg Side* (1939), Mikhail Kalatozov's* *Valerii Chkalov* (1941) and the Vasiliev* brothers' *Oborona Tsaritsyna/The Defence of Tsaritsyn* (1942). He also directed a number of minor films. RT

GERASIMOV, Sergei A.
Sarafanovo, Russia 1906 –
Moscow 1985

Soviet director and scriptwriter. Gerasimov began his career in 1924 as an actor with FEKS (Factory of the Eccentric Actor) and appeared in all the silent films made by Grigori Kozintsev* and Leonid Trauberg*. His most important films as a director were: *Semero smelykh/The Brave Seven* (1936), *Komsomol'sk* (1938), *Bol'shaya zemlya/The Great Earth* (1944), *Molodaya gvardiya/The Young Guard* (1948) and *Tikhii Don/And Quiet Flows the Don* (1957–8). As a teacher at VGIK* he exerted a major influence on younger directors, and between 1944 and 1946 he headed the Central Studio of Documentary Films, even though his own career was in features. RT

GERMAN, Alexei Yu
Leningrad 1938

Russian director. The son of the writer Yuri German, he graduated in 1960 from the Leningrad State Institute of Theatre, Music and Cinema, where he had studied with Kozintsev*. From 1964 he worked at Lenfilm, where in 1968 he co-directed *Sed'moi sputnik/The Seventh Companion* with Grigori Aronov. During the next twenty years German made only three feature films, each of them beset by delays, censorship and shelving, but between them they have brought him a reputation as one of the key directors of the period. *Proverka na dorogakh/Trial on the Road* (aka *Roadcheck*) was made in 1971 as *Operation 'Happy New Year!'*, from a story by his father. It describes the partisans' struggle against the Nazis without false heroics and gives a sympathetic portrait of an ex-deserter who eventually dies bravely with the partisans. It was immediately attacked by artistic censors for its lack of 'heroism', and banned, despite praise from Kozintsev, Kheifits* and the writer Konstantin Simonov. The film was not released until 1986. *Dvadtsat' dnei bez voiny/Twenty Days without War*, from a story by Simonov about a war correspondent's leave from the front in Tashkent, was made in 1976, and its unconventional picture of the war also led to attacks. It was called 'the shame of Lenfilm'. After being shelved for a year the film was surreptitiously released. German's startlingly original *Moi drug Ivan Lapshin/My Friend Ivan*

Lapshin, also from a story by his father, had a long and tortuous history. The screenplay was written in 1969, but German was not allowed to make it until 1979. Though his father's story about a criminal investigator was set in Leningrad, German moved it to a remote provincial town and introduced other changes, setting the film in 1935. 'The main things for us', he later said, 'was not the detective intrigue, nor the love story, but the time itself. It was the time we were making the film about.' And *Lapshin* succeeds extraordinarily in capturing the ambiguity of the period, the contrast between buoyant sloganising and the bleak horror seeping in from the margins, with visually stunning black-and-white photography and remarkable acting. It, too, caused scandals at Lenfilm and was shelved until 1984. When the film was eventually released it proved a major popular and critical hit. In a poll of Soviet film critics in 1989 it was selected as the best Soviet film of all time, garnering the votes of nine of the ten critics, and its aesthetic influence can be seen in such works as Yevgeny Tsymbal's* *Defence Counsel Sedov* and Vitali Kanevsky's* *Freeze, Die, Get Up Again*. Nevertheless, German made no new films during the 1980s. At the end of the decade he was very influential as head of a unit at Lenfilm dedicated to advancing the careers of young film-makers. In the early 1990s he began work on *Khrustalev, mashinu!/Khrustalev, My Car!*, a project set in 1953. This was to preoccupy him for most of the decade, with repeated delays caused by financial problems. It eventually premiered at Cannes in 1998. Shot in black-and-white in a succession of oppressive and labyrinthine interiors, and with German's trademark overlapping dialogue, it presents the days before Stalin's death as a horrifying absurdist nightmare. The hero, who is both a Red Army general and a surgeon, is drawn into the infamous 'Doctor's Plot' and shipped off to the camps, only to be brought back in a doomed attempt to save the dying leader. The film teems with marginal characters and densely portrayed subplots, initially disorientating the viewer but ultimately overwhelming him with an utterly persuasive picture of a hysterical, mad Russia reminiscent of the nineteenth-century literary tradition. German, one of the most ambitious and original directors working in Russia, here takes the formal inventions of *My Friend Ivan Lapshin* and pushes them further and deeper. JG

GETZ, Georgi Georgiev   Razpopovtzi 1926 – Sofia 1996

Bulgarian actor. Getz will be remembered as the actor best-able to combine austere roughness, moral dignity, and sublime tenderness in one part. He first played in cinema in *Utro nad rodinata/Dawn over the Fatherland* (1951), directed by Anton Marinović and Stefan Surchadžiev, while still studying at the theatrical academy in Sofia. Upon graduation in 1953 Getz was employed by the National Theatre where he worked throughout his long and versatile career. In the 1950s and 1960s he was cast in a number of films focusing on the anti-fascist struggle and on the socialist construction after World War II. His best-known roles include leads in Dako Dakovski's *Nespokoen pat/The Troubled Road* (1955), in Binka Željazkova's* *A biahme mladi/We Were Young* (1961), in Ducho Mundrov's *Pleneno iato/Captive Flock* (1962), in Zako Heskija's *Osmiat/The Eight One* (1969) and *Zarevo nad Drava/Glow over Drava* (1974), as well as in Valo Radev's* *Naidalgata nosht/The Longest Night* (1967). Getz was one of the leading peasant figures in Binka Željazkova's absurdist *Privarzaniat balon/The Attached Balloon* (1967) and was cast in Ljudmil Kirkov's* village–city migration classic *Seljaninat s koleloto/Peasant on a Bicycle* (1974), a role which became his most memorable screen appearance. Getz suffered a stroke during a stage performance in 1995 and died after a prolonged coma. DI

GLASNOST AND THE CINEMA

The Russian word *glasnost*, which literally means 'giving voice', attained international currency during the late 1980s, along with *perestroika*, meaning 'restructuring', as the main slogans of the attempt during the Gorbachev years to reform Soviet society. *Glasnost* was seen by Soviet politicians as the handmaid of the more important *perestroika*, but when the economic and political restructuring of the Soviet Union was shown to be impossible, this was mainly due to the spectacular success of *glasnost*. As a policy allowing greater freedom of expression in the media and the arts, it was introduced gradually and not unequivocally after Gorbachev's accession in 1985. In the press it allowed adventurous publications such as the weekly newspaper, *Moskovskie novosti/Moscow News* and the illustrated weekly magazine, *Ogonek/The Little Flame* to delve into the Soviet (and pre-Soviet) past and provide a continually more nuanced and polyphonic version of Russian history. Gradually they were allowed to turn their attention from the past to the present, and to expose the enormous economic, political and moral problems that beset the country. In the later 1980s, Soviet television joined in the process, though there were regular applications of the ideological brakes. In the field of literature, most daring was shown by the so-called 'thick journals', monthly magazines that combine publication of works of literature with serious journalism, and which have been in the forefront of Russian intellectual life for over a century. Such journals as *Novyi mir/New World* and *Znamya/The Banner* brought (or in some cases returned) to Soviet readers, the work of émigré writers from Nabokov and Zamyatin to Brodsky and, eventually, Solzhenitsyn, as well as hitherto banned works by writers who remained in Russia. Pasternak's *Doctor Zhivago*, for example, was finally published in the Soviet Union in 1988. This process boomed in 1988, with journals reaching hugely inflated print runs (the young people's monthly *Yunost'/Youth* was printing 3,100,000). But, perhaps inevitably, boom was followed by decline. Readers became sated with 'revelations'; and the withdrawal of state subsidies and the harsh intrusion of market economics led to paper shortages and a huge rise in book and magazine prices. In the post-Soviet Union the situation for serious publishing became precarious.

In cinema, the first hints of *glasnost* were provided by the release in the mid-1980s of some shelved films, such as Alexei German's* *Moi drug Ivan Lapshin/My Friend Ivan Lapshin*, a trickle which turned into a flood after the inauguration of a Conflict Commission at the Fifth Congress of the Union of Filmmakers* of the USSR, held in May 1986. Among the many scores of films released with the active intervention of the Commission were Tengiz Abuladze's* *Monanieba/ Repentance*, Alexander Askoldov's* *Komissar/The Commissar*, Andron Mikhalkov-Konchalovsky's* *Istoriya Asi Klyachinoi/The Story of Asya Klyachina*, Irakli Kvirikadze's* *Plovets/The Swimmer*, and a number of important works by Kira Muratova* and Alexander Sokurov*. The appearance of these films substantially altered our understanding of the Soviet cinema of the Brezhnev period.

The new board of the union also took measures to encourage younger film-makers, and it is notable that most of the key films of the next decade were made by new directors. The loosening of ideological control was soon apparent in a wave of hard-hitting documentaries on both historical and contemporary topics. Remarkable among the former is Marina Goldovskaya's *Vlast' solovetskaya/Solovki Power* (1988), a history of the notorious northern labour camp complex. Contemporary documentaries covered a range of hitherto taboo issues from ecological neglect to drugs, prostitution and AIDS. The ambitious work of such directors as Herz Frank*, Stanislav Govorukhin*, Iosif Pasternak* and Juris Podnieks* opened a window on a parallel Soviet reality long known to exist but scarcely acknowledged officially.

The new freedom of expression allowed to feature directors also led to polemical new readings of the Soviet past in the work of such directors as Yevgeni Tsymbal* and Vitali Kanevsky*, and films like Alexander Proshkin's *Kholodnoe leto pyat'desyat tret'ego/The Cold Summer of '53* (1987). Nor did the version of the lives of contemporary Soviet young people revealed in Vasili Pichul's* *Malen'kaya Vera/Little Vera*, Valeri Ogorodnikov's* *Vzlomshchik/The Burglar*, Rashid Nugmanov's* *Igla/The Needle* or, most notably, in Kira Muratova's *Astenicheskii sindrom/The Asthenic Syndrome* conform to official stereotype. But by the end of the decade the ideological and aesthetic free-for-all that characterised the move to the 'market economy' in Russian film-making was responsible for the release of a torrent of sub-American gangster films and 'sex thrillers'. Ambitious examinations of contemporary Russian life continued to be made, but the simultaneous breakdown of the old Soviet distribution system and a popular yearning for hitherto inaccessible cinematic Americana (of however dubious quality) made their path to the audience increasingly fraught. JG

GODINA, Karpo   Acimovic-Godina; Skopje, Macedonia
1943

Yugoslav director and cinematographer of Slovene origin. After several successful short films (of which *Zdravi ljudi za razonodu/Healthy People for Enter-tainment/Litany of Healthy People* won the Grand Prix at Oberhausen in 1971) and more than 200 commercials, Godina directed his first feature film, *Splav Meduze/The Raft of Medusa*, in 1980. The famous painting by Géricault not only provided the title and the opening sequence, but was also used as a metaphor for the story itself: a road movie about a group of young artists gathered round Ljubomir Micić, a founder of 'Zenitism', an anarchist avant-garde art movement based in the Balkans of the 1920s. Visually stunning (Godina was director of photography for more than twenty films between 1960 and 1980), the film uses silent movie features such as iris shots and intertitles. *Rdeči boogie/Red Boogie* (1982) repeated the theme of misunderstood artists on the road: a group of jazz musicians travels around Slovenia during the postwar socialist reconstruction. *Umetni raj/Artificial Paradise* (1990), Godina's most ambitious project to date, is based on the discovery of several sculptures made by Fritz Lang as a young officer of the Austrian army during World War I, while he was stationed with a pioneer of Slovene cinema, Karol Grosmann*. The film, although somewhat pretentious in suggesting the importance of this period for Lang's development, was shown at a special tribute screening at the 1991 Cannes film festival on the occasion of the centenary of Lang's birth. SP

GOGOBERIDZE, Lana L.   Tbilisi, Georgia [USSR] 1928

Georgian director. After graduating from Tbilisi University in 1951 and from VGIK*, where she studied with Sergei Gerasimov*, in 1959, Gogoberidze co-directed the documentary *Tbilisi 1500 let/Tbilisi is 1500 Years Old* (1959). She began directing features in 1961, and her greatest success was with *Neskol'ko interv'yu po lichnym voprosam/Several Interviews on Personal Problems* (1979), the story of a Tbilisi journalist whose professional success is soured by her errant husband's complaints of neglect. The film has an autobiographical strand for Gogoberidze in scenes in which the heroine recalls being reunited with her mother, returned from the camps, scenes which, in their stillness and concentration, contrast with the energetic visual style of the rest of the film. Gogoberidze approached this material directly in *Valsi Pecoraze/Waltz on the Pecora River* (1992). Set in the late 1930s, it tells the parallel stories of a mother exiled as the wife of an 'enemy of the people', and her daughter, who runs away from an orphanage to find the family flat now occupied by a KGB officer. JG

GOVORUKHIN, Stanislav S.
Bereziki, Russia [USSR] 1936

Russian actor, director and scriptwriter of feature films and documentaries. Govorukhin completed his studies at VGIK* in 1966, and began work in the Odessa film studios. His first film, co-directed with Vladimir Durov in 1967, was *Vertikal'/Vertical*, an adventure film starring the legendary actor and singer Vladimir Vysotsky. Among early features directed by Govorukhin are *Zhizn' i udivitel'nye priklyucheniya Robinzona Kruzo/The Life and Extraordinary Adventures of Robinson Crusoe* (1973), the television series *Priklyucheniya Toma Soyera i Gekl'berri Finna/The Adventures of Tom Sawyer and Huckleberry Finn* (1981), and *Desiat' negriat/Ten Little Niggers* (1987), from the Agatha Christie story, but his best-known feature was the five-part television film *Mesto vstrechi izmenit' nel'zya/The Meeting Place Cannot Be Changed* (1979). A police thriller set at the end of World War II, and again starring Vysotsky, it was one of the most popular films of the era. In the late 1980s and early 1990s, Govorukhin was active both as an actor, notably in Sergei Solovyov's* *ASSA*, and as a polemical journalist, but his greatest fame resulted from a trilogy of documentaries on the fate of Russia. *Tak zhit' nel'zya/We Cannot Live Like This* (1990) was a combative assessment of the failures of Soviet communism. *Rossiya, kotoruyu my poteryali/The Russian We Have Lost* (1991) offered an enthusiastic portrait of pre-Revolutionary Russia. *Velikaya kriminal'naya revoliutsiya/The Great Criminal Revolution* (1994) looked at the underside of the allegedly democratic New Russia. A television documentary, *Alexander Solzhenitsyn* (1992), relates a journey by the director to the writer's Vermont home. In 1993 he was elected a deputee of the State Duma. A number of feature films have been made by other directors from Govorukhin's screenplays, most notably Valeri Todorovsky's* *Podmoskovnye vechera/Katia Ismailova* (1994). Govorukhin's most recent feature film, *Voroshilovskii strelok/Rifleman of the Voroshilov Regiment* (1999), caused controversy for the starkness of its condemnation of the Russian present in a tale of a provincial pensioner and war veteran, played by the veteran star actor Mikhail Ul'ianov, who embarks upon a trail of vengeance after his granddaughter is raped by thugs. JG

GRLIĆ, Rajko
Zagreb, Yugoslavia (now Croatia) 1947

Yugoslav director of Croatian origin, now in the US. Having graduated from FAMU* Grlić is one of the members of the Yugoslav Prague Group*. Besides directing features, he also worked for television and collaborated on some of his scripts with Srdjan Karanović* and Dubravka Ugrešić. His first success came with the socially critical *Bravo Maestro* (1978) starring Rade Serbedzija* which tells the story of an opportunistic musician who readily adapts to social conditions. Grlić's award-winning *Samo jednom se ljubi/You Love Only Once* (aka *That Melody Haunts My Reverie*, 1981) with Miki Manojlović* is a riveting personal drama set in the 1950s about a former partisan who marries into a bourgeois family and is gradually rejected by his former comrades. Set in 1970s' Zagreb, *U raljama života/In the Jaws of Life* (1984) is a tongue-in-cheek adaptation of Ugresić's popular feminist novel about simple-minded Štefica Cvek and the more complex but equally insecure female television director who is working on a series about Štefica. *Djavolji raj/That Summer of White Roses* (1989), starring Tom Conti and Rod Steiger, won 'grand prix' and best director at the Tokyo film festival. Set during World War II, it opened up Grlić's interest in historical topics. The director then made another historical film, *Čaruga/Charuga* (1990), this time set after World War I and featuring a peasant anarchist who struggles to impose his self-styled idea of social justice. In the early 1990s Grlić emigrated to the US where he teaches at Ohio University. He is involved with the development of a multimedia CD-ROM offering state-of-the-art training in film production. DI

Other Films Include: *Pricam ti pricu/Tellin' You a Tale* (1973); *Kud puklo da puklo/If It Kills Me* (1974); *Plava laguna Porec/Blue Lagoon Porec* (1981); *Zagreb* (1982); *Za srecu je potrebno troje/Three for Happiness* (1986); *Pitke vode i slobode/Give Us Drinking Water and Freedom* (1986); *Pitke vode i slobode II* (1987).

GROSMANN, Karol

Drakovci, Slovenia 1864 – Ljutomer, Slovenia 1929

Pioneer of Slovene cinema. His two-minute 17.5 mm *Sejem v Ljutomeru/Ljutomer's Fair* (1905) is the first known Slovene movie. *Odhod od maše/Return from the Church* (1905) and *Na domačem vrtu/Home Garden* (1906) later confirmed his Lumière-like vision of cinematographic views as fragments of everyday life. A lawyer and intellectual, Grosmann was well known for his fascination with modern techniques. A pure coincidence brought a slightly wounded German soldier named Fritz Lang into his house during World War I. Lang stayed for a few weeks and made some sculptures, visible in Karpo Godina's* *Umetni raj/Artificial Paradise* (1990). SP

GRUBČEVA, Ivanka

Sofia 1946

Bulgarian director. Best known internationally for her award-winning films for children and youth. Upon graduating from the Babelsberg Film School in Potsdam (GDR) with the diploma film *Hlapeto/The Brat* (1968), based on a Georgi Mišev* story, Grubčeva worked as assistant director for Metodi Andonov* and Ivan Terziev before embarking on an anti-fascist theme in *Edin mig svoboda/A Moment of Freedom* (1970). The film's failure, both artistically and commercially, prompted a return to the world of children to make a string of highly praised films, as well as television productions such as *Deca igrajat văn/Children Play out of Doors* (1972), *Izpiti po nikoe vreme/Exams at Any Odd Time* (1974), *Pri nikogo/With Nobody* (1975), and the five-part television serial *Vojnata na taraležite/The Hedgehogs' War* (1979). Working principally with scriptwriters Georgi Danailov and the Mormarev brothers, who often used the children's film to deal critically with general social problems, Grubčeva was instrumental in raising the Bulgarian children's film to a high standard. In 1987, with Gorbachev's rise to power in the USSR, she was appointed artistic director of the newly formed Alfa production unit at Boyana* Studios. In the 1990s she was able to complete an action-adventure, *Zhrebiyat/Lot* (1993) which looks back at the years between the two world wars and chronicles a banker's turbulent career. RH

GUBENKO, Nikolai N.

Odessa, Ukraine [USSR] 1941

Russian actor, director and screenwriter. Gubenko graduated from the acting faculty of VGIK* in 1964, and from the directing faculty, where he studied in the workshop of Sergei Gerasimov* and Tamara Makarova*, in 1970. His film acting debut was as Kolya Fokin in Marlen Khutsiev*'s *Zastava Il'icha/The Ilyich Gate* (1963). Gubenko directed his first feature *Prishel soldat s fronta/The Soldier Returns from the Front* in 1972. Among his best films are *Podranki/Orphans* (1977), which considers the lives of children orphaned by World War II; the satirical comedy *Iz zhizni otdykhayushchikh/Holiday People* (1981); and *I zhizn', i slezy, i lyubov'/Life, Love, Tears* (1984), the story of a group of pensioners living in an old people's home. In 1987 Gubenko directed *Zapretnaya zona/Forbidden Zone*, about the devastating effect of a hurricane on the inhabitants of a small Volga village. From 1987 to 1991 he served as the director in chief of the legendary Taganka Theatre in Moscow, at which he had first acted in the 1960s. In the last years of the Soviet Union, from 1989 to 1991, he served as Minister of Culture and was a member of the Presidential Council. JG

GYPSIES IN EAST EUROPEAN CINEMA

Various minority groups inhabit Eastern Europe: Vlahs scattered in pockets across South Eastern Europe, Germans in Romania and Poland, Hungarians in Romania and Serbia, ethnic Turks and Pomaks in Bulgaria, Albanians in Serbia and Macedonia. Numerous documentaries are made about these minorities and they often appear in features as well. Besides the Jews, a group that is found in all East European countries is the Gypsies (Romany), and many films have been made about them. The interest in Romany and their identity-building process in cinema has repeatedly brought up issues of authenticity versus stylisation, of a tendency to patronise and exoticise. Rather than being given the chance to portray themselves, Romany have usually been depicted by others. A large number of documentaries were made about Gypsies, particularly in post-communist times – expressing concern for their socio-economic conditions and growing racial hatred. While documentaries tend to sympathise with the plight of this group and question the social framework of minority policies, feature film, although conscious of the social problems, still exploits their freewheeling lifestyles. Gypsy plots are characterised by several recurring motives: passionate and self-destructive infatuations; feast in time of plague; the astonishing maturity of streetwise teenager protagonists; the extended family and complex family relations; mistrust of outsiders; the forced urbanisation and conversion of the semi-nomadic lifestyle.

Well-represented in the Soviet cinema, where as early as in the 1930s films told stories of Gypsies happily integrating within the new social structures, the ultimate Soviet Gypsy film, made by Moldovan Emil Loteanu, remains the 1975 adaptation of Maxim Gorky's *Tabor ukhodit v nebo/Gypsies Are Found near Heaven*, a lavish feast for the eye depicting Gypsies as independent strong spirits. Most prominently, however, the Gypsies are present in the cinema of the East Central European and Balkan countries where their stories have been used in films aiming to make critical statements about social issues. Many films from Hungary, the Czech Republic and Poland have Gypsy subplots, and most recently films such as the socially-critical Czech *Marian* (1996, Petr Vaclav) and the King Lear-type story *Romani kris – Cigánytörvény/Gypsy Lore* (1997, Bence Gyöngyössy) were acclaimed at film festivals around the world. The Hungarian tradition of Gypsy films is quite strong, with prominent features such as Sándor Sára's* *Cigányok/Gypsies* (1962), Pal Schiffer's *Cséplö Gyuri/Gyuri* (1978), and Lívia Gyarmathy's *Koportos* (1979). The debut feature of promising young Polish director, Dorota Kedzierzawska, *Diably, diably/Devils, Devils* (1991) is the timeless story of a group of travellers who are ostracised by the inhabitants of a Polish village where nevertheless a tender attraction develops between a Gypsy girl and a Polish boy.

Most films about Gypsies, however, were made in Yugoslavia.

Gypsy women emerged as romantic passionate protagonists in early films like Slavko Vorkapich's* *Hanka* (1955). The classical Cannes' winner, Alexandar Petrović's* *Sakupljaci perja/I Even Met Happy Gypsies* (1967) was the first high-profile Gypsy film. It tells the story of Bora, a ne'er-do-well Gypsy who gambles and gets involved in a number of shady business ventures and love pursuits. Slobodan Sijan's* *Ko to tamo peva?/Who's Singing over There?* (1980) is believed to be the most popular Yugoslav film ever. It features two Gypsy musicians on their way to Belgrade on the first day of World War II. During the journey they are harassed and bullied by the other passengers, but after a bomb hits the bus they are, symbolically, the only survivors. Goran Paskaljević's* *Andjeo cuvar/Guardian Angel* (1987), a gritty film, with strong documentary power, features a journalist who comes to suspect that Gypsy children are sold abroad into slave labour and tries to help a teenage boy to escape this grim fate. The award-winning *Dom za vesanje/Time of the Gypsies* (1989) by Emir Kusturica* features Gypsy life in a spectacularly beautiful, magical-realist manner. The protagonist, Perhan, a teenager with telekinetic gifts, gets involved with a flamboyant crime lord and is then taken to Italy to run a crime ring of children pickpockets and beggars.

Kusturica returned to the Gypsy topic in his flamboyant *Crna macka, beli macor/White Cat, Black Cat* (1998) shot on the shores of the Danube in Belgrade. In 1997, Macedonian director Stole Popov who had previously made a documentary on Gypsy life, *Dae* (1979), won an award at the Montreal Film Festival for his new film, *Gypsy Magic*. Romania has the largest Romany population of all. The worst reports of anti-Romany violence come from there. Scenes of pogroms by Romanians over Gypsies appeared in the 1995 Cannes' contender *Senatorul melcilor/Senator's Snails* (1995) by Mircea Daneliuk, as well as in French-Romany director Tony Gatlif's *Gadjo Dilo* (1997), set in Wallacchia. Bulgarian Georgi Dyulgerov's* *Chernata Lyastovitza/The Black Swallow* (1995) looked at the complex social situation of the Gypsies in the periphery of today's Europe. The interest in Gypsies, particularly in recent years, may be connected to the marginalisation which people in the Balkans experience themselves. The Gypsies serve merely as a picturesque backdrop for the more universal concern of rejection. DI

H

HAAS, Hugo
Brno [then Austria-Hungary] 1901 – Vienna, Austria 1968

Czech actor, director and scriptwriter. Haas studied music and acting, and was a member of several theatre companies. He became a popular comic actor in films such as *Muži v offsidu/Men in Offside* (1931) and *Život je pes/A Dog's Life* (1933, part of a sequence of seven films directed by Martin Frič*). He turned to direction in the late 1930s, notably with his film version of Karel Čapek's anti-fascist play *Bílá nemoc/The White Sickness* (1937), in which he also played the part of Doctor Galén. The film was withdrawn after Nazi protests but the Jewish-born Haas completed two more films before leaving for Hollywood, where he played cameos and became a B-movie director/writer/lead actor in a sequence of nine films. *Pickup* (1951) and *One Girl's Confession* (1953) were based on Czech novels, and *Edge of Hell* (1956) was a remake of Frič's *Ulička v ráji/A Street in Paradise*, in which Haas had starred. Haas's last films were made in Austria, but plans to return to his home country in 1968 were thwarted by the Soviet invasion and he died the same year. PH

Other Films Include: **As Actor** – *Dobrý voják Švejk/The Good Soldier Švejk* (1931); *Načeradec, král kibiců/Načeradec, King of the Kibitzers* (1932); *Ulička v ráji/A Street in Paradise* (1936). **As Actor/Director** – *Velbloud uchem jehly/Camel through the Eye of a Needle* [co-dir.] (1936); *Děvčata, nedejte se!/Girls, Defend Yourselves!* [co-dir.], *Kvočna/Mother Hen* [dir. only] (1937); *Co se šeptá/What is Whispered* (1938). **As Actor/Writer/Director in the US** – *Girl on the Bridge* (1951); *Strange Fascination* (1952); *Thy Neighbour's Wife* (1953); *Bait, The Other Woman* (1954); *Hold Back Tomorrow* [writer/director only] (1955); *Hit and Run, Lizzie* (1957); *Night of the Quarter Moon* [dir. only]; *Born to be Loved* (1959). **In Austria** – *Der Nachbar/The Neighbour* (1966); *Verrückt/Crazy Idea* (1967).

HAITOV, Nikolai
Javorovo 1919

Bulgarian scriptwriter and dramatist, whose tales about rustic life in his native Rhodope mountains provided the materials for several commercially successful film productions, most notably Georgi Djulgerov's* *Izpit/The Test* (1971). By the 1970s, Haitov was one of the most sought-after scriptwriters at Boyana* Studios. When *Izpit* was paired with another Haitov adaptation, Milen Nikolov's *Gola săvest/Naked Conscience*, and released as the two-part *Šaren svjat/*

Colourful World (1971), the combined message of proving one's manhood and safeguarding natural resources appealed to the sensibilities of a people forced to abandon its rural roots and migrate to industrial centres during the postwar period. At the same time, another Haitov story, *Krajat na pesanta/The End of the Song* (1971), was adapted by Nikolov, and his play *Lamjata/The Dragon* – filmed by Todor Dinov in 1974 – was enjoying a popular run in the theatres as a fairy tale set in medieval Bulgaria.

It was a stage director turned film-maker, Metodi Andonov*, who then collaborated with Haitov on *Kozijat rog/The Goat's Horn* (1972), the most successful film in the history of Bulgarian cinema. Set in the Middle Ages, this tale of vengeance drew on familiar mountain ballads and folk traditions for its action-packed story. But in Haitov's hands the screenplay was also honed to a legend along the lines of an ancient myth – a tale handed down through the centuries from ancient Thrace, in much the same manner as the more familiar legend of Orpheus had originated. Later, Haitov and director Eduard Zahariev* were to rework the same legends of manhood and valour in their *Măžki vremena/Manly Times* (1977).

Not all of Haitov's stories made successful film productions. But his respect for the outsider, his deeply moral attitude to nature, and his belief that even a lonely 'fight for right' has its own rewards raised him to the eminence of a national balladeer. In the 1990s Haitov became an outspoken nationalist. He continued his involvement with cinema by rewriting his script for *Kozijat Rog/The Goat's Horn* and presenting an updated version for the remake in 1994 by director Nikolai Volev. RH

HAMMID, Alexander

Alexander Hackenschmied;
Linz, Austria 1907

Czech director, cinematographer and editor. The principal exponent in Czechoslovakia of what he called the 'independent film', Hammid originally studied graphics before moving to architecture and photography. In 1930 he organised the first week of avant-garde films in Prague as well as a New Photography exhibition. His first film, *Bezučelna procházka/Aimless Walk* (1930), was shown alongside René Clair's* *Entr'acte* and Jean Vigo's *A Propos de Nice*. An unusual view of Prague, reflected in its title, it hinged on the idea of the separation of one human being into two. In *Na Pražskem hradě/Prague Castle* (1932) he sought the relationship between architectonic and musical form. His interest in the relation between image and music is further evidenced in the Venice award-winner *Zem spieva/The Earth Sings* (1933), where he edited Karel Plicka's footage of Slovak folklore to a specially commissioned score. He took a major credit as 'artistic collaborator' on Gustav Machatý's *Ze soboty na neděli/From Saturday to Sunday* (1931), and in the late 1930s worked as photographer and edi-

94

tor of Herbert Kline's *Crisis* (1939), a documentary on Czechoslovakia from the Anschluss to the German invasion. In the US, where he changed his name from Hackenschmied to Hammid, he continued to follow an idiosyncratic path, co-directing *Meshes of the Afternoon* (1943) with Maya Deren and *The Medium* (1950) with Gian-Carlo Menotti, as well as many documentaries, and pioneering films using multi-screen and IMAX. PH

Other Films Include: *Listopad/November* [short, ph] (1934); *Poslední léto/The Last Summer* [short, co-ph, co-ed] (1937). **In the US**: *Lights Out in Europe* [ph, ed] (1939); *The Forgotten Village* [co-d, ph, ed] (1940); *At Land* [short, co-ph, co-ed], *Valley of the Tennessee* [d], *Toscanini: Hymn of the Nations* [short, d] (1944); *A Study in Choreography for the Camera* [co-ph, co-ed], *The Private Life of a Cat* [short, d] (1945); *Ritual in Transfigured Time* [short, co-ph, co-ed] (1945–6); *To Be Alive* [short, co-d, ph] (1964); *We Are Young* [short, co-d, ph] (1967); *US* [short, co-d, ph] (1968); *To Fly* [sup. ed] (1976).

HANÁK, Dušan
Bratislava 1938

Slovak director. One of the leading Slovak directors to emerge in the late 1960s, Hanák graduated from FAMU* in 1965 and made his feature debut with *322* (1969), which won the Grand Prix at Mannheim. A visionary but pessimistic film, it was banned until 1988. His remarkable documentary *Obrazy starého sveta/Pictures from an Old World* (1972), a compelling portrait of peasant life, suffered a similar fate, while his comedy *Ja milujem, ty miluješ/I Love, You Love* (1980, released 1988) also proved too abrasive for the authorities. In those films that were released, *Ružové sny/Rose-tinted Dreams* (1976) and *Tichá radost'/Silent Joy* (1985), he treated, respectively, Slovak–Gypsy relations and the problems of the independent woman. In neither film did a more accessible surface compromise his fundamental honesty of treatment. He also directed *Súkromné životy/Privatlieben/Private Lives* in 1990. Hanák's internationally acclaimed 1996 film *Papierove Hlavy/Paper Heads* makes use of previously unseen documentary footage. The film is a personal reflection on freedom and censorship in the absurd totalitarian universe of communist Czechoslovakia. PH

HAS, Wojciech Jerzy
Cracow 1925

Polish director. Among the leading directors of the 1950s and 1960s, but distinct from the 'Polish School' in his rejection of World War II themes and heroic action. His alienated and solitary protagonists are more likely to be passive than heroic. In *Pętla/The Noose* (1958), Has adapted a story by Marek Hłasko (Poland's answer to Jack Kerouac) about a day in the life of an alcoholic. Has is known for his transpositions of 'impossible' literary classics, in particular the hugely successful *Rękopis Znaleziony w Saragossie/The Saragossa Manuscript* (1965), starring Zbigniew Cybulski*. His 1988 feature, *Niezwykła Podróz Baltazara Kobera/The Fabulous Journey of Balthazar Kober*, explores the territory of epic quests and magical medieval worlds. Has is currently director of the Łódź* Film School. AW

Other Films Include: *Lalka/The Doll* (1968); *Sanatorium pod Klepsydrą/The Hourglass Sanatorium* (1973); *Piśmak/Write and Fight* (1985); *Osobisty Pamiętnik Grześnika . . . Przez Niego Samego Spisany/ Memoirs of a Sinner* (1985).

HEIFITS, Josef – see KHEIFITS, Iosif E.

HISTORY AND HERITAGE IN EAST EUROPEAN FILM

East European cinemas were often involved in producing massive scale historical blockbusters usually chronicling episodes of the glorious past of the country and fulfilling the needs of romanticised representations of national history. Such were the Polish adaptations of Henryk Sienkiewicz's epics *Krzyzacy/Knights of the Teutonic Order* (1960, Aleksander Ford*), or the trilogy *Pan Wolodyjowski/Colonel Wolodyjowski* (1969), *Potop/The Deluge* (1974), and *Ogniem i mieczem/With Fire and Sword* (1999), directed by Jerzy Hoffman*. Epic works of similar scale were Bulgarian Ljudmil Staikov's* *Han Asparuh/Khan Apsarukh* (1981) and *Vreme na nasilie/Time of Violence* (1988), Romanian Sergiu Nicolaescu's* *Dacii/The Dacians* (1966) and *Mihai Viteazu/Michael the Brave* (1971), and many of the Yugoslav 'Partisan Films'*. Such productions involved elaborate props and costumes, and thousands of extras engaged in massive battle scenes with cavalry and artillery. Within the system of the centralised film industry the politically correct directors of these blockbusters usually had the army at their disposal, an arrangement significantly cutting down the production costs. East European filmmaking had a vested interest in exploring philosophical aspects of history – metaphorically, as in Kawalerowicz's* *Matka Joanna od aniolow/Mother Joan of the Angels* (1961) and *Faraon/Pharaoh* (1966) and Wojciech Has's* *Rekopis znaleziony w Saragossie/The Saragossa Manuscript* (1965) or allegorically, as in the intellectual but some what pretentious work of Hungarian András Jeles* *Angyali üdvözlet/Annunciation* (1984). A number of fine East European films deal with the problems of the individual versus history. The work of Miklós Jancsó*, whose best-known films are set in the past (*Szegénylegények/The Round-up*, 1965; *Csillagosok, katonák/The Red and the White*, 1967; *Magyar rapszódia/Hungarian Rhapsody*, 1979), is

96

particularly notable in this respect. The latter is particularly notable in this respect. *The Round-up*, for example, features a minor episode of nineteenth-century Hungarian history which allows the director to explore the relationship between public and private and to re-examine concepts of power and personal ethics. The aesthetics of the film glorify the beauty of the barren landscape of the Hungarian *puszta*. There are multiple visual and semantic layers in each frame and an elaborate interplay of light and shadow, an approach which Jancsó brings to perfection in his later work. The ironies of individual fate intersecting with historical streamlining are remarkably captured by István Szabó* in his *Mephisto* (1981) and, most of all, in the Austro-Hungarian period character study, *Oberst Redl/Colonel Redl* (1985). Another example of study of recent history through an individual's fate is Wajda's early war trilogy. The first part, *Pokolenie/A Generation* (1954), depicts the underground struggle of a group of young Poles. *Kanal/Canal* (1957) chronicles the 1944 Warsaw uprising and focuses on the doomed escape of a group of rebels through the sewers of the city. *Popiól diament/Ashes and Diamonds* (1958), the concluding part and Wajda's recognised masterpiece, is another treatise on individual limitations in confronting the mighty flow of history set on the last day of World War II. Wajda has revisited topics of Polish history on many other occasions, mostly working on literary adaptations like the epics, *Popioli/Ashes* (1966), based on the work of Stefan Zeromski, *Ziemia obiecana/Promised Land* (1974), based on Stanislaw Reymont, and *Pan Tadeusz* (1999), based on Adam Mickiewicz. The heritage aspect of village life has often formed a subject for film in East Central Europe with works like Jan Rybkowski's adaptation of Wladyslaw Stanislaw Reymont's *Chlopi/The Peasants* (1973). Wajda's *Brzezina/ Birch Wood* (1970) and *Wesele/Wedding* (1973), based respectively on works by Jaroslaw Iwaszkiewicz and Stanislaw Wyspianski, reveal the subtle tensions between the parallel village and town cultures. Two quintessential Czech films are set in small villages and deal with the humorous intricacies of communal village life – Vojtěch Jasný's* *Vsichni dobrí rodáci/All My Good Countrymen* (1968) and Jiří Menzel's* *Vesnicko má stredisková/My Sweet Little Village* (1985). While industrial development in East Central Europe led to the growth of cities, in the Balkans villages remained the predominant mode of communal organisation much later into the twentieth century. Respectively, film-makers from the Balkan countries have maintained a persistent attention on village life, tradition, folklore and minorities. The village is a special community where traditions are nurtured, where patriarchy is often intact, where reputation easily falls prey to ill-intended gossip, and where hard, agricultural labour is an everyday reality. All these dimensions of village life are reflected in Balkan cinema. Visually stunning works such as Zivko Nikolić's *Jovana Lukina* (1979) set in Montenegro or Metodi Andonov's* *Kozijat rog/The Goat's Horn* (1972) set in Bulgaria's Rhodopi Mountains tell tales of proud mountain dwellers. Patriarchal culture is the topic of Albanian mother-in-law-as-oppressor picture *Perralle Nga e Kaluara/A Tale from the Past* (1988, d. Dhimiter Anagnosti), of Bulgarian bride-snatching story *Mazki vremena/Manly Times* (1977, d. Eduard Zahariev*), and of Yugoslav 'padre padrone'-style *Virdzina/ Virgina* (1991, d. Srdjan Karanovic*). A number of Balkan films deal with the difficult years of the village during and after the wars and with the period of forced collectivisation in the 1950s. Industrial growth in the 1960s and 1970s led to the desertion of villages and to massive village–city migrations that have been explored in many of the region's masterpieces like the Bulgarian migration cycle films from the 1970s such as Ljudmil Kirkov's* *Seljaninat s koleloto/Peasant on a Bicycle* (1974) and *Matriarhat/Matriarchy* (1977) and in Hristo Hristov's* *Darvo bez koren/A Tree with No Root* (1978). Films featuring village life, like the Romanian *Nunta de piatra/Stone Wedding* (1972, d. Dan Pita* and Mircea Veroiu*) and the Bulgarian *Lacenite obuvkii na neznajnija vohn/The Patent Leather Shoes of the Unknown Soldier* (1979, d. Rangel Vălčanov*), often reveal magical realist elements and display a meticulous attention to folkloric detail. DI

HOFFMAN, Jerzy   Cracow 1932

Polish director. Hoffman will remain in the annals of Polish filmmaking as the director of epic super-productions, mostly for his ambitious adaptation of the trilogy of nineteenth-century Polish novelist and Nobel laureate Henryk Sienkiewicz which he made over a period of thirty years. Each part of the trilogy deals with a different struggle of the Polish nobility during the eventful seventeenth century, and in each one the epic setting serves as a backdrop for a passionate love story. Political considerations imposed an order of filming differing from the sequence of the novels. *Pan Wolodjowski/Colonel Wolodyjowski* (1969), which depicted the resistance against the invading Turks, was made first. The second film, *Potop/The Deluge* (1974), was set against the backdrop of a Swedish invasion. *The Deluge* was nominated for an Academy Award and holds the all-time Polish box-office record. The third part, focusing on the awkward subject of Polish–Ukrainian relations, was filmed by Hoffman twenty-five years later. This third and last film, *Ogniem i mieczem/With Fire and Sword* (1999), is an adaptation of the first part of the trilogy and deals with a Cossack uprising in the Ukraine, under Polish rule at the time. It took Hoffman nearly a decade to secure the funding for this most lavish Polish superproduction ever, budgeted at eight million US dollars. The three hour epic employed over 10,000 extras and 250 horses, and used a number of shooting locations and custom-built sets. The other best-known films of Hoffman are the class-conscious melodrama *Tredowata/Leper* (1976), and *Znachor/The Quack* (1982), the story of an amnesiac healer based on the novel by Tadeusz Dolega-Mostowicz. DI

Other Films Include: *Gangsterzy i filantropi/Gangsters and Phil-anthropists* (1963); *Chwila wspomnien: rok 1956/1957/A Moment's Remembrance: The Year 1956/1957* (1964); *Trzy kroki po ziemi/Three Steps on Earth* (1965); *Prawo i piesc/The Law and the Fist* (1966); *Jarmark cudów/Miracle Fair* (1966); *Do krwi ostatniej/To the Last Drop of Blood* (1978); *Wedle wyrokow twoich/After Your Decrees* (1984); *Prekrasnaya neznakomka/Beautiful Stranger* (1992).

HOLLAND, Agnieszka Warsaw 1948

Polish director and scriptwriter. Holland graduated from FAMU* in Prague in 1971 and began her career as assistant to Krzysztof Zanussi* on *Iluminacja/Illumination* (1973). A member of Andrzej Wajda's 'X' film unit, she was a prominent exponent of the 'cinema of moral un-rest'. Her distinctive personal style, influenced by the Czech New Wave* and reflecting strong political views, was evident from her first feature, *Aktorzy Prowincjonalni/Provincial Actors* (1979), which re-ceived the FIPRESCI (international film critics) award at Cannes. While Holland was not popularly perceived as a feminist in Poland, her *Kobieta Samotna/A Woman Alone* (1981), the story of a middle-aged postwoman, was critically acclaimed for its perceptive portrayal of women in Poland. She scripted several of Wajda's films, including *Człowiek z Żelaza/Man of Iron* (1981) and *Korczak/Korczak* (1990). Holland's international reputation failed to shield her from adverse repercussions for her pro-Solidarity stance, and she was forced to em-igrate when martial law was imposed. Based in Paris since 1981, she is one of the few Polish directors to have forged a successful European career, with the commercial and critical successes of *Bittere Ernte/Angry Harvest* (1984, nominated for an Academy Award for Best Foreign Film) and *Europa, Europa* (1990). Her first wholly 'French' film, the intense *Olivier Olivier* (1991), is based on the true story of a young boy who disappears from home and is 'found' six years later wandering the streets of Paris, his true identity in question. For her first Hollywood production, *The Secret Garden* (1993), Holland joined forces with scriptwriter Caroline Thompson to adapt the popular British children's novel by Frances Hodgson Burnett. Holland was a screenplay consultant on Kieślowski's *Three Colours* series, and continues to have a successful and prolific career as a di-rector in Europe and North America. AW
Website: http://www.perfectnet.com/holland

Other Films Include: *Gorączka/Fever* (1980); *To Kill a Priest* (1988, US/Fr.); *Total Eclipse* (1995, Fr.); *Faux monnayeurs* (1995, Fr.); *Washington Square* (1997, US); *The Third Miracle* (1998, US); *Julie Walking Home* (1999, Can.).

HOLOCAUST FILM

The Holocaust largely unravelled in Eastern Europe, and it was mostly East European Jews who perished. Many remarkable films on the Holocaust have been made in the region ranging from gritty and grim realism to poetic cathartic tragedy. Before World War II, East European film-makers produced a number of films that focused on the East European Jewry in the region, and Poland had a well-established Yiddish-language film production in the early 1930s. More recently, numerous documentaries and feature films have revisited the subject of Jewish life and anti-Semitism – Polish Jerzy Kawalerowicz's* *Austeria/The Inn* (1983), and Hungarian Judit Elek's *Tutajosok/The Raft* (1989), and *Mondani a mondhatatlant: Elie Wiesel üzenete/To Speak the Unspeakable: The Message of Elie Wiesel* (1996) in which Holocaust author Elie Wiesel returns to his native Transylvania. A number of works explore the Nazi period, usually including a subplot about Jewish persecution – from Yugoslav *Balkan Ekspres/Balkan Express* (1983, Branco Baletic) or *That Summer of White Roses* (1989, Rajko Grlić) to Wajda's* *Eine Liebe in Deutschland/A Love in Germany* (1983, Ger.). Best known is Istvan Szabó's* award-winning *Mephisto* (1981), based on Klaus Mann's novel and telling the real life story of German actor Gustav Gründgens (Klaus-Maria Brandauer), notorious for his conformity to the Nazi regime. Szabó's 1988 *Hanussen*, again with Brandauer, replays the *Mephisto* motif, but this time it tells the story of a Berlin clairvoyant who came into prominence in the early 1930s with his involvement in political conspiracies around the Reichstag fire. A whole series of films from Eastern Europe focus on life in the ghettos. The Nazi 'model city' of Terezin appears in Alfred Radok's work, in Zbynek Brynych's *Transport z raje/Transport from Paradise* (1962), and in Karel Kachyňa's* *Posledni motyl/The Last Butterfly* (1990, Fr./Czech./UK) about a mime who entertains the children in the ghetto. Aleksander Ford's* *Ulica Graniczna/Border Street* (1948) and Wajda's *Samson* (1961) show different aspects of ghetto life. Set in the Warsaw ghetto and offering an unforgettable portrait of moral self-sacrifice is Wajda's portrayal of educator Janusz, *Korczak* (1991), a film which strongly influenced the visual style of Spielberg's *Schindler's List* (1993) largely due to the fact that set designer Allan Starski worked on both films. Films focusing on the camps and the Final Solution are Polish Wanda Jakubowska's* *Ostatni etap/The Last Stage* (1948) and Slovak Peter Solan's *Boxer a smrt/The Boxer and Death* (1963), as well as East German *Nackt unter Wölfen/Naked among Wolves* (1962) directed by Frank Beyer based on the novel by Bruno Apitz. Hungarian *Hideg napok/Cold Days* (1966, András Kovács*) is a grim post-factum reconstruction of the extermination of the Jews of the Serbian town Novi Sad. Jan Nemec's* masterpiece *Démanty noci/Diamonds of the Night* (1963), a black-and-white film with little dialogue, is based on the work of Arnost Lustig* and shot with a dynamic expressionist camera by Hynec Bocan and

Miroslav Ondricek*. It is the story of two teenage boys who have escaped from a transport and who run through a forest, desperate to stay alive. The protagonists are fully dependent on nature and experience hunger, cold, exhaustion. Nemec uses surrealist elements scattered throughout the film, juxtaposing the contrasting dark shots of the escape and the shining shots of silent sunny flashbacks. A wide range of films focus on those who tried to help the Jews and the moral dilemmas they faced. These include the poetic love stories of Bulgarian-East German *Zvezdi/Sterne/Stars* (1959) directed by Rangel Vălčanov* and Konrad Wolf and written by Angel Wagenstein* and the melancholic *Romeo, Julia a tma/Sweet Light in a Dark Room* (aka *Romeo, Juliet and Darkness*, 1960, Jirí Weiss). Elmar Klos and Jan Kadar's* *Obchod na korze/Shop on a Main Street* (1965, Czech.) is probably the best work about moral ambiguity and indecisiveness. Starring Ida Kaminska as the old Jewish shopkeeper and Joseph Kroner as her newly appointed Arian supervisor, it is the story of a reluctant Nazi supporter who is, however, too hesitant to take sides. The complex and controversial experiences of those hiding Jews are the subject of Agnieszka Holland's* claustrophobic *Bittere Ernte/Angry Harvest* (1985, Ger.) and Andrzej Wajda's theatrical *Wielki tydzien/Holly Week* (1995). Post-Holocaust traumas are explored in Antonín Moskalyk's *Dita Saxova* (1967) based on the work of Arnost Lustig* and in Andrzej Wajda's *Krajobraz po bitwie/Landscape after Battle* (1970) based on the work of Tadeusz Borowski. DI

HRABAL, Bohumil   Brno 1914 – Prague 1997

Czech writer. Hrabal's versatile oeuvre balanced humour and sadness in an inimitable manner, making the seemingly petty preoccupations of his protagonists evoke laughter and tears from the audiences. Hrabal studied law at Charles University, worked in various jobs, and only became a writer at the age of forty-eight. His works were banned after 1968 and since 1975 have only been published in limited editions but he never left Czechoslovakia where he enjoyed somewhat of a cult status. His fans regularly gathered around him at the Prague's *Golden Tiger* pub. He died after he fell through a hospital window while feeding pigeons. Many of Hrabal's works were adapted for the cinema, most notably Academy Award-winning Jirí Menzel's* *Ostre Sledované Vlaky/Closely Watched Trains* (1966) as well as Menzel's subsequent bittersweet comedies *Skrivanci na niti/Larks on a String* (1969), *Postriziny/Cutting It Short* (1980), and *Slavnosti snezenek/The Snowdrop Festival* (1983). Produced by Barrandov* and shot by Jaromir Sofr, *Closely Watched Trains* is a tragicomedy about a young provincial stationmaster during World War II who, while preoccupied with his humorous sexual initiation, becomes involved in a serious anti-fascist conspiracy. After the writer's death, a noisy public controversy between Menzel and a private producer unfolded over the adaptation rights of another of Hrabal's novels, *Jak jsem obsluhoval anglického krále/I Served the King of England*. Other films based on the work of Hrabal are *Perlicky na dne/Pearls of the Deep* (1965) directed by Czech New Wave's* Menzel, Chytilová* and Jireš*, and *Nezny barbar/Tender Barbarian* (1989), directed by Petr Koliha. DI

HRISTOV, Hristo Plovdiv 1926

Bulgarian director. Widely respected for tackling some controversial socio-political themes, Hristo Hristov graduated from the Sofia Academy of Dramatic Art (VITIS) in 1958. Until 1966 he worked as a stage designer and director of plays and operas, then spent two years at the Mosfilm studios in Moscow assisting Marlen Khutsiev*, Andron Mikhalkov-Konchalovsky* and Mikhail Romm*. His first feature, *Ikonostasăt/Iconostasis* (1969), co-directed by animation director Todor Dinov, was a breakthrough in Bulgarian cinema because of its original treatment of iconography and religious art as integral to Bulgaria's historical and cultural tradition. Then, after making a heavily theatrical epic on national hero Georgi Dimitrov and the infamous Leipzig trial, *Nakovalnja ili čuk/Anvil or Hammer* (1972), co-produced by the Soviet Union and East Germany, he broke another taboo by adapting Jordan Radičkov's* controversial novel *Posledno ljato/The Last Summer* (1972–4) for the screen; two years on the shelf and released only in a drastically edited version, the film mourned the passing of village life and peasant traditions in surrealist style.

Hristov tested the patience of the authorities again in the 1980s by making a series of gripping psycho-dramas on the ills of Eastern bloc socialism: *Kamiona`t/The Lorry* (1980, about the transport of a worker's body to his native village for burial), *Edna žhena na trideset i tri/A Woman at 33* (1982, about a divorced office secretary unjustly victimised), *Sabesednik po žhelanie/Question Time* (1984, about a popular actor suffering from cancer who reviews the options left to him), and *Harakteristika/Reference* (1985, about honesty versus corruption among taxi drivers) – all withdrawn from theatrical circulation after a token release.

During Hristov's years as First Secretary of the Bulgarian Filmmakers union (1974–82), several talented directors and scriptwriters at Boyana* Studios received his moral support to experiment with genres and challenge the fixed ideological formulas of socialist filmmaking. In the 1990s Hristov worked mostly for television and in documentary. His feature *Sulamit* (1997) was a period biopic of a Jewish actress from the first half of the twentieth century. RH

HRUŠÍNSKÝ, Rudolf   Nový Etynk 1920 – Prague 1994

Czech actor. One of Czechoslovakia's leading stage and screen actors, Rudolf Hrušínský also exerted great moral authority. In 1989, when Russian troops were again assembling outside Prague, his radio appeal calmed the nation, and in 1990–2 he served as an MP in the newly resurrected democracy. Born of a touring theatrical family, he had no formal training but joined E. F. Burian's youth theatre group and was a member of the National Theatre from 1960, in recent years appearing as Falstaff and as Ekdal in *The Wild Duck*. His film career began in 1937 when he appeared as the youthful lead in a sequence of films, before consolidating his comic talents as Švejk in *Dobrý voják Švejk/ The Good Soldier Švejk* (1957). He appeared opposite Anne Heywood in Jiří Weiss's Anglo-Czech *Třicet jedna ve stínu/90° in the Shade* (1965), but is best known to international audiences for the nonchalant comedy of his roles in Jiří Menzel's* *Rozmarné léto/Capricious Summer* (1967), *Postřižiny/Cutting it Short* (1980) and *Slavnosti sněženek/The Snowdrop Festival* (1983). The range of his abilities is represented by a terrifying portrait of evil in Juraj Herz's *Spalovač mrtvol/The Cremator* (1968) and his restrained and moving performance as the doctor in František Vláčil's* *Dým bramborové natě/Smoke on the Potato Fields* (1976). PH

HUNGARY

The first film screening in Hungary took place just a few months after the Lumière brothers' first public show in Paris. Starting in May 1896, a representative of the Lumière company organised regular screenings in a Budapest hotel café for almost a year. The first footage produced in Hungary was also made by the same company. However, regular film production started relatively late. The first Hungarian film – *A tánc/The Dance* by Béla Zsitkovszky – was made in 1901. It consisted of twenty-seven one-minute reels, each representing a different kind of folk dance, and was commissioned by a cultural-scientific society. For some time, production and distribution were not separated in the Hungarian film industry. The first independent production company was created in 1911, but it failed a year later. The first full-length feature film, *Ma és holnap/Today and Tomorrow*, was made by the biggest production and distribution company, Projectograph, in 1912. It featured Mihály Kertész* (later Michael Curtiz in Hollywood) as an actor, and it is likely that Kertész was also the director.

In the following decade, film production developed quickly. While by 1913 only ten Hungarian feature films had been made, by 1918 this number had increased to 109, and there were as many as thirty-seven film production companies. Three names stand out as pioneers of early Hungarian cinema. Jenő Janovics, a former actor and theatre director, was one of the most important producers of the time; and both Sándor

Korda (later Alexander Korda) and Mihály Kertész began their apprenticeship as directors in his company. In 1918 Korda bought Janovics' company and founded a studio called Corvin, whose facilities became the basis of later Hungarian film production. The period 1918–19 was a high point in Hungarian silent film production since the revolutionary governments from the autumn of 1918 until the summer of 1919 strongly supported cinema. During the short period of communist dictatorship in 1919 more than thirty films were produced, of which only two have survived. Since virtually all important filmmakers of the time supported the revolution, after its downfall many of them had to leave Hungary. Understandably, the counter-revolutionary government did not trust film industry people, which caused an almost total disintegration of Hungarian film production during the following decade.

The next boom period for Hungarian cinema began in the mid-1930s. It was assisted by a law requiring theatres to devote 10 (later 20) per cent of their programmes to Hungarian films. Most of the films produced in this period were light comedies written by popular playwrights of the time, which gave Hungarian cinema a domestic success it has never achieved since. A significant part of this popularity was due to comedy and melodrama stars such as Gyula Kabos, Kálmán Latabár, Pál Jávor or Katalin Karády*. Film production continued to increase during the war, and in 1943 reached a peak of fifty-four films, a figure never since equalled. Hungarian cinema also achieved its first international artistic success in the early 1940s: István Szőts'* *Emberek a havason/Men on the Mountains* (1942), which won first prize at the Venice Biennale. The end of the war, however, brought a halt to significant popular film-making in Hungary.

The subjection of Hungarian film production to politics began in the immediate postwar period, though for a few years this did not mean a unilateral or monolithic influence. Independent private producers could find money for production, albeit with great difficulty, whereas the major political parties participating in the coalition government founded their own production companies, evidently obtaining finance quite easily. The Hungarian film industry was entirely nationalised in 1948, after the communist takeover. But during this short transitional period some remarkable films were made, such as Géza Radványi's *Valahol Európában/Somewhere in Europe* (1947) and Szőts' *Ének a búzamezőkről/Song of the Cornfields* (1947). These films signalled a new beginning for Hungarian cinema, moving away from popular genres and adopting an *auteur* film perspective. However, this opening was blocked by communist ideological control for at least eight years, and the impact that Italian neo-realism had on Szőts' and Radványi's work did not extend to Hungarian cinema generally – Radványi left Hungary in 1948, Szőts in 1957. After 1948, production dropped to five or six films per year and it remained at that level until 1955. Most films of this period were made for direct propaganda purposes in the style of Socialist Realism*, and conformed to the ideological imperatives of the Communist Party. Political censorship was not institutional, but was built in at different levels of film production and distribution. All institutions were politically responsible for the product that went through them. Political authorities played an active role in initiating film scripts. Topics were designed at the highest level of cultural bureaucracy and directors were either selected by the political authorities themselves or approved by them. At this stage we cannot speak about censorship *per se*, since the highest level of political control was present right at the beginning of a film's production. Nevertheless, the popular comedy tradition of the 1930s and 1940s managed to survive in several communist propaganda films too. A number of musicals featuring fashionable songs and popular stars achieved considerable success even if the narratives concentrated on the ubiquitous communist hero fighting imperialist agents and saboteurs. Production began to increase after 1955, with a significant jump in 1961, to around twenty films annually, a level sustained over the next twenty-five years. Production dropped significantly again after 1988. In the early 1990s, in the wake of political democratisation and the introduction of a market economy, the volume of feature film production has fallen below ten films a year. On the other hand, the drop in feature film production has been accompanied by a boom in documentaries.

The year 1955 is considered a turning point in Hungarian film history. Films made in this year signal a considerable loosening of ideological control, and a chance for the neo-realist trend initiated in the early 1940s by István Szőts to continue. The key film in this respect is Zoltán Fábri's* 'peasant film' *Körhinta/Merry-go-round* (1955), which achieved great international success. Other 1955 films, like Félix Máriássy's *Budapesti tavasz/Spring in Budapest* and *Egy pikkoló világos/A Glass of Beer*, or Károly Makk's* *9-es kórterem/Ward no. 9*, also show a re-emergence of *auteur* film in Hungary, though this trend was blocked again for a short period after the Soviet invasion of 1956.

In 1962, however, a 'new wave' of Hungarian art cinema began [> CZECH NEW WAVE]. Two generations came to film-making at virtually the same time. Some directors of the first postwar generation – Zoltán Fábri, Károly Makk, János Hersko and Félix Máriássy – had already made important films in the 1950s, but others, like Miklós Jancsó*, András Kovács*, Márta Mészáros* and Péter Bacsó*, made their first feature film at the same time as the generation that graduated from the Film Academy in the early 1960s (Ferenc Kósa, István Szabó*, Judit Elek, Sándor Sára*, István Gaál and others). While the 'new wave' of the younger generation mainly concentrated on personal problems, such as young people's difficulties in adapting to society or conflicts between the value systems of different generations, the older film-makers turned to history and politics. Perhaps not surprisingly, after the Hungarian uprising of 1956, the strongest theme evident centred on problems of national identity, the relationship between the individual and history, and the individual's moral autonomy in the face of political pressures and repression. In this period,

Hungarian cinema and politics were inextricably linked. Film-making became the prototype of politically conscious activity in Hungary, for political censorship was less severe in the case of films than for other cultural forms. Topics were not prescribed as in the 1950s, and decisions about scripts were made by a middle-ranking official at the Ministry of Culture, though the final decision whether or not a film should be released was still in the hands of the highest political officer of cultural policy. Directors could consider themselves important agents of political liberties in another sense, many of them having direct contact with high-ranking political leaders, which allowed them to function as an intellectual pressure group. In this period began the practice of 'political bargaining' between directors and political authorities, to negotiate changes and the release of politically controversial films. Although popular genre films reappeared (the historical melodrama and comedy in particular), they were few in number compared to the *auteur* films made in this period.

In the 1970s the political-historical analysis of the *auteur* cinema of the 1960s permutated into a distinctive sub-genre: the historical allegory or parable. This form had been initiated by Miklós Jancsó in 1965 with *Szegénylegények/The Round-up*, as a way of circumventing censorship, and it was at first used only by him. Historical events were given a highly symbolic and abstract treatment and were used to exemplify moral conflicts caused by dictatorial oppression. After 1968, however, many directors who had never before treated political or historical themes directly also adopted and modified this genre, creating a realist trend of political and historical parables: András Kovács' *A magyar ugaron/Fallow Land* (1972) and *Bekötött szemmel/Blindfold* (1975); István Gaál's *Magasiskola/The Falcons* (1970); Ferenc Kósa's *Nincs idő/Beyond Time* (1972). Finally, in the late 1970s, the political preoccupation of films centred on the Stalinist Hungary of the 1950s. These films were no longer allegorical; rather, they made more or less direct political allusions to the inevitable failure of the regime: Pál Gábor's *Angi Vera* (1978) and *Kettévált mennyezet/Wasted Lives* (1984); Kovács' *A Ménesgazda/The Stud Farm* (1978); Kósa's *Mérkőzés/ The Match* (1980); Makk's *Egymásra nézve/Another Way* (1982); Péter Bacsó's *Tegnapelőtt/The Day Before Yesterday* (1981), among others. The period was also characterised, however, by the banning of several films, mainly those made in the Balázs Béla Stúdió*.

Meanwhile popular film production underwent a real crisis when old-fashioned popular genres (classical melodrama and historical adventure films) were overtaken by the vogue for modern action, science-fiction and horror films. However, Western mass cultural trends were out of favour with the conservative communist culture policy of the time, and in any event these genres were too expensive for the Hungarian film industry. Moreover, most Hungarian filmmakers refused to 'prostitute' themselves by making popular films, and when some of them tried to initiate a Hungarian 'quality popular' genre, as György Szomjas did in the late 1970s, they were hampered

106

by the lack of 'positive myths' of everyday life upon which to base it. In the early 1980s the international market became increasingly important for Hungarian cinema, partly as a consequence of the declining political significance of Hungarian films at home, although some films were still banned. On the other hand, growing economic problems led a number of directors to seek financial support for their films from abroad. The most successful in this respect was István Szabó, whose *Mephisto* (1981) won an Academy Award in 1982. The most successful attempts at popular film-making of the period were imitations of foreign movies, like István Bujtor's *Az Elvarázsolt dollár/ Enchanting Dollar* (1985), a Hungarian version of an Italian series.

In the late 1980s and early 1990s, with the coming of a new film-making generation (more than a dozen first films were made in the early 1990s), and after the collapse of the communist regime and the ideologically controlled and state-supported production system, no single trend dominated. In the early 1990s, Hungarian cinema was characterised by a significant documentary film production dealing with contemporary political and social issues, as well as with historical investigation; by the advent of the low-budget, amateur-style film supported by professional studios (András Szőke, Miklós Ács, András Szirtes); by various kinds of lyrical-subjective forms (Attila Janisch, Can Togay, Ildikó Enyedi, Tibor Klöpfler); and by an abstract metaphysical or utopian style (Béla Tarr*, György Fehér, András Monory, Zoltán Kamondy). In a country where the intellectual tradition of *auteur* cinema remains such a powerful influence, and where resources for film production have been dramatically reduced, 'popular' film has come to be represented by foreign – almost exclusively American – films. Internationally established directors such as Marta Mészaros, Miklós Jancsó and István Szabó continued adding new films to their filmographies, but it was the work of younger directors such as Péter Gothár (*Hagyjállógva Vászka/Váska Easoff*, 1996), György Fehér (*Szenvedély/Passion*, 1998), János Szász (*Woyzeck*, 1994; *Witman fiúk/The Witman Boys*, 1997), Ildikó Szabó (*Gyerekgyilkosságok/Child Murders*, 1993; *Csajok/Bitches*, 1995), Ildikó Enyedi (*Büvös vadász/ The Magic Hunter*, 1994), and Ibolya Fekete (*Bolshe Vita*, 1996) which attracted most international attention and acclaim. KAB

HUSZÁRIK, Zoltán   Domony 1931 – Budapest 1981

Hungarian film director and designer. Huszárik was the most original talent of his generation; his distinctive personal and artistic character, and the fact that he did not follow any major cinematic trend or current but created his own unique artistic universe, made him a legendary figure of modern Hungarian cinema. He started his studies at the Academy of Theatre and Film Art in 1949, but was considered politically unreliable by the school authorities and had to leave in 1952. He went back after 1956, graduating in 1961. For ten years he made only short films, which earned him an international reputation, beginning with *Elégia/Elegy* (1965), awarded the Oberhausen prize. He made only two full-length feature films. The first, *Szindbád* (1971), is a masterpiece of non-linear narration and pictorial composition. It is also a summary of the particular inspiration that can be found in all his works: a melancholia generated by the disappearance of an organic sense of life in which sensual pleasures and the consciousness of mortality are closely entwined. Huszárik was also unique in the Hungarian cinema of the 1960s and 1970s in that his work remained untouched by any political, social or historical involvement. In all his short films he favoured a non-narrative lyrical and pictorial style which expressed a nostalgia for a relationship to nature and to cultural traditions on the verge of extinction. KAB

Other Films Include: *Amerigo Tot* [short] (1969); *Tisztelet az öregasszonyoknak/Tribute to Old Women* [short] (1972); *Csontváry* (1979).

I

IDZIAK, Slawomir
Katowice 1945

Polish cinematographer. Idziak's debut in cinema was as a camera operator for Andrzej Wajda's* *Wesele/The Wedding* (1972), a superior example of relentlessly moving hand-held camera. But Idziak has won most international acclaim for his impressive work with colour filters and lenses which helped him to create the unique visual style of Krzysztof Kieślowski's* acclaimed films, *Krótki film o zabijaniu/A Short Film about Killing* (1988), *Podwojne zycie Weroniki/La double vie de Véronique/The Double Life of Véronique* (1991), and *Trzy kolory: Niebieski/Trois couleurs: Bleu/Three Colours: Blue* (1993). Idziak is a proponent of the *auteur*ist view of the cinematographer. To him, the cinematographer is the most important collaborator of the director and has a decisive impact on the overall aesthetic approach. By directly controlling the style of the film via camera positioning, colour and perspective, the cinematographer is nothing less than a co-author. This conviction is revealed in his long-lasting commitment to cultivating the tasteful and unobtrusive cinematic style of Krzysztof Zanussi* with whom Idziak worked on *Bilans kwartalny/The Quarterly Balance* (1975), *Constans/The Constant Factor* (1980), *Kontrakt/Contract* (1980), *Imperative/Imperative* (1982), *Paradigma/Paradigm* (1985), *Stan posiadania/Inventory* (1989), and on several made-for-television

European projects. Idziak also shot Wajda's *Dyrygent/Conductor* (1979) and Kieślowski's earlier *Przejscie podziemne/Pedestrian Subway* (1973) and *Blizna/The Scar* (1976). Internationally Idziak has been a cinematographer on many Western productions, most notably John Sayles' *Men with Guns* (1997) and Andrew Niccol's *Gattaca* (1997). He also directed two films – *Nauka latania/Flying Lessons* (1978) and *Enak* (1992). Idziak teaches film production in Poland. DI

ILIU, Victor   Sibiu 1912 – Rome, Italy 1968

Romanian director, whose *Morea cu noroc/The Mill of Good Luck* (1955) is regarded as a pioneering achievement in Romanian film. Iliu attended Eisenstein's* lectures on direction in 1946–7, and learnt from veteran Romanian director Jean Georgescu. From 1951, starting with *In sat la noi/In Our Village*, he made a series of rural Socialist Realist* dramas reflecting the ruling party's priority of collectivisation of agriculture in the semi-literate countryside. *Morea cu noroc*, a tale of Transylvanian peasants' poverty in the nineteenth century, shows Iliu transcending political diktat through creative film-making, looking to many European influences and fully utilising Romanian technical and acting talents. His next and last film – *Comoara din Vadul Veche/The Treasure of Vadu Vechi* (1963) – is a sombre psychological drama of sabotage. Until his early death he was a leading influence on the industry as president of the Association of Film-Workers, editor of *Cinema* and head of the I. L. Caragiale Institute for Theatre and Film Art (IATC), where he taught another generation, including Dan Piţa* and Mircea Veroiu*. MM

ILLÉS, György   Eger 1914

Hungarian cinematographer, teacher and mentor of many generations of Hungarian cinematographers. He started in the film industry in 1935 and made his first film as a cinematographer in 1949. The same year, he became a teacher at the Academy of Theatre and Film Arts, and later was appointed director of the cinematography department, a post he still occupies. In the 1950s, Illés initiated a new realist style of cinematography, using natural lighting and flexible camera handling. He always considered that the cinematographer's work does not start with shooting, but at the script stage. Illés has shot more than fifty films, and many important Hungarian and international cinematographers – Vilmos Zsigmond, László Kovács, Jean Badal, Lajos Koltay – consider themselves his disciples. It is commonly held in Hungary that the worldwide reputation of Hungarian cinematography is primarily due to Illés' teaching and professional influence. KAB

Other Films Include: *9-es kórterem/Ward no. 9, Budapesti tavasz/ Spring in Budapest* (1955); *Husz ora/Twenty Hours* (1965); *141 perc a befejezetlen mondatból/141 Minutes from the Unfinished Sentence* (1975).

ILYINSKY, Igor V. Moscow 1901–87

Soviet actor. Ilyinsky was for many years the leading comic actor in Soviet cinema. He worked in both the Moscow Art and Meyerhold Theatres and first appeared on screen in Yakov Protazanov's* *Aelita* (1924), in which he played a comic detective. He appeared in Fyodor Otsep's* *Miss Mend* (1926), played leading roles in Sergei Komarov's *Potselui Meri Pikford/The Kiss of Mary Pickford* (1927) and *Kukla s millionami/The Doll with the Millions* (1928), and also appeared in three other Protazanov silent films, including *Prazdnik svyatogo Iorgena/The Feast of St Jorgen* (1930). But he was probably best remembered by Soviet audiences for his portrayal of archetypal philistine bureaucrats, Byvalov in Grigori Alexandrov's* musical comedy *Volga-Volga* (1938) and Ogurtsov in Eldar Ryazanov's* *Karnaval'naya noch'/Carnival Night* (1957). RT

IOSELIANI, Otar D. Tbilisi, Georgia [USSR] 1934

Georgian director. In 1965 Ioseliani graduated from VGIK*, where he had studied with Alexander Dovzhenko*. His 1962 short film *Aprel'/April* is about the life of a newly-married couple; his 1964 documentary *Chugun/Cast Iron* observes a day in the life of a metal works. In 1968 Ioseliani made his first full-length feature *Listopad/When Leaves Fall*, also set in a factory. In *Zhil pevchii drozd/Once Upon a Time There Was a Singing Blackbird* (1970), the charming, feckless hero, a percussionist at the Tbilisi Opera, has not a care in the world and is continually at the disposal of his many friends until, in the film's shockingly unexpected final scene, he is knocked down by a car and killed. *Pastoral'/Pastoral* (1975) examines the effect a summer visit by a string quartet has on the inhabitants of a Georgian village. Since 1984 Ioseliani has been based in Paris. His 1984 film *Les favoris de la lune/Favourites of the Moon*, a Parisian comedy, has been compared to the work of René Clair and Jacques Tati, and won the Jury Prize in Venice. The documentary *Un petit monastère en Toscane/A Little Monastery in Tuscany* (1988) was followed by *Et la lumière fut/And Then There Was Light* (1989), set in a Senegalese village in which a timber company has arrived to cut down the trees, and informed with Ioseliani's concern that the noble and primitive traditions of thousands of years are disappearing. In the melancholy allegorical comedy *La chasse aux papillons/The Butterfly Hunt* (1992), Ioseliani turns to Russian themes. When an elderly émigrée dies in a French provincial town, her château is inherited by her sister, who still lives in the Soviet Union. This woman and her daughter arrive for the funeral, and in very short order the daughter sells the château to some Japanese people, herself renting a fashionable apartment which her entourage soon reduces to the chaos of a Soviet communal flat. The mother, meanwhile, is sent off on a train, which is blown up by terrorists. Thus this film also laments the passing of moral and cultural traditions that have lasted for generations. It was followed by *Brigands (Chapitre VII)/Brigands* (1996), shot in Ioseliani's native Georgia, which offers a wry allegorical look at history as a succession of horrific yet comic disasters. As the film's hero moves from the medieval period through the Soviet Revolution and the rise of Stalin to post-Soviet ethnic conflict and emigration to Paris, Ioseliani's pessimism is tempered by his customary sense of the absurd. JG

J

JADRAN FILM

Croatian studio. The company was established in Zagreb in 1946, but its real growth began in 1955 when huge, Cinecittà-like studios were build in the Zagreb suburb of Dubrava. It soon became the biggest production studio in Yugoslavia, with more than a hundred national projects in total. It was also the main partner for international co-productions seeking untouched natural beauty and reasonably low production costs. Orson Welles' *The Trial* (1962), Alan Pakula's *Sophie's Choice* (1982) and the two-part television series *War and Remembrance* (co-produced with the US) are among some 200 international co-productions made at Jadran. SP

JAKUBISKO, Juraj   Kojšov 1938

Slovak director. Jakubisko graduated from FAMU* in 1965, where he made a number of internationally acclaimed experimental films, including his graduation film, *Čekají na Godota/Waiting for Godot* (1965). Coming from Eastern Slovakia, he was encouraged by his tutor, the director Václav Wasserman, to draw on the resources and traditions of folk culture. His trio of films, *Kristove roky/Crucial Years* (1967), *Zbehovia a pútnici/Il disertore e i nomadi/The Deserter and the Nomads* (1968, released in Czechoslovakia 1990) and *Vtáčkovia, siroty a blázni/Les Oiseaux, les orphelins et les fous/Birds, Orphans and Fools* (1969, released in Czechoslovakia 1991), revealed the cruelty of

111

peasant art (in *Zbehovia a pútnici*) and focused on alienated youth in an improvisatory style typical of the post-Godard generation. After the Soviet invasion, he was unable to make features again until 1979, when he returned with *Postav dom, zasad' strom/Build a House, Plant a Tree*, and the international success *Tisícročna včela/Die tausend-jährige Biene/The Thousand Year Old Bee* (1983), following this with an adaptation of Hans Andersen's *Perinbaba/Frau Holle/Mother Carey* (1985), featuring Giulietta Masina, and *Frankensteins Tante*, for West German television. His unfinished *Dovidenia v pekle, priatelia/ See You in Hell, Fellows!* (1970) was finally completed in 1990. He returned to his earlier style with *Sedím na konári a je mi dobre/I'm Sitting on a Branch and I Feel Well/Flying High* (1989), and its sequel *Lepšie byť bohatý a zdravý, ako chudobný a chorý/It is Better to Be Rich and Handsome Than Poor and Ugly* (1992). The latter satirised both the new world of capitalism and the delusions of Slovak nationalism. His 1997 film parable *Nejasná zpráva o konci svteta/An Ambiguous Report about the End of the World* (Czech Republic) was shown at the Montreal Film Festival and enjoyed international critical acclaim. PH

JAKUBOWSKA, Wanda   Warsaw 1907 – Warsaw 1998

Polish director. Poland's first woman director, Jakubowska was prominent in the START (Society of Devotees of Artistic Film) movement established in 1930 and the film-makers' cooperative SAF. In the 1950s she headed a production unit called START. *Ostatni Etap/The Last Stage* (1948), based on her own experiences as an Auschwitz internee, was the second film to be produced in postwar Poland and the first to receive international distribution. AW

Other Films Include: *Żolnierz Zwycięstwa/Soldiers of Victory* (1953); *Opowieść Atlantycka/Atlantic Story* (1955); *Koniec Naszegoswiata/The End of Our World* (1964); *150 na Godzine/At One Hundred and Fifty Km an Hour* (1971); *Zaproszenie/Invitation* (1985); *Kolory Kochania/ Colours of Love* (1987).

JANCSÓ, Miklós   Vác 1921

Hungarian film director. In the 1960s and 1970s, Jancsó was synonymous with Hungarian cinema among international audiences. He studied law and anthropology, and graduated in direction from the Hungarian Film Academy in 1951. During the 1950s, Jancsó made Stalinist newsreels. His first feature, *A harangok Rómába mentek/The Bells Have Gone to Rome* (1958), reveals none of the qualities that were later to become associated with the celebrated 'Jancsó style'. The earliest film that is characteristic of this style is *Oldás és kötés/Cantata*

(1963), primarily because of its very long takes. This is also Jancsó's first film made with scriptwriter Gyula Hernádi, with whom he still works. Jancsó claimed that he and Hernádi had watched Michelangelo Antonioni's *La notte* ten times before making this film, and indeed, technically speaking, Antonioni was a tremendous influence. Jancsó, however, was to develop a style of his own, whose main features are extremely long takes (up to ten minutes), minimal dialogue, a continuously moving camera choreographed with actors moving within a scene, and recurrent symbolic motifs and gestures.

The symbolic rendering of Jancsó's narratives dates back to *Így jöttem/My Way Home* (1964), where time and space are hinted at rather than specifically demarcated, characters are given little psychological delineation, and the film's central relationship between a young Hungarian man and a Russian soldier has to be deciphered through gestures and movements rather than dialogue. In his next film, *Szegénylegények/The Round-up* (1965) – for many critics his unparalleled masterpiece – all the elements of his style come together in an abstract historical parable about the nature of revolution and counter-revolution. It is also in this film that Jancsó's emphasis on the intricate mechanisms of political oppression testing the moral integrity of individuals appears for the first time. Though the story deals with the persecution of rebel prisoners who fought for the liberation of Hungary during the 1848 revolution against Austrian oppression, the film was interpreted by many as an allegory of the retaliations that followed the 1956 revolution. Subsequent films continued this focus on oppressive power, though, in Jancsó's increasingly abstract stylistics, characters functioned less as representatives of particular historical forces than as the embodiments of conflicting ideas.

In the early 1970s, at the height of his international reputation, Jancsó made four films in Italy about the rituals of power. In the 1980s the main subject of his work was the dissimulating and mystical character of politics. More recently, the stories again derive from actual political events. Jancsó now makes increasing use of video techniques, primarily to intensify an atmosphere of spatial and temporal confusion. He has also directed plays, though his theatrical work has never achieved the same importance as his films. KAB

Other Films Include: *Három csillag/Three Stars* (1960); *Csillagosok, katonák/The Red and The White* (1967); *Csend és kiáltás/Silence and Cry, Fényes szelek/The Confrontation* (1968); *Sirokkó/Winter Wind* (1969); *Égi bárány/Agnus Dei, La pacifista/The Pacifist* (1970, It.); *Még kér a nép/Red Psalm* (1971); *La tecnica ed il rito/The Technique and the Rite* (1972, It.); *Roma rivuole Cesare/Rome Wants Another Caesar* (1973, It.); *Szerelmem Elektra/Elektreia* (1974); *Vizi privati, pub-bliche virtù/Private Vices, Public Virtues* (1976, It.); *Életünket és vérünket: Magyar rapszódia I./Hungarian Rhapsody* (1978); *Allegro Barbaro: Magyar rapszódia II./Allegro Barbaro* (1979); *A zsarnok szíve, avagy Boccaccio Magyarországon/The Tyrant's Heart, or Boccaccio in*

Hungary (1981); *Hajnal/Dawn* (1986); *Szörnyek évadja/The Monsters'*
Season (1987); *Jézus Krisztus horoszkópja/Jesus Christ's Horoscope*
(1988); *Isten hátrafelé megy/God Goes Backwards* (1991); *Kék Duna*
keringő/Blue Danube Waltz (1992); *Szeressük egymást gyerekek!/Let's*
Love One Another (1996); *Nekem lámpást adott kezembe az Úr,*
Pesten/Lord's Lantern in Budapest (1999).

JANDA, Krystyna   Starachowice 1952

Polish actress. Janda shot to stardom in her first film role as the as-
sertive film student Agnieszka in Andrzej Wajda's* *Człowiek z*
Marmuru/Man of Marble (1977). She has had a long association with
Wajda, appearing in *Bez Znieczulenia/Rough Treatment* (1978) and
Człowiek z Żelaza/Man of Iron (1981), among other films. She received the Best Actress award at Cannes in 1990 for her role in
Przesłuchanie/The Interrogation (1981, rel. 1989), Ryszard Bugajski's*
film, in which she plays a woman subjected to humiliating tortures by
the Stalinist authorities of 1950s Poland. Her film career now extends
to France and Germany. A popular theatre and television actress, she
won popular and critical acclaim for her television portrayal of the
nineteenth-century Polish actress, Helena Modrzejewska. AW

Other Films Include: *Polowanie na Muchy/Hunting Flies* (1972);
Mephisto (1981, Hung.); *Laputa* (1986, Ger.); *Tato/Daddy* (1995, Pol.);
Pestka/Pip (1995, Pol.); *Palais de la Santé* (1996, Fr.)

JASNÝ, Vojtěch   Kelč 1925

Czech director. One of the first graduates of FAMU* in 1951, Jasný
began his career in conjunction with Karel Kachyňa*, with whom he
directed a number of documentaries as well as their joint feature
debut, *Dnes večer všechno skončí/It Will All Be Over Tonight* (1954).
In the late 1950s his films *Zářijové noci/September Nights* (1956) and
Touha/Desire (1958) were in the forefront of those challenging the
status quo, while the allegorical *Až přijde kocour/That Cat/Cassandra*
Cat (1963), featuring Jan Werich*, and *Všichni dobří rodáci/All My*
Good Countrymen (1968) were among the most important Czech films
of the 1960s. The latter (banned between 1969 and 1989) was considered the first Czech film to tell the truth about the collectivisation
of the countryside. Yet it was also a lyrical hymn to nature which refused to demonise its villains. After 1969, Jasný pursued a less significant international career, making films in Austria, West Germany,
Finland and Canada. His Austrian films included an adaptation of
Heinrich Böll's *Ansichten eines Clowns/Face of a Clown/The Clown*
(1975). He returned to Czechoslovakia in 1991 to make the documentary *Proč Havel?/Why Havel?* His most recent film, the US–Czech pro-

114

duction *Návrat ztraceného ráje/Return to Paradise Lost* (1999), is a semi-autobiographical tale of a film-maker's return from New York to his native Moravia. PH

Other Films Include: *Přežil jsem svou smrt/I Survived Certain Death* (1960); *Procesí k panence/Pilgrimage to the Virgin* (1961); *Dýmky/ Pipes* (1966); *Česká rapsodie/Czech Rhapsody* [short] (1969); *Fluchtversuch/Attempt to Escape* (1976, Aust.); *Rückkehr/The Return* (1977); *Gospodjica/Das Fräulein/The Maiden* (1980, Yug.); *Eläköön it-semurhaaja/Bis später/The Suicide* (1984, Fin.); *The Great Land of Small* (1987, Can.); *Gladys* (1999, *Can.*); *Freezing Sunlight* (1996, US).

JELES, András   Jászberény 1945

Hungarian film and theatre director. Next to Gábor Bódy*, Jeles is perhaps the most powerful and original Hungarian director of his generation. In common with many directors, his career began in the Balázs Béla Stúdió*, in the mid-1970s. In his first feature, *A kis Valentino/Little Valentino* (1979), he used the documentary-fiction film style [> DOCUMENTARY (HUNGARY)] in a very particular way. Rather than reinforcing the story's verisimilitude, Jeles deliberately pushed it in an absurd-surrealist direction, constructing by the film's end a gloomy atmosphere of reality. The film provoked both scandal and an enthusiastic reception. His next two films were no less controversial; *Álombrigád/The Dreambrigade* (1983, released 1987) achieved notoriety as the only Hungarian feature film to be banned in the 1980s. In this film Jeles deploys an esoteric, theatrical style to deal with the conflicts of political self-expression among Hungarian workers. Despite the esoteric form, the message contained in the film's depiction of the relationship between workers and political leaders was clear enough to offend Hungarian officialdom. *Angyali üdvözlet/The Annunciation* (1984) was even more obscure: an adaptation of a Hungarian classic drama performed entirely by children. Many viewed it as a travesty of Hungary's 'sacred' literary tradition. In the meantime, Jeles organised an amateur theatre group called the Monteverdi birkózókör (Monteverdi Wrestling Club), whose performances achieved considerable international success. Since 1984 he has devoted most of his energies to the theatre. His latest film, *Dieu n'existe pas/God Does Not Exist* (1997), is a strange, visionary story about a young Jewish girl in Hungary during World War II, elements of which are taken from the diaries of Anne Frank and Dickens' *David Copperfield*. KAB

JIREŠ, Jaromil   Bratislava 1935

Czech director. Jireš studied at FAMU*, graduating in photography in 1958 and in direction in 1960. His first feature, *Křik/The Cry* (1963), dealt with the life of a television repairman whose wife is expecting a baby. Its complex narrative, involving flashbacks and flashforwards, establishes a mental world in which past, present, the individual and society intermingle. The film established Jireš as one of the leaders of the Czech New Wave* but he was unable to gain approval for a second feature until 1968, when he made *Žert/The Joke* in conjunction with novelist Milan Kundera. Planned before the publication of Kundera's book, the film used similar techniques to *Křik* to juxtapose the absurdities and idealism of 1950s Stalinism with the compromises and defeats of the present. Jireš maintained his technique through two very different films, an adaptation of Vítězslav Nezval's surrealist novel *Valerie a týden divů/Valerie and Her Week of Wonders* (1970), and the World War II story *... a pozdravuji vlaštovky/... And My Greetings to the Swallows* (1972). Although *Žert* was banned 'for ever' in 1973, Jireš maintained a continuity of production and, albeit working on a variety of simplistic subjects, produced notable documentaries focusing on Czech music. His adaptations of novels by Vladimír Páral (*Mladý muž a bílá velryba/Young Man and the White Whale,* 1978; *Katapult/Catapult,* 1983) and a series of social problem films showed something of his former talent, but this only re-emerged with his post-1989 film, *Labyrinth* (1992), German-financed and widely seen as a necessary counterbalance to Steven Soderbergh's *Kafka*. PH

Other Films Include: *Perličky na dně/Pearls of the Deep* [episode *Romance*] (1965); *Útěky domů/Escapes Home* (1980); *Opera ve vinici/ Opera in the Vineyard* (1981); *Neúplné zatmění/Partial Eclipse* (1982); *Prodloužený čas/Extended Time* (1984); *Lev s bílou hřívou/Lion with a White Mane* (1986); *Antonín Dvořák* [TV] (1990); *Popis věčného zápasu/Beschreibung eines Kampfes/Description of a Battle* (1991); *Helimadoe* (1993); *Učitel tance/The Dance Teacher* (1994); *Dvojrole/ Double role* (1999, Czech./Fr.).

K

KACHYŇA, Karel   Vyškov 1924

Czech director. Educated at FAMU*, Kachyňa was trained as a cinematographer and was one of the first graduates to enter the industry. Between 1950 and 1955, he worked on a series of documentaries with co-director Vojtěch Jasný*. They made their first feature together but then followed separate paths. In the 1960s, Kachyňa began an important collaboration with the writer Jan Procházka, which was to test the limits of what was then permitted in Czech cinema. Perhaps the most impressive of their films were *Naděje/Hope* (1963), *At' žije republika/ Long Live the Republic* (1965), *Kočár do Vídně/Coach to Vienna* (1966), and *Noc nevěsty/Night of the Bride* (1967), in which script, cinematography and music were matched in a kind of counterpoint. Approved themes such as the war, collectivisation or the revolution were given an unorthodox treatment, focusing on the complexity of human motivation and frequently critical of the communist role. Procházka became head of the Writers Union during the 'Prague Spring', and his last two films with Kachyňa, *Směšný pán/Funny Old Man* (1969) and *Ucho/The Ear* (1969, rel. 1990), were banned in the aftermath of the Soviet invasion. Kachyňa filmed, as *Už zase skáču přes kaluže* (1970), Procházka's adaptation of Alan Marshall's *I'm Jumping Over Puddles Again*, with another writer taking the credit (Procházka died in 1971). Kachyňa continued to make films but never achieved quite the same standard again, insubstantial themes frequently collapsing under an excess of imagery. His most notable later films have included *Lásky mezi kapkami deště/Love among the Raindrops* (1979), *Smrt krásných srnců/Death of the Beautiful Roebucks* (1986), and *Poslední motýl/The Last Butterfly/Le Cri du papillon* (1990), a co-production with Britain and France. In 1993, he successfully returned to another Procházka subject with *Kráva/The Cow* (1993), made for television. His most recent works are the psychological drama *Fany* (1995), and *Hanele* (1999), an exploration of anti-Semitism in Central Eastern Europe. PH

KADÁR, Ján

Budapest, Hungary 1918 –
Los Angeles, US 1979

and
KLOS, Elmar

Brno [then Austria-Hungary] 1910 –
Prague 1993

Slovak and Czech directors, writers and producers. Ján Kadár studied law and then photography in Bratislava in the 1930s. Imprisoned in Nazi concentration camps during the war, he made three films in Slovakia in the late 1940s before moving to Prague and beginning his career with Elmar Klos. Klos began in cinema by helping his scriptwriter uncle, Josef Skružný, in the late 1920s and acting in small parts. He was co-founder and directed films for the film unit set up by the Baťa shoe company in Zlín (subsequently Gottwaldov, now Zlín again), which pioneered documentary and advertising films in the late 1930s.

Kadár and Klos took co-credits on eight features, with Klos as producer and Kadár as director. Their films were characterised by their critical stance and a variety of stylistic approaches, ranging from a modern fairy story such as *Tři přání/Three Wishes* (1958, rel. 1963),

117

which attacked social hypocrisy and corruption, to an almost documentary assault on Stalinist justice in *Obžalovaný/The Accused* (1964). Their film about the partisan struggle in Slovakia, *Smrt si říká Engelchen/Death is Called Engelchen* (1963), intercut past and present in a way that provoked comparisons with Alain Resnais' *Hiroshima, mon amour*, while their Oscar-winning *Obchod na korze/A Shop on the High Street/The Shop on Main Street* (1965) mixed comedy, tragedy and fantasy in a compelling portrait of the Jewish experience under fascism. In 1968, Kadár emigrated to the United States where he followed an uneven career, although the Canadian-made *Lies My Father Told Me* (1975) enjoyed both critical and commercial success. Klos remained at home in obscurity, emerging in 1989 to collaborate with the Syrian-born Moris Issa on *Bizon*. PH

Other Films Co-Directed, Written and Produced by Kadár and Klos Include: *Únos/Kidnapped* (1952); *Hudba z Marsu/Music from Mars* (1955); *Tam na konečné/House at the Terminus* (1957); *Touha zvaná Anada/Adrift/Desire is Called Anada* (1969, rel. 1971).

KADARE, Ismail   Gjirokaster 1936

Albanian writer. Albania's leading poet and novelist, translated worldwide and nominated several times for a Nobel prize. Born and raised in a historical city near the Greek border, Kadare studied in Tirana and at the Maxim Gorky Literary Institute in Moscow. The gripping magical realist style of Kadare takes the reader to a claustrophobic universe where innocent protagonists wander in the oneiric labyrinth-like spaces of totalitarianism. Two of Kadare's novels have been adapted for the cinema. Kujtim Cashku's *Te paftuarit/Broken April* (1985), a beautifully shot story of clashing revengeful mountaineers and treacherous townsmen, is influenced by Miklós Jancsó's* visual style. Dhimiter Anagnosti's *Kthimi i Ushtrisë së vdekur/The Return of The Dead Army* (1989) is an adaptation of Kadare's classic debut novel, *The General of the Dead Army* (1962), a tale of desire, mistrust and betrayal. In 1990 Kadare, who had been a member of the Communist Party for decades, entered open opposition to the government which led to his emigration in 1992. He now resides in Paris. DI

KAIDANOVSKY, Alexander L.   Rostov on Don 1946 – Moscow 1995

Russian actor, director and scriptwriter. After studies at the Shchepkin Theatre Academy, Kaidanovsky worked as an actor in both the Vakhtangov Theatre and the Moscow Art Theatre, while also appearing in such films as Nikita Mikhalkov*'s *Svoi sredi chuzhikh, chuzhoi sredi svoikh/At Home among Strangers, Alone among Friends* (1974).

Perhaps his greatest success in over forty film roles was the title role in Andrey Tarkovsky*'s *Stalker* (1980). As a director he made the short films *Sad/The Garden* (1983), based on a Borges story, and *Iona, ili khudozhnik za rabotoi/Jonah, or the Artist at Work* (1984). His first full-length film, *Prostaya smert'/A Simple Death* (1987) was based on Tolstoy's *The Death of Ivan Ilich*, and starred Alisa Freindlikh*, who played Kaidanovsky's wife in *Stalker*. Kaidanovsky's most ambitious film is *Zhena kerosinshchika/The Kerosene Seller's Wife* (1988), from his own script. The film is set in a town in former East Prussia in 1953, the year of Stalin's death, and superficially concerns the efforts of a visiting investigator to pursue charges of corruption laid against the head of the town's Party committee. But Kaidanovsky's range is considerably greater, taking in questions of history and myth, truth, chance and lies, in a febrile and often hallucinatory narrative that is visually, along with the work of Sokurov*, among the most ambitious and exciting achievements of recent Russian cinema. After his death the director Yevgeni Tsymbal* made two documentaries about him, a contribution to the television series *Chtoby pomnili* [Lest We Forget], 1996, and *Sny Stalkera/Stalker's Dreams* (1998). JG

KALATOZOV, Mikhail K. Mikhail Kalatozishvili; Tbilisi, Georgia [Russian Empire] 1903 – Moscow 1973

Georgian Soviet director, who began as a jack-of-all-trades in Georgian cinema in 1923. His first film as director, the poetic documentary *Sol' Svanetii/Salt for Svanetia* in 1930, portrayed the benefits brought by Soviet power and the construction of a new road to an isolated part of the Caucasian mountains. In 1936 he became director of the Tbilisi film studios, was Soviet cinema's representative in the US from 1943 to 1945, and between 1945 and 1948 was in overall charge of Soviet feature film production. During this period he made *Muzhestvo/Courage* (1939), *Valerii Chkalov* (1941) and the Cold War propaganda vehicle *Zagovor obrechënnykh/The Conspiracy of the Damned* (1950), for which he was awarded the Stalin Prize in 1951. He gained an international reputation with *Letyat zhuravli/The Cranes Are Flying*, which won the Palme d'Or at Cannes in 1958. His last film was *Krasnaya palatka/The Red Tent* (1970), a co-production with Italy which dealt with the polar expedition of the Italian explorer Nobile. RT

KAMINSKI, Janusz Ziembice, Poland 1959

Polish-born American cinematographer. Kaminski emigrated from his native Poland at the age of twenty-two to the US where he graduated at Columbia College in Chicago. Although he has never made a Polish film, his work is a direct continuation of the best in Polish cinematography and brings an international recognition to the Polish cinematic tradition. In the early 1990s he worked on a number of low-budget Hollywood thrillers. His breakthrough came in 1992 when Stephen Spielberg invited him to come to Poland and do the camerawork on *Schindler's List* (1993). The project also employed other Poles like designer, Allan Starski (designer of Wajda's* *Korczak, Holly Week*, and *Pan Tadeusz*) whose work enjoyed international acclaim. Since 1993 Kaminski has been an indispensable member of Spielberg's team. He was the cameraman for all Spielberg's subsequent films – *Amistad* (1997), *The Lost World: Jurassic Park* (1997), and *Saving Private Ryan* (1998), and is scheduled to be DP on all of Spielberg's forthcoming projects – *Memoirs of a Geisha* (2000), *Jurassic Park 3* (2000), and *Minority Report* (2000). In 1994 Kaminski won an Oscar for the cinematography of *Schindler's List* and in 1999 for *Saving Private Ryan*. His work on *Amistad* was nominated for an Oscar in 1997. In 1999 he made a directorial debut with the New Line production, *Lost Souls* (1999). He married the American actress, Holly Hunter, in 1995. DI

KANEVSKY, Vitaly   Suchan, Siberia [USSR] 1935

Russian director. Kanevsky was born in the Soviet Far East, and in 1960 began studies at VGIK* in the workshop of Mikhail Romm*. In 1962 he played the leading role in *Proshlym letom/Last Summer*, a short film by Viktor Tregubovich set on a collective farm. In 1966, falsely accused of theft, he was sentenced to eight years' imprisonment. Released in 1974, he finally received his director's diploma in 1977 and made a short film *Chetvertaya taina/The Fourth Secret* at the studios of Belorusfilm. In 1981 he directed his first feature, *Derevenskaia istoriia/A Village Story*, but the film was re-edited without his being consulted, and the final version does not represent his vision. In 1989, encouraged by Alexei German*, he made the autobiographical film *Zamri, umri, voskresni/Freeze, Die, Get Up Again*. Set in 1947, it relates the experiences of twelve-year-old Valerka and his friend Galiya among 'enemies of the people' and Japanese prisoners of war. *Freeze, Die, Get up Again* succeeded as miraculously as German's *My Friend Ivan Lapshin* in evoking provincial life in Stalinist Russia. The British director Alan Parker saw part of the film and persuaded the director of the Cannes film festival to accept it. In 1990, at the age of fifty-five, Kanevsky won the Caméra d'Or for first features. Kanevsky's next film *Samostoyatel'naya zhizn'/An Independent Life* (1992) continues Valerka's story, as he grows to manhood in a world of everyday violence and degradation. In 1993 Kanevsky made a documentary *My, deti dvadtsatogo veka/We, the Children of the Twentieth Century*, a direct and depressing series of interviews with juvenile criminals in St Petersburg, one of whom is Pavel Nazarov, the young actor who played Valerka in Kanevsky's earlier films. JG

120

KARÁDY, Katalin
Budapest 1912 – São Paulo, Brazil 1989

Hungarian actress, who became the only Hollywood-type movie star in Hungary. Karády's career as an actress was fairly short but nonetheless dazzling. She was already a well-known popular singer when she appeared in her first and most successful movie, *Halálos tavasz/Deadly Spring* (1939). The film scandalised the fascist authorities, who condemned its sentimentality and lack of patriotic feeling. Karády's alto voice and the erotic mood she generated made her the Hungarian equivalent of the Marlene Dietrich type of *femme fatale*. Her unwillingness to take part in Nazi propaganda campaigns during the war led to rumours of her being a British spy, rumours that were reinforced by her arrest by the Gestapo in 1944. Her participation in the resistance is still not clear (she claimed to have hidden refugees in her apartment). Karády left Hungary after the communist takeover in 1949 and this ended her career as an actress. Her films could not be shown for thirty years, which only helped to nourish the mythology surrounding her. It was only in the late 1970s that her songs were re-released and her films shown theatrically, to huge acclaim. KAB

Other Films Include: *Erzsébet királynő/Queen Elizabeth, Hazajáró lélek/Haunting Spirit* (1940); *Ne kérdezd, ki voltam/Don't Ask Who I Was, Kísértés/Temptation* (1941); *Sziriusz/Sirius, Halálos csók/Deadly Kiss, Egy szív megáll/A Heart Stops Beating* (1942); *Valamit visz a víz/ Something is in the Water, Szováthy Éva* (1943); *Forró mezők/Hot Fields* (1948).

KARANOVIĆ, Srdjan
Belgrade 1945

Yugoslav director of Serbian origin. Karanović studied directing at FAMU* and belongs to the Yugoslav Prague Group*. Throughout his career he has been interested in exploring contemporary Yugoslavian issues, as well as peasant life and patriarchal society. Karanović developed a distinctive visual style in which the use of landscape is particularly important. Most of his work has been as a feature director but he also worked for television in the 1970s and co-wrote scripts for other members of the Prague Group (R. Grlić*) as well as for his own adaptation of Dragoslav Mihajlović's novel, *Petrijin Venac/Petria's Wreath* (1980). His first major success came with the critic's award at Cannes for *Miris poljskog cveca/The Scent of Wild Flowers* (1977), the story of the failed attempt of an intellectual to preserve his privacy by escaping an overwhelmingly busy, urban lifestyle. *Petria's Wreath*, which won the Golden Arena Prize at the Pula* festival, was shot by the acclaimed cameraman, Tomislav Pinter and starred Mirjana Karanović, one of the finest actresses of Yugoslavian cinema. It tells the heartbreaking life story of a simple peasant woman in a remote Serbian coal-mining town between World War I and World War II. Karanović's next film, *Nesto izmedju/Something In-between* (1983), contained a premonition of war which came true only a decade later. The plot featured an American woman who, while visiting Belgrade, gets involved with two Yugoslav lovers (Miki Manojlović* and Dragan Nikolić) and who leaves after seeing herself unable to choose between them. *Za sada bez dobrog naslova/A Film with No Name* (1988) is an inter-ethnic Romeo-and-Juliet tragedy involving Macedonians and Albanians. Karanovic continued his interest in studies of traditionalist relations in his *Virdzina/Virgina* (1991), a film dealing with issues of sexual identity in the patriarchal society of the Balkans. The story, set in the Bosnian mountains of the late nineteenth century, concentrates on the fate of a young girl (Marta Keller, Cézar award for best actress) who is raised as a boy in order to save face for her family who have only had girls. The oppressed protagonist, however, does not endure the transvestism and ends up committing a liberating move, revealing her feminine identity and calling for an anti-patriarchal revolt. DI

Other Films Include: *Stvar srca/The Matter of Heart* (1968); *Paní vrátná* (1969); *Neblbni* (1969); *Drustvena igra/Social Game* (1972); *Jagode u grlu/A Throatful of Strawberries* (1985).

KARLOVY VARY

Czech film festival. The first international film festival in Czecho-slovakia was held at Mariánské Lázně (Marienbad) and Karlovy Vary (Carlsbad) in 1946. It became competitive in 1948, with the venue moving permanently to Karlovy Vary in 1950. To accommodate the introduction of the Moscow Festival in 1959, it went biennial, the two festivals alternating until 1992. Both Karlovy Vary and Moscow func-tioned as Eastern bloc alternatives to Cannes and Venice but, despite a blatant ideological role (juries were frequently told which politically acceptable film to vote for), Karlovy Vary often provided a genuine meeting-place for film-makers. Important films to win its major award include Jiří Menzel's* *Rozmarné léto/Capricious Summer* (1967) and Ken Loach's *Kes* (1969). Long before Nantes and London took up the cause, Karlovy Vary was promoting 'Third World' cinema and it be-came one of the principal channels through which Latin American, Asian and African cinema reached audiences in Europe. The first 'post-revolutionary' festival in 1990 concentrated on the Czech and Slovak film-makers whose work had been banned during the previous twenty years. Under the direction of Eva Zaoralova the festival con-tinues to showcase the best output of East European cinema. PH

KARMITZ, Marin

French film producer of Romanian descent. Karmitz emigrated to France at the age of nine and studied at the French film school. He was involved with the leftist movement of the late 1960s, directing an award-winning documentary and two feature films. In the mid-1970s he entered the distribution and production business on his own and developed his company, MK2, which is considered to be one of the foremost independent European film enterprises. Karmitz also runs a prestigious distribution operation, *MK2 Diffusion*, following a niche marketing approach to the art house circuit and integrating an exhibition chain, foreign sales, and a film library. One of the leading European film developers, Karmitz has produced most of Claude Charbrol's films since 1985, and worked with internationally recognised directors such as Ruy Guerra, Alain Resnais, Alain Tanner, the Taviani Brothers, and Arturo Ripstein. Karmitz has a long-standing interest in promoting directors from Eastern Europe. He produced Yilmaz Güney's *Duvar/The Wall* (1983) and Pavel Lungin's* *Taski-Blyuz/ Taxi Blues* (1990). In the 1990s he helped re-launch the career of Romanian Lucian Pintilie*, acting as producer for his *Prea târziu/Too Late* (1996) and *Terminus paradis/Last Stop Paradise* (1998). Karmitz's biggest artistic and financial success was the production of Kieślowski's* *Trzy kolory/Trois couleurs/Three Colours: Niebieski/Bleu/Blue* (1993), *Bialy/ Blanc/White* (1994) and *Czerwony/Rouge/Red* (1994) which brought him international recognition and considerable financial reward. DI

KATOWICE FILM AND TELEVISION SCHOOL (WYDZIAŁ RADIA I TELEWIZJI, UNIWERSYTET ŚLĄSKI, KATOWICE)

Polish film school. The Department of Radio and Television at the University of Śląsk in Katowice, founded by Polish Television and intended as a television school, has become Poland's second film school, with many of its graduates working in cinematography. The student strikes and political manoeuvring in the faculty at Łódź* in the mid-1970s drew students and lecturers to Katowice, which also has better technical facilities. The department runs courses in cinematography for film and television, production management and direction, and promotes a strong documentary tradition with lecturers such as Krzysztof Kieślowski* and documentarist Irena Kamieńska. AW

KAUFMAN, Mikhail A.

Soviet director and cameraman, brother of Dziga Vertov* and Boris Kaufman (later cameraman on Jean Vigo's films) and one of the founders of the Soviet school of documentary film-making. Kaufman was the cameraman for Vertov's silent newsreels and documentary films up to and including *Chelovek s kinoapparatom/The Man with the Movie Camera* (1929). He wrote, directed and shot the feature-length documentaries *Moskva/Moscow* (1927) and *Vesnoi/Springtime* (1929) and a series of documentaries in the 1930s, including *Nebyvalyi pokhod/An Unprecedented Campaign* (1931), *Bol'shaya pobeda/A Great Victory* (1933), *Aviamarsh/The Aviators' March* (1936) and *Nasha Moskva/Our Moscow* (1939). From 1941 he concentrated on popular educational films and his career went into a decline with works such as *Kompozitor Tikhon Khrennikov/The Composer Tikhon Khrennikov* (1967), a study of the Stalinist head of the Composers' Union. RT

KAWALEROWICZ, Jerzy   Gwóździec, Ukraine 1922

Polish director. Kawalerowicz is one of the leading figures of the 'Polish School' of the 1950s and early 1960s. He was born in the Ukraine and graduated from the short-lived Cracow Film Institute, along with Wojciech Has*. His first solo features, *Celuloza/A Night of Remembrance* and *Pod Gwiazdą Frygijską/Under a Phrygian Star* (1954), were a two-part adaptation of I. Newerley's novel *A Night of Remembrance*. An epic tale of prewar Polish society, the films centre on one man's political development as a communist and his tempestuous romance with a fellow activist. In 1955 Kawalerowicz became head of the Kadr Film Unit with Tadeusz Konwicki* as his literary chief. Their work together on *Matka Joanna od Aniołów/Mother Joan of the Angels/The Devil and the Nun* (1961) won a Special Jury Prize at Cannes. Kawalerowicz was also prominent in the 'second wave' of Polish films of the 1960s. His taut psychological thriller, *Pociąg/Night Train* (1959), is comparable to the best of American B-movies, its reflections on mob violence and persecution adding a distinctly contemporary political overtone. Kawalerowicz's ambitious move into the epic genre with *Faraon/The Pharaoh* (1966), billed as the 'communist *Cleopatra*', is more memorable as an exercise in logistics and locations than for the film itself. Kawalerowicz turned again to Polish history with *Śmierć Prezydenta/Death of a President* (1977), which looked at the story of Gabriel Narutowicz, Poland's first elected president, and *Austeria/The Inn* (1983), dealing with World War I and the Hasidic Jewish community. His *Bronsteins Kinder/Bronstein's Children* (1990) is a German production about the revenge of three Jewish men on their German concentration camp warden many years after the war. AW

Other Films Include: *Za chto?/Why?* (1995).

KERTÉSZ, Mihály

Michael Curtiz; Budapest 1888 –
Hollywood 1962

Hungarian-American director. Michael Curtiz, one of the most prolific directors in the history of cinema, was born Mihály Kertész to a
Hungarian Jewish family in Budapest. He studied acting and directed
stage productions as well as numerous silent films in his native country.
Kertész's debut was the first feature-length Hungarian film, *Az Utolsó
bohém/The Last Bohemian* (1912). He was influenced by the Scand-
inavian silent film tradition having worked shortly in Denmark in
1913. Kertész's early Hungarian films, which include over thirty
silents, had a strong impact on the development of the film industry in
his native country, where he worked alongside the other distinguished
Hungarian director of the time, Sándor (Alexander) Korda*. In 1919
Kertész emigrated to Vienna, as a reaction to the nationalisation of the
Hungarian film industry by the short-lived communist government.
Eventually he moved to the US in 1926, where he worked for Warner
Bros., 20th Century-Fox and Paramount until his death and made over
100 films. His best-known Hollywood films are *The Adventures of
Robin Hood* (1938), *Angels with Dirty Faces* (1938), *Casablanca*
(1942), *Mildred Pierce* (1945), *White Christmas* (1954), and *We're No
Angels* (1955). DI

Other Hungarian-made Films Include: *Ma és holnap/Today and
Tomorrow* (1912); *Rablélek/Slave Souls* (1913); *Házasodik az uram/
My Man Is Getting Married* (1913); *Az Éjszaka rabjai/The Slaves of the
Night* (1914); *A Kölcsönkért csecsemők/The Borrowed Babies* (1914);
Bánk Bán/Governor Bank (1914); *Akit ketten szeretnek/The One Who
Is Loved by Two* (1915); *Makkhetes/Seven Clubs* (1916); *A Magyar
föld ereje/The Power of the Hungarian Land* (1916); *Farkas/Wolf*
(1916); *Az Ezüst kecske/The Silver Goat* (1916); *Doktor úr/Dear
Doctor* (1916); *Árendás zsidó/The Jewish Tenant* (1917); *A Vörös
Sámson/The Red Samson* (1917); *Az Utolsó hajnal/The Last Dawn*
(1917); *Tavasz a télben/Spring in Winter* (1917); *Tatárjárás/The Tartar
Invasion* (1917); *A Szentjóbi erdõ titka/The Secret of the Szentjob Forest*
(1917); *A Kuruzsló/The Charlatan* (1917); *Halálc-sengõ/Deathbell*
(1917); *Az Ezredes/The Colonel* (1917); *A Béke útja/The Way of Peace*
(1917); *Az Ördög/The Devil* (1918); *A Wellingtoni rejtély/The Mystery
of Wellington* (1918); *Lulu* (1918); *Júdás/Judas* (1918); *A Csúnya
fiú/The Ugly Boy* (1918); *Alraune/Alraune* (1918); *99/Kilencvenkilenc/
99/Ninety-nine* (1918); *Liliom* (1919); *Jön az öcsém/John the Younger
Brother* (1919).

KHANZHONKOV, Alexander A.   1877 – Yalta, Crimea [USSR] 1945

Russian film producer. Khanzhonkov began importing films from France in 1906 and set up his own production company in 1908, concentrating mainly on Russian themes. He produced one of the first full-length feature films, *Oborona Sevastopolya/The Defence of Sebastopol* (1911), and employed most of the leading figures in pre-Revolutionary Russian cinema, including Evgeni Bauer*, Vera Kholodnaya*, Ivan Mosjoukine*, Lev Kuleshov* and Ivan Perestiani*. He became the major Russian film producer and his company owned cinemas and published film journals. In spring 1917 he moved to the Crimea for health reasons and later emigrated, returning, like Yakov Protazanov*, to work for Rusfilm (later Mezhrabpom*) in 1923. He became director of Proletkino, which, as its name implies, was supposed to produce films for the proletariat. When it failed, Khanzhonkov and others were charged with fraud in a sensational trial. He was never convicted but was thereafter forbidden to work in cinema as a 'disenfranchised person'. In 1934, on the fifteenth anniversary of Soviet cinema, he was rehabilitated and given a state pension. RT

KHEIFITS, Iosif E. [HEIFITS, Josef]   Minsk, Belorussia [Russian Empire] 1905 – St Petersburg 1995

Soviet director and scriptwriter. Kheifits joined the Leningrad studios in 1928 and worked with Alexander Zarkhi on a Communist Youth League production brigade, making *Veter v litso/Wind in the Face* (1930) and *Polden'/Noon* (1931). Their best-known film in a long collaboration was undoubtedly *Deputat Baltiki/Baltic Deputy*, which portrayed the conversion of a professor to the revolutionary cause and won a Grand Prix at the 1937 Paris International Exhibition. Their other films included: *Chlen pravitel'stva/A Member of the Government* (1940), *Ego zovut Sukhe Bator/His Name is Sukhe Bator* (1942) and *Razgrom Yaponii/The Rout of Japan*, awarded a Stalin Prize in 1946. They achieved international recognition much later with three Chekhov adaptations: *Dama s sobachkoi/The Lady with the Little Dog* (1960), which won a prize at Cannes, *V gorode S/In the Town of S* (1967) and *Plokhoi khoroshii chelovek/The Duel* (1973). RT

KHOKHLOVA, Alexandra S.   Berlin, Germany 1897 – Moscow 1985

Soviet actress and teacher, who began working in cinema in 1916, when she met her lifelong companion Lev Kuleshov*. Khokhlova studied at the State Film School (where she later taught, after it had become VGIK*) from 1919, and between 1920 and 1923 was a leading participant in the 'Kuleshov collective', appearing in his *Na krasnom fronte/On the Red Front* (1920). She appeared in most of his subsequent films, with leading roles in *Luch smerti/Death Ray* (1925), *Po zakonu/By the Law* (1926) and *Velikii uteshitel'/The Great Consoler* (1933), but is best remembered for her distinctive performance as the Countess in his *Neobychainye priklyucheniya Mistera Vesta v strane bol'shevikov/The Extraordinary Adventures of Mr West in the Land of the Bolsheviks* (1924). She exemplified the school of 'model' acting that Kuleshov tried to develop and was held up by Sergei Eisenstein* as a fitting contrast to the Hollywood female stereotype. RT

KHOLODNAYA, Vera V.　　Poltava, Ukraine [Russian Empire] 1893 – Odessa, Ukraine 1919

Russian actress. Trained as a ballerina at the Bolshoi, Kholodnaya began making films in 1914. After her appearance in Yevgeni Bauer's* *Pesn' torzhestvuyushchei lyubvi/The Song of Love Triumphant* (1915), she became the most popular actress in pre-Revolutionary Russian cinema. She made five more films with Bauer, including *Deti veka/ Children of the Age* (1915) and her greatest screen triumph, *Zhizn' za zhizn'/A Life for a Life* (1916). Her portrayal of women's sadness and suffering gave her immense popularity in a Russia torn apart by war and revolution. In the summer of 1918, while filming in Odessa, Kholodnaya fell victim to the epidemic of Spanish influenza sweeping Europe. The funeral for this 'queen of the screen', as her contemporaries hailed her, was a Russian equivalent to the later obsequies for Rudolph Valentino in Hollywood. RT

KHOTINENKO, Vladimir I.　Slavgorod, Altai Region, Russia [USSR] 1952

Russian director. Khotinenko graduated from the Sverdlovsk Institute of Architecture in 1976. From 1978 to 1982 he worked at the Sverdlovsk Film Studio as a designer. In 1981 he completed the Higher Courses for Scriptwriters and Directors in the workshop of Nikita Mikhalkov*. He presently lectures in feature film direction at VGIK*. In his early films Khotinenko investigates the past: *Odin i bez oruzhiya/Alone and Unarmed* (1984), co-directed with Pavel Fattakhutdinov, is about a Red commander, Vorontsov, who is alone in his fight against a criminal during the Civil War; in *Zerkalo dlya geroya/A Mirror for a Hero* (1987), two men meet during the shooting of a film and return together to their childhood in the immediate postwar period. Khotinenko's next films were set in contemporary Russia, and concerned themselves with the theme of fate. *SV/Sleeping Car* (1989) is set on a train, underscoring the element of fate that is present even in seemingly chance meetings; *Patrioticheskaya komediya/Patriotic Comedy* (1992) is set in Sverdlovsk, and explores the Russian folk figure of the house spirit in the context of contemporary life. In *Makarov* (1993), the poet Alexander Sergeyevich Makarov, played by Sergei Makovetsky*, returns home, having bought a Makarov pistol. The pistol changes the poet's life, depriving him of friends, family and his muse. 'Doroga'/'The Road' was his contribution to the almanac made to mark the centenary of cinema, *Pribytie poezda/The Arrival of a Train* (1995); in this film the spiritual values of the character played by the singer Yevgeniya Smolyaninova cannot be bought for money by a rich businessman. With *Musul'manin/The Muslim* (1995) Khotinenko began a new phase in his career: the film explored the power belief has over human lives: the Russian soldier Kolya returns to his native village after years in captivity, having espoused the Muslim religion; his changed faith serves to highlight the corruption of Russian traditions. BB

KHUTSIEV, Marlen M.   Tbilisi, Georgia [USSR] 1925

Russian director and scriptwriter. Khutsiev began work as an assistant director at the Tbilisi studios in 1944. In 1952 he graduated from Igor Savchenko's* workshop at VGIK*. His first film, *Vesna na Zarechnoi ulitse/Spring in Zarechnaya Street*, co-directed with Felix Mironer in 1956, is a study, lyrical and melodramatic by turn, of the life of a young woman teacher. In 1959 he made his first solo feature *Dva Fedora/The Two Fyodors*, which saw Vasili Shukshin's* debut as an actor. Khutsiev's masterpiece is *Zastava Il'icha/The Ilyich Gate* (Ilyich is the patronymic of Lenin), also known as *Mne dvadtsat' let/I Am Twenty*, which Khutsiev co-scripted with Gennadi Shpalikov. Work on this portrait of 1960s youth continued over five years, from 1959 to 1964, with constant harassment from the Soviet censors, and in the face of the disapproval of Khrushchev himself, who denounced the film in March 1963 for its failure to represent young people as builders of a communist society. The version of the film which, as *I Am Twenty*, won the Special Jury Prize in Venice in 1964 had had ninety minutes and whole sections removed from it. The full film was not restored and shown until 1989, after a 1987 decision of the Conflict Commission set up by the Union of Filmmakers* following its radical Fifth Congress in 1986. Despite his problems with *The Ilyich Gate*, Khutsiev made another film devoted to the lives of young people, *Iyul'skii dozhd'/July Rain* in 1967, followed, in 1970, by the war film, *Byl mesyats mai/It Was the Month of May*, and, in 1971, by the documentary *Alyi parus Parizha/The Red Sail of Paris*. In 1976, after the death of Mikhail Romm*, he joined Elem Klimov* and G. N. Lavrov in completing that director's *I vse-taki ya veryu/And Nonetheless I Believe*, which was followed by *Posleslovie/Postscript* in 1983. His most recent project, also made over several years, from 1988 to 1991, is *Beskonechnost'/Infinitas*, a three-and-a-half-hour philosophical parable, in which a middle-aged intellectual sets off on a mysterious journey through space and time, constantly encountering his younger self. Though the film was envisaged on the epic scale of *The Ilyich Gate*, its critical reputation is nowhere near as high. JG

KHVAN, Alexander F. Cheboksary 1957

Russian director, scriptwriter and actor. Khvan graduated from the Directors' Faculty of VGIK* in 1980, having studied with Lev Kulidzhanov* and Tatiana Lioznova. He played episodic roles in the films *Maniya Zhizeli/Giselle's Mania* (1995), directed by Alexei Uchitel, and *Nauchnaia sektsiia pilotov/Scientific Section of Pilots* (1996), directed by Andrei I. He made his debut as a director with the short 'Khoziain'/'The Master' in the film almanac, *Dominus* (1988). His first feature, *Diuba-Diuba* (1992), defines one of Khvan's main concerns: mental escape into other worlds. Andrei is a student of scriptwriting in Moscow, but he has no role, no function in this context. He creates a scenario for the escape of his former girlfriend Tanya from prison, and carries through with it right to the end. When he has secured her escape, it becomes clear that he did not act out of love, but meddled in Tanya's life without any right to do so: like a scriptwriter, like an author, he has taken control of her life. Finally, Andrei is on his own, in an American airport; as though nothing had ever happened, he embarks on what seems to be the training course in the US for which he had been nominated at the beginning of the film. Khvan's contribution to an almanac devoted to the centenary of cinema, *Pribytie poezda/The Arrival of a Train* (1995), consisted of the short 'Svadebnyi marsh'/'The Wedding March', which revolves around the love triangle of a film-maker father, his student son and his fiancée who is at the same time the father's mistress. His film *Dryan' khoroshaia, dryan' plokhaya/Good Trash, Bad Trash* (1998) explores the escape of a killer into a dream world of his own, which contrasts with his brutal behaviour in reality. *Umirat' legko/Dying Is Easy* (1999) is a thriller about a man who tries to attract the attention of the woman he loves by killing those around her. Khvan's films are set in a contemporary, crime-ridden Russia, while his heroes escape into dream worlds, separate from the worlds which they inhabit. BB

KIEŚLOWSKI, Krzysztof Warsaw 1941– 96

Polish director. A distinctive voice in Polish cinema, known for his uncompromising moral stance, Kieślowski first came to attention in the early 1970s for his incisive (often shelved) documentaries and shorts on the political reality of life in Poland. His features of the late 1970s

129

explored the relationship between the personal and the political with style, directness and a raw edge of realism, making him a key figure in the 'cinema of moral unrest'. Although the authorities banned *Przypadek/Blind Chance* (1981), Kieślowski was undeterred and made *Bez Końca/No End* in 1984. In the late 1980s he turned to television, directing *Dekalog*, a series of ten films thematically inspired by the Ten Commandments. The international release of one of these, *Krótki Film o Zabijaniu/A Short Film about Killing* (1988), and the subsequent massive success of the whole series, was greeted with surprise by Polish critics, who compared *Dekalog* unfavourably with Kieślowski's earlier work. His next feature, *Podwójne Życie Weroniki/The Double Life of Véronique* (1992), was a co-production between the Tor Film Unit and French producers; it enjoyed critical and commercial success, especially in France. Kieślowski's last work was a trilogy based on the French flag: 'liberty' (*Trois couleurs Bleu/Three Colours: Blue*, 1993), 'equality' (*Trois couleurs Blanc/Three Colours: White*, 1993) and 'fraternity' (*Trois couleurs Rouge/Three Colours: Red*, 1994). They have secured for Kieślowski – hailed as 'the most truly European director' – a place in the pantheon of European art cinema. He died in 1996 in Warsaw of complications during heart surgery. A documentary on Kieślowski features some of his last interviews *Krzysztof Kieślowski: I'm So-So ...* (1995, dir. Krzysztof Wierzbicki). Since 1998 an international competition for young film-makers, *Prix Kieślowski*, has been established by his French producer Marin Karmitz*. AW

Bib: Danusia Stok, *Kieślowski on Kieślowski* (1993); Paul Coates (ed.), *Lucid Dreams: The Films of Krzysztof Kieślowski*, 1999; Christopher Garbowski, *Krzysztof Kieślowski's Decalogue Series: the Problem of the Protagonists and their Self-transcendence*, 1996.

KIRKOV, Ljudmil   Vraca 1933–95

Bulgarian director, respected for his social themes and an ability to make films with which a young audience could easily identify. After graduating from the Sofia Academy of Dramatic Art (VITIS), Kirkov enrolled in 1959 for a course in film direction at Moscow's VGIK* under Mikhail Romm*. After two insignificant feature films, he hit his stride with *Švedski krale/Swedish Kings* (1968), a social comedy contrasting Western tourists on the Black Sea coast with the native working class.

Kirkov's best films were made in collaboration with scriptwriter Georgi Mišev*: *Momčeto si otiva/A Boy Becomes a Man* (1972) and its sequel *Ne si otivaj!/Don't Go Away!* (1976) are about a youth coming of age; *Seljaninăt s koleloto/Peasant on a Bicycle* (1974) and *Matriarhat/ Matriarchy* (1977) are nostalgic perspectives on fading village life. Kirkov also collaborated with dramatist-scriptwriter Stanislav Stratiev on three contemporary themes with a strong moral message: *Kratko* *slănce/Brief Sunlight* (1979), *Orkestăr bez ime/A Nameless Band* (1982), and *Ravnovesie/Balance* (1983). Moral and social issues were also the focus of his acclaimed last two dramas, *Ne znam, ne chuh, ne vidiah/Don't Know, Didn't Hear, Didn't See* (1984) and *Petuk vecher/ Friday Night* (1985). RH

KLIMOV, Elem G.   Stalingrad, Russia [USSR] 1933

Russian director. After studying at the Higher Institute of Aviation, Klimov worked as an engineer and a journalist before entering the workshop of Efim Dzigan at VGIK*, graduating in 1964. His first two features, the satirical comedies *Dobro pozhalovat', ili postoronnim vkhod vospreshchen/Welcome, or No Unauthorised Admittance* (1964), set in a summer camp for Young Pioneers, and *Pokhozhdeniya zubnogo vracha/Adventures of a Dentist* (1965), set in a provincial town, both encountered censorship difficulties for their mordant analysis of Soviet values and of Khrushchevian delusions in particular. *Sport, sport, sport* (1971) combined factual and feature material. *Agoniya/Agony*, Klimov's epic survey of the baleful influence of Rasputin on the last year of the Tsarist regime, though completed in 1975, was not released in Russia until 1984. After the death of Mikhail Romm*, Klimov and Marlen Khutsiev* completed his film *I vse-taki ya veryu/And Nonetheless I Believe* (1976), a strident survey of negative aspects of twentieth-century life. In 1980 Klimov made *Larisa*, a short documentary in memory of his wife, the director Larisa Shepitko*. His next project was *Proshchanie/Farewell* (1981), an anguished version of Valentin Rasputin's 1976 story about the flooding of a Siberian village. The film had been begun by Shepitko, and was taken over by Klimov after her untimely death. Like most of Klimov's films, it was initially shelved, this time because its desperate ecological warning did not please the Soviet authorities. In 1985 Klimov made *Idi i smotri/Come and See*, a savage epic about Nazi atrocities in Belorussia during World War II. In May 1986 he was elected new First Secretary of the Union of Filmmakers of the USSR* at its revolutionary Fifth Congress, and he spent the following years presiding over the renewal of the union and the industry. At the end of the decade he worked on a projected film of Mikhail Bulgakov's novel *The Master and Margarita*, but the plans did not come to fruition and the novel was eventually filmed by Yuri Kara. JG

KLOPČIČ, Matjaž   Ljubljana, Slovenia 1934

Yugoslav director, scriptwriter, art director and critic of Slovene origin. After studying architecture, Klopčič began directing short films in 1959. His first feature, *Zgodba, ki je ni/On the Run/Non-existing Story* (1967), clearly influenced by the French New Wave, established him as a typical *auteur*. In his later films, especially *Oxygen* (1970) and *Strah/Fear* (1974), he successfully deployed unusual narrative strategies, building up an impressive personal universe of split personalities and identity problems. While French critical acclaim (he was 'discovered' by *Positif* and the La Rochelle festival) opened the door to several important festivals, he seduced the Slovene public with a classical adaptation (both for film and television) of a famous Ivan Tavčar story, *Cvetje v jeseni/Autumn Flowers* (1973), about a tragic love affair between an elderly lawyer and a young country girl. *Iskanja/Search* (1979), based on a travel diary by Slovene writer Izidor Cankar, can be considered Klopčič's film manifesto: beautifully shot in Venice (by Tihomir Pinter), the film is full of metaphysical contemplations on art and life. Klopčič now teaches at the Ljubljana Film Academy, as well as writing for *Ekran** and occasionally directing for television. SP

Other Films Include: *Na papirnatih avionih/Paper Planes* (1967); *Sedmina/Funeral Feast/Regards to Maria* (1969); *Vdovstvo Karoline Žašler/The Widowhood of Karolina Žašler* (1976); *Dediščina/Heritage* (1984); *Moj ata, socialistični kulak/My Dad, the Socialist Kulak* (1988); *Triptih Agate Schwarzkobler/The Tryptich of Agata Schwarzkobler* (1997).

KLOS, Elmar – see KADÁR, Ján

KOLTAI, Lajos   Budapest 1946

Hungarian cinematographer. Lajos Koltai will be remembered as the cinematographer of István Szabó's* acclaimed trilogy – the Academy Award-winning *Mephisto* (1981), Cannes and BAFTA-winning *Oberst Redl/Redl ezredes/Colonel Redl* (1985), and *Hanussen* (1988), all featuring *tour-de-force* performances by Austrian actor Klaus-Maria Brandauer. Koltai has filmed almost all of Szabó's films since the late 1970s. He was also the cinematographer on the seminal early black-and-white works of Márta Mészáros*. Koltai was the Director of Photography for Pál Gábor's internationally acclaimed *Angi Vera* (1979), Péter Gothár's* landmark *Ajándék ez a nap/A Priceless Day* (1979) and *Megáll az idö/Time Stands Still* (1981) and for many more Hungarian directors. In the 1990s Koltai worked predominantly in the US as a cinematographer on films by Luis Mandoki, Andrei Konchalovsky* and Jodie Foster. In Europe he shot two films directed by Klaus-Maria Brandauer and one directed by Giuseppe Tornatore. His main contributions to the art of cinematography are his dynamic camera work and his mastery of colour. DI

KOKANOVA, Nevena

Bulgarian actress. A popular stage and screen actress, Kokanova is considered the 'first lady' of Bulgarian cinema. Having made her initial appearance on the screen as a nineteen-year-old in Jianko Jiankov's *Godini za ljubov/Years of Love* (1957), she achieved international fame in Vălo Radev's* *Kradetsăt na praskovi/The Peach Thief* (1964), in which she plays a prison commandant's wife who falls tragically in love with a Yugoslav POW. Married to actor-director Ljubomir Šarlandjiev, Kokanova appeared in almost all his films as the lead actress; upon his sudden death in 1979, she completed his last production: *Trite smărtni grjaha/Three Deadly Sins* (1980). RH

KOMOROWSKA, Maja

Polish actress, originally trained with the world-famous experimental theatre director and theorist, Jerzy Grotowski. His approach to performance, emphasising the physical and the expression of emotion, clearly informs her work. She has worked closely with Krzysztof Zanussi*, notably in his early film *Bilans Kwartalny/Quarterly Balance/ A Woman's Decision* (1975), in his wartime drama *Rok Spokojnego Słońca/The Year of the Quiet Sun* (1984) and more recently in *Stan posiadania/Inventory* (1989) and *Cwal/In Full Gallop* (1996). Komorowska appeared in the lead role in the first part of Kieślowski's* *Decalogue – I Am the Lord Thy God* (1988). With her haunted and melancholy eyes and an air of physical and emotional vulnerability, Komorowska is typically cast as a victim of fate, as in Tadeusz Konwicki's* *Jak Daleko Stąd Jak Blisko/So Far, So Near* (1972), or as a willing female martyr. Komorowska is a popular and respected actress who works in theatre and television as well as film. She lectures at the Warsaw Drama School. AW

KONCHALOVSKY, Andrei – see MIKHALKOV-KONCHALOVSKY, Andron

KONWICKI, Tadeusz
Nowa Wilejka, Lithuania 1926

Polish writer and director. Konwicki is one of Poland's best-known and highly regarded modern novelists. He was born in a small village near Vilnius, historical capital of Lithuania, then part of Poland but in the postwar period in the Soviet Union. The evocation of this homeland became a central theme in Konwicki's novels and films. For some time after the war his novels followed the style of Socialist Realism*, but with the post-1956 political and cultural liberation he employed a more individual style which attracted the disapproval of the authorities. His involvement in film dates back to the 1950s when he was literary head of the Kadr Film Unit and collaborated on screenplays for films such as *Matka Joanna od Aniołów/Mother Joan of the Angels* (1961) by Jerzy Kawalerowicz*. He made his directorial debut with *Ostatni Dzień Lata/The Last Day of Summer* (1958). An intimate and melancholy story about a chance meeting between a man and woman at the end of the war, the film was internationally acclaimed and won a prize at Venice in 1958. Konwicki's films offer personal reflections on the individual, and yearn for the mythical Lithuanian homeland of Polish literature. In *Jak Daleko Stąd Jak Blisko/So Far, So Near* (1972) Konwicki questioned the morality of war, creating a world where there was no 'absolute right' and individuals bore responsibility for their own actions. It was the first Polish film to take this critical standpoint. Other Polish directors have turned to Konwicki's novels for inspiration, most notably Andrzej Wajda*, who filmed *Kronika Wypadków Miłosnych/ A Chronicle of Love Affairs* in 1986. Costa-Gavras's 1993 *La petite apocalypse/The Little Apocalypse* (Fr./Pol./It.) was based on Konwicki's novel. AW

Other Films as Director/Scriptwriter Include: *Dolina Issy/The Issa Valley* (1982); *Lawa/Lava* (1989).

KORNGOLD, Erich Wolfgang
Brünn (Brno), Czechoslovakia 1897 – Hollywood, California 1957

Bohemian-born composer of modern opera (*Die tote Stadt*), who toured as a conductor and in 1931 was named Professor of Music at the Akademie der Schönen Künste in Vienna. His second career as one of the great Hollywood composers started inconspicuously with his Strauss arrangements for Alfred Hitchcock's *Waltzes from Vienna* (1934), continued with a Mendelssohn adaptation for *A Midsummer Night's Dream* (d. 1935, Max Reinhardt* and Wilhelm Dieterle, US), and finally earned him a generous contract with Warner Bros. Korngold received his first Oscar in 1936 for the score of *Anthony Adverse*, and his second for *The Adventures of Robin Hood* (1938). His film music was both an effective background for dramatic action and, where necessary, serious music in its own right, as with his 'Cello concerto in C-major, op. 37', featured in *Deception* (1946). From 1946, he composed again for concert halls in Europe while keeping his job in Hollywood. KU

Bib: Brendan G. Carroll, *Erich Wolfgang Korngold* (1984).

Other Films Include: *Captain Blood* (1935); *Give Us This Night* (1936); *The Private Lives of Elizabeth and Essex* (1939); *The Sea Wolf* (1941); *Devotion* (1943); *Between Two Worlds* (1944).

KORDA, (Sir) Alexander
Sándor László Kellner; Puszta Turpósztó, Hungary 1893 – London 1956

British producer and director of Hungarian origin. Korda entered the film industry in his native Hungary, where he directed his first film in 1914, *Tutyu és Totyo*. After arrest under the Horthy regime, he fled to Vienna in 1919. He continued producing in Austria and Germany and spent three undistinguished years in Hollywood, before moving to Paramount's subsidiary in Paris in 1930, where he notably directed the classic *Marius* for Marcel Pagnol. In 1932, he arrived in Britain, where he founded London Films, and worked with his brothers, Zoltan and Vincent. JC

Bib: Karol Kulik, *Alexander Korda: The Man Who Could Work Miracles* (1975).

KOVAČEVIČ, Dušan
Belgrade 1949

Yugoslav playwright and screenwriter of Serbian origin. If there is such a thing as a Balkan social character, Kovačevič is the expert on it. With his trademark dark humour he creates a grotesque world, inhabited by protagonists who find themselves caught between an underworld of enterprising mobsters and the compelling rhetoric of nationalist bullies. Kovačevič is responsible for at least two of the most impressive Yugoslav movies ever made and enjoys something of a cult status within the country. He wrote the script for Slobodan Šijan's* Gypsy story *Ko to tamo peva?/Who's Singing over There?* (1980), considered to be the most popular Yugoslav film of all time and set on the day of the notorious Nazi bombing of Belgrade in April 1941. Kovačevič then worked with Emir Kusturica* on the controversial and grim war-goes-on-forever satire *Underground* (1995) which initially bore the working title *Once Upon a Time There Was a Country* and after winning at Cannes became the best-known film on the disintegration of Yugoslavia. With Bozidar Nikolić, Kovačevič directed his own satirical play *Balkanski spijun/Balkan Spy* (1984) which ridiculed the paranoia of the Yugoslav secret services. Two of his other scripts were directed by the Yugoslav Prague Group's* Goran Marković. *Sabirni centar/Meeting Point* (1988) is a satirical take on a fictional encounter between the living and the dead. Set in 1990s Belgrade, the Bulgarian–French co-production *Urnebesna tragedija/Burlesque Tragedy* (1995) is a metaphor for the state of Yugoslav affairs in the 1990s. It tells the eerie and farcical story of a group of psychiatric patients released from the hospital where they can no longer receive proper care. DI

KOVÁCS, András
Chidea, Romania 1925

Hungarian director. In the 1960s and 1970s, Kovács played an important role in Hungarian cinema both as a director and as president of the Association of Hungarian Film-makers, a vital organisation that mediated between political power and film-makers. He moved to Hungary from Romania in 1946 and graduated from the Academy of Theatre and Film Art in 1950. Between 1951 and 1957 he headed the Central Script Department of MAFILM, the state production company.

Kovács made his first film, *Zápor/Summer Rain*, in 1960, and his most important films were produced during this decade. His style is generally characterised by tight narrative structures and an abundance of dialogue; he also brought cinéma vérité* to Hungary in the 1960s. *Nehéz emberek/Difficult People* (1964) consists of parallel interviews based on part-fictional situations drawn from the lives of five Hungarian inventors who find it difficult to get their inventions approved by the authorities. Kovács' early films reveal a commitment to the idea that cinema should be the social and historical conscience of the nation. In his most important work, *Hideg napok/Cold Days* (1966), he deals with the atrocities committed by Hungarian fascists against Serbs and Jews during the war and raises the question of personal responsibility for historical events. During the 1970s, Kovács continued to make documentaries and cinéma vérité-type films, focusing on the political rigidity of the period and the powerlessness of socially conscious people. Though in the 1980s Kovács turned to more personal topics (such as the life of the wife of Count Károlyi, the first president of the Hungarian republic), in *Két választás Magyarországon/ Two Elections in Hungary* (1987), he returned to the more controversial political themes of his early works, here dealing with the abuse of the Hungarian parliamentary elections in 1985. KAB

Other Films Include: *Pesti háztetők/On the Roofs of Budapest, Isten őszi csillaga/Autumn Star* (1962); *Falak/Walls* (1968); *Extázis 7-10-ig/ Ecstasy from 7 to 10* (1969); *Staféta/Relay Race* (1970); *A magyar ugaron/Fallow Land* (1972); *Bekötött szemmel/Blindfold* (1975); *Labirintus/Labyrinth* (1976); *A Ménesgazda/The Stud Farm* (1978); *Októberi vasárnap/A Sunday in October* (1979); *Ideiglenes paradicsom/Temporary Paradise* (1980); *Szeretők/Lovers* (1983); *A vörös grófnő/The Red Countess* (1985); *A Nehéz emberek ma/Difficult People Today* (1996); *Egy Nehéz ember Kaliforniában/A Difficult Man in California* (1996).

KOVALOV, Oleg A.
Leningrad 1950

Russian director, critic and film historian. Kovalov graduated in 1983 from the film critics' faculty of VGIK*. He has made a number of montage films using archival footage which he reassembles to tell a story, such as *Ostrov mertvykh/Island of the Dead* (1992) about the demise of *art nouveau* as embodied in the great Russian film star of the silent era Vera Kholodnaya* (1893–1919), to whom this film is a tribute. Kovalov uses fragments from her films, and binds them into a surrealist collage of documentary, animation and feature film. *Sady skorpiona/The Gardens of the Scorpion* (1991) is a collage of fragments from documentaries and features made between 1925 and 1958. At the centre of the film stands the plot of a Cold War thriller of 1955 about Vasya Kochetkov, who visits the sales girl Valya and her grandmother and falls in love with the girl; but he is told that they are spies, and he adopts the role of fiancé to catch them and have them arrested. Kochetkov is played by the actor Vadim Grachev, who also featured in educational reels about alcohol abuse, which Kovalov discovered in the archives. Kochetkov's exposure to military instruction is shown to be as hypnotic as the treatment alcoholics receive in the clinic. Kovalov tries not to unify history or to create a myth, but rather to fragment and undermine the mythical perfection of the 1950s with their polished surface. *Kontsert dlya krysy/Concert for Rat* (1995) is a feature film based on the work of the Russian absurdist writer Daniil Kharms. For the centenary of cinema Kovalov wrote the script for *Russkaya Ideya/The Russian Idea* (1995) a film co-financed by the British Film Institute and directed by Sergei Selyanov*. In recent years he has been working on Sergei Eisenstein*; he has made a documentary about Eisenstein's life with extracts from his films entitled *Sergei Eizenshtein. Avtobiografiya/Sergei Eisenstein. An Autobiography* (1995), and he has reconstructed a film which Eisenstein might have made from the footage filmed in Mexico at the time of *¡Que Viva México!*, entitling it *Meksikanskaya fantaziya/A Mexican Fantasy* (1998). BB

KOZINTSEV, Grigori M. Kiev, Ukraine [Russian Empire] 1905 – Leningrad 1973

Soviet director and writer, who studied art with Alexandra Exter in Kiev and became involved in the production of street theatre after 1917. Kozintsev moved to Petrograd in 1920 and in 1921 co-founded FEKS with Leonid Trauberg*, with whom he worked closely until 1945, initially in theatre and from 1924 in cinema. Their joint films began with *Pokhozhdeniya Oktyabriny/The Adventures of Oktyabrina* (1924) and ended with *Prostye lyudi/Simple People* (1945, rel. 1956). Whereas Trauberg's subsequent career as a film-maker went into severe decline, Kozintsev went on to make two biographical films, *Pirogov* (1947) and *Belinskii/Belinsky* (1953), and an adaptation of Cervantes' *Don Quixote* (1957), with Nikolai Cherkasov* in the title role. This prepared Kozintsev for the Shakespeare adaptations that initiated his international reputation: *Gamlet/Hamlet* (1964), starring Innokenti Smoktunovsky*, and *Korol'Lir/King Lear* (1971).

Kozintsev also taught in various institutions, including VGIK* from 1922 until 1971, and published widely. His books include *Nash sovremennik Vil'yam Shekspir* (1962), published in English as *Shakespeare: Time and Conscience* (1966); *Prostranstvo tragedii* (1973), translated as *The Space of Tragedy* (1977); and *Glubokii ekran 'The Deep Screen'*. RT

KRAUZE, Antoni
Warsaw 1940

Polish director, who studied Fine Art and was active in the Students' Satirical Theatre before graduating from Łódź* in 1966. He was assistant to Krzysztof Zanussi* on *Struktura Kryształu/The Structure of Crystal* (1969). Krauze was involved in the documentary movement of the late 1960s which gave rise to the 'cinema of moral unrest'. His debut feature, *Palec Boży/The Finger of God* (1973), the story of an individual's fight against the system in pursuit of his ambition to be an actor, is based on an autobiographical novel by Tadeusz Zamechura. Krauze's great talent for comedy was revealed in his second feature, *Prognoza Pogody/Weather Forecast* (1983). Set in an old people's home, this farce manages to avoid cliché while making both serious and hilarious points about the Polish welfare state. The film fell foul of the authorities and was shelved during the period of martial law. Krauze had to wait until the political thaw of the late 1980s to make his next film, *Dziewczynka z Hotelu Excelsior/Girl from the Hotel Excelsior* (1988), about the holiday romances and obsessions of a middle-aged couple at a seaside health spa. AW

KULESHOV, Lev V.
Tambov, Russia 1899 – Moscow 1970

Soviet director and theorist. After studying art, Kuleshov joined Alexander Khanzhonkov's* studio in 1916 and worked as set designer for Yevgeni Bauer*. His first film as director was *Proekt inzhenera Praita/Engineer Prait's Project* (1918), which displayed elements of Constructivist machine worship. During the Civil War, he made newsreels and a feature combining documentary and acted footage, *Na Krasnom fronte/On the Red Front* (1920). In 1919 he organised his own workshop, the 'Kuleshov collective', at the State Film School (later VGIK*), which included Boris Barnet* and Vsevolod Pudovkin*. Since there was no film stock, they practised their ideas in a series of experiments called 'films without film' and developed the notion of the 'Kuleshov effect' in which, through montage*, each shot acquired a different shade of meaning according to its place in the sequence. But Kuleshov never believed in Sergei Eisenstein's* notion of 'typage', preferring instead to train actors or, as he called them, 'models' (*naturshchiki*), aiming for maximum screen expressivity with minimum gesture and effort. These ideas were further developed in *Neobychainye priklyucheniya Mistera Vesta v strane bol'shevikov/The Extraordinary Adventures of Mr West in the Land of the Bolsheviks* (1924), starring Alexandra Khokhlova*. Kuleshov next made a science-fiction film, *Luch smerti/Death Ray* (1925), and the Gold Rush drama *Po zakonu/ By the Law/Dura Lex* (1926). His first sound film was *Velikii uteshitel'/ The Great Consoler* (1933), a work of extraordinary complexity: superficially a biographical study of the American writer O. Henry, it examined the role of the artist in society, with clear implications for the Soviet artist under the new guidelines of Socialist Realism*. Subsequently his film-making career declined and his last film was *My s Urala/We Are from the Urals* (1944), but he continued to teach at VGIK until his death. Kuleshov was also a prolific writer, the first to use the term montage and to use it to define the specificity of cinema: his books include *Iskusstvo kino* ('*The Art of Cinema*', 1929), *Repetitsionnyi metod v kino* ('*The Rehearsal Method in Cinema*') and *Praktika kinorezhissury* ('*The Practice of Film Direction*', both 1935), and *Osnovy kinorezhissury* ('*The Foundations of Film Direction*', 1941). Kuleshov was the founding father of Soviet cinema: Pudovkin once remarked, 'We make films, Kuleshov made cinema.' RT

Bib: R. Levaco (ed., trans.), *Kuleshov on Film: Writings of Lev Kuleshov* (1974).

KULIDZHANOV, Lev A.   Tbilisi, Georgia [USSR] 1924

Soviet director. Kulidzhanov graduated from VGIK*, where he had studied with Sergei Gerasimov*, in 1955. His first film, *Damy/Ladies* (1954), based on a short story by Chekhov, was co-directed with Genrikh Oganisyan. Among his important early works were *Dom, v kotorom ya zhivu/The House I Live in* (1957), which follows the inhabitants of a new apartment block on the outskirts of Moscow from 1935 until after the war; *Otchii dom/My Father's House* (1959), in which a young woman discovers life on a collective farm; and *Kogda derev'ya byli bol'shimi/When the Trees Were Big* (1962), about the social regeneration of a drunken widower. It is on these three films that Kulidzhanov's reputation as a director increasingly rests. *Sinyaya tetrad'/The Blue Notebook* (1964) is about Lenin's life before the Russian Revolution. In 1970 Kulidzhanov made a version of Dostoyevsky's novel *Prestuplenie I nakazanie/Crime and Punishment*. The feature documentary *Zvezdnaya minuta/The Starry Minute* (1975) is about space flight and the first Soviet cosmonaut, Yuri Gagarin. It was followed by the television film *Karl Marks. Molodye gody/Karl Marx. The Early Years* (1980). Kulidzhanov's main claim to fame later, however, is as one of the leading cinematic bureaucrats of the Brezhnev years, and as a proponent of the conservative tendency in Soviet cinematography. The range of the positions of authority he occupied is indicative of the symbiotic relationship between the Soviet state and its 'loyal' artists. He was First Secretary of the Union of Film-makers of the USSR* from 1965 until he was ousted in 1986. He also served as a deputy of the Supreme Soviet over several years, and was, after 1976, a candidate member of the Central Committee of the Communist Party of the USSR. He has been the recipient of several official prizes and awards. JG

KUSTURICA, Emir   Sarajevo, Bosnia-Herzegovina 1954

Yugoslav film director of Bosnian origin. The most successful film-maker of the former Yugoslavia. Awards for his amateur films during high school led him to the FAMU* film school in Prague, and his third-year film *Guernica* gained first prize at the 1977 Karlovy Vary* film festival. After two films for Sarajevo television (*Nevjeste dolaze/The Brides are Coming*, 1978, and *Buffet Titanic*, 1980), he was given his first chance to shoot a feature in 1981. His debut was a triumph: *Sječaš li se Dolly Bell?/Do You Remember Dolly Bell?* (1981), a story of Sarajevo teenagers sampling the first taste of pop culture in the 1950s, was awarded the Golden Lion at Venice. With his second film, *Otac na službenom putu/When Father was away on Business* (1985), he stayed in Sarajevo but went back in time to 1948, mixing the political (Tito's break with Stalin) with a picturesque portrayal of old family traditions falling apart. Winning the 1985 Palme d'Or at Cannes and an Oscar nomination for Best Foreign Language Film established Kusturica as a film-maker of international standing. He turned down interesting of-fers in order to shoot *Dom za vešanje/Time of the Gypsies* (1989) in his typical slow-motion way: the production took almost two years. The film won the 1989 Best Director award at Cannes and established Kusturica as an 'oneiric' film-maker. Miloš Forman* invited him to teach at Columbia University in New York, where he turned a stu-dent's original screenplay into *Arizona Dream* (1993), dreamt up mostly for French money and combining his own stylistic tics with rather bizarre casting (Jerry Lewis, Faye Dunaway). His pro-Yugoslav position during the war in Bosnia made him 'unwanted' in his native city, Sarajevo. His 1995 *Bila jednom jedna zemlja/Underground*, a co-production with France, Germany and Hungary (with some partici-pation from Serbia) scripted by Dusan Kovacević*, won the Palme d'Or at the Cannes film festival. The film, starring Miki Manojlović* and Lazar Ristovski, tackles the history of Yugoslavia between 1941 and the break-up in the 1990s. It was received internationally with a mixture of admiration and criticism. The allegations that the film was nothing else but Serbian propaganda led to Kusturica's short-lived public withdrawal from film-making in 1996. Soon thereafter he re-turned to the Gypsy topic in his consciously non-political compendium of exotic imagery, *Crna macka, beli macor/Black Cat, White Cat* (1998), set on the shores of the Danube in Belgrade and revolving

140

around the intricate interactions between several extended Romany families. The film won the director a Silver Lion at the Venice Film Festival. Kusturica's next project is a Holocaust drama based on D. M. Thomas's *The White Hotel*. SP

KUTZ, Kazimierz
Szopienice, Silesia 1929

Polish director. Kutz started his prolific career as assistant to Andrzej Wajda* on *Pokolenie/A Generation* (1955). One of the 'Polish School', his early features drew on his adolescence and on the war experience. In his debut feature, *Krzyż Walecznych/Cross of War* (1959), he linked three stories by Joseph Hen about society coming to terms with the end of the war. Kutz is best known for his 'Silesian' trilogy – *Sól Ziemi Czarnej/Salt of the Black Country* (1970), *Perła w Koronie/The Pearl in the Crown* (1972) and *Paciorki Jednego Różańca/The Beads from a Rosary* (1980) – in which he examines different aspects of his native region and its long, troubled history (there have been disputes over the ownership of Silesia, in western Poland on the border with Germany, for centuries). Kutz has worked extensively for theatre and television, as director of the Cracow Television Centre. His *Smierc jak kromka chleba/Death as a Slice of Bread* (1994) explored the 1981 killing of striking miners in the Wujek mine by the authorities, a tragic postscript to the Silesian trilogy. AW

Other Films Include: *Slowo honoru/A Word of Honour* (1953); *Jesienny dzien/An Autumn Day* (1959); *Nikt nie wola/Nobody's Calling* (1960); *Ludzie z pociagu/Night Train* (1961); *Tarpany/Wild Horses* (1962); *Milczenie/Silence* (1963); *Upal/Heat* (1964); *Ktokolwiek wie.../Whoever May Know* (1966); *Skok/The Leap* (1967); *Znikad do nikad/From Nowhere to Nowhere* (1975); *Linia/The Line* (1975); *Na strazy swej stac bede/I Shall Always Stand Guard* (1984); *Wkrotce nadejda bracia/The Brothers Will Come Soon* (1986); *Straszny sen Dzidziusia Gorkiewicza/The Terrible Dream of Babyface Gorkiewicz* (1993); *Zawrocony/Converted* (1994, Pol.); *Pulkownik Kwiatkowski/Colonel Kwiatkowski* (1995).

KVIRIKADZE, Irakli M.
Tbilisi, Georgia [USSR] 1939

Georgian director and scriptwriter. After growing up in Batumi and a period studying journalism in Tbilisi, Kvirikadze moved to Moscow, graduating from Grigori Chukhrai's* workshop at VGIK* in 1970. He returned there to teach for a period in 1985. Kvirikadze writes the screenplays for his own films, including the short *Kuvshin/The Jar* (1971), *Gorodok Anara/The Little Town of Anara* (1976), *Plovets/The Swimmer* (1981) and *Vozvrashchenie Olmelsa/The Return of Olmels*

141

(1985), and for such films as *Robinzonada, ili moy angliiskii dedush-ka/Robinsonada, or My English Grandfather* (1987), directed by his wife, Nana Dzhordzhadze, and Valeri Ogorodnikov*'s *Bumazhnye glaza Prishvina/Prishvin's Paper Eyes*. His most important film, *The Swimmer*, a tragi-comedy of great lyrical beauty, uses the experience of three generations of Georgian swimmers, in 1913, 1947 and 1980, to effect what is both a pointed allegory of life under three political regimes and a questioning of our ability to represent the past adequately. It was shown in a version shorn of much of the central Stalin section, and not released as Kvirikadze made it until 1987. Kvirikadze returned to the subject of Stalin in *Puteshestvie Tovarishcha Stalina v Afriku/Comrade Stalin Goes to Africa* (1991), in which a Jewish Georgian bottle-factory worker is prevailed upon to become Stalin's double. The film continues Kvirikadze's interrogation of history and its representation. During the 1990s he has written several screenplays, notably the one for Dzhordhzadze's *Mille et une recettes du cuisinier amoureux/A Chef in Love* (1996). JG

L

LAMAČ, Karel
also Karl or Carl; Prague [then Austria-Hungary] 1897 – Hamburg, West Germany 1952

Czech actor and director. Karel Lamač originally studied as a pharmacist, produced film reportage during World War I, and subsequently gained employment as a film technician. Admired for his 'matinee idol' good looks, he was first famous as an actor, then as a prolific and cosmopolitan director, working, according to some estimates, on over 200 films. He built the independent Kavalírka film studios in 1926, and in conjunction with his then wife Anny Ondra* formed the Ondra-Lamač company in Berlin in 1930. Lamač directed the first two films based on Hašek's *The Good Soldier Švejk* in 1926: *Dobrý voják Švejk/The Good Soldier Švejk* and *Švejk na frontě/Švejk at the Front*. Working regularly in Western Europe, particularly Germany, he also made numerous multi-language versions and popular light comedies starring Vlasta Burian* and Ondra. During World War II, he directed features in Britain. PH

Other Films Include: *Gilly po prvé v Praze/Gilly's First Visit to Prague* (1920); *Chyt'te ho!/Catch Him!*, *Bílý ráj/The White Paradise* (1924); *Karel Havlíček Borovský* [co-dir], *Lucerna/The Lantern* (1925); *Velbloud uchem jehly/Camel through the Needle's Eye* (1926);

142

Saxophon Susi (1928, Ger.); *Das Mädel mit der peitsche/The Girl with the Whip* (1929, Ger.); *On a jeho sestra/He and His Sister, Die Fledermaus* (1931, Fr.); *Funebrák, Lelíček ve službách Sherlocka Holmese/ Lelíček in the Service of Sherlock Holmes, Baby* [Fr.] (1932); *Die Tochter des Regiments/Daughter of the Regiment* (1933, Aust.); *Polská krev/Polish Blood, Klein Dorrit/Little Dorrit* [Ger.], *Knock-Out* [Ger.] (1934); *Der Hund von Baskerville/The Hound of the Baskervilles* (1936, Ger.); *They Met in the Dark* (1943, UK); *It Happened One Sunday* (1944, UK); *La Colère des Dieux/Anger of the Gods* (1946, Fr.); *Die Diebin von Bagdad/The Thief of Bagdad* (1952, Ger.).

LATINOVITS, Zoltán
Budapest 1931 –
Balatonszemes 1976

Hungarian actor. From 1959 until his suicide in 1976, Latinovits played leading roles in forty-seven films and twenty-one television movies, acted in more than two dozen important stage productions, directed two plays, and published two books. He studied architecture, and though he never went to acting school he became the most employed actor in the Hungarian cinema of the 1960s. His talent was remarkably versatile, although he mostly played the energetic, impatient, non-conformist intellectual. His 'intellectual masculinity' was close to that of Marcello Mastroianni (Latinovits dubbed Mastroianni's voice in *La dolce vita*, 1960) but he was more energetic and much more volatile. His powerful character led many directors to cast him in aggressive or negative roles, often as evil officers or other diabolical types.

Latinovits was a non-conformist, and he had many conflicts with Hungarian cultural bureaucracy. He tried to create his own theatre with selected actors and directors but the cultural and political authorities thwarted his plans. His suicide was a great shock in Hungary. Many poems were written in tribute, and he became a symbol of the intellectual and moral integrity of the artist. KAB

Other Films Include: *Gyalog a mennyországba/Walking to Heaven* (1959); *Oldás és kötés/Cantata* (1960); *Szegénylegények/The Round-up* (1965); *Hideg napok/Cold Days* (1966); *Falak/Walls, Fiúk a térről/ Boys from the Square* (1967); *Csend és kiáltás/Silence and Cry* (1968); *Isten hozta őrnagy úr!/The Tót Family, Utazás a koponyám körül/ Journey round My Skull* (1969); *Szindbád* (1971); *A magyar ugaron/ Fallow Land* (1972); *Az ötödik pecsét/The Fifth Seal* (1976).

LENICA, Jan
Poznań 1928

Polish animator and poster designer. A member of the left-wing avant-garde, Lenica was instrumental in establishing animation as an art form in Poland. Films like *Był Sobie Raz/Once Upon a Time* (1957, made with Walerian Borowczyk*) and *Nowy Janko Muzykant/Janko the Musician* (1960) used graphic techniques to create surreal and often darkly humorous parables of life. Winning international acclaim allowed Lenica to find finance in the West and maintain a relatively independent status. A growing political disillusionment is evident in his later films, for example *Landscape* (1975), where Lenica grapples with the totalitarianism that had seduced and betrayed him. AW

Other Films Include: *Dom/House* (1958); *Monsieur Tête* (1959, Fr.); *Labirynt/Labyrinth* (1963); *La Femme fleur* [Fr.], *A* [Fr.] (1964); *Adam II* (1969); *Ubu et la Grande Gidouille* (1979, Fr.).

LENIN, Vladimir I.

Simbirsk, Russia 1870 – Moscow 1924

Soviet revolutionary leader. Lenin, who led the October Revolution in 1917, was one of the first to realise the political potential of cinema in a backward and illiterate country like post-Revolutionary Russia, remarking: 'Of all the arts, for us cinema is the most important.' Unlike many of his contemporaries, he also appreciated that, as a successful propaganda medium, cinema would have to entertain its audiences as well as persuade them, hence his suggestion of a ratio between propaganda and entertainment films, later known as the 'Lenin proportion'. On 27 August 1919 he signed the decree creating the first nationalised film industry in the world. RT

LINDA, Bogusław

Toruń 1952

Polish actor and director. As one of the leading young actors associated with the 'cinema of moral unrest', Linda became an 'everyman' figure, the average young man trying to make his way in contemporary Polish society. His starring roles in films like Krzysztof Kieślowski's* *Przypadek/Blind Chance* (1987), Agnieszka Holland's* *Kobieta Samotna/A Woman Alone* (1981), Janusz Zaorski's* *Matka Królów/ Mother of the Kings* (1982; first shown 1987) and a whole body of work which was finally seen in the political thaw of 1987, won him a popular following. Linda tried to move away from his politically symbolic roles in the mid-1980s, taking a diverse range of parts which were well received by the public. In 1990 he made his directorial debut with *Seszele/Seychelles*, about the longing to escape from everyday realities, as experienced by two psychiatric patients who subsequently take refuge in the labyrinthian passages of an opera building. The film was panned by Polish critics almost before it was finished, and was poorly distributed and promoted. However, *Seszele* soon became a cult hit with audiences, both in Poland and in Paris, where it won two student festival awards. He continues to act in Polish and Czech films. AW

144

LITVINOVA, Renata M.

Russian actress and scriptwriter. In 1989 Litvinova graduated from the scriptwriting faculty of VGIK*, where she had studied in the workshop of Kira Paramonova and Ivan Kuznetsov. Her earliest screenplays are those for *Ochen´ lyubimaya Rita, poslednyaya s nei vstrecha/ Very Beloved Rita, the Last Meeting with Her*, a short film directed by A. Ayapova in 1988; with Oleg Morozov and Andreas Schmidt, for *Leningrad. Noyabr´/Leningrad. November* (1990), also directed by Morozov and Schmidt, which tells of an émigré who returns from Cologne to visit his native city for the last time; and for Valeri Rubinchik's *Nelyubov´/Not Love* (1991), the melodramatic story of a girl who cannot return the love of either of her suitors. In 1992 she wrote the script for the film *Traktoristy-2/Tractor Drivers 2*, a parodic 're-make' by the alternative film-makers, the brothers Gleb and Igor Aleinikov of the classic 1939 collective farm musical *Tractor Drivers* by Ivan Pyriev*. The script displays both a precise engagement with the original and a wild and increasingly outrageous imagination. In recent years Litvinova's career has been closely associated with that of the director Kira Muratova*. In 1994 she played the part of Liliya and wrote the nurse's ecstatic monologues for the film *Uvlechen'ya/Enthusiasms*. In Muratova's 1997 *Tri istorii/Three Stories*, the longest, central episode *Ofeliya/Ophelia* is also written by Litvinova, and she plays the part of the coolly murderous, eponymous heroine. Litvinova's unique, mannered acting style and delivery, and her stunning Monroesque blonde looks have turned her into one of the most fashionable personalities of the new Russian cinema, but this should not detract from her great talents as a scriptwriter, with an acute ear for the absurdities of contemporary speech. It is this that has made her collaboration with Muratova so fruitful, but she continues to provide material for other contemporary directors. She wrote the scripts for both Aleksandr Sukochev's tale of female desperation *Printsipial´nyi i zhalostlivyi vzgkuad/A Principled and Pitiful Glance* (1995) and Yuri Grymov's *Muzhskie otkroveniia/Male Revelations* (1996), and the latest film by Valeri Todorovsky*, *Strana glukhikh/ Land of the Deaf* (1998) was based on a Litvinova story and contains another of her extraordinary female characters, the deaf and dumb Yaya, who wishes to escape from contemporary Moscow into the paradisiacal world of the deaf. JG

LIVNEV, Sergei D.
Born 1964

Russian director, producer and scriptwriter. Livnev graduated from VGIK*, where he had studied scriptwriting and cinematography, in 1987. He began his career as a scriptwriter with the script for Sergei Solovyov's* *Assa* (1988). In 1993 he set up the studio L-Film, turning himself into a producer. Between 1995 and 1998 he was the director of the Gorky Film Studios, Moscow, launching a 'low budget project' designed to cater primarily for the video market. His film *Kiks* (1991) deals with doubles and the confused identities of a rock singer who is a drug addict and is therefore 'replaced' by her twin sister. *Serp i molot/Hammer and Sickle* (1994) explores the discrepancy between reality and model, this time in a historical context. The film is about a demand made by Stalin in 1936 that the country should have more soldiers: Yevdokiya Kuznetsova turns into Yevdokim Kuznetsov, a model worker of the metro construction brigade. The 'hero' is awarded a medal and married to Liza Voronina, a *kolkhoz* worker. They become the models for Vera Mukhina's famous Moscow statue, 'The Worker and the Peasant', and an exemplary Soviet family: they adopt a girl who has been orphaned during the Spanish Civil War. Then Yevdokim rebels: he wants to live his own life, not a model Soviet existence. He challenges Stalin's control of his life, attacks the leader, and is shot. Paralysed and unable to speak, Yevdokim is once more turned into a 'hero': he has supposedly saved Stalin's life and is exhibited as a museum piece. Livnev is a postmodernist, who parodies the culture of the rock underground and of Stalinism in these two films. He exposes the inability of people to live up to the expectations and ideals set by the society in which they live. BB

ŁÓDŹ Film School (Państwowa Wyższa Szkoła Filmowa, Telewizyjna i Teatralna Im. Leona Schillera)

Polish film school. The Łódź Film School was established in 1947 after the dissolution of Poland's first film school in Cracow. It has a world-wide reputation for excellence and its graduates (among them Andrzej Wajda*, Roman Polanski, Jerzy Skolimowski* and Krzysztof Zanussi*) have become some of the most accomplished directors and cinematographers of world cinema. For many years, attending the school was the only route into the profession in Poland, and graduation secured a place in one of the industry's film units. Some of Poland's finest film-makers lectured at the school: Aleksander Ford* (1948–68), Andrzej Munk* (1957–61) and Jerzy Kawalerowicz* (since 1980). The school's current director, Professor Wojciech Has*, has the difficult job of guiding it into the post-communist world. A panorama of films by alumni of the school was organised by the Museum of Modern Art in New York and toured various locations in the US in 1998–9. AW

LOPUSHANSKY, Konstantin
Dnepropetrovsk, Ukraine [USSR] 1947

Russian director and screenwriter. After studying music at the Kazan and Leningrad Conservatoires, Lopushansky completed the Higher Courses for Directors at Goskino, and worked with Andrey

146

Tarkovsky* on *Stalker*. His first film, the short *Solo* (1979), which is about a performance of Shostakovich's Fifth Symphony, shows the influence of that work. It was followed by *Pis'ma mertvogo cheloveka/Letters from a Dead Man* (1986), a vision of the world after nuclear war, on which one of the scriptwriters was Boris Strugatsky, also the co-author of the source for *Stalker*. The dead man of the title is a professor, played by Rolan Bykov, who writes to his lost son of his despair at the hubris of modern science. Lopushansky returned to the subject of a post-catastrophic world in the religious and ecological fable *Posetitel' muzeya/A Visitor to a Museum* (1989). In 1994 he made *Russkaya simfoniya/Russian Symphony*, a fantastic meditation on contemporary experience in which a Russian intellectual attempts to save children from imminent apocalypse. JG

LUGOSI, Béla
Béla Ferenc Dezsö Blaskó; Lugos, Austria-Hungary, (now Lugoj, Romania) 1882 – Los Angeles, US 1956

Hungarian-American actor. Béla Lugosi used the name of his birthplace as his alias and brought it to legendary fame through his evil screen personae. He began as a stage actor early in the century and played in a number of Hungarian silents, such as Mihály Kertész's* *Az Ezredes/The Colonel* (1917) and *Kilencvenkilenc/99* (1918), Alfréd Deésy's *A Leopárd/The Leopard* (1917), *Leoni Leo* (1917), and *Casanova* (1918). For these early roles he occasionally used the alias, Arisztid Olt. In 1919 he emigrated, first to Germany, and then to the US in 1921 where he started on Broadway and eventually moved on to Hollywood. His most famous role was Count Dracula in Tod Browning's classic, *Dracula* (1931). Lugosi has played in over eighty films, mostly typecast as villains, vampires, ghosts, monsters and Frankenstein. Toward the end of his career he appeared in the films of maverick director, Ed Wood. DI

LUNACHARSKY, Anatoli V.
Poltava, Ukraine [Russian Empire] 1879 – Menton, France 1933

Soviet politician and writer. As People's Commissar for Enlightenment from 1917 to 1929, Lunacharsky held overall political responsibility for Soviet cinema in its formative period. A liberal by nature, he tolerated in his interpretation of Lenin's* views on cinema a wide variety of approaches, reminding film-makers that 'boring agitation is counter-agitation'. His wife, Natalia Rozenel, regularly appeared in vamp-like parts in films such as Konstantin Eggert* and Vladimir Gardin's* *Medvezh'ya svad'ba/The Bear's Wedding* (1926), which Lunacharsky co-scripted. He also wrote the scripts for a number of other popular melodramas, including Gardin's *Slesar' i kantsler/*

The Locksmith and the Chancellor (1924, co-scripted by Vsevolod Pudovkin*) and Grigori Roshal's *Salamandra/The Salamander* (1928), in which he made a cameo appearance. He published a book, *Kino na zapade i u nas* (*Cinema in the West and Here*, 1928), and numerous articles on cinema. RT

LUNGIN, Pavel S.   Moscow 1949

Russian director and scriptwriter. The son of the famous scriptwriter and playwright Semyon Lungin, Pavel Lungin studied structural linguistics at Moscow University, and then completed the Higher Courses for Scriptwriters in 1975. He worked for several years as a scriptwriter before making his directorial debut with *Taksi-Blyuz/ Taxi-Blues* (1989), a Franco-Russian co-production about the relationship between an alcoholic musician, played by Pyotr Mamonov, from the group *Zvuki mu*, and the Moscow taxi driver Shlykov. The film drew attention for its bold, if only partially successful attempt to blend Russian elements – an unblinking evocation of the poverty and misery of modern urban life – with an energy, rapid montage and excess familiar from American crime thrillers. Lungin attracted further controversy with his next feature *Luna Park* (1992), in which a young anti-Semitic Muscovite muscle-builder, whose group are devoted to achieving a racially pure Russia, discovers that he is half-Jewish. In 1992 he also made the documentary film *GULag – Sekret schast'ia/The GULag – The Secret of Happiness*. In 1995 he contributed *La Mer de toutes les Russies/The Sea of All the Russias* to the portmanteau film in homage to Jean Vigo, *À Propos de Nice, La Suite/À Propos de Nice, Part Two*. His 1996 thriller *Liniia zhizni/The Line of Life* did not attract the attention his first two features did. JG

LUSTIG, Arnost   Prague 1926

Czech-American writer and screenwriter. A Holocaust survivor, award-winning Arnost Lustig wrote a number of short stories which became the literary source for some of the best-known Czech films about the Holocaust. Zbynek Brynych's *Transport z raje/Transport from Paradise* (1962) is an account of the shocking reality of life and death existing side-by-side in the Nazi model-ghetto of Terezin. Jan Nemec's* shattering masterpiece, *Démanty noci/Diamonds of the Night* (1964) follows the desperate escape of two Jewish boys from a camp-bound convoy. Antonín Moskalyk's *Dita Saxova* (1967), starring the beautiful Krystyna Mikolajewska, focuses on postwar traumatic syndrome. *Modlitba pro Katerinu Horovitzovou/A Prayer for Katherina Horovoitzova* (1969) is a moral treatise about the American practice of trading Jewish lives for imprisoned Nazis. The film was banned for twenty-one years and only released in 1990. After 1968,

Lustig emigrated to the US. He has been an active proponent of Czech culture abroad, and is currently a literature professor at American University in Washington, DC. DI

M

MACEDONIA – see YUGOSLAVIA (former)

MACHATÝ, Gustav
Prague [then Austria-Hungary] 1901 – Munich, West Germany 1963

Czech director. Gustav Machatý worked as a pianist in a movie theatre, actor and scriptwriter before directing the farce *Teddy by kouřil/ Teddy'd Like a Smoke* (1919). He left for Hollywood in 1920, where he reputedly worked on films by D. W. Griffith and Erich von Stroheim. He returned to Czechoslovakia, and in 1926 made a highly acclaimed feature, *Kreutzerova sonáta/The Kreutzer Sonata*, based on the Tolstoy story and notable for its impressive sets and expressionist influence. He consolidated his reputation with the enormously successful *Erotikon* (1929), and his first two sound features, *Ze soboty na neděli/From Saturday to Sunday* (1931), and *Extase/Ecstasy* (1932), which earned the condemnation of the Vatican at the time and subsequent cult status for Hedy Lamarr's nude scene. His films brought together several talents, including the poet Vitězslav Nezval, one of the co-founders of Czech surrealism, who worked on all three of the latter films, Alexander Hammid*, the avant-garde director and future documentarist, as well as the key figures of the 'Czech school' of cinematography, Jan Stallich, Václav Vich and Otto Heller. The three films provide an often subtle analysis of male–female relations, given an added force through the poetic lyricism of Machatý's style. *Extase* marked the end of Machatý's Czech career and, after films in Italy and Austria, he was signed to a Hollywood contract. He did second unit work on *The Good Earth* (1936) and *Madame X* (1937), and directed *Jealousy* (1945). He also made a 'Crime Does Not Pay' short and the B-feature *Within the Law* (1939). After directing *Suchkind 312/Missing Child 312* (1956) in West Germany, he was appointed professor at the Munich Film School. Attempts to negotiate further projects in Czechoslovakia came to nothing. PH

Other Films Include: *Švejk v civilu/Švejk in Civilian Life* (1927); *Načeradec, král kibiců/Načeradec, King of the Kibitzers* (1932); *Nocturno* (1934, Aust.); *Ballerine* (1936, It.); *The Wrong Way Out* [short] (1938, US).

MACHULSKI, Juliusz
Olsztyn 1955

Polish director and actor. Machulski graduated from film school in 1978 and heads the Zebra Film Unit. Poland's answer to a 'Hollywood Movie Brat', Machulski is known for his fast-paced popular comedies. His second feature, *Seksmisja/Sexmission* (1984), a sci-fi comedy starring Jerzy Stuhr*, attracted rave reviews and a large public in Poland, although his uninspired and stereotyped portrayal of women in a world without men was criticised abroad. His later films include *Kingsajz/Kingsize* (1987), a whimsical comedy/political allegory starring Stuhr and the new Polish sex symbol, Katarzyna Figura. His latest action-adventure comedies *Kiler/Killer* (1997) and *Kilerów 2-óch/ Killer 2* (1999) enjoyed wide popularity in Poland. AW

Other Films Include: *Vabank* (1981); *Vabank II czyli Riposta/Revenge* (1984); *Szwadron/Squadron* (1992); *Déjà vu* (1989); *V.I.P.* (1991); *Girl Guide* (1995); *Kilerów 2-óch/Killer 2* (1999).

MAKAROVA, Tamara F.
St Petersburg 1907

Soviet actress. Makarova started in film in 1927. Although she subsequently appeared in films by Vsevolod Pudovkin* (*Dezertir/The Deserter*, 1933) and Mikhail Chiaureli* (*Velikoe zarevo/The Great Dawn*, 1938, and *Klyatva/The Vow*, 1946), her career is closely associated with the director Sergei Gerasimov*, for whom she played leading roles in *Semero smelykh/The Brave Seven* (1936), *Komsomol'sk* (1938), *Bol'shaya zemlya/The Great Earth* (1944) and *Molodaya gvardiya/The Young Guard* (1947). Makarova usually embodied women in extremity and, with Lyubov Orlova*, was one of the key figures in defining the officially determined role of women in the Stalin* period. She taught at VGIK* from 1943 and shared a workshop with Gerasimov. RT

MAKAVEJEV, Dušan
Belgrade, Serbia 1932

Yugoslav film director and scriptwriter of Serbian origin. The most controversial Yugo-slav director began his film career with shorts after graduating in psychology and film and writing film criticism. From the beginning, his films were marked with a sweet smell of forbidden fruit, making him one of the most original members of the 'Black Wave'*: *Čovek nije tica/A Man Is Not a Bird* (1965) aimed to 'ironise the working class'; *Ljubavni slučaj ili tragedija službenice PTT/Love Affair, or the Case of the Missing Switchboard Operator/Switchboard Operator* (1967) focused on a love story between a rat exterminator and a telephone operator; *Nevinost bez zaštite/Innocence Unprotected* (1968) combined a 1942 semi-documentary of the same name with images of the participants twenty-five years later. But the real breakthrough came in 1971, with *W. R. – Misterije organizma/W. R. – Mysteries of the Organism*. This film collage, starring Milena Dravić*, and based on the theories of sexual psychologist Wilhelm Reich, was an international hit but was judged so 'subversive' in Yugoslavia that it was not officially shown there until 1986. Makavejev was forced to work abroad: he shot *Sweet Movie* (1974) in France and Holland, *Montenegro* (1981, also *Pigs and Pearls*) in Sweden, and *The Coca Cola Kid* (1985) in Australia. These films did not receive the critical acclaim of his early work, and *Manifesto* (1988, US/Yugoslavia) and *Gorilla Bathes at Noon* (1993, Ger.) failed to revive his fortunes. Makavejev was involved in various consultancy projects in Europe and the US and in 1994, his film, *A Hole in the Soul* (1994, produced by BBC Scotland), was an intimate self-portrait which was shown at the Edinburgh Film Festival. SP

Bib: Daniel J. Goulding, 'Makavejev', *Five Film-makers* (1994).

MAKK, Károly   Berettyóújfalu 1925

Hungarian director. Makk is one of the most productive Hungarian directors of his generation. He graduated from the Academy of Theatre and Film Art in 1950 and has been an active and versatile film-maker for forty years. He tried his hand at many different genres and styles, including light comedy (*Liliomfi*, 1954), social drama (*Megszállottak/The Obsessed*, 1961), and lyrical psychological drama (*Szerelem/Love*, 1970). He has also made films for television. Whatever the genre, the distinctive features of Makk's work are his talent for directing actors and his ability to evoke the precise psychological atmosphere of a situation. His unquestionable masterpiece is *Szerelem*, which won several international prizes. This film was based on two autobiographical short stories by the Hungarian writer Tibor Déry, who spent four years in prison after 1956 for his activities in the revolution. During his prison years Déry wrote letters to his aged and ailing mother, and, to make his absence bearable for her, pretended he was abroad making a film. Makk's film is a moving testimony to the strength of emotion and loyalty in defiance of the humiliations imposed by a dictatorial power. KAB

Other Films Include: *9-es kórterem/Ward no. 9* (1955); *Mese a 12 találatról/Tale of the Twelve Scores* (1956); *Ház a sziklák alatt/House Under the Rocks* (1958); *Mit csinált a feleséged 3-tól 5-ig?/His Majesty's Dates* (1964); *Macskajáték/Cat Play* (1974); *Egy erkölcsös éjszaka/ A Very Moral Night* (1977); *Két történet a félmúltból/Two Stories from the Recent Past* (1980); *Egymásra nézve/Another Way* (1982); *Játszani kell/Playing for Keeps* (1984); *Az utolsó kézirat/The Last Manuscript* (1987); *Magyar rekviem/A Hungarian Requiem* (1990); *Drága kisfiam/Dear Son* (1994); *Szeressük egymást gyerekek!/Let's*

Love Each Other, Chums (1996); *A Játékos/The Gambler* (1997, Hung./ UK).

MAKOVETSKY, Sergei V.   Kiev, Ukraine [USSR] 1958

Russian actor. Makovetsky studied at the Shchukin Theatre School from 1976 to 1980, when he began work as an actor at the Vakhtangov Theatre in Moscow. His cinematic career began in 1982. In 1990 he started to act at the Roman Viktiuk Theatre in Moscow. In 1992 he became an Honoured Artist of the Russian Federation. Makovetsky is the most gifted of the current generation of film actors with an extraordinary range from engaging comedy to neurotic inwardness to sinister threat. He has acted in films by many of the leading new directors of the 1990s including particularly Vladimir Khotinenko* and Alexei Balabanov*. For Khotinenko he was especially memorable in the title role in *Makarov* (1993), the story of a poet whose life is turned upside down when he purchases a Makarov pistol. For Balabanov he played the eponymous hero in *Trofim*, Balabanov's episode in *Pribytie poezda/The Arrival of the Train* (1995) a portmanteau film made by young directors to celebrate the centenary of cinema. Balabanov's film, made in sepia, potently evokes the atmosphere of pre-Revolutionary cinema in a story of a doomed peasant who comes to the capital, and he and Makovetsky would return to the underside of the pre-Revolutionary world in *Pro urodov i lyudei/Of Freaks and Men* (1998), a chilling tale of the pornography and sadomasochism that were also among the first fruits of cinema. This film won the Nike, the Russian Oscar, for best film of 1998, and Makovetsky gives a mesmeric performance as a sinister pornographer and blackmailer. Other notable recent roles include those in Kira Muratova's* *Tri istorii/Three Stories* (1997) and in Petr Todorovsky's* *Retro Vtroem/Ménage à Trois* (1998), a not entirely successful attempt to transpose Abram Room's* triangular love story *Bed and Sofa* to contemporary Moscow, in which Makovetsky reveals his skills and charm as a comic actor. Perhaps the most accomplished performance of his film career so far, however, is that of the intense and haunted Dmitri Shostakovich in Edgardo Cozarinsky's *Skripka Rotshil'da/Le Violon de Rothschild/Rothschild's Violin* (1996). JG

MAMIN, Yuri B.   Leningrad 1946

Russian director. Mamin graduated from the Leningrad State Institute of Theatre, Music and Cinema in 1969 as a theatrical director. In 1982 he completed the Higher Courses for Directors at Goskino, where he studied under Eldar Ryazanov*. His short 1986 comedy *Prazdnik Neptuna/Neptune's Feast* uses the device of Nikolai Gogol's play *The*

Inspector General – foolish provincials try to impress outsiders – to expose contemporary venality and bureaucratic incompetence. The satirical note prevails in his 1988 feature *Fontan/The Fountain*, in which events in a ghastly apartment block on the outskirts of Leningrad serve as a microcosm of all the absurdities and contradictions of the *perestroika* years. Mamin's next film, *Bakenbardy/Side Whiskers* (1990), is a savage dissection of the forces threatening to tear Russia apart in its story of the clash between the social misfits of the 'Capella' gang and their enemies, the muscle-bound 'Bashers'. The 'Bashers' are then co-opted into a new grouping, the 'Side Whiskers', who sport Pushkinian facial hair as a sign of their Russian nationalism. Mamin's films provide a picture of modern Russian life that is free of illusions, and *Okno v Parizh/Salades russes/A Window on Paris* (1993), in which a window in St Petersburg magically opens on to the rooftops of Paris, offers further scope for irony, this time over the unresolved ambivalence that Russians feel towards the rest of Europe. In 1998 Mamin co-directed *Gor'ko!/Kiss the Bride!*, a comedy about a wedding ceremony that goes disastrously wrong, with Arkadi Tigai. JG

MANAKI BROTHERS
Milton   Avdela, Greece 1882 – Bitola, Macedonia 1964
and
Yanaki   Avdela, Greece 1879–1960

Macedonian photographer, pioneer of Yugoslav cinema. His brother Yanaki taught Manaki photography and sent him a Bioscope No. 300 camera from London in 1905. His first views of family life, religious rituals and craftsmen's work still have great ethnological value. He later specialised in more structured documentary reportage of political visits and meetings, such as Sultan Reshad's visit to Bitola in 1911. He was official court photographer to the Turkish sultan and the kings of Romania and Yugoslavia. In 1921 he opened, with his brother, the 'Manaki' film theatre in Bitola, which was destroyed by fire in 1939. After World War II he was recognised as a pioneer of Yugoslav cinema and the press award given at the national film festival in Pula* was named after him. The film festival in Bitola, Macedonia, is named after the Manaki Brothers. In his Cannes' winner, *To Vlemma tou Odyssea/Ulysses' Gaze* (1995), Greek director Theo Angelopoulos symbolically explored the life-path of Milton Manaki. SP

MANCHEVSKI, Milcho   Skopje 1959

A Macedonian-born and US-educated film-maker, Manchevski's 1994 film *Pred dozhdot/Before the Rain* (1994), starring Rade Serbedzija*, was hailed as one of the best cinematic representations of the cultural and ethnic problems of the Balkans. A co-production between Great Britain, France and Macedonia, with dialogue in several languages, and relying on a non-conventional narrative structure, beautiful cinematography and music, *Before the Rain* was seen as part of an important new trend which took East European film beyond the confines of a specific region or country. The film won the Golden Lion at the Venice Film Festival. Manchevski, who also works in experimental film and music videos, is constantly on the move between Europe and North America. He quit the set of Miramax's *Ravenous* over creative differences and is now working on his next *auteur*ist project which will be set in Macedonia around the turn of the century and in present-day New York. DI

MANOJLOVIĆ, Miki   Predrag Manojlović; Belgrade 1950

Yugoslav actor of Serbian origin. Manojlović has been cast in a wide range of roles, but is at his best when playing womanising, wheeler-dealer Balkan subjects. He is best-known internationally for the roles of Mesa in *Otac na sluzbenom putu/When Father Was Away on Business* (1985) and Marko in *Underground* (1995), both Cannes-winning films by Emir Kusturica*. Starting his career in the early 1970s, Manojlović appeared in many of the films of the Prague Group* – like Rajko Grlić's* *Samo jednom se ljubi/You Love Only Once* (1981), and Srdjan Karanović's* *Nesto izmedju/Something In-between* (1983) and *Jagode u grlu/A Throatful of Strawberries* (1985). By the 1990s, the expressive face of Manojlović was an indispensable presence in many Serbian productions. He played the lead in Goran Marković's *Tito i ja/Tito and I* (1992) and in Goran Paskaljević's* *Tudja Amerika/ Someone Else's America* (1995), as well as in Macedonian Stole Popov's *Gypsy Magic* (1997). In 1998, Manojlović had parts in all three internationally acclaimed and award-winning Yugoslavian films – Paskaljević's *Bure baruta/Powder Keg* (1998), Kusturica's *Crna macka, beli macor/Black Cat, White Cat* (1998), and Srdjan Dragojević's* *Rane/Wounds* (1998). In the 1990s Manojlovic also acted in a number of French productions, most notably as Agostino Tassi in Agnès Merlet's *Artemisia* (1997). DI

MARCZEWSKI, Wojciech   Łódź 1944

Polish director. Marczewski finished his studies at Łódź* in 1969, making several television films before *Zmory/Nightmares* in 1979. Set in turn-of-the-century Poland, *Zmory* looks at a young boy's coming of age before World War I. Acclaimed for his visual style, Marczewski turned to his own childhood in the 1950s for inspiration in *Dreszcze/Shivers* (1981), which uses freeze-frames and camera angles to startling effect to elicit a child's perception of the world. Along with

154

films like Feliks Falk's* *Był Jazz/And There Was Jazz* (1984) and Jerzy Domaradzki's *Wielki Bieg/The Great Race* (1987), *Dreszcze* is one of a series of films within the 'cinema of moral unrest', commenting on Poland in the Stalinist years. Although artistically acclaimed, *Dreszcze* was shelved for political reasons. Marczewski had to wait nine years to make *Ucieczka z Kina Wolność/Escape from Liberty Cinema* (1990), a homage to Woody Allen's *Purple Rose of Cairo* which skilfully comments on self-censorship in the new political regime while making fun of the old communist censorship. A subtle yet incisive film, the very successful *Ucieczka z Kina Wolność* upholds the promise of Marczewski's earlier work while bringing a new perspective to post-communist Polish cinema. His 1997 film, *Czas Zdrady/Time of Treason*, was about Niccolo Machiavelli. AW

MASHKOV, Vladimir L. Tula 1963

Russian actor and director. Mashkov studied in the Actors' Studio School of the Moscow Arts Theatre under Oleg Tabakov in 1989–90 and has continued to act since then in the Oleg Tabakov Theatre, playing both classical and contemporary roles. He has directed a number of plays for Tabakov's theatre. He has also had a prolific cinematic career in the 1990s, and has become perhaps the most popular star of the new Russian cinema, specialising in attractive but dangerous and corrupt heroes. Among his greatest successes have been the parts of the computer specialist and New Russian entrepreneur hero of Denis Evstigneyev's *Limita* (1994); and the lover in *Podmoskovnye vechera/Katya Ismailova* (1994), Valeri Todorovsky'*s contemporary remake of Nikolai Leskov's classic story of fatal passion 'A Lady Macbeth of the Mtsensk District'. International recognition came with the main part in Pavel Chukhrai's* *Vor/The Thief* (1997), a period film in which Mashkov plays another of his dubious but irresistible heroes. The film won five Nikes, including those for Best Film and Best Actor (for Mashkov), and was then shortlisted for the Oscar for Best Foreign Language Film. Also in 1997 Mashkov made his first film as a director, *Sirota kazanskaya/The Sympathy Seeker* (1997) a sentimental tale that won popular success but earned him no critical plaudits. In 1998 he played the scholar hero of Roman Balayan's thriller *Dve luny, tri solntsa/Two Moons and Three Suns*. In 1999 he acted for the first time with two other major stars of the new Russian cinema, Oleg Menshikov* and Evgeni Mironov*, and also with Nonna Mordiukova, who played Alexander Askoldov's* Commissar, in Denis Evstigneyev's *Mama*, a sequel to the true-life story of the Seven Simeons, the subject of a 1989 documentary by Herz Frank*. But though the scope of the story and the starriness of its cast were intended to make it into a huge popular film about the post-Soviet fate of Russia, its improbable plot and uneasy acting style made it a critical disaster. JG

MEDVEDKIN, Alexander I.
Penza, Russia 1900 –
Moscow 1989

Soviet director and scriptwriter. A committed communist from the day he joined the Party in 1920, Medvedkin participated in the Civil War of 1917–21 and from 1927 worked in the Gosvoyenkino army film studio. In 1932 he headed the film train that travelled to the major construction projects of the first Five Year Plan and used film to improve productivity: in one year the brigade shot seventy-two films. He made a number of films that used satire and grotesques to attack bureaucracy, and in 1935 his comic masterpiece *Schast'e/Happiness*, an attack on opponents of collectivisation, was released, followed in 1937 by *Chudesnitsa/Miracle Worker*. During World War II Medvedkin worked at the front. In the early 1950s he filmed the agricultural campaign to conquer the Virgin Land, satirising that in turn in *Bespokoinaya vesna/The Unquiet Spring* (1956). He became a cult figure among left-wing intellectuals in the West in the 1970s and is the subject of two films by Chris Marker, *Le Train en marche/The Train Rolls on* (1973) and *Le Tombeau d'Alexandre/The Last Bolshevik* (1993). RT

MENSHIKOV, Oleg E.
Serpukhov, Russia [USSR]
1960

Russian actor. Menshikov graduated in 1982 from the Shchepkin Theatre School in Moscow. He worked in a number of theatres in Moscow including the Maly, the Soviet Army Theatre, the Ermolova Theatre and the Mossovet Theatre. He made his reputation as a stage actor for his roles as the dictator Caligula (1991), the dancer Nijinsky (1993), and the poet Sergei Esenin in the London production of *When She Danced ...* (1992), where he performed alongside Vanessa Redgrave. He has also acted in a London production of Dostoevsky's *The Gamblers* (1992). In 1998 he made his debut as a stage director with a production of Griboedov's *Woe from Wit*, in which he also played the hero Chatsky. He has acted in films since 1981. He had early successes as Kostik in Mikhail Kozakov's *Pokrovskie vorota/The Pokrov Gates* (1982); as Sergei Sinitsyn in Yuri Kushnerev's *Moi lyubimyi kloun/My Favourite Clown* (1986); and as Arteniev in Alexander Muratov's *Moonzund* (1987). He has often played characters who need to forge a mask for themselves in order to create, however artificially, a sense of meaning in their lives: Andrei Pletnev in Alexander Khvan's* *Diuba-Diuba* (1992), a scriptwriter who devises a plan to help his ex-girlfriend escape from prison, only to realise that she does not love him any longer; or the NKVD agent Dmitri in Nikita Mikhalkov's* *Utomlennye solntsem/Burnt by the Sun* (1994) who returns as a storyteller, dancer, singer and entertainer to the house of his lost love, only to arrest her husband at the end of the day. Menshikov

156

has risen to stardom not least because of this part, for which he received major awards, including the State Prize (1996). As Sasha Kostylin, the soldier in captivity in Sergei Bodrov's* *Kavkazskii plennik/The Prisoner of the Mountains* (1996), he has no family whilst inventing stories about his past. Most recently he has starred in Mikhalkov's *Sibirskii tsiriul'nik/The Barber of Siberia* (1999) in the role of the cadet Andrei Tolstoi. BB

MENSHOV, Vladimir V.   Baku, Azerbaijan [USSR] 1939

Russian director. Menshov graduated from the Moscow Arts Theatre School in 1965 and was a postgraduate student at VGIK*. He has played a number of roles in cinema, while his debut as a director came at Mosfilm in 1977 with *Rozygrish/The Practical Joke*, for which he was awarded the State Prize. The film, whose action evolves in a school, explores the conflict between two pupils accused of cheating, and their potential for leadership as revealed in their attempts to defuse the issue. In 1979 he made *Moskva slezam ne verit/Moscow Does Not Believe in Tears*, which won him both the Oscar for Best Foreign Language Film and the State Prize of the USSR. Three women represent different models of family and happiness: Tonya devotes her life to a happy marriage with children in the countryside; Lyudmila wants to climb the social ladder through marriage to a sportsman, who turns out to be an alcoholic, and causes the marriage to fail; while Katya brings up her child on her own when she realises that its father would not be a good partner, makes a career and devotes her life to social progress. Eventually she meets the man she loves, Gosha, who will take over the leading role in the family. Katya's personal happiness is thus a reward for her earlier sacrifice of the personal to the social good. In *Lyubov' i golubi/Love and Doves* (1984) Kuzyakin finds fulfilment during a stay in a sanatorium where he is sent after an accident, and rejects his stale family happiness with children, wife and doves in favour of genuine love. *Shirli Myrli* (1995) begins in Russia, but ends with the entire cast of characters on a flight to the Canary Islands. A giant diamond discovered in the depths of Siberia could secure Russia's future and save its economy. As it is transported back to Moscow, it is, of course, stolen, though it is eventually recovered. Menshov's films explore themes of the individual's happiness and love, while placing his characters into unusual and unreal situations which make them realise their genuine and real feelings. BB

MESKHIEV, Dmitri D.   Leningrad 1963

Russian director. Meskhiev graduated from VGIK* where he had studied direction with Marlen Khutsiev*, in 1988, and made his debut with *Gambrinus* (1990), based on a story by the turn-of-the-century writer, Alexander Kuprin. His film *Tsiniki/The Cynics* (1991), taken from the novel by Anatoli Mariengof, encapsulated in a detached and cynical manner the period of the Russian Revolution and the Civil War: the hero is a historian, the heroine is from a well-off family, and both feel unnecessary in the new society, forcing them into irony and cynicism as a defence mechanism. *Nad temnoi vodoi/Over Dark Waters* (1993) based on a script by Valeri Todorovsky*, explores the life of a man who tries to make things work out for him, but who tragically fails in the end. Meskhiev contributed 'Esksersis No. 5'/'Exercise No. 5' to the film almanac made for the centenary of cinema, *Pribytie poezda/The Arrival of a Train* (1995). His film *Amerikanka/The American Bet* (1998) set in the early 1970s, deals with the first love of the teenager Alesha for Tanya, the girlfriend of his dead brother. *Zhenskaya sobstvennost'/Women's Property* (1999) is a melodramatic love story about a young actor who, while still a student at the film institute, falls in love with his professor, whom he marries, but who tragically dies of cancer. While his friends believe that he embarked upon the love affair merely to promote his career, it gradually emerges that the young man really loved the much older woman and did not act for material reasons. Meskhiev's films are shot in a very detached way as though there was no emotional connection between the director and the story. BB

MENZEL, Jiří   Prague 1938

Czech director and actor. Menzel graduated from FAMU* in 1962 and worked as an assistant to Věra Chytilová* before becoming a director. A self-proclaimed student of comedy (particularly the Czech comedies of Martin Frič*, and Jiří Voskovec* and Jan Werich*), his films are mostly based on collaborations with leading writers. Most of his best films have been in partnership with the novelist Bohumil Hrabal – *Perličky na dně/Pearls of the Deep* (1965, episode *Smrt pana Baltazara/The Death of Mr Balthazar*), *Skřivánci na niti/Skylarks on a String* (1969, rel. 1990, Berlin Golden Bear award), *Postřižiny/Cutting It Short* (1980), *Slavnosti sněženek/The Snowdrop Festival* (1983), and especially *Ostře sledované vlaky/Closely Observed Trains* (1966, Academy Award-winner, 1967), the most popular abroad. Its story of a young station assistant more concerned with losing his virginity than promoting the Führer's New Order was very much in the Švejkian tradition of the little man finding his own ways of subverting dominant ideologies. Menzel also adapted two novels by Vladislav Vančura* and worked with Ladislav Smoljak* and Zdeněk Svěrák*. He was active in theatre as director of the Činoherní klub (Drama Club), and after the fall of the communist government in 1989 he became head of the direction department at FAMU. In 1990 he made a film of his stage production of Václav Havel's *Žebrácká opera/The Beggar's Opera*. He has combined directing with acting, some of his best-known parts

158

being the philandering doctor in Chytilová's *Hra o jablko/The Apple Game* (1976), Hrabal in Petr Koliha's *Něžný barbar/Tender Barbarian* (1989), and the leading role in Costa-Gavras' *Petite apocalypse/A Minor Apocalypse* (1992). While always adopting a respectful attitude towards literary sources, Menzel's direction is distinguished by balanced ensemble playing, a gentle lyricism, and a humanist attitude to his characters reminiscent of Jean Renoir and François Truffaut. He continues to act, mostly in the Czech Republic and other parts of Europe and, in 1995, directed *Audience*. PH

Other Films as Director Include: *Zločin v dívčí škole/Crime in the Girls School* [title episode] (1965); *Rozmarné léto/Capricious Summer* (1967); *Zločin v šantánu/Crime in the Nightclub* (1968); *Kdo hledá zlaté dno/Who Looks for Gold* (1974); *Na samotě u lesa/Seclusion near a Forest* (1976); *Báječni muži s klikou/Those Wonderful Men with a Crank/Those Wonderful Movie Cranks* (1978); *Vesničko má, středisková/My Sweet Little Village* (1985); *Konec starých časů/The End of Old Times* (1989); *Život a neobyčejná dobrodružství vojáka Ivana Čonkina/The Life and Extraordinary Adventures of Private Ivan Chonkin* (1994).

MÉSZÁROS, Márta   Budapest 1934

Hungarian director. Mészáros, one of Hungary's best-known filmmakers, spent her early childhood in the Soviet Union where her family was exiled for being communists. Her father was later arrested and 'disappeared' during Stalin's political purges. Mészáros studied film at VGIK* in Moscow and in the 1950s and most of the 1960s she made short films, newsreels and documentaries, some of them in Romania. Her career as a feature film director began in 1968 with *Eltávozott nap/The Girl*. In her early films Mészáros dealt with the fate of young women subjected to social and emotional deprivation. Her later films often focus on women's issues such as child-bearing and adoption and women's personal integrity, while most display an interest in the father–daughter relationship. At the same time, she is one of the few directors whose films have dealt openly and powerfully with the specific conditions faced by women in Eastern Europe. It is perhaps symptomatic of this situation that her work is better known and appreciated abroad than in Hungary. In the 1980s Mészáros directed an autobiographical trilogy – *Napló gyermekeimnek/Diary for My Children* (1984), *Napló szerelmeimnek/Diary for My Loves* (1987), *Napló apámnak, anyámnek/Diary for My Mother and Father* (1990) – in which she analyses her childhood and adolescence as profoundly disturbed by Stalin's political atrocities, as well as by repression in Hungary. KAB

Bib: Catherine Portuges, *Screen Memories: The Hungarian Cinema of Márta Mészáros* (1993).

Other Films Include: *Holdudvar/Binding Sentiments* (1969); *Szép lányok, ne sírjatok/Don't Cry, Pretty Girls* (1970); *Örökbefogadás/ Adoption* (1975); *Kilenc hónap/Nine Months, Ök ketten/The Two of Them* (1977); *Olyan, mint otthon/Just Like Back Home* (1978); *Útközben/On the Way* (1979); *Örökség/The Heiresses* (1980); *Anna* (1981); *A magzat/Fetus* (1993); *Siódmy pokój/Settima Stanza/The Seventh Room* (1995, It.); *Kisvima/The Last Diary* (1998, Ger./Hung.); *A szerencse lányai/Cory Szczescie/Daughters of Luck* (1999, Pol.).

MEZHRABPOM (also Mezhrabpomfilm)

Soviet film studio. Originally founded in 1924 as an arm of the International Workers' Relief (for which Mezhrabpom is the Russian acronym) and based on the pre-Revolutionary 'Rus' film-making co-operative, the studio remained outside direct centralised state control. It was organised as a limited company and run as a commercial operation, and therefore oriented its production towards a mass audience, notably in co-productions, especially with the similar German organisation Prometheus-Film, and films aimed at overseas markets. At the same time, Anatoli Lunacharsky* wrote a number of scripts for the studio, including *Salamandra/The Salamander* (1928). Among Mezhrabpom's leading directors were Vsevolod Pudovkin*, from *Shakhmatnaya goryachka/Chess Fever* (1925) to *Dezertir/The Deserter* (1933); Lev Kuleshov*, from *Vesëlaya kanareika/The Happy Canary* (1929) to *Krayzha zreniya/Theft of Sight* (1934, not released); Yakov Protazanov*, from *Aelita* (1924) to *Marionetki/The Marionettes* (1934); and Boris Barnet*, from *Miss Mend* (1926) to *U samogo sinego morya/By the Bluest of Seas* (1936), which was one of the studio's last productions.

From 1928 to 1936 the studio was renamed Mezhrabpomfilm and brought under closer political and financial control. During this period one of its engineers Pavel Tager, developed the sound system used for the first Soviet sound films, including Nikolai Ekk's* *Putëvka v zhizn'/The Path to Life* (1931). But the studio's international and commercial orientations rendered it vulnerable to accusations of ideological deviation in the era of 'socialism in one country', and in 1936 it became the Soyuzdetfilm children's film studio, renamed again in 1948 after Gorky. RT

MIKHALKOV, Nikita S.   Moscow 1945

Russian actor, director and scriptwriter. The son of the Soviet writer Sergei Mikhalkov and the younger brother of the director Andron Mikhalkov-Konchalovsky* (Andrei Konchalovsky), Mikhalkov studied at the Shchukin Theatre School from 1963 to 1966 and then at VGIK*, where he graduated in 1971 from the workshop of Mikhail

160

Romm*. Among his early acting roles was that of Kolya in Danelia's*
Ya shagayu po Moskve/I Walk around Moscow (1963). His first feature film as a director was *Svoi sredi chuzhikh, chuzhoi sredi svoikh/At
Home among Strangers, a Stranger at Home* (1974), an adventure story
set during the Russian Civil War. It was followed by *Raba lyubvi/A
Slave of Love* (1975), which tells of the tribulations of a group of actors trying to complete a film melodrama (A Slave of Love) in post-
Revolutionary Odessa, and the political awakening of the star, played
by Yelena Solovei. In 1976, Mikhalkov made *Neokonchennaya p'esa
dlya mekhanicheskogo pianino/An Unfinished Piece for Mechanical
Piano*, based on Chekhov's early play, *Platonov*. The moving *Pyat'
vecherov/Five Evenings* (1978), from the play by Alexander Volodin,
is set in 1957, and chronicles a new encounter between a couple separated at the outbreak of World War II. Mikhalkov's visually stunning
but lugubriously (and inappropriately) sentimental version of
Goncharov, *Neskol'ko dnei iz zhizni I. I. Oblomova/Several Days in
the Life of I. I. Oblomov* (aka *Oblomov*) (1979) was followed by the
family dramas *Rodnya/Kinfolk* (1981) and *Bez svidetelei/Without
Witnesses* aka *A Private Conversation* (1983). Mikhalkov also continued his career as an actor, notably in Ryazanov's* *Vokzal dlya
dvoikh/Station for Two* (1983) and *Zhestokii romans/Cruel Romance*
(1984). Mikhalkov was outspokenly sceptical about the changes in
Soviet cinema introduced at the Fifth Congress of the Union of Film-
makers* in 1986, and his feature films since then have been international co-productions. *Ochi chernye/Dark Eyes* (1987) was made in
Italy, and starred Silvana Mangano and Marcello Mastroianni, who
won the Best Actor prize at Cannes in a confection loosely based on
'The Lady with the Little Dog' and other Chekhov stories. In 1989
Mikhalkov set up the highly successful Tritè film production company
in Moscow. *Urga. Territoriya lyubvi/Urga. Territory of Love* (1991), a
French co-production, was a glorious return to form, and won
Mikhalkov the Golden Lion at Venice in 1991 and a European Film
Award in 1993. A film with an acute sense of history and geography,
which captures the desolate, compelling grandeur of the steppes, it
tells the story of a Mongol family's gradual accommodation to a
modernity which seems likely to exclude Russians, and of the Russian
protagonist's growing sense of his own anachronism. It was followed
by the documentary *Anna ot 6 do 18/Anna from Six to Eighteen* (1993),
which consists of a series of interviews filmed with his daughter on her
successive birthdays, soliciting her opinions on questions both topical
and eternal. *Utomlennye solntsem/Soleil trompeur/Burnt by the Sun*
(1994), set in 1936, was Mikhalkov's belated contribution to the wave
of interrogations of Soviet history. It shared the Jury Prize at Cannes
and won the Oscar for Best Foreign Language Film in 1995. In it,
Mikhalkov himself plays Kotov, a Red Army Divisional Commander,
whose family's idyllic life in the country is thrown into turmoil by the
arrival of a mysterious stranger. Dark secrets of the political past are
revealed and eventually Kotov is arrested, beaten up and driven away

to his death. The film is graced by a memorably affecting performance in the role of Kotov's young daughter by Mikhalkov's own daughter, Nadia. Mikhalkov's most recent film is the lavish historical epic, *Sibirskii tsiriul'nik/The Barber of Siberia* (1999), which had its première in the Kremlin Palace of Congresses in February 1999. One of the most expensive films ever made outside Hollywood, it stars the Western actors Julia Ormond and Richard Harris, as well as the leading Russian actor Oleg Menshikov*. Mikhalkov himself plays the part of Tsar Alexander III. It tells the story, beginning in 1885, of an American woman who travels to Russia to assist a Western adventurer who has invented a machine (the barber of the title) which can chop down Siberian forests with chilling efficiency. Once in Russia the American woman falls in love with a young officer cadet. The epic story, which ends in 1905, returns to the immemorial and obsessive Russian debates over their uniqueness and their relationship with the West and is envisaged as a fillip for Russian self-esteem in a time of trouble. Mikhalkov has occupied several important cultural positions in recent years. At the Third Congress of the Union of Filmmakers of the Russian Federation* in December 1997 he was elected chairman of the union. He has since attempted to introduce plans for the resuscitation of the Russian film industry in a time of economic and cultural crisis. JG

MIKHALKOV-KONCHALOVSKY, Andron S.
Andrei Konchalovsky; Moscow 1937

Russian director and scriptwriter. The son of the Soviet writer Sergei Mikhalkov and the elder brother of the director Nikita Mikhalkov*, Mikhalkov-Konchalovsky studied at VGIK* in the workshop of Mikhail Romm*, graduating in 1965, the year in which his *Pervyi uchitel'/The First Teacher* was made at Kirgizfilm. Taken from a story by the Kirgiz writer Chingiz Aitmatov, it tells of a young man's struggle to impose Soviet ways in a distant Kirgiz village. His next film, *Istoriya Asi Klyachinoi, kotoraya lyubila, da ne vyshla zamuzh/The Story of Asya Klyachine, Who Loved But Did Not Marry* (aka *Asya's Happiness*) (1967), which showed life on a collective farm with unflinching realism, was banned until 1988, when Konchalovsky belatedly won the Nike, for best direction. He followed it with more conventional projects, adaptations of Turgenev's novel *Dvoryanskoye gnezdo/A Nest of Gentlefolk* (1969) and of Chekhov's *Dyadya Vanya/Uncle Vanya* (1971). *Romans o vlyublennykh/Romance about Lovers* (1974) was followed by his last Soviet film *Sibiriada/Siberiade* (1979), an inordinately long epic of life in a Siberian village from 1900 to the 1970s. Andrei Konchalovsky (as he signs his Western films), made his first American film, *Maria's Lovers*, in 1984. Starring Nastassja Kinski, Keith Carradine and Robert Mitchum, it successfully transposes a poignant love story by the Russian writer Andrei Platonov to a small town in Pennsylvania. This was followed by *Runaway Train* (1985), from a script by Akira Kurosawa; *Duet for One* (1986); *Shy People* (1987); *Homer and Eddie* (1988); and the Sylvester Stallone thriller *Tango and Cash* (1989), which Konchalovsky left halfway through shooting. With *The Inner Circle* (Russian title *Blizhnii krug*, 1991), an Italian–Russian co-production, Konchalovsky turned back to Russian material. Tom Hulce plays Ivan Sanshin, Stalin's cinema projectionist, and Bob Hoskins plays Beria in an unimaginative version of the Soviet 1930s, captured far more persuasively in Soviet films of the Gorbachev period. *Kurochka Ryaba/Riaba My Chicken* (1994) a disappointing return to the characters of *The Story of Asya Klyachina* (Asya is now played by Inna Churikova*, an actress who has achieved great renown playing in the films of her husband, Gleb Panfilov*), finds them perplexed and defeated by the advent of the 'free market' in the Russian village. In 1997 Konchalovsky made a version of *The Odyssey* for NBC TV, with Armand Assante as Odysseus and Greta Scacchi as Penelope. Cinematically, the promise of Konchalovsky's earliest films has not been fulfilled. In recent years he has published two extensive volumes of memoirs, *Nizkie istiny* (*Low Truths*), Moscow, 1998 and *Vozvyshayushchii obman* (*Elevating Deceit*), Moscow, 1999. JG

MIRONOV, Evgeni V.   Saratov, Russia [USSR] 1966

Russian actor. Since his graduation from the Saratov Theatre School in 1986 and from the Moscow Arts Theatre School in 1990, Mironov has acted at the Moscow Arts Theatre and at Oleg Tabakov's Studio Theatre. His stage work includes the part of Orestes in Peter Stein's production of Aeschylus's *Oresteia*, Ivan Karamazov in a production taken from Dostoevsky's *The Brothers Karamazov* by Valeri Fokin, and Hamlet in Stein's 1998 Moscow production. In film his work has included Sasha in Valeri Todorovsky's* *Liubov'/Love* (1991), for which he was awarded the Best Actor award at the *Kinotavr*, the Sochi film festival; Poletaev in Petr Todorovsky's* *Ankor, eshche ankor!/ Encore, Another Encore!* (1992); Misha in Denis Evstigneyev's *Limita* (1994); and Khlestakov in Sergei Gazarov's *Revizor/The Government Inspector* (1995), taken from Nikolai Gogol's play, where he was cast alongside the most outstanding actors of contemporary Russia. His major role of the 1990s is, however, the part of the Afghan war veteran, Kolya Ivanov, in Vladimir Khotinenko's* *Musul'manin/The Muslim* (1995), for which he received the Russian Film Academy's Nike award. In Kolya, Mironov portrays a Russian soldier who converted to Islam while in captivity; upon his return to his village, Kolya remains an outsider as his abstinence and pacifism is at odds with the corruption and violence which reign in the Russian community; he is a 'stranger at home'. In Denis Evstigneyev's epic, *Mama* (1999) he plays the drug-addicted son alongside his 'brothers' Vladimir Mashkov* and Oleg Menshikov*. BB

MIŠEV, Georgi
Yoglav 1935

Bulgarian scriptwriter. A prolific author of popular comedies and a highly skilled satirist, whose original stories and scripts helped to boost the fortunes of the Bulgarian cinema during its revival in the 1970s. Born and raised in a village, Mišev sometimes returns to memories of his youth for material, but for the most part his stories deal with the friction that results when rural traditions clash with the more impersonal and anonymous urban life.

As a scriptwriter, Mišev has collaborated mostly with three directors: Eduard Zahariev*, Ljudmil Kirkov* and Ivan Andonov. The best films are those with Zahariev, which reveal a penchant for the absurd in everyday life, particularly among ordinary people who strive to be better than they really are. In their first effort together, *Ako ne ide vlak/If the Train Doesn't Arrive* (1967), an absurd hunt takes place at night for a missing person about whom no one really knows anything. In *Prebrojavane na divite zajci/The Hare Census* (1973, winner of several festival awards), a government official appears suddenly in a village with nonsensical orders to count the number of wild hares in the district. And in *Vilna zona/Villa Zone* (1975) a suburban garden party on a summer night erupts into an out-of-control battle with the neighbours. Each of these films offered ample room for Zahariev and Mišev to satirise the conniving parvenu and the greedy petit bourgeois in contemporary socialist society.

Mišev collaborated with Ljudmil Kirkov on a series of nostalgic, yet quite bitter, films about disintegrating village life and the steady migration of rural populations to cities and industrial areas: *Momčeto si otiva/A Boy Becomes a Man* (1972), *Seljaninăt s koleloto/Peasant on a Bicycle* (1974), *Ne si otivaj!/Don't Go Away!* (1976), and *Matriarhat/ Matriarchy* (1977). And although his screenplays for Ivan Andonov – *Samodivsko horo/Fairy Dance* (1976) and *Dami kanjat/Ladies' Choice* (1980) – reveal a mellowed Mišev, he can still poke some light-hearted fun at the foibles of the established middle class, the 'privileged' in a socialist society with a taste for ostentation.

Mišev's characters, carefully observed from everyday life, are readily recognisable to a home audience. However, as clearly delineated universal types, they also contributed to the acceptance of Bulgarian cinema abroad – and to the maturing of a now sophisticated national cinema. RH

MONTAGE – see SOVIET MONTAGE

MONTENEGRO – see YUGOSLAVIA (former)

MOSJOUKINE [MOZZHUKHIN], Ivan I. Penza, Russia 1890 – Neuilly-sur-Seine, France 1939

Russian actor. After studying law Mosjoukine began acting, first in theatre and then from 1911 in comic roles in films such as *Domik v Kolomne/The House at Kolomna* (1913). He began playing lead roles in Yevgeni Bauer's* films for Alexander Khanzhonkov*, such as *Zhizn' v smerti/Life in Death* (1914), in which he first shed the 'Mosjoukine tears' that became his hallmark. After a disagreement with Bauer over casting, Mosjoukine left to make films for the rival Yermolev company under the direction of Yakov Protazanov*, frequently playing distraught demonic characters caught between duty and (usually) secret passion: *Nikolai Stavrogin, Chaika/The Seagull* and *Ya i moya sovest'/I and My Conscience* (all 1915), *Vo vlasti grekha/In the Realm of Sin, Pikovaya dama/The Queen of Spades* (one of his greatest popular successes), *Plyaska smerti/The Dance of Death* and *Sud Bozhii/Divine Judgment* (all 1916), *Prokuror/The State Prosecutor, Satana likuyushchii/Satan Triumphant* and *Malyutka Elli/Little Ellie* (all 1917), and *Otets Sergii/Father Sergius* (1918). The effectiveness of Mosjoukine's performances depended on his ability to communicate psychological states through expression and gesture, and this gave rise to the term the 'Mosjoukine style of screen acting', whose elements he himself attempted to define. He left Russia for France with Protazanov in 1920, starring in *Justice d'abord/Justice First* (1921, released in the USSR in 1923 as *Sluga slepogo dolga/The Servant of Blind Duty*), *L'Angoissante aventure/The Agonising Adventure* (1923, which he co-scripted) and *Le Brasier ardent*, which he directed himself and which is supposed to have persuaded Jean Renoir to 'forget ceramics and try his hand at cinema'. He attempted to relaunch his career in Hollywood, then in Germany and again in France, but his later films never achieved the success that he had enjoyed earlier in Russia. RT

MOSKVIN, Andrei N. St Petersburg 1901 – Leningrad 1961

Russian cameraman. The bulk of Moskvin's career as one of the leading Soviet cameramen was spent with Grigori Kozintsev* and Leonid Trauberg*, from their early FEKS days to their 'Maxim trilogy'. He is, however, probably best-known internationally as the cameraman for the studio shots in Sergei Eisenstein's* *Ivan Groznyi/Ivan the Terrible* (1943–6), for which Eduard Tisse* worked on the outdoor shooting. RT

165

MUNK, Andrzej
Cracow 1921 – Łowicz 1961

Polish director. One of the giants of the 'Polish School' of the 1950s, Munk studied architecture and law before going to Łódź*. After several fine documentaries, he made his first feature, *Człowiek na Torze/ Man on the Track* (1957), which examines four different 'explanations' for a man jumping on to a train track (a structure echoed in Krzysztof Kieślowski's* 1987 *Przypadek/Blind Chance*). The film won Munk Best Director award at the 1957 Karlovy Vary* festival. His highly individual style and uncompromising analysis of the Polish nation – for example his ironic view of the Polish heroism cult in *Eroica* (1958) – signalled the emergence of the 'second wave' of Polish film-making. *Zezowate Szczęście/Bad Luck* (1960), his next film, continued exploring the concept of heroism in Poland with the same incisiveness and sarcasm. Munk taught at Łódź from 1957 until his untimely death in a car crash in 1961. This happened while he was shooting *Pasażerka/The Passenger*, a harrowing view of World War II and the concentration camps. The film was completed (using existing footage and stills) by Witold Lesiewicz and released in 1963. His influence on a generation of film-makers, among them Roman Polanski*, has earned him an important place in Polish film history. AW

Other Films Include: *Kolejarskie Słowo/A Railwayman's World* (1953); *Gwiazdy Muszą Płonąć/The Stars Must Shine* (1954); *Spacerek Staromiejski/A Walk in the Old City of Warsaw* (1958).

MURATOVA, Kira G.
Soroca, Romania 1934

Russian director, actress and scriptwriter. Muratova studied at VGIK* in the workshop of Sergei Gerasimov*, who, she says revealingly, taught her to listen to words and intonation, graduating in 1962. Her first two films, the short, *U krutogo yara/By the Steep Ravine* (1962) and *Nash chestnyi khleb/Our Honest Bread* (1963) were co-directed with her then husband, Alexander Muratov. *Korotkie vstrechi/Short Meetings* (1967), her first film as a solo director, concerns the triangular relationship between Valentina (played by Muratova), a woman who runs the water supply in a Soviet city, the geologist Maxim (played by Vladimir Vysotsky) and a young village girl. Goskino raised 'moral objections', and the film had a very limited release in film clubs. Her next film, the marvellously observant *Dolgie provody/Long Goodbyes* (1971), tells of the poignantly complex relationship between a feckless divorcée and her sixteen-year-old son. This film, about the ordinary lives of ordinary people, originally accepted by Goskino, was banned as 'non-socialist, bourgeois realism' (objections were made even to the way the characters danced). Muratova was then deprived of her VGIK qualifications and banned from directing. After an abortive attempt to return to direction with a version of Lermontov's 'Princess Mary', she

166

was allowed to make *Poznavaya belyi svet/Getting to Know the World*, a romantic triangle set on a construction site, for Lenfilm in 1979. In *Sredi serykh kamnei/Among the Grey Stones* (1983), Muratova adapted a nineteenth-century story by Korolenko, but the film was heavily cut on completion. Muratova removed her name and the film was released as directed by 'Ivan Sidorov'. With the intervention of the Conflict Commission, set up by the Union of Filmmakers* in 1986, *Short Meetings* and *Long Goodbyes* were released to lavish international praise, and Muratova was revealed as one of the most talented directors of the period. Her next move was unexpected – she made *Peremena uchasti/Change of Fate* (1987), a version of W. Somerset Maugham's story 'The Letter', moving it to an unspecified Central Asian country. *Astenicheskii sindrom/The Asthenic Syndrome* (1989) can be seen as the key film dissection of the *perestroika* years. It begins in black-and-white, with a story of a troubled woman, reminiscent of Muratova's early work, but this time the woman is inconsolable in her bereavement and the tone is desperately bleak. Suddenly her tale is revealed to be a film, being shown at a Moscow cinema to an audience which includes the narcoleptic teacher hero of the 'main' film. This Moscow is shown with unflinching, sometimes comic acuteness, to be a place of hysterical, aggressive women and passive, inert men, all suffering from the syndrome of the film's title, a debility that provokes both of these reactions to extreme stress. Muratova's vision of late-Soviet life was so merciless that she achieved the by now rare distinction of having her film banned until it won the Special Jury Prize at Berlin in 1990. If *The Asthenic Syndrome* showed a society in moral agony, *Chuvstvitel'nyi militsioner/The Sensitive Policeman* (1992), made as the Soviet Union was collapsing, shows people as marionettes who spout nothing but a succession of Soviet clichés. The device of dialogue repetition, familiar from Muratova's earlier films, is here taken to absurd extremes. The bold formalism of *The Sensitive Policeman* offers a vision perhaps even darker than that of *The Asthenic Syndrome*. Both films reveal Muratova as a director continually capable of aesthetic innovation, an innovation she pushed even further in *Uvlechen'ya/ Enthusiasms* (1994), a film about the hopes and dreams of a circus artiste, Violetta, and a jockey, Sasha, which as good as dispenses with plot but is acutely alert to the passions (linguistic as well as physical) of its characters. This film which was awarded the Nike as best Russian film of 1994, marks the beginning of Muratova's collaboration with Renata Litvinova*, who acted in the film and wrote some of the dialogue. In 1997 Muratova made *Tri istorii/Three Stories*, three tales of violent death told with her customary brilliant and chilling formality, staring Sergei Makovetsky*, Litvinova and the veteran actor Oleg Tabakov. The longest and most remarkable episode, *Ofeliia/ Ophelia*, is scripted by and stars Litvinova, as a misanthropic blonde who murders the mother who abandoned her. In 1999, she made the short film *Pis'mo v Ameriku/Letter to America*. Her recent work has cemented Muratova's reputation as, with Sokurov* and German*, one

trandafirului/Memory of the Rose (1963), which took many international prizes. *Dacii/The Dacians* (1966), his first epic, is a mythic reinterpretation of Romanian history as a blending of the Roman and Dacian peoples 2,000 years ago, while *Mihai Viteazul/Michael the Brave/The Last Crusade* (1971) glorifies the fight for Romanian unity in the sixteenth century. These two films (in which he appeared) helped inspire a new emotional Romanian nationalism. Nicolaescu represented Romania in a series of European film co-productions, and has also worked with French and German television. He still directs and co-scripts (and until the 1980s regularly starred in) craftsmanlike thrillers, comedy and adventure films, historical epics and contemporary dramas. *Revanşa/Revenge* (1978) is a typical fast-paced quality thriller in which Nicolaescu plays an indestructible police chief involved in shoot-outs and an improbable plot. In the 1990s he served as a member of the Romanian parliament. MM

Other Films Include: *Primavara obisnuita/A Habitual Spring* (1962); *Lectie în infinit/A Lesson in Infinity* (1965); *Vînatorul de cerbi/The Deerslayer* (1969); *Atunci i-am condamnat pe toti la moarte/Then I Sentenced Them All to Death* (1971); *Cu mîinile curate/With Clean Hands* (1972); *Ultimul cartus/The Last Bullet* (1973); *Un comisar acuza/A Police Inspector Calls* (1973); *Nemuritorii/The Immortals* (1974); *Piratii din Pacific/Pirates of the Pacific* (1975); *Insula comorilor/Treasure Island* (1975); *Zile fierbinti/Hot Days* (1976); *Osînda/Punishment* (1976); *Accident* (1976); *Razboiul independentei/The Independence War* (1977); *Ultima noapte de dragoste/The Last Night of Love* (1979); *Nea Marin miliardar/Uncle Martin, the Multimillionaire* (1979); *Mihail, cîine de circ/Michael, the Dog That Sang* (1979); *Capcana mercenarilor/Trap for Hired Guns* (1980); *Wilhelm cuceritorul/William the Conqueror* (1981); *Duelul/ Duel* (1981); *Intîlnirea/ The Encounter* (1982); *Viraj periculos/ Dangerous Curb* (1983); *Ziua Z/The Z Day* (1985); *Noi, cei din linia întîi/Us, the Front Line* (1985); *Ringul/The Ring* (1986); *Cautatori de aur/The Gold-diggers* (1986); *François Villon – Poetul vagabond/François Villon: The Maverick Poet* (1987); *Mircea/Proud Heritage* (1989); *Legenda carpatina/Carpathian Legend* (1989); *Oglinda/The Mirror* (1993); *Point Zero* (1995).

NORSTEIN, Yuri B.   Norshtein; Andreyevka [USSR] 1941

Russian animator. Norstein studied at the Soviet animation studio, Soyuzmultfilm and after 1961 worked there, participating in the making of dozens of films. His first film as a director was *25-e – pervyi den'/The 25th Is the First Day* (1968). Together with Ivan Ivanov-Vano, one of the founders of Soviet animation, he directed *Secha pri Kerzhentse/The Battle of Kerzhenets* (1971), which used extracts from Rismky-Korsakov's opera *The Tale of the Invisible City of Kitezh* and old Russian art. Norstein turned to the world of fable for *Lisa i* *zayats/The Fox and the Hare* (1973), *Tsaplya i zhuravl'/The Heron and the Crane* (1974) and *Ezhik v tumane/The Hedgehog in the Fog* (1975). *Skazka skazok/The Tale of Tales* (1979), his most ambitious project of the period, made with the writer Lyudmila Petrushevskaya, was described as a 'poetic meditation on life and creativity'. Despite initial difficulties with censorship (the film was shelved for six months), it won several prizes, including citation by an international panel of experts in 1984 as the greatest animated film of all time. Norstein, who acknowledges a debt to Dostoevsky, Platonov and Kafka in his work, has spent much of the time since the early 1980s working on an animated film of Nikolai Gogol's story 'The Overcoat'. This film too has encountered major difficulties, first with Soviet bureaucrats, then with market conditions which were inimical to Norstein's slow working speed, but against all the odds Norstein perseveres with it, describing the Gogolian source as like a chapter from the Bible for him, a 'storehouse of human conscience'. JG

NUGMANOV, Rashid
Alma Ata, Kazakhstan [USSR]
1954

Kazakh director. One of the leading exponents of the Kazakh 'new wave' of film directors, Nugmanov began making films while still a student of architecture in Almaty. *Ya-khkha/Ya-Ha-Ha* (1986), a short film made at VGIK*, where he studied in the workshop of Sergei Solovyov*, examines the Leningrad rock scene to a sound track of leading Russian rock groups including Kino. Kino's lead singer, the legendary Viktor Tsoi, stars, along with Pyotr Mamonov, from the group, *Zvuki mu*, in Nugmanov's graduation film *Igla/The Needle* (1988), an eclectic thriller set in Almaty, in which the hero's addict girlfriend leads him into encounters with the sinister and dangerous local underworld. *Dikii vostok/Wild East* (1993, a post-communist Western) combines Stalin and rock and roll in a futuristic parody of *The Seven Samurai*. JG

O

OGORODNIKOV, Valeri G.
Nizhnii Tagil, Russia [USSR]
1951

Russian director. After graduating from the Urals Polytechnical Institute in 1974, Ogorodnikov studied at the directors' faculty of

VGIK* in the workshop of Igor Talankin, graduating in 1984. His first feature, *Vzlomshchik/Burglar* (1986), drew attention for its sympathetic portrait of the uncertainties in the lives of modern Soviet young people. The hero's punk brother was played by Konstantin Kinchev, a Soviet rock idol, leader of the group, Alisa. In *Bumazhnye glaza Prishvina/Prishvin's Paper Eyes* (1989), from a screenplay by the Georgian director Irakli Kvirikadze*, he attempted something much more complex. The protagonist is a contemporary television director who, while acting in a film set in 1949, finds himself drawn into a nightmarish maelstrom of connections between the past and the present. It is one of the most sophisticated of a group of films from this period interrogating the Soviet past and its baleful legacy. After this Ogorodnikov made *Opyt breda lyubovnogo ocharovaniya/Experiment in the Delirium of Love's Fascination* (1991), a love story set in a madhouse. *Barak/The Hut* (1999), set in the year of Stalin's death, follows the lives and relationships of a group of families living in the hut of the title in the small Urals town where the director himself grew up. Using an array of cinematographic devices, it offers a visually stunning kaleidoscope of memories reminiscent of Fellini. JG

OLBRYCHSKI, Daniel   Łowicz 1945

Polish actor. Olbrychski was discovered by Andrzej Wajda*, who cast him as the lead in *Popioły/Ashes* (1965), an epic version of Żeromski's literary classic. With angelic good looks contrasted against a brooding persona, Olbrychski became an instant 1960s screen idol and successor to Zbigniew Cybulski* (a relationship explored in Wajda's *Wszystko na Sprzedasz/Everything for Sale*, 1969). Olbrychski's career flourished in Poland and abroad in films by Krzysztof Kieślowski*, Krzysztof Zanussi*, Jerzy Hoffman*, Nikita Mikhalkov*, Margarethe von Trotta, Claude Lelouch* and Volker Schlöndorff, among others. Closely associated with Wajda, he is best known for his performances in *Panny z Wilka/The Young Ladies of Wilko* (1979) and *Wesele/The Wedding* (1972) and *Pan Tadeusz* (1999). He continues to act in a wide range of European films. AW

ONDRA, Anny   Anny Ondráková; Tarnów, Galicia [then Austria-Hungary, now Poland] 1902 [3?] – Hamburg, West Germany 1987

Czech actress. After stage training in Prague, Anny Ondra became one of the leading stars of inter-war European cinema, working principally with her first husband, the actor-director Karel Lamač*. Once described as 'Buster Keaton in skirts', she was the first female comic in Czech film, appearing in a wide range of comedies. Her appeal rested on a slightly coquettish naïveté, and she appeared in musicals as well as playing an obligatory range of orphans and abandoned women. She appeared in four British films and, in 1929, Alfred Hitchcock put her fragile blonde beauty to rather different use in *The Manxman* and *Blackmail*, with her dialogue dubbed in the latter. Ondra-Lamač Film was founded in Berlin in 1930 and she played a central role in the production of most of her 1930s films. The second half of her career was based in Germany and she made her last screen appearance, for Helmut Käutner, in 1957. PH

Other Films Include: *Dáma s malou nožkou/Woman with Small Feet* (1919); *Zpěv zlata/Song of Gold, Gilly po prvé v Praze/Gilly's First Visit to Prague* (1920); *Tu ten kámen/Tutankhamun/This is the Stone, Únos bankéře Fuxe/The Kidnapping of Banker Fuxe* (1923); *Bílý ráj/The White Paradise, Chyt'te ho!/Catch Him!* (1924); *Karel Havlíček Boro-vský, Lucerna/The Lantern* (1925); *Velbloud uchem jehly/Camel through the Needle's Eye* (1926); *Der erste Küss/The First Kiss, Saxophon Susi* (1928, Ger.), *God's Clay* (1928, UK); *Blackmail, Glorious Youth, The Manxman* (1929, UK); *Die Fledermaus, Mamsell Nitouche* [German versions of *La Chauve-souris* and *Mam'zelle Nitouche*, shot in Fr.], *On a jeho sestra/He and His Sister* (1931); *Baby* (1932, Fr.); *Kiki* (1933, Fr.); *Die Tochter des Regiments/Daughter of the Regiment* (1933, Aust.). **In Germany**: *Klein Dorrit/Little Dorrit, Polská krev/Polish Blood, Knock-out* (1934); *Ein Mädel vom Ballett/A Girl from the Ballet, Donogoo Tonka* (1936); *Vor Liebe wird gewarnt/Beware of Love* (1937); *Himmel, wir erben ein Schloss/Heavens, We're Inheriting a Castle* (1943); *Schön muss man sein/One Has to Be Beautiful* (1951); *Die Zürcher Verlobung/Getting Engaged in Zurich* (1957).

ONDRÍCEK, Miroslav   Prague 1934

Czech cinematographer. Ondrícek's contribution to the Czech New Wave* equals the one of the directors with whom he worked. One of the pioneers of the hand-held camera, his unique visual style is best known from Miloš Forman's* early masterpieces, *Konkurs/The Competition* (1963), *Lásky jedné plavovlásky/Loves of a Blonde* (1965), and *Horí, má panenko/The Fireman's Ball* (1967). His collaboration with Forman continued in the US where Ondrícek worked on *Taking Off* (1971), *Hair* (1979), *Ragtime* (1981), *Amadeus* (1984), and *Valmont* (1989). The work on *Ragtime* brought him an Oscar nomination, and the cinematography for *Amadeus* – a BAFTA award and a second Oscar nomination. Ondrícek is responsible for the dynamic photography of many other works of the Czech New Wave – Jan Němec's* Holocaust masterpiece, *Démanty noci/Diamonds of the Night* (1964, with Hynec Bocan) and Ivan Passer's* *Intimni osvetleni/Intimate Lighting* (1966). He also worked with Jaroslaw Papousek and Otakar

Vávra*. Ondrícek has also worked with famous Western directors. He was the cameraman for Lindsay Anderson's British classics *If ...* (1968) and *O Lucky Man!* (1973), for George Roy Hill's *Slaughterhouse-Five* (1972) and *The World According to Garp* (1982), and for Mike Nichols' *Silkwood* (1983). In the 1990s Ondrícek worked on several films directed by the American, Penny Marshall. DI

ORLOVA, Lyubov P. Moscow 1902–75

Soviet actress. Orlova graduated from the Moscow Conservatoire, acting on stage from 1926 and on screen from 1934. Although she appeared in films made by a number of directors, she made her reputation in a series of highly popular musical comedies directed by her husband Grigori Alexandrov*: they were known as the 'first couple' of Soviet cinema and Orlova was probably its most popular actress. She played what one critic has described as the 'ideal woman of the 1930s, the *femina sovietica*, a contemporary Valkyrie in a white sweater with a severe perm'. Her characterisations appealed to a contemporary willingness to be deceived, depicted a paradise that audiences could believe in, and were designed to illustrate the possibility of self-improvement through effort and the benign influence of the Party and Stalin. This is above all implicit in *Vesëlye rebiata/The Happy Guys* (1934), *Tsirk/The Circus* (1936), *Volga-Volga* (1938), *Svetlyi put'/The Radiant Path* (1940) and *Vesna/Spring* (1947). She also appeared in Alexandrov's *Vstrecha na El'be/Meeting on the Elbe* (1949), *Kompozitor Glinka/The Composer Glinka* (1952) and, her last film, *Russkii suvenir/A Russian Souvenir* (1960). After her death Alexandrov co-directed a film about her, *Lyubov Orlova* (1983). RT

OTSEP, Fyodor A. [OZEP, Fédor] Moscow 1895 – Ottawa, Canada 1949

Russian director and scriptwriter. Coming to the cinema in 1916, Otsep jointly wrote scripts for a number of films, including *Polikushka* (1919), *Papirosnitsa iz Mosselproma/The Cigarette Girl from Mosselprom* and Yakov Protazanov's* *Aelita* (both 1924), *Kollezhskii registrator/The Station Master* (1925) and *Kukla s millionami/The Girl with the Millions* (1928). He directed the serial thriller *Miss Mend* (1926), *Zemlya v plenu/Earth in Captivity* (1928) and the Russo-German co-production of Tolstoy's *Zhivoi trup/The Living Corpse* (1929), after which he stayed in Germany, making *Der Mörder Dimitri Karamasoff/The Brothers Karamazov* (1931) as well as its French version *Les Frères Karamazoff* (also 1931). After the Nazis came to power he moved to France, where, under the name of Fédor Ozep, he contributed to the popular genre of exotic melodrama, making the French and German versions of *Mirages de Paris/Großstadtnacht/Mirages of*

Paris (1932), the Zweig adaptation *Amok* (1934), *La Dame de pique/The Queen of Spades* (1937), *Gibraltar/It Happened in Gibraltar*, and *Tarakanova/Betrayal* and its Italian version *La principessa Tarakanova* (all 1938). Interned as a displaced person, he was freed after the fall of France and fled to North America. He made his last film, *La Forteresse/Whispering City*, in Canada in 1947. RT

OVCHAROV, Sergei M.   Rostov on Don, Russia [USSR] 1955

Russian director and scriptwriter. After graduating from the Cinema and Photography Faculty of the Moscow Institute of Culture in 1976, Ovcharov entered the Higher Courses for Directors, from which he graduated in 1979, from the workshop of Gleb Panfilov*. He came to prominence with his films *Nebyval'shchina/Believe It or Not* (1983) and *Levsha/Lefty* (1986), based on a story by the nineteenth-century Russian writer Nikolai Leskov. The ambitious *Ono/It* (1989) also had its source in nineteenth-century literature, in Saltykov-Shchedrin's satire *The History of a Town*. But Ovcharov's reading of the novel includes all of Russian history, and finds roles for Lenin, Stalin, Beria, Khrushchev, Brezhnev and even Gorbachev on the way to an apocalyptic future. It was followed by *Barabaniada/Drum Rolls* (1993), a subject that had preoccupied Ovcharov for almost twenty years, and which he had embarked upon twice before, first as a student work in 1975 and then for TV in 1981. A picaresque, *faux-naïf* tale, completely devoid of dialogue, it follows the tribulations of a naive young man who is given a drum which takes control of his life as he wanders around Russia and experiences the chaos and contradictions of contemporary society. In 1998 he made the mixed animation and feature short *Faraon/Pharaoh*, in which ancient Egyptian frescoes come to life and tell their stories. The film shared the Golden Bear for the Best Short Film at the Berlin Film Festival in 1999. JG

OZEP, Fédor – see OTSEP, Fyodor

P

PANFILOV, Gleb A.   Magnitogorsk, Russia [USSR] 1934

Russian director and scriptwriter. While working as a chemical engineer after completing his studies at the Urals Polytechnic Institute, Panfilov saw Kalatozov's* *Letyat zhuravli/The Cranes Are Flying*, and this led him to a correspondence course in cinema and work in Sverdlovsk [Yekaterinburg] television. From 1960 to 1963 he studied cinematography at VGIK*, and in 1967 he completed the Higher Courses for Directors. His first feature *V ogne broda net/No Crossing under Fire* (1967), the story of a young woman whose commitment to the Revolution leads to her discovering her talent as a painter, gave a first starring role to his wife, Inna Churikova*. Churikova's remarkable talent is visible too in *Nachalo/The Debut* (1970), in which she plays an ordinary girl chosen to play Joan of Arc in a film; and in *Proshu slova/I Wish to Speak* (1975), in which she is the head of the Soviet of a provincial town whose party idealism is tested by the death of her teenage son. *Tema/The Theme* (1979), the story of a conformist writer forced to confront his own compromises, was shelved for seven years. During that time Panfilov made *Valentina* (1981), from a play by Alexander Vampilov, about the life of a young barmaid in a Siberian village café. In the 1980s Panfilov also made two grandiose films from the work of Maxim Gorky, both starring Inna Churikova. *Vassa* (1983), from the play *Vassa Zheleznova*, is a pre-Revolutionary family melodrama. It was followed by Panfilov's epic version of the revolutionary novel, *Mat'/Mother* (1989). Since 1991 he has been the artistic director of the Vera studio, where he returned to the years before the Russian Revolution, this time at the other end of the social scale, to make *Romanovy – Ventsenosnaya sem'ya/The Romanovs – An Imperial Family* (1998), which culminates in the shooting of the Tsar and his family and in which the Tsarina is played by the English actress Lynda Bellingham. JG

PARADZHANOV, Sergo   Tbilisi, Georgia [USSR] 1924 – Yerevan, Armenia 1990

Armenian Soviet director. Graduated from VGIK*, where he studied with Igor Savchenko*, and made a number of Ukrainian-language films, which he described as 'justified failures'. He first achieved international recognition with *Teni zabytykh predkov/Shadows of Our Forgotten Ancestors* (1965). All his subsequent films were infused with the spirit of folklore and ethnography: *Sayat Nova*, also known as *Tsvet granata/The Colour of Pomegranates* (1969), *Legenda o Suramskoi kreposti/The Legend of Suram Fortress* (1984), and *Ashik Kerib*

175

(1988). In 1974, because of his heterodoxy, all his film projects were blocked and he was imprisoned on various trumped-up charges and released in 1978 only after an international protest campaign. Describing cinema as a 'synthetic art', he developed Sergei Eisenstein's* concepts, using colour, rhythm, music, dancing and montage to move away from plot-constrained structures. RT

PASKALJEVIC, Goran   Belgrade 1947

Yugoslav director of Serbian origin, working in France. Paskaljević is one of the directors belonging to the Prague Group*, having graduated from FAMU* in 1972. Usually interested in exploring the lives of his ordinary contemporaries, Paskaljević's films treat the subject matter with a combination of humour and sympathy. Paskaljević first came into the critical spotlight with his *Cuvar plaze u zimskom periodu/ Beach Guard in Winter* (1976), a film approaching the concerns of average people with gentle humour. He continued this line of work in the internationally acclaimed *Pes koji je voleo vozove/The Dog Who Loved Trains* (aka *The Days Are Passing*, 1977) focusing on marginal people and their seemingly petty provincial concerns. Paskaljević has displayed a persistent interest in weak and disinherited protagonists. In *Poseban tretman/Special Treatment* (1980) he explored the crude ways society deals with alcoholics, and in *Andjeo cuvar/Guardian Angel* (1987) he focused on a journalist's (played by popular actor Ljubisa Samardzić) doomed attempt to help a disadvantaged Gypsy boy to escape the vicious circle of ghetto life. In the 1990s, in collaboration with screenwriter Gordan Mihić, Paskaljević directed the somewhat sentimental *Tango Argentino* (1992) about the relationship between a little boy and an old man, and *Tudja Amerika/Someone Else's America* (1995), a story of global migrants and displacement. A co-production with France, Great Britain, Germany and Greece that takes place in New York and Texas and features Spaniards, Montenegrin and Chinese, it is a film which explores the cross-cultural mixing of peoples and places and is simultaneously nostalgic and invigorating. Paskaljević's most mature work is the internationally acclaimed *Bure baruta/Powder Keg* aka *Cabaret Balkan* (1998) which explores the bewildered state of mind of the inhabitants of rump Yugoslavia's capital under Milosević's regime. This violent, depressing and gritty film stars a pleyade of the best-known Yugoslav actors, like veterans Milena Dravić* and Miki Manoilović*. DI **Website**: http://www.paskaljevic.com

Other Films Include: *Pan Hrstka/Mr Hrstka* (1969); *Nekolik slov o lásce/Some Words about Love* (1970); *Legenda o Lapotu/The Legend of Lapota* (1972); *Sluga/Servant* (1973); *Deca/Children* (1973); *Teret/ Burden* (1974); *Potomak/Descendent* (1974); *Kapetan Janko/Captain Janko* (1974); *Iz pobede u pobedu/From victory to victory* (1975); *Zemaljski dani teku/Earthly Days Unfold* (1979); *'Sipad'/Sipad* (1979);

176

Stuon/Twilight (1983); *Varljivo leto '68/Summer of '68* (1984); *Vreme cuda/Time of Miracles* (1989).

PASSER, Ivan   Prague 1934

Czech director. Educated at FAMU*, Passer began his career as an assistant on films by Ladislav Helge, Zbyněk Brynych and Vojtěch Jasný* before collaborating with Miloš Forman* on all four of his principal Czech films. He directed a short film, *Fádní odpoledne/A Boring Afternoon*, in 1964, and a feature, *Intimní osvětlení/Intimate Lightning*, in 1965. Adapted from a story by Bohumil Hrabal, *Fádní odpoledne* is a beautifully observed study of an afternoon in a Prague pub, focusing on the minutiae of life in a way that is both captivating and lyrical. *Intimní osvětlení* is the story of a weekend in the country where two musicians meet and reflect on the meaning of life. Almost without plot, its gentle observation of the mundane seems a logical extension from the style of Forman's early films. Passer left Czechoslovakia in 1968 for a career in the US, where his films have assumed quite different forms. Films such as *Law and Disorder* (1974) and *Silver Bears* (1978) are interesting satires on modern corruption, but his best-known works are *Born to Win* (1971), an unusual approach to the drug scene, and *Cutter's Way* (also *Cutter and Bone*, 1981), a classic *film noir* that is also a disturbing portrait of the post-Vietnam experience. PH

Other Films Include: *Crime and Passion* [also *An Ace up My Sleeve*] (1976); *Creator* (1985); *Haunted Summer* (1988); *Stalin* [TV] (1992); *Kidnapped* [TV] (1995, US); *The Wishing Tree* (1999, US).

PASTERNAK, Iosif   Kiev, Ukraine [USSR] 1950

Russian documentary director. After studies at the Kiev Conservatoire, Pasternak worked from 1973 at the Kiev Nauchfilm Studios, before moving to Mosfilm in 1983. His *Chernyi kvadrat/The Black Square* (1988) surveys the experience of the non-conformist artists of the 1960s–1980s, and provides a striking visual record of their work, while its archival footage of the Stalin and Khrushchev periods expands the analysis of the relationship between artists and power to cover the entire Soviet period. *Alexandre Galich. Moscou-Paris/Aleksandr Galich: Izgnanie/Alexander Galich: Exile* (1989) uses the fate of the exiled poet to examine the history of the Soviet emigration. After 1990 Pasternak made a number of documentaries for French television, including *De la Petite Russie à l'Ukraine/From Little Russia to the Ukraine* (1990); *Moscou* (1990), showing the city as imagined by the Russian avant-garde artist, Francisco Infante; and *Moscou. Trois jours en Août/Moscow. Three Days in August* (1991), which contains remarkable footage shot inside the Moscow White House during the abortive 1991 coup. The brilliantly acute and evocative *Le Fantôme Efremov/The Phantom of Efremov* (1992) visits a typical central Russian town to discover how little it was affected by the events of 1991. In recent years Pasternak has continued to make documentaries in France on Russian themes. JG

PAVLENKO, Pyotr A. St Petersburg 1899 – Moscow 1951

Russian writer and scriptwriter. Pavlenko co-scripted Sergei Eisenstein's* *Aleksandr Nevskii/Alexander Nevsky* (1938), Mikhail Chiaureli's* *Klyatva/The Vow* (1946) and *Padenie Berlina/The Fall of Berlin* (1949), and Grigori Alexandrov's* *Kompozitor Glinka/The Composer Glinka* (1952). He was elected to the USSR Supreme Soviet and awarded a Stalin Prize in 1948. RT

PAVLOVIĆ, Živojin Šabac, Serbia 1933 – Belgrade 1998

Yugoslav director and writer of Serbian origin. A leading figure of the Yugoslav 'Black Wave'*, Pavlović discovered movie treasures in the Belgrade film archive during his studies of decorative painting in the late 1950s. He soon began to give lectures, travelling around Serbia and talking about films. He never lost his intimate contact with the realities of provincial life, but he was at the same time capable of transforming them into cinematographic moments of truth. His existentialism is evident in two of the most interesting Yugoslav films of the 1960s: *Budjenje pacova/Awakening of the Rats* and *Kad budem mrtav i beo/When I Am Dead and White* (both 1967). Both films are tragic and depressive – so depressive that Pavlović was subsequently deprived of work by the communist authorities for more than fifteen years. He 'escaped' to Slovenia, where he directed two rural dramas (*Rdeče klasje/Red Wheat*, 1971; *Let mrtve ptice/Dead Bird's Flight*, 1973) and a controversial evocation of war, *Nasvidenje v naslednji vojni/Farewell until the Next War* (1980), based on a best-selling Slovene novel by Vitomil Zupan [> YUGOSLAV 'PARTISAN FILMS']. The prophetic title of this film became true ten years later, when the rest of what used to be Yugo-slavia was plunged into bloodshed. His last film, *Dezerter/Deserter* (1994) is loosely based on a plot from Dostoyevsky and is set in Vukovar at the time of the Yugoslav break-up*. SP

Other Films Include: *Neprijatelj/The Enemy* (1965); *Povratak/Homecoming* (1966); *Zaseda/Ambush* (1969); *Hajka/Pursuit* (1977); *Zadah tela/Body Scent* (1983); *Na putu za Katangu/On the Road to Katanga* (1987).

PERESTIANI, Ivan N.
Taganrog, Ukraine [Russian Empire] 1870 – Moscow 1959

Georgian Soviet director, scriptwriter and actor. A stage actor from 1886 and in cinema from 1916, he played about twenty roles before the 1917 Revolution. Perestiani made agit-films* during the Civil War and taught at VGIK*. He directed the first Soviet Georgian feature *Arsen Dzhordzhiashvili* (1921) but is best remembered for *Krasnye d'yavoly-ata/The Little Red Devils* (1923), in which he used the techniques of the American adventure film to tell a revolutionary tale, thus appealing to a broad and youthful audience. After working in Odessa and Armenia, Perestiani returned to Tbilisi in 1933 and subsequently concentrated on acting and scriptwriting for the Georgian studios. RT

PETROV, Valeri
Sofia 1920

Bulgarian writer, who contributed significantly to the artistic development of postwar Bulgarian cinema. Valeri Petrov took up freelance writing in 1956 and became famous a few years later through his collaboration with director Rangel Vălčanov* on the breakthrough film *Na malkija ostrov/On a Small Island* (1958). He collaborated with Vălčanov on two more films, *Părvi urok/First Lesson* (1960) and *Slănceto i sjanka-ta/Sun and Shadow* (1962); and these three films were hailed internationally as evidence of a poetic awakening in Bulgarian cinema.

When the Bulgarian 'new wave' ground to a halt shortly after the downfall of Khrushchev, Petrov turned to writing poems, essays and plays, while also translating Shakespeare into modern Bulgarian for the stage. His penchant for writing stories and plays for children eventually brought him back to Boyana* Studios in the mid-1960s: his scripts for Borislav Šaraliev's *Ricar bez bronja/Knight without Honour* (1966) proved to be such a commercial success among both young and adult audiences that children's films thereafter became a production factor at Boyana. More than a decade after he first worked with Vălčanov, Petrov collaborated with him again on *S ljubov i nežnost/ With Love and Tenderness* (1978), in which an ageing sculptor and a young girl confront bureaucrats, hangers-on and a cross-section of ordinary citizens enjoying the 'Black Sea Riviera'. But, attractive as the film was on the aesthetic level, its theme appeared outmoded at the time, a throwback to the 1950s when Bulgarian 'poetic realism'* was in style.

Critics have speculated on how Bulgarian cinema might have developed, and been recognised abroad, had Petrov been able to devote more of his considerable talents to writing for the cinema. In the 1990s he scripted only one film, *Vsichko ot nula/Everything from Scratch* (1996, d. Ivan Pavlov). RH

PETROV, Vladimir M.   St Petersburg 1896 – Moscow 1966

Soviet director and scriptwriter, who studied acting at the Alexandrinsky Theatre in Petrograd and made his stage debut in 1917. Petrov worked with Gordon Craig in England in 1918 and went into film-making in 1925. He made a series of films for children and young people, beginning with *Zolotoi mëd/Golden Honey* (1928) and ending with *Fritz Bauer* (1930). His first great success was a film adaptation of Ostrovsky's play *Groza/The Storm* (1934). Petrov is principally re-membered for his two-part historical epic *Pëtr I/Peter the Great* (1937–9), with Nikolai Cherkasov* as the tsarevich, which won the Grand Prix at the Paris International Exhibition in 1937 and the Stalin Prize in 1941. In 1944 he turned to the Napoleonic Wars with *Kutuzov* and in 1950 contributed to the Stalin cult with *Stalingradskaya bitva/The Battle of Stalingrad*. In his last films he concentrated on adaptations of the Russian classics from Gogol to Kuprin. RT

PETROVIĆ, Aleksandar   Paris, France 1929–94

Yugoslav director and scriptwriter of Serbian origin. One of the most prominent film-makers of the former Yugoslavia, with Dušan Makavejev* and Emir Kusturica*. After film criticism and several doc-umentaries, Petrović made two feature films – *Dvoje/Couple/When Love Is Gone*, 1961, and *Dani/Days*, 1963 – clearly influenced by the French New Wave* tendency of deconstructing conventional nar-ration into fragments of everyday life and love, and heralding a Yugoslav 'new wave' known as the 'Black Wave'*. His real break-through came in 1965 with *Tri/Three*, a complex interweaving of three stories reflecting on death. With his next film, *Skupljači perja/I Even Met Some Happy Gypsies* (1967), which shared the Special Jury Prize at Cannes, Petrović achieved international recognition. He later needed this accolade, since his domestic career was in trouble: his adaptation of Bulgakov's novel *Majstor i Margarita/The Master and Margarita* (1972) was perceived as a direct offence to the communist regime, and Petrović was out of work for some time. Another scandal involving his student Lazar Stojanović's graduate film, *Plastic Jesus*, was used as an excuse to remove Petrović from the Belgrade Film Academy in 1973. His comeback should have been the European epic adaptation of Serbian writer Miloš Crnjanski's 'roman fleuve' *Seobe/Migrations* (1985, released 1994), but Petrović became em-broiled in endless judicial procedures, financial problems and bad timing. SP

Other Films Include: *Jedini izlaz/The Only Way Out* (1958); *Biče skoro propast sveta/It Rains in My Village* (1968); *Gruppenbild mit Dame/Group Portrait with Lady* (1977, Ger./Fr.).

180

PICHUL, Vasili V.　　　Zhdanov, Ukraine [USSR] 1961

Russian director. After studying at VGIK* from 1977–83 in the first workshop of Marlen Khutsiev*, Pichul worked in television. In 1986 he joined the Gorky Film Studios, Moscow, where in 1988 he made *Malen'kaya Vera/Little Vera*, a film which came to epitomise the *perestroika* period [>GLASNOST AND THE CINEMA]. Set in Pichul's home town of Maryupol (Zhdanov) in the southern Ukraine, and scripted by his wife, Maria Khmelik, *Little Vera* amazed Soviet audiences by its sexual frankness, and made something of an international celebrity of its star, Natalya Negoda. Several years on, the film's importance can be seen to lie more in its bleak evocation of Soviet working-class life. Holed up in a cramped high-rise flat with her drunken father and overworked mother, poorly-educated Vera is destined for a dead-end job as a telephonist until she meets workshy student Sergei. ... The film was seen by over fifty million people in Russia and variously interpreted, in the acres of press coverage devoted to it, as exposing or condoning all that was wrong in the late-Soviet society. Pichul's independently made *V gorode Sochi temnye nochi/Dark Nights in Sochi* (1989), was, by contrast, a commercial flop. After that he made *Mechty idiota/Dreams of an Idiot* (1993), an eclectic and challenging version of *The Golden Calf*, a classic work by the Soviet satirists, Ilf and Petrov. During 1994–7 Pichul worked as one of the directors of the popular satirical television series, *Kukly/Puppets*, based on the British *Spitting Image* programme. In 1999 he directed the comedy action thriller *Nebo v almazakh/The Diamond-studded Sky*. JG

PICK, Lupu　　　Jassy, Romania 1886 – Berlin 1931

Romanian-born director and actor, who as an actor played in Richard Oswald* fantasy films, Henny Porten comedies and the Joe Jenkins and Stuart Webb detective series. His last and best-known role was as the Japanese diplomat Massimoto in Lang's *Spione/Spies* (1928).

Pick's first directorial assignments were popular star vehicles, including a futuristic anticipation of television (*Der Weltspiegel/The Mirror of the World*, 1918). In the early 1920s he collaborated closely with writer Carl Mayer on *Kammerspielfilme**, which they inaugurated with *Scherben/Shattered* (1921) and *Sylvester* (1923). The films' critical success and aesthetic influence on Weimar cinema are traditionally attributed to Mayer, but it was as much due to Pick's distinctive use of camera movement, sparse decors, and the natural flow of *mise-en-scène* (with only one intertitle in *Scherben*) that the genre generated an atmospheric intensity around its sociological representation of the everyday. A trilogy was conceived that would have included *Der letzte Mann/The Last Laugh* (1924), but a disagreement between Pick and Mayer led Pick to leave the project and the assignment went to F. W. Murnau. Thereafter, Pick made only a few films, some

181

unjustly forgotten, like the intriguingly offbeat *Gassenhauer* (1931). MW/TE

Other Films Include: *Mr Wu* (1918); *Herr über Leben und Tod/Master of Life and Death* (1919); *Zum Paradies der Damen/To the Ladies' Paradise* (1922); *Eine Nacht in London/A Night in London* (1928); *Napoleon auf St Helena/Napoleon on St Helena* (1929).

PINTILIE, Lucian   Tarutyne [then Romania, now Ukraine] 1933

Romanian director, who helped achieve international credibility for Romanian cinema with *Reconstituirea/The Reconstruction* (1969), went into exile and returned after twenty years, in 1990, as Director of Film at the Ministry of Culture. After attending theatre and film school Pintilie made his reputation as a stage director, and first worked in film as assistant director to Victor Iliu*. *Duminică la ora 6/Sunday at Six* (1965), his directorial debut, was a skilfully shot war film devoid of cliché – highly original for Romania. *Reconstituirea*, about two students forced to reconstruct a fight in a bar, is a complex allegorical tragi-comedy of collective irresponsibility, with striking use of camera and crowd scenes. Despite official criticism and delays in domestic release, it was hailed in Europe as a breakthrough for Romanian cinema. Following criticism of his stage work at home Pintilie worked in Yugoslavia, France and America as a stage and opera director, returning to film with *Paviljon 6* (1978), a stylish Chekhov adaptation made in Yugoslavia; and briefly to Romania for *De ce bat clopotole Mitică?/Carnival Stories* (planned for a 1981 release but shelved until the 1989 revolution). Adapted from I. L. Caragiale's grotesque and satirical play, it echoes Gogol's *Inspector-General*. Pintilie's 1990 return to Romania resulted in *Le Chêne/Steiarul/The Oak* (1992), a French–Romanian co-production and the major depiction to date of the degradation of the late Ceauşescu years. Pintilie worked intensively throughout the 1990s. Most of his later films were Romanian–French co-productions, such as *O Vara de neuitat/Un été inoubliable/ An Unforgettable Summer* (1994), shown at Cannes, exploring fragile inter-ethnic relations in the Balkans, and the socially critical dramas, *Prea târziu/Too Late* (1996), and *Terminus paradis/Last Stop Paradise* (1998). MM

Bib: Anca Visdei, 'Entretien avec Lucian Pintilie', *L'Avant-Scène du cinéma* (October 1992).

PIȚA, Dan   Dorohei 1938

Romanian director and scriptwriter, who with *Nuntă de piatră/Stone Wedding* (1972, co-directed and scripted with Mircea Veroiu*)

achieved a breakthrough in the international recognition of Romanian film. A medical assistant for ten years before studying under Victor Iliu*, his silent student film about a driver and cyclist, *Viaţa in roz/La Vie en rose* (1969), was shown worldwide. In *Nuntă de piatră*, Piţa's quiet observation of social subversion at a traditional wedding subtly understates the conflict between conformism and individuality. The film is complemented by its sequel, *Duhul aurului/Lust for Gold* (1973). The contemporary drama *Filip cel bun/Philip the Good* (1975) is comparable to Lucian Pintilie's* *Reconstituirea* in its attention to social realism. Piţa directed some films in a popular series parodying the Western, starting with *Profetul, aurel şi Ardelenii/The Prophet, the Gold and the Transylvanians* (1977), which played on the incongruousness of Transylvanian peasants transplanted to Texas. *Concurs/The Contest* (1982) is a gripping commentary on leadership and psychology. *Dreptate în lanturi/Chained Justice* (1983) deploys elegant black-and-white photography in a Robin Hood-style adventure. *Pas în doi/Paso Doble* (1986), also co-scripted by Piţa, breaks Romanian social taboos in its handling of a *ménage-à-trois*. Piţa's claims to magic realism are extended in *Noiembrie, ultimul bal/November, the Last Ball* (1989), with its mirage-like tragic relationships in a nineteenth-century provincial town. *Hôtel de lux* (1991) was well received at Venice shortly after Piţa's new administrative powers had embroiled him in an industry-wide strike. Piţa's films in the 1990s mainly focus on the drab post-communist reality, such as the festival favourites, *Pepe si Fifi/Pepe and Fifi* (1994), *Sominul insulei/The Island Asleep* (1994); *Eu Adam/My Name Is Adam* (1996), and *Omul zilei/Man of the Day* (1997). MM

PODNIEKS, Jūris   Riga, Latvia [USSR] 1950 – Alsunga, Latvia 1992

Latvian documentary director. Podnieks graduated from the cinematography faculty of VGIK* and earned a reputation as a cinematographer. He directed his first film *Sozvezdie strelkov/Constellation of Riflemen* in 1982, but international success came with the pioneering and timely *Legko li byt' molodym?/Is It Easy to Be Young?* (1987), a series of interviews with young people in his native Riga. Podnieks' secret was to let these young people speak in their own words, and the unprecedented authenticity of what they had to say led to sensationally high audiences for a documentary film. The success and originality of Podnieks' film led British Central Television to commission him to make a series of five hour-long documentaries, broadcast in Britain in 1990 as *Hello, Do You Hear Us?*, Russian title *My/We*, which remains a key document for understanding the last years of the Soviet Union. Here, too, though Podnieks includes all the major events of the period, it is the testimonies of individuals, from the Baltic to Central Asia, that are most effective. From 1991 Podnieks became increasingly involved in documenting the struggle of the Baltic peoples to regain their independence, the subject of his film, *Homeland/Krestnyi put'/Calvary* (1991). In January 1991, an attempt to repress this movement led to violence in Vilnius and Riga. While Podnieks and his team were filming in Riga, his cameramen, Andris Slapins and Gvido Zvaigzne, were shot dead by troops, events captured in the short *Postscript/Posleslovie* (1991) to *Homeland*. Podnieks' final completed film for Central, *End of Empir/Krushenie imperii* (1991) combined footage of Moscow during the August 1991 coup and sequences from his earlier films. Podnieks, who said he never made films but filmed life, was shooting another film, *Unfinished Business*, set in several parts of the former Soviet Union, and thinking of moving into feature films, when he died in a freak diving accident. JG

POLAND

At the birth of cinema Poland was 'officially' non-existent. Since 1795 the country had been partitioned between Austria, Prussia and Russia, and Polish artistic and cultural life had mostly relocated to Paris. However, a strong sense of national identity survived. In the late 1890s several Poles made attempts to develop 'moving pictures', but only Kazimierz Proszynski's 'Pleograf' enjoyed any success; in 1902 and 1903 he shot around fifteen documentary and comedy shorts, which were very popular. The success of the Pleograf was short-lived and, after its first screening in Cracow on 14 November 1896, the Lumière Cinematograph soon led the field. Poland's first cinema was established in Łódź in 1899, and by 1902 the first film studio was making and distributing short films. It was not until 1908, however, that the first Polish feature was produced: *Antoś po raz Pierwszy w Warszawie/Anthony's First Trip to Warsaw*, made by Pathé cameraman Josef Meyer.

In the years that followed, film production grew slowly but steadily. Antoni Fertner, a comic inspired by Max Linder, became a celebrity in Poland and Eastern Europe. Alexander Hertz established the Sfinks studio in 1909 and was soon the most important figure in the development of a Polish national cinema. Hertz produced films of excellent technical quality – if rather theatrical style – and was responsible for discovering and fostering Poland's first stars. Pola Negri's debut in *Niewolnica Zmysłów/Slave of Sin* (1914, d. Jan Pawłowski) was a major hit and Hertz also introduced Jadwiga Smosarska in Danny Kaden and Władysław Lenczewski's *Strzał/The Shot* (1922); Smosarska subsequently became a major Polish screen actress of the 1930s. Hertz was joined by directors Richard Ordyński and Edward Puchalski as cinema blossomed during the war. By 1919 there were 400 cinemas in the newly independent Poland and, with state support, the industry produced twenty-one features and sixty-one shorts. This boom was short-lived, and by 1922 American films dominated the

184

market. Three main Polish film companies functioned in the 1920s and 1930s: Sfinks, Falanga and Leofilm. Apart from popular comedies, farces and melodramas, historical films like Ryszard Bolesławski's *Cud nad Wisłą/Miracle on the Vistula* (1921) and adaptations of classic literary texts were popular genres. There was also a growing Yiddish cinema*, developed by Joseph Green and catering for the large Polish-Jewish community.

A strong critical tradition was established in Poland as early as 1898 with Bolesław Matuszewski's recognition of film as an art form. Karol Irzykowski, an eminent philosopher and literary critic, published many articles on cinema, culminating in his book *Dziesiąta Musa* ('The Tenth Muse', 1921). This lively atmosphere of debate surrounded the success of popular film-makers like Wiktor Biegański, whose *Wampiry Warszawy/Vampires of Warsaw* (1925) was widely acclaimed for its use of a truly cinematic language. In 1928 Poland had its first international success with *Huragan/Hurricane*, Joseph Lejtes' debut feature, and in the following year Michal Waszyński won a prize for the erotic *Kult Ciała/Cult of the Flesh*, Poland's first sound film.

Despite these critical and box-office successes, Polish film production declined in quality and quantity during the late 1920s. The arrival of sound in the midst of an economic depression stretched the young industry to its limit. An attempt to create an alternative cinema was made by START (Stowarzyszenie Miłośników Filmu Artystycznego/ Society of Devotees of Artistic Film), an organisation which prefigured the French New Wave and British 'Free Cinema'. Established in 1930 by such directors as Aleksander Ford*, Wanda Jakubowska*, Stanisław Wohl, Jerzy Bossak and Eugeniusz Cekalski, START called for a cinema based in social reality, higher artistic and technical standards and support from the state (Ford, Jakubowska and others, with Franciszka and Stefan Themerson*, also founded the world's first film-makers' cooperative, SAF, in 1935). The films made by START's members were artistically ambitious, influenced by German expressionism and Soviet montage*, and many won prizes abroad, notably Cekalski and Wohl's *Trzy Etudy Chopina/Three Chopin Studies* at Venice in 1937. The government responded in the mid-1930s by improving tax conditions and in 1937 a record number of twenty-seven features and 102 shorts were produced. Although START was short-lived, its ideas and personnel provided a base for the postwar Polish film industry. Following the German occupation of Poland in 1939, film production was suspended and German films dominated the screens. The war, in which about one in five of the Polish population were killed, also devastated the film industry: equipment, facilities and prints were destroyed in the bombing.

The new communist Poland regarded film as an important asset, and in 1945 the 'industry' was nationalised. Based on the Czołówka Filmowa (a war film unit which operated on the Soviet front in June 1943), Film Polski*, with Ford at its head, was established as the leading production house. Technical equipment was 'acquired' from

185

the Soviet-held part of Germany and the precursor of the famous
Łódź* film school was established in Cracow. By 1947 production
was again under way. The first international success was Jakubowska's *Ostatni Etap/The Last Stage* (1948), about the horror of the
concentration camps. Indeed, the war – occupation, resistance, the
disintegration of Polish society – provided the subject matter for
many films of this period: Leonard Buczkowski's *Zakazane Pio-
senki/Forbidden Songs* (1948), Ford's *Ulica Granicowa/Border Street*
(1949), Andrzej Wajda's* *Pokolenie/A Generation* (1955). But under
the impact of the official ideology, these themes soon fell prey to
rigid formulae: the communist underground was portrayed as the
singular embodiment of the resistance in relation to the suspect
Home Army, the collective hero was celebrated at the expense of
the individual, and general adherence to Socialist Realism* was
required.

By the mid-1950s film production had risen to an average of eight
features annually, with cinemas numbering 2,672. The political thaw
following Stalin's death (1953) allowed a significant restructuring of
film production, giving film-makers greater artistic control. A new
'zespół', or production unit system, was established at Film Polski,
lasting until 1990. The eight (state-funded) units, headed by eminent
film-makers, had nominal artistic and financial autonomy. However,
decisions still had to be verified by the Central Office of Cinematography, so that censorship occurred at script stage, and political content rather than economic or artistic considerations determined the
distribution and exhibition fate of any title.

Under these conditions of limited autonomy and ideological constraint, a new era in Polish film-making was launched. Between 1954
and 1963 a group of films known as the 'Polish School' emerged, characterised by romantic pessimism, a preoccupation with the subjection
of the individual to the forces of history, and a re-examination of
Poland's tragic war years. Films like Wajda's *Kanał/Canal* (1956) and
Popiół i Diament/Ashes and Diamonds (1958), Andrzej Munk's*
Eroica (1958) and Wojciech Has's *Pożegnania/Farewells* (1958) turned
the constraints of the censor to their advantage, using striking visual
symbols, allusion and tone to create a rich subtext. International audiences and critics were fascinated, though at times symbols and
allusions were so nationally specific as to be lost on non-Polish
audiences.

The 1960s, as in Hungary and Czechoslovakia, produced a new generation or 'second wave' of film-makers. Directors like Roman
Polanski*, with *Nóz w Wodzie/Knife in the Water* (1962), and Jerzy
Skolimowski*, with *Walkower/Walkover* (1965), dealt with individual
morality in contemporary Poland, in a style influenced by the French
New Wave. Historical themes were also explored in epic films, including adaptations of Polish literature like Has's *Rękopis Znaleziony w
Saragossie/The Saragossa Manuscript* (1965) and *Lalka/The Doll*
(1968), and Ford's *Krzyżacy/Knights of the Teutonic Order* (1960).

186

The political disruptions of the late 1960s and early 1970s prompted some reorganisation of the industry with the number of film units reduced from eight to six; Ford, Jerzy Toeplitz (head of the Łódź Film School) and Jerzy Bossak (head of the Kamera film unit) lost their administrative positions. The student demonstrations and workers' protests of this period gave impetus to a reappraisal of documentary by a group of young film-makers. Krzysztof Kieślowski*, Marcel Łozinski, Antoni Krauze* and others explored the form to its limits, making a series of exciting, incisive, engaging and often political films. While many of these films were banned or shelved for several years, audience interest was strong and it was not uncommon to go to the cinema just to see the short film.

Wajda's *Człowiek z Marmuru/Man of Marble* (1976) signalled a new mood of social consciousness, witnessed in the rise of the trade union 'Solidarity' and the intense political battles of the period. It also paved the way for the so-called 'cinema of moral unrest'. These films, by Kieślowski, Agnieszka Holland*, Janusz Zaorski*, Filip Bajon, Wojciec Marczewski*, Ryszard Bugajski* and others, eschewed symbolism and allusion in order to comment more directly on the Polish malaise. Thus Kieślowski's *Bez Końca/No End* (1984), Holland's *Kobieta Samotna/A Woman Alone* (1981) and Marczewski's *Dreszcze/Shivers* (1981) evoked a deep unease about the bankruptcy of Polish society. Drawing on their documentary roots, these film-makers focused on everyday realities and moral quandaries with which their audiences could identify. With the growing strength of Solidarity and the popular Lech Wałęsa's vocal criticism of the government, films also became more direct in their approach, examining contemporary society and recent history. Felix Falk's* *Wodzirej/Top Dog* (1979) deals with the corruption of small town politics. Wajda's *Człowiek z Żelaza/Man of Iron* (1981, Palme d'Or at Cannes) mixes documentary footage with fiction, showing tanks descending on protesting crowds in the 1970s and the resulting casualties. And Krauze's *Prognoza Pogody/Weather Forecast* (1983) provided a comic treatment of contemporary issues. (Many of these films, however, were not seen by audiences until martial law was lifted in 1989.)

When General Jaruzelski imposed martial law in 1981, the subsequent imprisonments and retaliations forced many of the film-makers most closely associated with Solidarity to leave Poland or stop working. Others survived by conforming to censorship, which, while stringent politically, became tolerant towards sex and violence. The public responded by largely avoiding cinemas and turning instead to a thriving underground culture. A network of film clubs and cultural activities flourished, using churches as venues. Foreign films were borrowed from embassies, and pirate videos and 16mm copies of shelved titles were screened. A few films continued to be made, like Janusz Zaorski's* *Matka Królów/Mother of Kings* (1982, rel. 1987). Meanwhile established directors such as Wajda and Zanussi* turned to foreign financing. As the economic depression grew worse, young

187

filmmakers concentrated on documentaries and shorts. The largest commercial successes proved to be a new strand of 'science-fiction' comedies, notably Juliusz Machulski's* *Seksmisja/Sex Mission* (1983). By 1986 the industry, like the country, was in severe financial crisis.

The dawn of Poland as a new democracy in 1989 brought hopes for a cinematic revival. Dozens of shelved films were shown domestically and internationally; Bugajski's *Przesłuchanie/The Interrogation* (1981) was particularly applauded. Polish cinema and television productions were concerned once more with setting the historical record straight about, this time, the most recent past. Documentaries by Marcel Łoziński, Maria Zmarz-Koczanowicz and Andrzej Titkow had audiences queuing round the block. However, the euphoria soon vanished when the gravity of Poland's financial crisis became apparent. Those who could, turned to foreign co-productions, 'the today and tomorrow of Polish cinema' as *Kino* put it: Kieślowski to France for *Podwójne Życie Weroniki/The Double Life of Véronique* (1991) and the *Three Colours* trilogy (1993–4), Zanussi to Britain and Denmark for *Dotknięcie/The Touch* (1990). As elsewhere in Eastern Europe, the Polish government opted for privatisation of the film industry, backed by a strong industry lobby, and the hitherto predominantly *auteur*-based cinema turned towards commercialism. Interest in 'serious' film magazines like *Film* and *Kino* has also diminished, while new, more gossipy publications are popular. Censorship has been abolished. Some film units survive as private companies, raising money on a project-by-project basis. A new Ministry of Film offers production monies for projects selected by a panel of experts, on a matching fund basis. Many film-makers, working independently, often have to raise finance through advertising and television. Further problems occur in the distribution and exhibition areas, for Hollywood has been quick to exploit the 'free' Polish market, establishing links with new distribution and exhibition chains and investing heavily in advertising and promotion. Against a background of rising ticket prices and falling wages, and a steady decline in the number of cinemas (from 2,500 in the 1970s to 900 in 1992), America has taken over the screens. Whereas in the 1980s there had been an opening towards Western European film, by 1991 all top twenty box-office successes were US productions. Despite some subsidies to art-house cinemas and distribution companies via the Film Ministry, it is hard to see a Polish film on a Saturday night. Paradoxically Hollywood has boosted the international reputation of Polish production. With art director Allan Starski and director of photography Janusz Kamiński* winning Oscars for their contribution to Spielberg's *Schindler's List* (1993), which was shot in Poland, Polish film professionalism has never been held in higher regard. During the 1990s the veterans of Polish cinema such as Andrzej Wajda, Krzysztof Zanussi, Janusz Zaorski, and others continued to make films, and some new directors made their debut features. The decade was marked by the triumphant international success of Krzysztof Kieślowski's *Three Colours* but also by the untimely death of Kieślowski in 1996 and by the

loss of the veteran of Polish cinema, Wanda Jakubowska in 1998. Actor Jerzy Stuhr* made a compelling directorial debut and was responsible for some of the most acclaimed films of the decade including *Historie milosne/Love Stories*, 1997. Some Polish film-makers managed to adjust to the changing audience tastes and created cinematic works with indisputable mass appeal. Action adventures such as *Psy/Pigs* (1992), directed by Wladyslaw Pasikowski and starring Boguslaw Linda* or the witty features of popular Juliusz Machulski* (*Killer*, 1997) performed more than well at the box-office. In 1999 Jerzy Hoffman* finally released his three-hour epic *Ogniem i mieczem/With Fire and Sword* (1999), an adaptation of Henryk Sienkiewicz's work, the most expensive Polish super-production to date. AW
Website: http://wwwtech.net.pl/filmy

POLANSKI, Roman
Raymond Polanski; Paris, France 1933

Polish director. Perhaps the most famous expatriate Polish film-maker. Polanski's international success, as well as his tragic and infamous private life, have been well documented. Polanski first made shorts, including the much noticed *Dwaj Ludzie z Szafą/Two Men and a Wardrobe* (1958). He shot to fame with his feature debut *Nóż w Wodzie/Knife in the Water* (1962), making the cover of *Time* magazine as the face of new foreign cinema. Subsequently moving to the West, he consolidated his promise with *Repulsion* (1965) and *Cul-de-Sac* (1966), both made in Britain, before moving on to Hollywood. Polanski nonetheless maintained his connection to Poland; his association with composer Krzysztof Komeda continued up to his first Hollywood success, *Rosemary's Baby* (1968), and he often uses Polish cinematographers. Versatile and idiosyncratic, his best work is characterised by his ability to look at the dark side of human nature with a sharp irony and a sense of the absurd. His Hollywood success continued with *Chinatown* (1974), starring Jack Nicholson and Faye Dunaway, but was then cut short when Polanski's private life was brought under legal scrutiny; he moved to France in 1977 to avoid prosecution by US courts. Polanski's European films have ranged from a successful adaptation of Thomas Hardy's classic novel *Tess of the d'Urbervilles* (*Tess*, 1979), through the Hitchcockian overtones of *Frantic* (1988), to the commercial failure of his comedy romp on the high seas, *Pirates* (1986). *Lunes de fiel/Bitter Moon* (1992) refers back to Polanski's earlier work, with echoes of *Nóż w Wodzie* in a tale of sexual obsession. In 1995, he directed *Death and the Maiden*, starring Sigourney Weaver and Ben Kingsley. Polanski continues to make acting contributions in his own films and others, including, *Grosse fatigue* and *Une pure formalité*, the latter co-starring Gérard Depardieu* (both 1995, Fr.). His latest film is the French–Spanish thriller, *The Ninth Gate* (1999) with Johnny Depp. He continues to direct, mainly in Europe, making *Double* (1996, Fr.) and *Angeli* (1996, It.). AW

POPESCU-GOPO, Ion
Bucharest 1923–89

Romanian animator and director, who was largely responsible for modern Romanian animation's success with a worldwide audience. A graduate of the Bucharest Fine Arts Institute and a former sculptor, cartoonist, journalist and book illustrator, Gopo founded the first Romanian animation department in 1950 (which became AnimaFilm* in 1964). After following the Disney line prevalent in Eastern Europe, he created in *Scurtă istorie/A Short History* (1956) the 'little man with the flower' – a character both grotesque and funny, cruel and opportunist, determined to survive, travelling through time and human culture always grasping his flower. It won the Palme d'Or at Cannes, and formed the first of a trilogy. The series inspired UNESCO to sponsor a sequel, *Allo, allo* (1961). In the 1960s Gopo abandoned pure animation. After *S-a furat o bombă/A Bomb was Stolen* (1962), a parody thriller against nuclear war, he concentrated on children's films, science-fiction and live-action animation, even combining all three. *Maria, Mirabella* (1981) is a magical children's musical. In the 1970s Gopo revived the 'little man with the flower': in *Ecce homo* (1978), faced by hunger, pollution and war, he departs the planet leaving his flower behind. *Quo vadis homo sapiens* (1982) is an anthology of Gopo's shorts, and a new film in its own right, in which the 'little man' looks at the history of inventions, philosophy and the failings of humanity. Gopo was chairman of the Romanian Film-makers' Association and maintained a prolific output of features and animation almost until his death. MM

PREISNER, Zbigniew
Bielsko-Biala, Poland 1955

Polish composer. Preisner is Poland's foremost film music composer whose work employs classical Baroque elements in a postmodern blend of sounds. Along with screenwriter Krzysztof Piesiewicz, Preisner was the closest collaborator of director, Krzysztof Kieślowski*, for almost a decade. He wrote the scores for the acclaimed TV series, *Dekalog/Decalogue* (1987–8), for *Bez konca/No End* (1984), *Podwojne zycie Weroniki/La double vie de Véronique/The Double Life of Véronique* (1991), and for the trilogy *Trzy kolory/Trois couleurs/Three Colours: Niebieski/Bleu/Blue* (1993), *Bialy/Blanc/White* (1994) and *Czerwony/Rouge/Red* (1994). Preisner wrote the score for Krzysztof Wierzbicki's documentary, *Krzysztof Kieślowski: I'm So-So ...* (1995). In 1998, Preisner created a unique musical opus, combining voice and instrumental music. *Requiem for My Friend* (1998), dedicated to the memory of Kieślowski, was recorded in Warsaw and Cracow and features performances by numerous outstanding Polish singers, including soprano Elzbieta Towarhicka whose voice was used in Kieślowski's films. Preisner also worked for Polish directors, Agnieszka Holland* on *To Kill a Priest* (1988), *Europa, Europa*

190

(1990), *Olivier, Olivier* (1991), and *The Secret Garden* (1993) and Magdalena Lazarkiewicz on *Przez dotyk/By Touch* (1985) and *Ostatni dzwonek/The Last Schoolbell* (1989). He has written music for many directors worldwide – for Louis Malle's *Fatale/Damage* (1992), Charles Sturridge's *Fairy Tale: A True Story* (1997), and Hector Babenco's *At Play in the Fields of the Lord* (1991) and *Corazón iluminado/Foolish Heart* (1998) and has won a number of international awards. He occasionally uses the alias, Van den Budenmayer. DI

PREOBRAZHENSKAYA, Olga I.   Moscow 1881–1971

Soviet director, actress and scriptwriter. Preobrazhenskaya studied acting at the Moscow Art Theatre Studio and first appeared on screen in the popular *Klyuchi schast'ya/The Keys to Happiness* (1913); she was a leading actress of the pre-Revolutionary cinema. In 1916 she co-directed *Baryshnia-krestianka/The Lady Peasant* with Vladimir Gardin*. Her first film as solo director was *Viktoriia/Victoria* (1917). Though she continued directing until 1941, she is best known for her film about the oppression of women in the pre-Revolutionary Russian countryside, *Baby ryazanskie/Peasant Women of Ryazan* (1927). Preobrazhenskaya taught at VGIK* from 1927 to 1941. RT

PROKOFIEV, Sergei S.   Sontsovka, Russia 1891 – Moscow 1953

Russian composer. Prokofiev wrote his first film score for Alexander Fainzimmer's* *Poruchik Kizhe/Lieutenant Kijé* (1934), but is better known for his work for Sergei Eisenstein* on *Aleksandr Nevskii/Alexander Nevsky* (1938) and *Ivan Groznyi/Ivan the Terrible* (1943–6), which explore Eisenstein's ideas on 'orchestral counterpoint' where the music not merely supports the image but also clashes with and comments on it. The most famous instance of these techniques is the 'Battle on the Ice' sequence in *Aleksandr Nevskii*. RT

PROTAZANOV, Yakov A.   Moscow 1881–1945

Russian director. Protazanov studied at the Moscow Commercial Academy, but after a trip to Paris, where he visited the Pathé Brothers' factory, he joined the Gloria company in Moscow, working first as a translator for the foreign cameramen. His first screenplay was for a 1909 version of Pushkin's *Bakhchisaraiskii fontan/The Fountain of Bakhchisarai*, and the first film he directed was *Pesn' katorzhanina/The Convict's Song* (1911). Of the seventy-three films he made before the Revolution, only seven are extant, but they include such remarkable work as *Ukhod velikogo startsa/The Departure of a Great Old Man* (1912), about the last days of Tolstoy, and, after his move to the Ermolev company, a masterly version of Pushkin's *Pikovaya dama/The Queen of Spades* (1916), with a mesmeric performance by Ivan Mosjoukine* as Ierman. Mosjoukine worked for him again in the proto-expressionist *Satana likuyushchii/Satan Triumphant* (1917), in the bleak northern tale of repression *Malyutka Elli/Little Ellie* (1918), and in a version of Tolstoy's *Otets Sergii/Father Sergius* (1918). After the Revolution, Protazanov moved with Ermolev first to Yalta, and then into emigration, to Paris in 1920, where he gave René Clair his first chance in cinema as an actor in *Le Sens de la mort/The Meaning of Death* (1921), and then to Berlin. In Berlin he was persuaded by Moisei Aleinikov to return to Soviet Russia to work in the new Mezhrabpom-Rus* studio.

His first film on his return was *Aelita* (1924), from Alexei Tolstoi's story, which is famous as the first Soviet science-fiction film, for its Constructivist sets, and for the costumes designed by Alexandra Exter, but it is also remarkable for its acute vision of Russia under the New Economic Policy. Though a popular success, it aroused criticism from both the Party and younger film-makers, and Protazanov followed it with the conventional *Ego prizyv/His Call* (1925), a melodrama which ends with its 'fallen' heroine responding to Lenin's injunction. Throughout the 1920s Protazanov produced a steady stream of melodramas and comedies. *Sorok pervyi/The Forty-First* (1926), from Boris Lavrenev's story, is about a Red Army girl, Maryutka, marooned on a desert island with a White officer who is her prisoner. Despite falling in love with him, she eventually remembers her duty and makes him her forty-first victim. *Chelovek iz restorana/The Man from the Restaurant* (1927) is set in 1916 and chronicles the social awakening of its little man hero. Among Protazanov's successful comedies of the period are *Zakroishchik iz Torzhka/The Tailor from Torzhok* (1926), with Igor Ilyinsky* as the eponymous hero who eventually finds love and wealth when he wins the state lottery; *Protsess o trëkh millionakh/The Three Millions Trial* (1926), a satire, set in Italy, about the world of banking; and *Don Diego i Pelageya/Don Diego and Pelageia* (1927), which mocks provincial bureaucrats. Protazanov's first sound film was *Tommi/Tommy* (1931), in which an English soldier serving in the intervention forces during the Russian Civil War is brought to political awareness. During the 1930s Protazanov's projects encountered increasing difficulties and he was less prolific, but among his most important films of this decade was a powerful version of Ostrovsky's play, *Bespridannitsa/Without a Dowry*, in 1936. His final film, *Nasreddin v Bukhare/Nasreddin in Bukhara* (1943), is a kind of Uzbek *Thief of Baghdad*. The sheer scope and variety of Protazanov's output mean he is increasingly recognised as one of the leading Russian directors.
JG

PUDOVKIN, Vsevolod I.
Penza, Russia 1893 – Riga, Latvia [USSR] 1953

Soviet director, actor and theorist. Pudovkin originally studied chemistry and physics at Moscow University but was called up in 1914 and later captured and imprisoned by the Germans. After the Revolution he became a founder member of Lev Kuleshov's* workshop at the State Film School (later VGIK*) and acted in his *Neobychainye priklyucheniya Mistera Vesta v strane bol'shevikov/The Extraordinary Adventures of Mr West in the Land of the Bolsheviks* (1924), *Luch smerti/Death Ray* (1925) and *Veselaya kanareika/The Happy Canary* (1929). Pudovkin's own first film as a director was a short comedy, *Shakhmatnaya goryachka/Chess Fever* (1925), and this was followed by a short, *Mekhanika golovnogo mozga/The Mechanics of the Brain* (1926). His three major silent films were *Mat'/The Mother* (1926), based loosely on Gorky's account of the 1905 Revolution; *Konets Sankt-Peterburga/The End of St Petersburg* (1927), made to celebrate the tenth anniversary of the October Revolution; and *Potomok Chingis-khana/The Heir to Genghis Khan* (1928, released in the West as *Storm over Asia*), his treatment of British involvement in Mongolia.

Influenced by Kuleshov, Pudovkin laid greater emphasis on the role of the actor than did Sergei Eisenstein* but he was nevertheless co-signatory with Eisenstein and Grigori Alexandrov* of the 1928 'Statement on Sound', which warned of the dangers of the abandonment of montage and the re-theatricalisation of cinema through the use of purely illustrative sound. But, unlike Eisenstein, Pudovkin did not pursue these ideas thoroughly in practice, apart from his first experimentation with sound in *Prostoi sluchai/A Simple Chance* (1932) and *Dezertir/The Deserter* (1933). He used professional actors and his films all had individual heroes. Pudovkin's writings developed these ideas and he was the first Soviet film director to have his works published in English, in *Film Technique* (1929) and *Film Acting* (1935), not published fully in Russian until after his death. Pudovkin also proved more pliable than some other film-makers during the Great Terror and was not always averse to protecting his own interests at the expense of others. His later work deteriorated for reasons that were not entirely within his control, as can be seen from *Pobeda/Victory* (1938), *Admiral Nakhimov* (1946) and *Vozvrashchenie Vasiliya Bortnikova/ The Return of Vasili Bortnikov* (1953). Nevertheless he remains one of the great names from the formative period of Soviet cinema. RT

PULA

National film festival of the former Yugoslavia. This annual presentation of Yugoslav feature films was first held in 1954 in the Croatian town of Pula on the northern Adriatic coast. The films were shown in a Roman arena dating from the first century, transformed into a huge open-air film theatre (with a capacity for 13,000 people). In 1955 the festival began to award prizes, for direction, acting, photography, art direction and music. The award for the best film of the year was the 'Golden Arena'. For the next thirty-five years Pula was the main Yugoslav film event. With the collapse of Yugoslavia, the festival experienced organisational problems, and in 1993 it was remodelled as the National Croatian film festival. SP

PUTTI, Lya de
Vesce 1897 – New York 1931

Hungarian-born actress, best remembered as the seductive Bertha-Marie in E. A. Dupont's *Varieté /Variety* (1925). She began her career in a string of supporting roles, as in Richard Oswald's *Die Liebschaften des Hektor Dalmore* (1921) and *Othello* (1922) with Emil Jannings. In 1922 she appeared in two films by F. W. Murnau, *Der brennende Acker* and *Phantom*. By the mid-1920s, de Putti starred in Lothar Mendes' *S.O.S. Die Insel der Tränen* (1923, opposite Paul Wegener) and in Karl Grune's *Eifersucht* (1925, opposite Werner Krauß). After the success of *Varieté*, Adolph Zukor invited her to Hollywood in 1926, where she was typecast as the exotic, European *femme fatale* in five films, including D. W. Griffith's *Sorrows of Satan* (1926) and as a Russian revolutionary in *The Scarlet Lady* (1928). MW

Bib: Johannes Zeilinger, *Lya de Putti: Ein vergessenes Leben* (1991).

PYANKOVA, Natalya
Mytishchi, Russia [USSR] 1958

Russian director and scriptwriter. Pyankova studied with Sergei Solovyov* and Valeri Rubinchik at VGIK* from 1990 to 1994. Her first film, *S novym godom, Moskva/Happy New Year, Moscow* (1993), shot with long takes and an often static camera, is set entirely in the two rooms of a communal flat, and dissects the aspirations, the confusions, and above all the language of a group of youngish people (played by Pyankova's former fellow students at VGIK), drifting through the first years of a new era. *Strannoe vremya* (1997) consists of three connected stories, shot through with irony and self-consciousness, about the complex interrelationships of a group of men and women in their thirties. JG

PYRIEV, Ivan A.
Kamen, Russia 1901 – Moscow 1968

Soviet director and scriptwriter. After a brief career as an actor in the Proletkult and Meyerhold Theatres, Pyriev began scriptwriting in 1925. His first film as director was *Postoronnaya zhenshchina/A Woman on the Side* (1929), a satirical attack on bourgeois morality.

194

This was followed by a similar approach to bureaucracy in *Gosudarstvennyi chinovnik/A State Official* (1931). *Konveier smerti/The Assembly Line of Death* (1933) depicted the life of three women against the background of the rise of fascism in contemporary Germany. *Partiinyi bilet/Party Card* (1936) and *Sekretar' raikoma/ District Committee Secretary* (1942) carried a more overtly propagandist message, but Pyriev is best remembered for his musical comedies like *Bogataya nevesta/The Rich Bride* (1938), *Traktoristy/Tractor Drivers* (1939), *Svinarka i pastukh/The Swineherd and the Shepherd* (1941) and *Kubanskie kazaki/The Kuban Cossacks* (1950), all awarded the Stalin Prize. Towards the end of his career he devoted himself to adaptations of the works of Dostoyevsky, such as *Brat'ya Karamazovy/ The Brothers Karamazov* (1968). He was head of the Mosfilm studio for many years and was instrumental in setting up the Union of Filmmakers of the USSR*. RT

R

RADEV, Vălo

Vulo Radev; Lesidren 1923

Bulgarian cinematographer, director and writer. One of the key figures in the school of Bulgarian 'poetic realism'*. After graduating from the Moscow Film Theatre (VGIK*) in 1953 as a cameraman, Radev worked on various projects, notably Nikola Korabov's historical epic *Tjutjun/Tobacco* (1962). His first film as director was *Kradecăt na praskovi/The Peach Thief* (1964), for which he also wrote the script (adapted from a story by Emilian Stanev). The international success of *Kradecăt na praskovi* was due in large part to the performance of Nevena Kokanova*, who was to become Bulgaria's most popular screen star. Together with Rangel Vălčanov* and Binka Željazkova*, Radev spearheaded a Bulgarian 'new wave' with a pronounced trend towards 'poetic realism'.

Radev was often entrusted with major innovative productions designed to enhance the professional reputation of Bulgarian cinema. His *Tsar i general/Tsar and General* (1966), depicting the conflict between Tsar Boris and General Zaimov on the eve of World War II on both psychological and philosophical levels, was Bulgaria's first widescreen production. And *Čerhite angeli/Black Angels* (1970), an 'Eastern' about teenage partisans fighting fascists in the mountains, was Boyana* Studios' first commercially successful colour spectacle. RH

RADIČKOV, Jordan Kalimanitsa 1929

Bulgarian writer. Jordan Radičkov is sometimes referred to as the 'Bulgarian Gogol' for his mixture of the grotesque and the folkloric, while his surrealist vision, ironic sensibility and black humour lead others to compare him to Beckett and Ionesco.

Radičkov's prolific output of stories and plays during the 1960s and 1970s proved to be a rich source of inspiration for film directors seeking an alternative to the schematic formula of Socialist Realism*. Zako Heskija was the first to collaborate with him, adapting one of his stories to the screen: *Gorešto pladne/Torrid Noon* (1966), about a sleepy village on a hot summer's day that is stirred to life when a boy playing in a river suffers an accident. Then Binka Željazkova* adapted another of Radičkov's stories into the most controversial production in Bulgarian film history: *Privărzanijat balon/The Attached Balloon* (1967), withdrawn from circulation shortly after its release and banned until 1988. This modern fairy tale about village peasants faced with the opportunity to fly off in a big balloon appeared on the screen just when neo-Stalinism was being reintroduced in Warsaw Pact countries. Another controversial Radičkov adaptation was Hristo Hristov's* award-winning *Posledno ljato/The Last Summer* (1972–4), banned for two years and released only after being severely cut and re-edited. The protagonist – a stubborn peasant who refuses to leave an abandoned village that is soon to be flooded owing to the construction of a dam – was played by eminent stage and screen actor Grigor Vačkov*, making it all the more difficult for the authorities to ban the film altogether.

Other Radičkov adaptations proved less successful artistically and commercially. However, animation director Stojan Dukov paid Radičkov the ultimate compliment by satirising his highly successful, Beckett-like, one-man stage production of *Januari/January* in his cartoon *Fevruari/February* (1977). RH

RAIZMAN, Yuli Ya Moscow 1903–94

Soviet director and scriptwriter, who began his career as literary adviser to Mezhrabpomfilm* studio and assistant director to Yakov Protazanov*. His first major film was *Katorga/Penal Servitude* (1928). He next used sound experimentally in *Zemlya zhazhdet/The Earth Is Thirsty* (1930). In a long career as director and teacher his most important films were *Lëtchiki/Pilots* (1935), *Poslednyaya noch'/The Last Night* (1937, Grand Prix at the 1937 Paris Exhibition and Stalin Prize in 1941), *Mashenka* (1942), *Kavaler zolotoi zvezdy/The Cavalier of the Gold Star* (1951), *Kommunist/The Communist* (1957), *A esli eto lyubov'?/But What If This Is Love?* (1962), *Tvoi sovremennik/Your Contemporary* (1968), *Strannaya zhenshchina/A Strange Woman* (1978), *Chastnaya zhizn'/Private Life* (1982, USSR State Prize in 1983) and

Vremya zhelanii/A Time of Desires (1984). Although Raizman worked throughout the darkest period of Soviet history, his constant attempts to expand the thematic frontiers of Soviet cinema and his conscientious example made him one of the most respected of the older generation of Soviet film-makers, many of whom worked as his assistants at the Mosfilm studio. RT

REBENGIUC, Victor   1933

Romanian actor and occasional director, who gained European recognition in Liviu Ciulei's Cannes award-winning *Pădurea spînzuraţilor/ Forest of the Hanged* (1964). After graduating in Bucharest he became one of Romania's leading actors, helped by a striking stage presence and piercing eyes. Film roles – beginning with *Furtuna/The Storm* (1960) – tested his elegant and powerful presence in stories based on Romanian classics. In *Pădurea spînzuraţilor* he played a tragic hero refusing to fight fellow citizens in World War I, co-starring with his wife Mariana Mihut. In 1967 he played a British World War II officer in the Bulgarian *Noatta cea mai lungă/The Longest Night*, and has since regularly appeared in war films. A range of more realistic contemporary roles in the 1960s, such as *Poveste sentimentala/Sentimental Story* (1963), won Rebengiuc popular and critical acclaim. Through the 1970s and 1980s he balanced stage and screen careers, and in 1976 he co-directed with Dan Piţa* the powerful period drama *Tănase scatiu/A Summer Tale*. Rebengiuc has maintained his popularity by playing complex and heroic individuals who reject authority when necessary, as in the contemporary drama *Doctorul Poenaru* (1978), co-starring Stefan Iordache. He won the Best Male Performance award at San Remo for his role in the poignant peasant saga *Morometii* (1986). Following the 1989 revolution he played the mayor in Lucian Pintilie's* profound studies of late Ceauşescu Romania, *Le Chêne/Steiarul/The Oak* (1992) and *Terminus paradi's/Last stop Paradise* (1998). He continues to act in European films, most recently *Kinai vedelen/Chinese Defense* (1998, Hung.). MM

ROGOZHKIN, Alexander V.   Leningrad 1949

Russian director. Rogozhkin graduated in history and art history from Leningrad State University in 1972 and from the directorial faculty of VGIK*, where he had studied with Sergei Gerasimov*, in 1982. Between 1971 and 1977 he worked as a designer, first at Leningrad Television and then at Lenfilm studios; from 1980 to 1984 he made short films to order. He made his first feature film, *Radi neskol'kikh strochek/For the Sake of a Few Lines* in 1985, but his first successes were with *Karaul/The Guard* (1989), and *Chekist/The Member of the Cheka* (1991). This was followed by *Zhizn's idiotom/Life with an Idiot*

(1993), based on Viktor Erofeyev's eponymous novel about a humanist intellectual and his wife who adopt an idiot to fulfil a mission, not expecting to encounter violence. Rogozhkin achieved enormous popular success with *Osobennosti natsional'noi okhoty/Peculiarities of the National Hunt* (1995), which uses the notorious love Russians have for vodka as a motif for a social comedy. A Finn, who is researching the traditions of the Russian hunt from the time of the tsars to the present day, joins a group of five Russians from the military and police forces in the hunt. Yet things do not turn out as he expects. Drinking may be purposeless, but it is a habit which makes social and national differences disappear. The world returns to its purest form, without boundaries or limits. Rogozhkin has made two sequels to this very popular film, *Operatsiya s novym godom/Operation Happy New Year* (1996) with the same characters in a hospital ward, and *Osobennosti natsional'noi rybalki/Peculiarities of National Fishing* (1998) where the fishing party accidentally ends up in Finland. He has also recently made *Blokpost/Checkpoint* (1998), an anti-war film set in the belligerent Caucasus region, which portrays the day-to-day life of an army detachment: far from Moscow, people are left without support to defend the ideals of a fatherland whose values are crumbling and whose status is disintegrating. Rogozhkin is also the director of the very popular television series *Menty/Cops*. BB

ROMANIA

Though a Lumière brothers' screening took place in Bucharest in 1896, Romanian cinema development was slow and sporadic. The first feature of note was the epic *Războiul independenţei/War of Independence* (1912), directed by the actor Grigore Brezeanu. More artistically noteworthy was Jean Mihail's *Manasse* (1925). Lack of opportunity led Romanians with serious film ambitions, like Lupu-Pick and Jean Negulescu (later Negulesco), to emigrate, respectively to Germany and Hollywood. However, a network of cinemas developed in the 1920s, and films based on Romanian folk myths, which also drew on the American Western, were popular, such as *Haiducii* (1929). In 1934 a fund was set up to encourage production, and 1936 saw Romania's first regular film production, of newsreels and documentaries, under the auspices of the National Tourist Office. Romanian cinema won its first international accolade (first prize at Venice) with *Tara Moţilor/Land of the Motzi* (1938) by Paul Călinescu. Comedies and musicals also began to appear shortly before World War II.

Postwar production (the film industry was nationalised in 1948) was at first undistinguished, with limited range, technique and quantity. The decimated artistic community was alienated from the Soviet-imposed regime. Film strictly followed the Moscow line of popular instruction, though apart from Dinu Negreanu directors were locally trained. Calinescu's *Răsuna valea/The Valley Resounds* (1949) set the

198

Socialist Realist* style, concentrating on triumphs of progress and social justice in rural areas. Victor Iliu* dominated the genre with skill, beginning to pose artistic as well as political questions, but Jean Georgescu's attempts at socialist comedy showed its limitations. The regime's vulnerability made the 'thaw' slower than elsewhere, though in the late 1950s approved cultural links with other 'Romance' nations allowed the first of many co-productions, for example with France for *Ciulinii Baraganului/Baragan Thistles* (1957, dir. Louis Daquin). The wave of new film-makers from the I. L. Caragiale Institute of Theatre and Film Art (IATC) in Bucharest, founded in 1950, still had to conform, and their skills were needed at the Buftea* studios, which produced fifteen features a year from 1958. The Alexandru Sahia documentary and short film studio (founded in 1950 and named after the Marxist writer) also grew at this time under Ion Bostan. The animation skills of Ion Popescu-Gopo* led to the creation of another studio, AnimaFilm*. The making of children's films was pioneered by Elisabeta Bostan*.

Iulian Mihu and Manole Marcus' *Viaţa nu iartă/Life Will Not Forgive* (1958), based on Sahia's war stories, is a classic of the new generation. Liviu Ciulei, coming from the theatre, made three films, culminating in *Pădurea spînzuraţilor/Forest of the Hanged* (1964), a morality tale from World War I scripted by the skilled and prolific Titus Popovici, shot by Ovidiu Gologan and starring Victor Rebengiuc* and Silvia Popovici. It won the Best Director prize for Ciulei at Cannes. Mircea Dragan, the most versatile IATC graduate, promulgated the official line at IATC and in film criticism. His *Lupeni 29* (1962), based on a miners' strike, and Lucian Bratu's massive *Tudor* (1963), about a revolt against the Turks, paved the way for Dragan's and Sergiu Nicolaescu's* 'patriotic' film epics, glorifying Romanian history and spawning a whole series of historically-based adventure yarns. They reflect the new nationalism – and its apotheosis under Ceauşescu's regime (1965–89) – of controlled cultural emancipation from Moscow, creating an ideological orthodoxy more acceptable to the people and the intelligentsia.

In the late 1960s a less schematic representation of society was seen in more contemporary, realistic and challenging films. Andrei Bleier's *Diminetele unui băiat cuminte/The Mornings of a Sensible Youth* (1966) features young people unsure of their future. Gheorghe Vitandis's *O femeie pentru un anotimp/A Woman for One Season* (1969), scripted by Nicolae Breban, shows sensuality and emotional crisis. Theatre director Lucian Pintilie* broke through barriers of form and political acceptability in the subtle political subversion of *Reconstituirea/Reconstruction* (1969). These signs of a 'new wave' were hit by Ceauşescu's consolidation of power, and by delayed reaction to events in Czechoslovakia. Ceauşescu's Stalinism, anti-intellectualism and puritanism imposed a harder line on content, though allowing some experimentation in form. Adaptation to circumstance is evident in Dan Piţa* and Mircea Veroiu's* overpowering and

199

widely acclaimed *Nuntă de piatră/Stone Wedding* (1972); and in Manole Marcus' *Canarul şi viscolul/The Canary and the Storm* (1970), though here the striking visual effects tend to obscure the story. Radu Gabrea's biography of an anarchist hero, *Dincolo de nisipuri/Beyond the Sands* (1973), breached the limits on content, and the released version was rewritten and given a new slant.

Gabrea, Pintilie and Ciulei left Romania in the 1970s to find artistic freedom, and joined Romania's exiled communities in America and France. Piţa and Veroiu led, if not a new wave, perhaps a 'renaissance' into the 1980s, encouraged by praise for their work abroad. Alexandru Tatos* explored relations between individuals and authority in *Mere roşii/Red Apples* (1976) and other films. Iosef Demian's *O lacrima de fata/A Girl's Tear* (1981) showed the militia making a film 'for internal use' about a mysterious death. From the late 1970s Mircea Daneliuc* achieved a measure of subversion with psychology and magic realism, especially in *Probă de microfon/Microphone Test* (1979) and *Glissando* (1984), starring Stefan Iordache. Ada Pistiner's *Stop cadru la masă/ Freeze-Frame at Table* (1980) played ironically with personal frustration; and veteran director Malvina Ursianu's *O lumină la etajul 10/A Light on the Tenth Floor* (1985) also confronted contemporary issues in its story of a released female political prisoner (Irina Petrescu). Meanwhile box-office favourite Nicolaescu, together with Dragan, Marcus, Blaier and others, made competent and popular adaptations of literary classics, historical epics, war films, thrillers, comedies, and some contemporary dramas; while Transylvania* provided the backdrop to a series of Romanian 'Westerns' by various leading directors, starring Ilarion Ciobanu, Ovidiu Iuliu Moldovan and Mircea Diaconu.

The 1989 revolution brought in its wake political and economic paralysis in the film industry. While formal censorship ended, so did guaranteed state support, and film-makers went on strike to break free from the tainted Ministry of Culture. New financial and legal frameworks, and the powers of the new central budget authority – the National Cinematography Centre (CNC) – were slow to emerge; a strike in 1991 challenged Dan Piţa's alleged mismanagement of the CNC. Pintilie's appointment at the Ministry of Culture, and commissioning of Stere Gulea's documentary *Piata Universităţii – Romania/University Square – Romania* (1990), with its criticism of the new president Ion Iliescu, generated conflict with the ruling party. Pintilie's *Le Chêne/Stejarul/The Oak* (1992) is a powerful account of the last years of the Ceauşescu regime in Romania. A Romanian–French co-production which won international recognition, it represents some hope for a renewed Romanian cinema.

Buftea production peaked in the early 1980s at thirty-two features annually, while the Sahia documentary studio made 300 shorts, eighty of them on scientific subjects. Both studios suffered a steep decline, with only fourteen features completed in 1992. AnimaFilm significantly increased output through the 1980s, making sixty shorts and four long features in 1989. Its dominance (over 75 per cent) of film export earnings, and a Spanish link-up in 1991, indicate a more secure future.

Cinema has traditionally been a mass medium in Romania; typically half the population would see major releases, overwhelmingly domestic productions until the 1970s when the regime selectively imported the 'escapism' of American movies and Western television (non-Romanian films are subtitled). Audiences peaked in 1984 at 217 million (for a population of twenty-three million), boosted by the reduction in television output as part of the regime's economy drive. However, the boom in video, and since 1989 the transformation of television (with commercial channels in development), have cut cinema audiences by over 50 per cent. The number of cinemas has declined from a peak of 6,500 in 1965, and a first batch was offered for sale in 1992. Compared to other (former) Eastern bloc countries, American film penetration remains low (though it is rising) because of limited availability. In 1991 only four of the top ten films were American, the biggest hit being the Romanian *Adolescenţi/High School Rock* (1991). There are signs that, as the industry shows that it can be self-financing, the downturn may be at an end.

Romania has one specialist film magazine, *Cinema* (founded 1963). The Film Archive in Bucharest, established in 1957, contains 22,500 shorts. The national film festival has taken place at Costineşti since 1976, though its future is in doubt.

Film in Romania, first harnessed as a tool of ideology and economic development, became in the 1960s a central element in a new ideology based on Romanian national identity. It has remained partly in the shadow of theatre, sharing a directing and acting talent which considers theatre its first home. Its influence is currently small compared to television, which dominated the 1989 revolution and remains the central political arena. An East European-style 'new wave' or 'school' ultimately proved politically impossible, but the alternative paths taken have inspired in a few directors some of the subtlest and strongest imagery in world cinema – reflecting Romania's unique political and cultural experience. In the 1990s, Romanian cinema enjoyed international successes at festivals with the films of established directors such as Lucian Pintilie, Mircea Daneliuc, Dan Piţa, Mircea Veroiu, as well as with films by newcomers such as Radu Mihaileanu, who relied almost exclusively on foreign funding to make his *Trahir/Betrayal* (1993) and *Train de vie/Train of Life* (1998). MM
[> TRANSYLVANIA]

ROMM, Mikhail I.

Zaigraevo, Siberia [Russian Empire] 1901 – Moscow 1971

Soviet director and scriptwriter. Romm fought in the Red Army during the Civil War, studied sculpture, translated Flaubert and Zola, and wrote scripts before directing his first film, the Maupassant adaptation *Pyshka/Boule de Suif* (1934). Best known in the 1930s for his two revolutionary anniversary films, *Lenin v oktyabre/Lenin in October* (1938) and *Lenin v 1918 godu/Lenin in 1918* (1939, Stalin Prize in 1941), he then tended to toe the Party line with films such as *Mechta/The Dream* (1943), *Russkii vopros/The Russian Question* and *Vladimir Ilyich Lenin* (both 1948), *Sekretnaya missiya/Secret Mission* (1950) and *Ubiistvo na ulitse Dante/Murder on Dante Street* (1956), but much of his subsequent work was devoted to an exploration of sensitive moral dilemmas, as in *Devyat' dnei odnogo goda/Nine Days of One Year* (1962) and, above all, *Obyknovennyi fashizm/Ordinary Fascism* (1966). His last film, *I vse-taki ya veryu/Nonetheless I Believe* (1976), was completed by Marlen Khutsiev*, Elem Klimov* and German Lavrov. Romm taught at VGIK* from 1949 and his pupils included Tengiz Abuladze*, Grigori Chukhrai*, Vasili Shukshin*, Georgi Danelia* and Gleb Panfilov*. He was known in film circles for his outrageous anecdotes and imitations of his colleagues, which have since been issued on record and published in book form. RT

ROOM, Abram M.   Vilna, Lithuania [Russian Empire] 1894 – Moscow 1976

Soviet director and scriptwriter. After studying psychology, Room joined Meyerhold's theatre in 1923. He began teaching at VGIK* and made his first short comedy films in 1924. His first features were *Bukhta smerti/Bay of Death* and *Predatel'/The Traitor* (both 1926), but he achieved notoriety with his study of an eternal triangle in the social context of the New Economic Policy, *Tret'ya Meshchanskaya/Bed and Sofa/Third Meshchanskaya Street* (1927), from a script written with Viktor Shklovsky* and starring Nikolai Batalov*. *Prividenie, kotoroe ne vozvrashchaetsya/The Ghost That Never Returns*, set largely in a penal colony in Mexico, and *Plan velikikh rabot/Plan for Great Works*, the first Soviet sound feature film, followed in 1930. His next project, *Odnazhdy letom/Once One Summer*, was stopped during filming in 1932 and his next completed film, *Strogii yunosha/A Strict Young Man*, made in 1934, was banned because it dealt with the sensitive question of equality in Soviet society. After this, although he went on making films, his career as teacher ceased and as a film-maker he went into decline: he ended up making a series of literary adaptations of no great interest. RT

RUSSIAN AND SOVIET FILM PRESS

The film press has played a particularly important part in the history of Russian and Soviet cinema. Before the Revolution the established press tended to regard cinema as something like a toy and virtually ignored it. The rapid growth in cinema, and the cut-throat competition, led to different studios producing their own promotional magazines. In the 1920s a variety of regional and interest groups continued this tradition, but with the centralisation of the industry in the 1930s the situation changed. Since 1931 the principal theoretical and historical journal, which also reviews current films, has been *Iskusstvo kino* ('The Art of Cinema'), published monthly. Many leading film-makers, from Sergei Eisenstein* and Dziga Vertov* onwards, have published articles even when their film-making activities were officially out of favour. On the other hand, it was often through this journal that official disapproval was first made explicit as, for example, with the denunciation of Boris Shumyatsky* in January 1938. In the late Soviet period a mass-circulation popular illustrated magazine was also produced and translated into several languages, including English, under the title *Sovetskii ekran* ('Soviet Screen'). In these years *Iskusstvo kino* began to expand its coverage of Western films and Western popular culture, but new organs of scholarly research and historical documentation started work, in particular *Kinovedcheskie zapiski* ('Scholarly Film Notes'), produced by a group associated with the Cinema Research Institute of the Russian Cinema Committee in Moscow.

Kinovedcheskie zapiski has now produced over forty issues and has become the major journal of its kind, with a worldwide range of contributors. Also of major importance in the 1990s has been *Seans* ('Show') (eighteen issues to mid-1999). This beautifully produced and intellectually challenging St Petersburg-based journal concentrates on contemporary cinema and cultural theory. *Kinostsenarii* ('Film Scripts'), founded in 1973, publishes, in addition to the scripts of made and planned films, interviews, memoirs and archival material. At the other end of the spectrum are glossy magazines like the Russian version of *Premiere*, which started in 1996 and concentrates on Hollywood stars, while *Iskusstvo kino* continues successfully to straddle various cinematic worlds with increasingly serious attention paid to European and world art cinema and to new technologies. RT

RYAZANOV, Eldar A.   Samara, Russia [USSR] 1927

Russian director, scriptwriter and playwright. Ryazanov graduated from VGIK*, where he had studied with Kozintsev*, in 1950. After work making documentaries, he made the musical comedy, *Karnaval'naya noch'/Carnival Night* (1956), in which the humourless arts bureaucrat Ogurtsov is played by Igor Ilyinsky*. *Chelovek niotkuda/The Man from Nowhere* (1961) is a satirical comedy involving an anthropologist discovering a wild man and bringing him to Moscow. The hugely successful *Beregis' avtomobilya/Mind That Car!* (1966), the story of an eccentric thief who steals cars from crooks, sells them and gives the money to kindergartens, marked the beginning of a long and productive partnership with the playwright Emil Braginsky.

Ryazanov and Braginsky were responsible for some of the most popular comedies of the next two decades, including *Zigzag udachi/The Zigzag of Luck* (1968), *Ironiya sud'by, ili s legkim parom!/The Irony of Fate, or Have a Good Sauna!* (1975), *Sluzhebnyi roman/An Office Romance* (1977) and *Garazh/The Garage* (1980). In *Vokzal dlya dvoikh/Station for Two* (1983), the popular star Lyudmila Gurchenko, who made her debut for Ryazanov in *Carnival Night*, plays a middle-aged waitress who falls in love with a travelling musician. *Zhestokii romans/A Cruel Romance* (1984), starring Nikita Mikhalkov*, is a new version of the Ostrovsky play *Without a Dowry* earlier filmed by Protazanov*. *Zabytaya melodiya dlya fleity/Forgotten Melody for Flute* (1987) returns to satirising bureaucracy in the figure of Filimonov, head of the 'Central Leisure Directorate', a (fictitious) state institution devoted to deciding how Soviet citizens should spend their free time. *Dorogaya Yelena Sergeyevna/Dear Yelena Sergeyevna* (1988), based on a play by Lyudmila Razumovskaya, is an altogether darker piece, about a lonely teacher terrorised by her teenage students. After a long but ultimately unsuccessful attempt to film Vladimir Voinovich's *Chonkin* novels, Ryazanov made *Nebesa obetovannye/Promised Heavens* (1991), a social fantasy which he describes as a cry of both hope and desperate horror at the present state of Russia. This was followed, in 1993, by *Predskazanie/The Prophecy*, a social melodrama set in contemporary Moscow, the story of a middle-aged writer told by a Gypsy that he has twenty-four hours to live. *Privet, duralei!/Hallo, Little Fools!* (1996) is a tragicomic love story. Ryazanov is one of the few directors of the older generation to have managed to produce new and successful films regularly throughout the 1990s. His enormous popularity has been reflected over the years in his receipt of a number of state awards, including that of People's Artist of the Soviet Union. There have been several editions of the screenplays he wrote with Braginsky, and his book of memoirs, *Nepodvedennye itogi* ['Without Drawing Conclusions'], first published in Moscow in 1983, was reissued in expanded form in 1995. JG

RYBCZYŃSKI, Zbigniew   1949

Polish director. Rybczyński studied Fine Art in Warsaw and graduated as a cameraman from Łódź* in 1973. He made several experimental shorts for various animation studios in Poland, including *Tango* (1980), which won an Academy Award and first prize at Annecy. On the strength of his international reputation, he emigrated to America in the early 1980s and established his own studio, Zbig Vision. Rybczyński is at the forefront of video production, using high-definition technology and exploring film form in videos like *Steps* (1987, US) and *Orchestra* (1990, US). His experiments and achievements with the new possibilities offered by video have led to comparisons with film pioneer Georges Méliès. In 1994, Rybczyński directed, wrote and produced *Kafka*, part of the Genii series and in 1996 made an animated short, *Manhattan*. AW

Other Films Include: *Kwadrat/Square, Take Five* (1972); *Sklad* (1972); *Plamuz* (1973); *Zupa* (1974); *Nowa Ksiazka* (1975); *Swieto/Holiday, Weg zum Nachbar/The Road to the Neighbour* (1976); *Piatek-sobota/Friday-Saturday* (1977); *Mein Fenster/My Window* (1979); *Tango* (1980); *Media* (1980); *Angst* (1983); *The Day Before* (1984); *The Discreet Charm of Diplomacy* (1984); *Imagine* (1986); *Steps* (1987); *The Fourth Dimension* (1988); *The Duel* (1988); *Capriccio No. 24* (1989); *The Orchestra* (1990); *Washington* (1991); *Mistrz i Malgorzata/ The Master and Margarita* (1993).

S

SaGA

Led by Ademir Kenović, the Sarajevo Group of Auteurs (SaGA) was a loose collective which acted as a forum for those involved in all aspects of film-making in Sarajevo after Yugoslavia's break-up.* Working with a limited funding, the members of SaGA were enabled to make movies with financial assistance from organisations such as the Soros Foundation or Rotterdam Film Festival's Hubert Balls Fund. SaGA members documented the suffering of Sarajevo throughout the war, and coined the term 'Sarajevo hyperreality' when it became obvious that to describe their films as documentaries was insufficient. Footage shot and edited by SaGA members was widely used in a large number of documentaries about the Bosnian war made in the West. Besides Kenović, key figures in the group were Ismet Arnautalić, Mirza Idrizović and Pjer Zalica. Each of them directed a section of the compilation documentary *MGM Sarajevo: covjek, bog, monstrum/MGM Sarajevo: Man, God, The Monster* (1994) which was shown as part of Directors' Fortnight at Cannes in 1994, and which, along with Kenović's *Savrseni krug/Perfect Circle* (1997), remains one of the group's best-known films. DI

SÁNDOR, Pál   Budapest 1939

Hungarian director, one of the most distinctive and controversial talents of contemporary Hungarian cinema. Sándor graduated from the Academy of Theatre and Film Arts in 1964 and made a few shorts at the Balázs Béla Stúdió*. From his first feature, *Bohóc a falon/Clown on the Wall* (1967), Sándor's films have been concerned with the relationship between the individual and history, expressed with incisive humour but also a compassion rare in Hungarian film. The novelty of his approach lies in his ability to create microcosms which reflect history and society through a handful of characters, abolishing in the process the boundaries between the everyday and the historical. The need to belong is strong in many of his characters, presented as stumbling through a hostile world which they fail to understand while stubbornly clinging to their ideals. This is best seen in *Régi idők focija/Football of the Good Old Days* (1973). Minarik, the protagonist, is a direct descendant of Chaplin, and Sándor's irony and humanism merge in a burlesque tone which conceals the biting seriousness of his subject matter. Minarik (Dezső Garas) evolved into the more mature and solitary figure of Svéd in *Szabadíts meg a gonosztól/Deliver Us from Evil* (1978) and appeared as a cabaret clown in *Ripacsok/The Salamon and Stock Show* (1981), always struggling with the same problem: how to keep a group together, whether it be a ragged suburban football team, a disintegrating family in the midst of a nightmarish war, or two ageing clowns grotesquely sewn together in one pair of trousers.

Since *Ripacsok*, Sándor's idealism has gradually crumbled away, together with the tight narrative structure and abundant though disciplined imagery of his earlier films. Lately he has been working as a film and television producer. FC

Other Films Include: *Szeressétek Ódor Emíliát!/Love Emilia!* (1969); *Sárika, drágám/Sarah, My Dear* (1971); *Herkulesfürdői emlék/Improperly Dressed* (1976); *Szerencsés Dániel/Daniel Takes a Train* (1983); *Csak egy mozi/Just a Movie* (1985); *Miss Arizona* (1988, Hung./It.).

SÁRA, Sándor   Tura 1933

Hungarian cinematographer and director, one of the most important representatives of the traditionalist trend in Hungarian cinema. Sára graduated from the Academy of Theatre and Film Arts in 1957 and was among the founders of the Balázs Béla Stúdió*. As well as making some remarkable documentaries, he was cinematographer for a number of important Hungarian films by the young generation of the 1960s, like *Sodrásban/Current* by István Gaál (1963), *Tízezer nap/Ten Thousand Suns* by Ferenc Kósa (1965), *Apa/Father* by István Szabó* (1966), and *Szindbád* by Zoltán Huszárik* (1970). His distinctive cinematographic style is characterised by rather static but expressive compositions and his 1960s work, based on geometrically organised long shots, was a unique stylistic choice at the time. He made his first feature film as a director, *Feldobott kő/Upthrown Stone*, in 1969. This is a powerful story about the conflicts between different cultural traditions and ways of life in a political situation which turned cultural and ethnic minorities against each other. Sára continued to make feature films in the 1970s and 1980s, though they never matched the quality of his earlier work. Nevertheless, Sára was the initiator of a series of 'historical documentaries' – adopting an oral history-based reportage approach that was to dominate Hungarian documentary filmmaking in the 1980s and which occasionally provoked political controversy because of its critical stance towards official history. In the late 1980s and early 1990s, Sára continued to make documentaries dealing with the historical tragedies of the Hungarian people. Lately, he has been nominated as the President of Duna TV, the Hungarian satellite programme aimed at the Hungarian minorities living in neighbouring countries. KAB

Other Films Include: *Holnap lesz fácán/Tomorrow We Are to Have Pheasant* (1974); *80 huszár/80 Hussars* (1978); *Néptanítók/Schoolmasters* (1981); *Tüske a köröm alatt/Thorn under the Nail* (1987); *Könyörtelen idők/Harsh Times* (1991); *A Vád/Prosecution* (1996).

SASS-DORT, Barbara Łódź 1936

Polish director. Sass-Dort is popularly regarded in Poland as a feminist director. Her first feature, *Bez Miłości/Without Love* (1980), featured well-known actress Dorota Stalińska as a new type of heroine, intent on making a career rather than fulfilling her 'woman's role'. Sass-Dort's films follow a classical narrative structure, and characteristically look at women in Polish society, often featuring strong female protagonists who manipulate men and the system in order to get what they want. Sass-Dort directed television films for Andrzej Wajda's* 'X' production unit and features for the 'Kadr' unit headed by Jerzy Kawalerowicz*. Her 1993 feature *Pajęczarki/Web-spinners* looks at post-communist Poland, telling the story of two sisters who turn to crime in order to fund a trip to America. AW

Other Films Include: *Debiutantka/The Outsider* (1982); *Krzyk/The Scream* (1983); *Dziewczęta z Nowolipek i Rajska Jabłoń/The Girls from Nowolipek and the Apple Tree of Paradise* (1985); *W Klatce/Caged* (1987); *Historia niemoralna/An Immoral Story* (1990); *Pajeczarki/ Unlicensed Viewers* (1993); *Tylko strach/Only Fear* (1993); *Poluszenie/ Temptations* (1996); *Jak narkomk/Like a Dopehead* (1999).

SAVCHENKO, Igor A. Vinnitsa, Ukraine [Russian Empire] 1906 – Moscow 1950

Ukrainian Soviet director, scriptwriter and teacher. After training as an actor, Savchenko began directing agit-films* in 1931. He played a leading role in *Dvadsat' shest' komissarov/Twenty-Six Commissars*

207

(1933) and directed his first major film, the musical comedy *Garmon'/ The Accordion*, in 1934. The film provided a rather sanitised view of collectivisation in the Ukraine. During World War II he made several patriotic films but is probably best remembered for two epic depictions of Ukrainian history, *Bogdan Khmelnitsky* (1941) and *Taras Shevchenko* (1951). From 1946 he headed the Directors' Workshop at VGIK*, where he taught, among others, Marlen Khutsiev*, Alexander Alov and Vladimir Naumov. RT

SCHORM, Evald   Prague 1931–88

Czech director. Regarded as the 'philosopher' of the Czech New Wave*, Evald Schorm graduated from FAMU* in 1962. Noted for an impressive range of documentaries made between 1959 and 1964, he directed his first feature, *Každý den odvahu/Everyday Courage*, in 1964. A controversial analysis of the crisis of a party worker alienated from those he claims to represent, it was followed in 1966 by *Návrat ztraceného syna/Return of the Prodigal Son*, a study of suicide linked to an analysis of a society in crisis. Schorm's films can be characterised as intense moral reflections framed in a fairly conventional narrative form. After refusing to sign the obligatory acknowledgment of the correctness of the 1968 invasion, Schorm was unable to make films, and turned his attention to the stage, where he worked extensively on productions ranging from Janáček and Mozart to Shakespeare and Brecht. Schorm returned to the studios for *Vlastně se nic nestalo/ Killing with Kindness* (1988), in which the stars of *Každý den odvahu* and *Návrat ztraceného syna*, Jana Brejchová* and Jan Kačer, were reunited, but he died before the editing was completed. PH

Other Films Include: *Proč?/Why?* [short] (1964); *Zrcadlení/Reflections* [short], *Perličky na dně/Pearls of the Deep* [episode, *Dům radosti/House of Joy*] (1965); *Pět holek na krku/Saddled with Five Girls* (1967); *Pražské noci/Prague Nights* [episode, *Chlebove střevíčky/ The Bread Slippers*], *Farářův konec/End of a Priest* (1968); *Zmatek/ Confusion* [short] (1968, rel. 1990); *Den sedmý, osmá noc/Seventh Day, Eighth Night* (1969, rel. 1990); *Psi a lidé/Dogs and People* (1971).

SELYANOV, Sergei M.   Olonets, Karelia [USSR] 1955

Russian director, producer and scriptwriter. Selyanov studied at the Tula Polytechnic Institute from 1975 to 1978 and ran an amateur film studio there. He graduated from the scriptwriting faculty of VGIK*, where he had studied with Nikolai Figurovsky, in 1980, and completed the Higher Courses for Directors, studying with Rolan Bykov, in 1987–8. He is the head of STW, a film production company, which has

208

produced a number of recent films by Alexei Balabanov*, Oleg Kovalov*, and Alexander Rogozhkin*. Selyanov's first film, *Den' angela/Saint's Day* (1980–8), co-directed with Nikolai Makarov, was made without any funding, and not completed until 1988; it deals with the peasant community of the teenager Mafusail [Methuselah] whose father is a Civil War hero, whose brothers are criminals, but whose sisters are hardworking and devout. The mystical drama *Dukhov den'/Whit Monday* (1988), which stars the singer of the group DDT, Yuri Shevchuk, and *Vremya pechali eshche ne prishlo/The Time for Sorrow Has Not Yet Come* (1995) both deal with similar themes of life in the country. In *Time for Sorrow* the character Ivanov is first seen producing false bank notes in St Petersburg. He then features in a retrospective set in the countryside, in his native village, which is visited by a surveyor who explains to the inhabitants the impending eclipse of the sun. At the end of this flashback the camera tracks back on Ivanov, now on board an aeroplane which he hijacks and re-routes to Paris with the help of a gun he has made from chocolate. The plane lands in a Paris that is as false as the gun, and then turns out to be the right destination, the place Ivanov really dreamed of: the fields near his village. In *Russkaya ideya/The Russian Idea* (1995) with a script by Oleg Kovalov*, Selyanov traces the Russian Idea in Soviet cinema history through a montage of classic Russian and Soviet films. The early Soviet era is perceived as a golden age for the Russian Idea, and for the Socialist Realist utopian vision of paradise on earth. Selyanov usually juxtaposes the corruption of the city with sincerity and naïvety in the countryside, urban values spoiling and undermining rural ones. BB

ŠERBEDŽIJA, Rade   Bunic, Yugoslavia [now Croatia] 1946

Yugoslav actor of Serbo-Croatian origin. Šerbedžija started his career in the late 1960s and has appeared in over fifty feature films, mostly by Yugoslav directors such as Vatroslav Mimica, Živojin Pavlović*, Goran Marković, Rajko Grlić* and Boro Drasković. A handsome man with a memorable face, Šerbedžija has been cast in a large variety of roles – from Josip Broz-Tito in the TV drama *Bombaski proces* (1978) to a sexually-over-performing servant in Dušan Makavejev's* *Manifesto* (1988). In the early 1990s he became a dissident figure at odds with the nationalist regimes in Yugoslavia and Croatia and subsequently moved to the West where he has acted in a number of leading and supporting roles in films made by international directors – from Nicholas Roeg's adaptation, *Two Deaths* (1995) and Gregor Nicholas's tale of immigrants in New Zealand, *Broken English* (1996) through Francesco Rosi's Holocaust drama, *La Tregua/The Truce* (1996) and Stanley Kubrick's last film, *Eyes Wide Shut* (1999) to Hollywood entertainment flicks such as *The Saint* (1997) and *Mighty*

Joe Young (1999). At the same time he continued appearing in a number of features made throughout the various post-Yugoslav states in the 1990s. Šerbedžija's best role is the one of the weary Macedonian expatriate, the photographer Aleksandar in Milcho Mančevski's* *Pred dozhdot/Before the Rain* (1994). DI

SERBIA – see YUGOSLAVIA (former)

SHAKHNAZAROV, Karen G.   Moscow 1952

Russian director and screenwriter. Shakhnazarov studied at VGIK* in the studio of Igor Talankin, graduating in 1975. His film *My iz dzhaza/Jazzmen* (1983) follows the rise to fame of an Odessa jazz quartet in the 1920s, and was a great popular hit. It was followed by *Zimnii vecher v Gagrakh/A Winter Evening in Gagra* (1985) and *Kur'er/Messenger Boy* (1986), a coming-of-age comedy. *Gorod zero/ Zero City* (1989) is an absurd comedy in which an engineer's visit to a provincial Russian town turns into a nightmarish existential journey through Soviet experience.

Tsareubiitsa/Assassin of the Tsar (1991), a British–Russian co-production, starring Malcolm McDowell and the leading Russian actor Oleg Yankovsky, begins as a psychological drama, but lapses into a dull period piece about the last days of Russian imperial family. In 1993 Shakhnazarov and his regular scriptwriter Alexander Borodyansky co-directed *Sny/Dreams*, in which a late nineteenth-century countess 'dreams' contemporary Russian reality. *Amerikanskaia doch'/The American Daughter* (1995), one of several recent Russian films to ponder on the relationship with America, casts Vladimir Mashkov*, one of the most popular new stars of Russian cinema, as Varakin, whose former wife has now married an American, taking their daughter to San Francisco. Varakin kidnaps his daughter, and together they criss-cross America having a succession of adventures until he is arrested and imprisoned, only for his daughter to rescue him by helicopter and fly them back home to Russia. *The American Daughter*, though notable for being one of the first Russian films to be shot on location in the US, makes little pretension to originality. Shakhnazarov's most recent film *Den' polnoluniia/The Day of the Full Moon* (1997), however, is his most impressive and ambitious work to date, effectively using the original conceit of following a kaleidoscope of seemingly unconnected characters and episodes through a single day. From its initial Moscow setting the film expands into a disquisition on the whole of Russia and on recent history. In recent years Shakhnazarov has run his own Kur'er [Courier] film studio, and since 1998 he has been General Director of Mosfilm. JG

SHENGELAYA, Eldar N.   Tbilisi, Georgia [USSR] 1933

Georgian director. Eldar Shengelaya is the son of the director Nikolai Shengelaya, a key figure in the development of Georgian cinema, and the brother of Georgi Shengelaya*. He graduated from Sergei Yutkevich's* workshop at VGIK* in 1958. Among his early successes was *Neobyknovennaya vystavka/An Unusual Exhibition* (1969), a tragicomedy about the compromises in the life of a provincial sculptor. *Golubye gory/Blue Mountains* (1984), a whimsical comedy set in a Tbilisi publishing house, brought him international success. In a move away from the light, ironical humour of his early films, in 1993 Shengelaya made *Ekspress-Informatsiia/Express Information*, a dark absurdist comedy which chronicles the moral and political degradation of recent years. JG

SHENGELAYA, Georgi N.   Tbilisi, Georgia [USSR] 1933

Georgian director and actor. Georgi Shengelaya is the son of the director Nikolai Shengelaya, a key figure in the development of Georgian cinema, and the brother of Eldar Shengelaya*. He graduated from Alexander Dovzhenko's* and Mikhail Romm's* workshop at VGIK* in 1963. Shengelaya achieved early renown with his visually compelling 1971 film *Pirosmani*, a portrait of the brilliant Georgian primitive painter Niko Pirosmanashvili (1862–1918). *Melodii Veriiskogo kvartala/Melodies of the Veriisky Quarter* (1973) is a musical set in pre-Revolutionary Tiflis, and shows the influence of *Seven Brides for Seven Brothers*. *Pridi v dolinu vinograda/Come to Grape Valley* (1977) concerns the effect of construction work on a beautiful Georgian valley, while *Puteshestvie molodogo kompozitora/The Journey of a Young Composer* (1985) is set in 1907: while repression continues in the wake of the failure of the 1905 revolution, the young composer wanders eastern Georgia in search of folk songs. JG

SHEPITKO, Larisa E.   Artemovsk, Ukraine [USSR] 1938 – Kalinin District, Russia 1979

Russian director. Shepitko graduated from VGIK*, where she had studied in the workshop of Alexander Dovzhenko* (whom she always referred to as her mentor) and Mikhail Romm* in 1963. Her diploma work was *Znoi/Heat* (1963), made for Kirgizfilm from 'The Camel's Eye', a story by the Kirgiz writer, Chingiz Aitmatov about a clash of generations on a collective farm. It was followed by *Kryl'ya/Wings* (1966), in which a middle-aged woman, director of a civil engineering school, yearns for her days as a pilot in World War II and struggles to understand her daughter's generation. Shepitko's next project was the short film *Rodina elektrichestva/ Homeland of*

Electricity (1967), from the story by Andrei Platonov about the coming of electricity to a Russian village after the Revolution. Frequently compared to the work of her master Dovzhenko, this film, like Andrei Smirnov's* *Angel*, was shot as part of a portmanteau film *Nachalo nevedomogo veka/The Beginning of an Unknown Century*, made to mark the fiftieth anniversary of the Revolution. But the films were banned for twenty years, and *The Homeland of Electricity* only surfaced in 1987, long after Shepitko's death. In *Ty i ya/You and I* (1971) a brain surgeon suddenly experiences an identity crisis and goes to Siberia to sort out his life. Shepitko's greatest achievement is *Voskhozhdenie/The Ascent* (1976), taken from Vasil Bykau's story 'Sotnikov' and set in German-occupied Belorussia in 1942. The film, which concerns the tragic fate of a group of partisans, is suffused with spiritual strength and religious symbolism. It won the Golden Bear at Berlin in 1977. Shepitko died prematurely in a car crash in 1979, after beginning work on a version of Valentin Rasputin's lament for the Siberian village 'Farewell to Matyora'. The film was completed by her husband, Elem Klimov*, as *Proshchanie/Farewell* (1983). He is also the director of a short film made in her memory, *Larisa* (1981). JG

SHKLOVSKY, Viktor B.   St Petersburg 1893 – Moscow 1984

Soviet writer, critic and theorist. In the course of a long career Shklovsky scripted a number of films, including Lev Kuleshov's* *Po zakonu/By the Law* (1926) and *Gorizont* (1932); Abram Room's* *Bukhta smerti/Bay of Death*, *Predatel'/The Traitor* (both 1926) and *Tret'ya Meshchanskaya/Bed and Sofa/Third Meshchanskaya Street* (1927); Boris Barnet's* *Dom na Trubnoi/The House on Trubnaya* (1928); and Vsevolod Pudovkin's* *Minin i Pozharskii/Minin and Pozharsky* (1939). A leading Formalist, he also wrote a number of theoretical works on cinema and literature, including *Literatura i kinematograf* ('Literature and Cinema', 1923), *Gamburgskii schët* ('The Hamburg Reckoning', 1926), *Tret'ya fabrika* ('The Third Factory', 1926, translated into English in 1977), *Ikh nastoyashchee* ('Their Present-Day', 1927), *Kak pisat' stsenarii* ('How to Write a Script', 1931), a study of Sergei Eisenstein* (1978), a volume of memoirs (1966) and countless articles of film criticism and theory. RT

Bib: Viktor Shklovsky, *Third Factory* (1977).

SHOSTAKOVICH, Dmitri D.   St Petersburg 1906 – Moscow 1975

Russian composer. While studying at the Leningrad Conservatoire, Shostakovich earned money by playing piano accompaniment to films.

212

His first film score was for Grigori Kozintsev* and Leonid Trauberg's* *Novyi Vavilon/New Babylon* (1929) and he also scored their *Odna/ Alone* (1931) and 'Maxim trilogy' (1935–9), and Kozintsev's two Shakespearean films, *Gamlet/Hamlet* (1964) and *Korol' Lir/King Lear* (1971). Shostakovich also wrote music for Fridrikh Ermler* and Sergei Yutkevich's* *Vstrechnyi/Counterplan* (1932), Grigori Alexandrov's* *Vstrecha na El'be/Meeting on the Elbe* and Mikhail Chiaureli's* *Padenie Berlina/The Fall of Berlin* (both 1949). RT

SHUB, Esfir I.
Chernigov district, Ukraine [Russian Empire] 1894 – Moscow 1959

Soviet director. From 1922 to 1942 Shub worked as an editor of fiction films, rendering foreign films 'suitable' for Soviet audiences by excising politically incorrect aspects. She worked with Sergei Eisenstein* and they influenced one another considerably, a debt which both acknowledged. Shub was also involved in archival work on pre-Revolutionary newsreel and documentary footage, from which she made the compilation films for which she is most famous: *Padenie dinastii Romanovykh/The Fall of the Romanov Dynasty* (1927) and *Rossiya Nikolaya II i Lev Tolstoi/Lev Tolstoy and the Russia of Nicholas II* (1928). She went on to make compilations of contemporary Soviet footage, such as *Velikii put'/The Great Path* (1927); *Segodnya/Today* (1930); *KShE/Komsomol – Patron of Electrification*, with its highly experimental use of sound (1932); *Moskva stroit metro/ Moscow Builds the Metro* (1934); and *Strana sovetov/The Land of the Soviets* (1937). In 1939 she made a compilation of footage shot by Soviet cameramen in the Spanish Civil War, *Ispaniya/Spain*. Although less interesting aesthetically than the work of Dziga Vertov*, Shub's films did reach larger audiences. Her memoirs, *Krupnym planom* ('In Close-Up', 1959), are an important historical source, while her films preserve much footage that might otherwise have been destroyed. RT

SHUKSHIN, Vasili M.
Srostki, Siberia [USSR] 1929 – Kletskaya, Russia [USSR] 1974

Russian writer, director and actor. Shukshin worked on his local collective farm in the Altai region from the age of sixteen, and was then employed in a factory in Central Russia. He served as a sailor from 1949 to 1952 before returning to his village. In 1954 he began to study direction at VGIK* with Mikhail Romm*, graduating in 1960. In 1957 Shukshin began to act in films, starring in Khutsiev's* *Dva Fedora/ Two Fyodors* in 1959. His first short story was published in 1958, followed by his first collection, *Sel'skie zhiteli/Villagers* in 1963. His first film as a director, *Zhivet takoi paren'/There Is a Lad* (1964) is based, like all his subsequent films, on his own stories, and finds humour in both village innocence and urban pseudo-sophistication. In *Vash syn i brat/Your Son and Brother* (1966) a young man returns to his village between prison sentences. *Strannye lyud/Strange People* (1971) combines the tales of three eccentrics, while in *Pechki-lavochki/Happy Go Lucky* (1973) Shukshin himself stars, with his wife, Lydia Fedoseyeva-Shukshina, as a peasant couple leaving their Altai village for the first time on a long train journey to a southern resort. In his last completed film, *Kalina krasnaya/The Red Snowball Tree/Snowball Cherry Red* (1974), Shukshin again plays the hero, Yegor Prokudin, an ex-convict who makes an ultimately tragic attempt to start a new life in a remote village with a simple peasant woman (again played by his wife). After Shukshin's death, his screenplay *Pozovi menya v dal' svetluyu* ('Call Me From Afar', 1978) was directed by the actor Stanislav Lyubshin and the cinematographer German Lavrov. As well as acting in his own films, Shukshin appeared in such films as Gleb Panfilov's* *Proshu slova/I Wish to Speak* and Sergei Bondarchuk's* *Oni srazhalis' za rodinu/They Fought for Their Country* (1975), his last acting role. But Shukshin's major film project, about the seventeenth-century Cossack rebel Stepan (Stenka) Razin, which he fought to be permitted to make for several years, was never allowed by Soviet censors. The screenplay 'Ya prishel dat' vam volyu' ('I Have Come to Give You Freedom') was published as a novel in 1971. JG

SHUMYATSKY, Boris Z.

Near Lake Baikal
1886 – [?]1938

Soviet politician. Shumyatsky was an Old Bolshevik who had joined the Party in 1903 and played a leading part in the revolutionary movement in Siberia. He was Soviet plenipotentiary in Persia in the mid-1920s and it was there that he realised the propaganda potential of film, attracting large and enthusiastic audiences by showing Soviet films depicting unveiled women. This was his only experience of cinema when he was appointed head of the centralised state Soyuzkino organisation in late 1930. He followed Lenin's* and Lunacharsky's* dictum that cinema must both entertain *and* propagandise and set about establishing what he called a 'cinema for the millions' that would do just that. Thus he sponsored Grigori Alexandrov's* musical comedies and encouraged other directors to make films that were 'intelligible to the millions', like the 'Maxim trilogy' by Grigori Kozintsev* and Leonid Trauberg*. He mistrusted intellectuals and the avant-garde and stopped Sergei Eisenstein* completing *Bezhin lug/ Bezhin Meadow* (1935–7). As head of a delegation to Hollywood in 1935, he returned to propose a 'Soviet Hollywood', also known as 'Cine-City', in the Crimea, where the climate would allow filming throughout the year. But the decline in production, resulting from increased political controls and from the shadow cast by the purges, and his own growing power, made him appear to threaten Stalin* and in 1938 he was arrested, denounced and executed. RT

ŠIJAN, Slobodan

Belgrade, Serbia 1946

Yugoslav director of Serbian origin. After graduating in painting and film at the Belgrade Academy, Šijan shot several films for television which clearly expressed his fascination with the classical American tradition of Ford and Hawks. His critically acclaimed feature debut, *Ko to tamo peva?/Who's Singing over There?* (1980), was one of the box-office hits of the 1980s in Yugoslavia. The story of a group of people journeying by bus to Belgrade on the eve of the World War II bombardments was more than grotesque comedy: it was a clever and authentic tribute to John Ford's *Stagecoach* (1939). Šijan repeated this strategy in later films, with references to Ealing comedy and classical horror, but his first direct encounter with American cinema, the 1988 co-production *The Secret Ingredient*, was a failure. SP

Other Films Include: *Maratonci trče počasni krug/Marathon Lap of Honour* (1982); *Kako sam sistematski uništen od idiota/How I Was Systematically Destroyed by an Idiot* (1983); *Davitelj protiv davitelja/ Strangler vs. Strangler* (1984).

SKOLIMOWSKI, Jerzy

Łódź 1938

Polish director. A poet, actor, athlete and ex-boxer, Skolimowski co-scripted Andrzej Wajda's* *Niewinni Czarodzieje/Innocent Sorcerers* (1960) and Roman Polanski's* *Nóż w Wodzie/Knife in the Water* (1962). His first feature, *Rysopis/Identification Marks: None* (1965) was made while studying at Łódź* and revealed an ironic and cynical attitude to the political optimism of the times. A distinctive film talent, Skolimowski has garnered international awards for his subsequent films. His 1967 anti-Stalinist allegory, *Ręce do Góry/Hands Up*, was banned (and not shown until 1985) and Skolimowski settled in Britain. His imaginative and original exploration of sexual awakening in *Deep End* (1970, UK) quickly established his international reputation. However, his subsequent career has fared better when he has dealt with a Polish theme: both in *Moonlighting* (1982, UK), his response to the imposition of martial law, and in *Success is the Best Revenge* (1984, UK), he deftly intertwines his experience as a Polish artist abroad with astute insights into the eccentricities of the British. Skolimowski returned to Poland to film *Ferdydurke/30 Door Key* (1991), an adaptation of a novel by Gombrowicz, one of Poland's most distinguished modern writers. He continues to act and direct in both Europe and the US. AW

215

Other Films Include: *Walkower/Walkover* (1965); *Bariera/Barrier* (1966); *Le Départ* (1967, Belg.); *The Adventures of Gerard* (1970, UK); *King, Queen, Knave* (1972); *The Shout* (1977, UK); *The Lightship* (1985, US); *Acque di primavera/Torrents of Spring* (1989, Fr./It.).

SLOVAKIA

Usually considered alongside the Czech cinema, the Slovak cinematic tradition had not been looked upon as a really independent national cinema until the split of Czechoslovakia in 1993. The Koliba studios in Bratislava were established in 1947 but their production was secondary to that of Barrandov. Slovak directors who worked most actively during the Czechoslovak period were Jan Kadar and Elmar Klos* who made the Oscar-winning *Obchod na korze/Shop on a Main Street* (1965, Czech.), and Peter Solan (b. 1929), well-known for his Holocaust feature *Boxer a smrt/The Boxer and Death* (1963). Stefan Uher (b. 1930) was one of the most active Slovak directors. In 1962 he made the beautiful *Slnko v sieti/Sun in the Net* which marked the beginning of the Czech New Wave. Dusan Hanák's* work focused on life in Slovakia. He used a unique combination of documentary and feature for his highly original *Papierove Hlavy/Paper Heads* (1996). The best-known director from Slovakia is Juraj Jakubisko*, working mostly in the surrealist genre. He, however, left Slovakia after the split and resettled in the Czech Republic where he worked on two features. The best-known director of the younger Slovak generation is Martin Sulik, the director of the acclaimed *Záhrada/The Garden* (1995). Sulik most recently contributed a short to the Czech film compendium *Praha ocima/Prague Stories* (1999). In the 1990s, a new art film festival was established in Trencianske Teplice. DI

SLOVENIA – see YUGOSLAVIA (former)

SMIRNOV, Andrei S.   Moscow 1941

Russian director and scriptwriter. Smirnov studied in Mikhail Romm's* workshop at VGIK*, graduating in 1962. His 1967 short film *Angel*, from the story by Yuri Olesha, was made as part of a planned portmanteau film to mark the fiftieth anniversary of the Revolution, *Nachalo nevedomogo veka/The Beginning of an Unknown Century*, but the films' bleak vision, and in particular *Angel*'s shocking account of the savagery of the Civil War, caused them to be shelved for twenty years, until *Angel*, and Larisa Shepitko's* *Rodina elektrichestva/ Homeland of Electricity*, were finally released in 1987. In *Belorusskii vokzal/The Belorussian Station* (1971), Smirnov uses an encounter between four war veterans to contrast the idealism of their life at the front with the compromises of the postwar period. His next film, *Osen'/Autumn* (1975), an intimate story of a passionate love affair, had restrictions placed on its release, and his 1979 *Veroi i pravdoi/By Faith and Truth* was so radically altered by censorship that Smirnov abandoned direction in disgust and turned to play- and scriptwriting. In May 1986, at the Fifth Congress of the Union of Filmmakers*, Smirnov was elected to the board, and from 1988 to 1990 he served as acting First Secretary of the Union. In the late 1980s Smirnov played a leading part in getting hitherto-banned films to Soviet viewers and in the encouragement of new talent. JG

SMOKTUNOVSKY, Innokenti M.   Tatyanovka, Siberia
[USSR] 1925 – Moscow 1994

Russian actor. Smoktunovsky trained in Krasnoyarsk and began acting on stage in 1946 and on screen in 1957. He first came to prominence with one of the leading roles in Mikhail Romm's* *Devyat' dnei odnogo goda/Nine Days of One Year* (1962) and achieved international recognition in the title role of Grigori Kozintsev's* Shakespeare adaptation, *Gamlet/Hamlet* (1964), which won him the Lenin Prize in 1965. He played a wide range of roles from the comic to the composer *Chaikovskii/Tchaikovsky* (Igor Talankin, 1970), a prize-winner at San Sebastian. He was Mozart in *Motsart i Sal'eri/Mozart and Salieri* (1962) and Salieri in *Malen'kie tragedii/The Little Tragedies* (1980), and after 1976 regularly appeared with the Moscow Art Theatre. RT

SMOLJAK, Ladislav   Prague 1931
and
SVĚRÁK, Zdeněk   Prague 1936

Czech writers, actors and directors. Smoljak and Svěrák made their reputations as the principal playwrights and producers of the Jára Cimrman Theatre. Their success in the 'normalised' cinema of the 1970s and 1980s was all the more remarkable given their reputation for black and absurdist humour. After an initial success as actors/writers on *Marečku, podejte mi pero!/Mareček, Pass Me a Pen!* (1976) and *Jáchyme, hod' ho do stroje!/Joachim, Put It in the Machine!* (1974), directed by the veteran comedy film-maker Oldřich Lipský, they moved to the production of their own scripts with Smoljak as director. These ranged from the absurdist *Rozpuštěný a vypuštěný/Dissolved and Let out* (1983), a detective story in which the main character is twinned with a clockwork replica, to perhaps their best film, *Kulový blesk/Ball Lightning* (1978), a brilliant ensemble film about how to move apartments in Prague. Familiar for their cameo roles in other people's films, they also worked with Jiří Menzel* (*Na samotě u lesa/Seclusion near a Forest*, 1976), while Svěrák wrote the scripts for two Oscar-nominated films: Menzel's *Vesničko má, středisková/My Sweet Little Village* (1985), and his son Jan Svěrák's *Obecná škola/The Elementary School* (1991). In 1993, Svěrák scripted Menzel's *Život a neobyčejná dobrodružství vojáka Ivana Čonkina/The Life and Extraordinary Adventures of Private Ivan Chonkin*, and collaborated on Jan Svěrák's *Akumulátor 1*. In 1995, Svěrák scripted and starred in the Academy Award-winning *Kolya* (1996, d. Jan Svěrák), in which Smoljak also had a cameo role. PH

Other Films as Writers Include: *At' žijí duchové!/Long Live Ghosts!* [Svěrák only] (1977); *Vrchní, prchni!/Run, Waiter, Run!* [dir. Smoljak], *Trhák/Smash Hit* (1980); *Jára Cimrman, ležící, spící/Jára Cimrman, Lying, Asleep* (1983, dir. Smoljak); *Nejistá sezóna/Uncertain Season* (d. Smoljak, 1987); *Lotrando a Zubejda/Lotrando and Zubejda* (1997, d. Karel Smyczek).

SNEZHKIN, Sergei O. Leningrad 1954

Russian director. Snezhkin studied at VGIK*, in the workshop of Efim Dzigan*. His first major success was *ChP raionnogo masshtaba/ Emergency on a Regional Scale* (1988), from the story by Yuri Polyakov, which exposed corruption and cynicism in the Young Communist League, a subject sensitive enough to cause the film to be widely banned. He followed it with *Nevozvrashchenets/Non-returnee* (1990), from the popular story by Alexander Kabakov, a dystopian vision of the imminent Russian future. In 1998 he made *Tsvety kalenduly/Marigolds*, a film set in the dacha of a deceased Soviet poet, now occupied by his impoverished widow, their daughter and three granddaughters, each with their own plans for the house and for their personal future. But suddenly a New Russian and former peasant drives up, intent on buying the property. Thus Snezhkin looks at post-Soviet history through a Chekhovian prism. Since 1991 he has been artistic director of the Barmalei film studio in St Petersburg. JG

SOCIALIST REALISM

Socialist Realism was the official doctrine supposedly governing all artistic practices in the Soviet Union and its dependent states (it was imposed as a constituent part of the Soviet hegemony over Central and Eastern Europe after 1945) from its proclamation at the First Congress of Soviet Writers in August 1934 until the collapse of the Soviet system in 1991. Socialist Realist art had, above all, to be easily accessible and 'intelligible to the millions'. It therefore eschewed experimentation in both form and content. It consisted of two fundamental elements. The first was 'Realism', in the tradition of nineteenth-century critical realism, depicting a reality that audiences would recognise and feel familiar with. This realism could be critical, but only if the criticism furthered the revolutionary cause, as defined by the authorities of the moment. The second element was 'Revolutionary Romanticism', a romanticism that looked forward to the future communist utopia and explained and justified whatever sacrifices or difficulties were currently required. This meant in practice that Socialist Realism could mean different things to different people in different situations at different times. As Stalin's cultural henchman Zhdanov noted in 1934, the artist had to depict life 'not simply as "objective reality", but to depict reality in its revolutionary development'. Probably the most succinct definition of Socialist Realism was given in 1933 by a somewhat cynical Anatoli Lunacharsky*: 'Socialist Realism depicts not reality as it is, but as it *ought* to be.' RT

SOKUROV, Alexander N.
Podorvikha, Russia
[USSR] 1951

Russian director. After a career in television from 1969 to 1975 in Gorky (Nizhny Novgorod) where he attended the university, Sokurov studied at VGIK* from 1975 to 1978, though he would later state categorically: 'I got nothing out of VGIK.' Though he is now recognised as one of the most important Russian directors of the last two decades, Sokurov's work was not recognised until the intervention of the Conflict Commission of the Union of Filmmakers*, set up in 1986. This released from the notorious 'shelf' the feature films, *Odinokii golos cheloveka/The Solitary Voice of Man* (1978), a poetic version of the Platonov story filmed so differently by Mikhalkov-Konchalovsky* as *Maria's Lovers*, and his free adaptation of Shaw's *Heartbreak House* known as *Skorbnoe beschuvstvie/Mournful Indifference/Anaesthesia Dolorosa* (1983), as well as a number of documentaries. *Maria* (1975/88) began as a study of a typical collective farm worker, but when Sokurov returned in 1988 Maria was dead and her husband and daughter parted by feuding. Among the other shelved documentaries eventually released were *Sonata dlya Gitlera/Sonata for Hitler* (1979); *Al'tovaya sonata. Dmitrii Shostakovich/Sonata for Viola. Dmitri Shostakovich* (1981); *Zhertva vechernaya/Evening Sacrifice* (1984), which shows a montage of people returning from a demonstration in Leningrad; and *Elegiya/Elegy* (1985), a vision of Russia's fate based in the career of the great bass, Chaliapin. In the late 1980s Sokurov continued to be a prolific maker of both documentaries and features. His documentaries included *Moskovskaya elegiya/Moscow Elegy* (1987), made in memory of Tarkovsky*; and *Sovetskaya elegiya/Soviet Elegy* (1989) and *Primer intonatsii/An Example of Intonation* (1991), both concentrating on the figure of Boris Yeltsin. The feature film *Dni zatmeniya/Days of Eclipse* (1988) casts a young Russian doctor adrift in a remote Central Asian town, and deploys a continually dynamic camera and inventive sound track to create a haunting picture of alienation. *Spasi i sokhrani/Save and Protect* (1989) is a challenging version of *Madame Bovary* set in the Caucasus. In *Krug vtoroi/The Second Circle* (1990), a young man returns to the flat of his deceased father, and Sokurov provides a relentlessly austere vision of the Soviet way of death, an examination he deepens in *Kamen'/Stone* (1992). Sokurov's concern with death and the significance of human life continued in two films made in 1993, the documentary *Elegiya iz Rossii/Russian Elegy*, which incorporates late nineteenth-century photographs and early twentieth-century war footage to observe a number of people at the point of death; and the feature *Tikhie stranitsy/Whispering Pages*, set in a St Petersburg of the mind and steeped in the dark world of the 'insulted and the injured" of nineteenth-century Russian literature. In 1995 Sokurov made the five-hour documentary *Dukhovnye golosa. Iz dnevnikov voiny. Povestvovanie v piati chastiakh/Spiritual Voices. From the Diaries of War. A Narration in Five Episodes*, a mesmerising rumination provoked by observing the life of Russian soldiers guarding the Tadjik–Afghan frontier during the local civil war. In *Vosto-chnaya elegiya/Oriental Elegy* (1996) a poetic journey around a small island provokes thoughts about man and nature. *Mat' i syn/Mother and Son* (1997), scripted by the regular writer of his feature films, the poet Yuri Arabov – over the years Sokurov has established a closely-knit group of collaborators – is the culmination of the creative investigations of two decades, paring plot to a minimum: in a large, dilapidated house in the country a man tends his dying mother. But this almost non-existent narrative is the framework for an extraordinarily powerful composition in sound and colour that addresses questions of love, death and grief with majestic power. It was the film with which Sokurov, so long spoken of as a genius, achieved worldwide success. Also in 1997, Sokurov made *Uzel/The Knot*, a documentary to celebrate the eightieth birthday of Alexander Solzhenitsyn. Sokurov spends time with the writer in his country house and his admiration and respect for him seems absolute. In 1998 Sokurov continued his prolific production of documentaries and in 1999 he made *Molokh*, the love story of Hitler and Eva Braun, which won Arabov the scriptwriting prize at Cannes. JG

SOLNTSEVA, Yuliya I.   Moscow 1901–89

Russian actress and director. After studies in the Historical-Philological Faculty of Moscow University, Solntseva graduated from the State Institute of Music and Drama in 1924. In 1923 she had also begun to work as an actress in the Mezhrabpom-Rus* and Odessa film studios. Her memorable first cinematic role was as the heroine of Yakov Protazanov's* *Aelita*, in which she was the eponymous queen of Mars, her striking beauty set off by costumes and headgear designed

220

from sketches by the artist Alexander Exter and by the Constructivist sets of Viktor Kozlovsky. She showed her flair for comedy in the leading role in *Papirosnitsa ot Mossel'promad/The Cigarette Girl from Mossel'prom* (1924), directed by Yuri Zhelyabuzhsky. From the late 1920s she began a lifelong personal and professional relationship with her husband, the director Alexander Dovzhenko*. She was assistant director on his *Zemlya/Earth* (1930), in which she also acted, on *Ivan* (1932), *Aerograd* (1935), *Shchors* (1939), and *Michurin* (1948). In 1940 she directed the documentary film, *Bukovina, zemlya ukrainskaya/ Bukovina is Ukrainian Land*, and after the Soviet Union entered World War II she collaborated with Dovzhenko on the documentaries, *Bitva za nashu Sovetskuyu Ukrainu/The Battle for Our Soviet Ukraine* (1943) and *Pobeda na Pravoberezhnoi Ukraine/Victory in Right-Bank Ukraine* (1944). She began her independent career as a director with a film of a stage production of Maxim Gorky's play, *Egor Bulychev i drugie/Yegor Bulychev and Others* (1953). After Dovzhenko's death in 1956, Solntseva made two films from his screenplays, *Poema o more/Poem of the Sea* (1958), about the creation of the Kakhosk hydro-electric station, and *Povest' plamennykh let/The Flaming Years* (1960), a war film, which was also the first Soviet widescreen film. This was followed by *Zacharovannaya Desna/The Enchanted Desna* (1964), based on Dovzhenko's childhood memoirs, and by *Nezabyvaemoe/Unforgettable* (also known as *Ukraina v ogne/Ukraine on Fire*, 1967), taken from his wartime stories. *Zolotye vorota/The Golden Gates* (1969) was devoted to Dovzhenko's artistic career, and includes extracts from his films and documentary material. Her continued commitment to his legacy also involved her in directing the restoration of *Earth* in 1973 and in helping prepare his collected writings for publication. *Takie vysokie gory/How High Are the Mountains* (1974) is the story of a village teacher, played by Sergei Bondarchuk*, while Solntseva's last film as a director, *Mir v trekh izmereniyakh/The World in Three Dimensions* (1979) is about the life of a brilliant welder who spurns scientific research for practical work in a pipe-rolling mill. She was made People's Artist of the USSR in 1981. JG

SOLOVYOV, Sergei A.   Kem, Russia [USSR] 1944

Russian director and scriptwriter. After work in Leningrad television from 1960 to 1962, Solovyov studied at VGIK*, graduating in 1968 from the workshop of Mikhail Romm* and Alexander Stolper. His first work as a director was from literary sources, two episodes from Chekhov stories in the 1970 film, *Semeinoe schast'e/Family Happiness*, a version of Gorky's *Egor Bulychev i drugie/Yegor Bulychev and Others* (1971), and the television film *Stantsionnyi smotritel'/The Stationmaster* (1972), from Pushkin. But Solovyov's main focus in film has been the lives of modern young people. *Sto dnei posle detstva/One*

Hundred Days after Childhood (1975), *Spasatel'/Lifeguard* (1980) and *Naslednitsa po pryamoi/Direct Descendant* (1982) are all about the growing pains of young adults. In *Chuzhaya belaya i ryaboi/The Wild Pigeon* (1986) the cosmonaut hero recalls his postwar childhood and his craze for pigeons. During the 1980s Solovyov taught at VGIK. In the late 1980s he ran the Krug (Circle) production division for new projects, and made two eclectic films with the artists and the aesthetics of the new rock culture. *ASSA* (1988) is a tale of the Soviet mafia and the new youth set in wintry Yalta, with music by Boris Grebenshchikov and a central role for Viktor Tsoi, singer with the legendary group, Kino. It was followed by the eccentric farce, *Chernaya roza – emblema pechali, krasnaya roza – emblema lyubvi/Black Rose Stands for Sadness, Red Rose Stands for Love* (1989). Eccentricity also features prominently in Solovyov's next film, *Dom pod zvezdnym nebom/A House beneath the Starry Sky* (1991), at the end of which the heroes abandon Soviet reality for the heavens. From April 1994 to December 1997 he was Chairman of the Union of Filmmakers* of the Russian Federation. JG

SOVIET MONTAGE

Early Russian film critics homed in on movement and space as the distinctive characteristics of cinema as opposed to theatre, and it fell to Lev Kuleshov* to define the manner in which film images were cut together as the key element in marking the specificity of cinema. In 1917 he wrote: 'The essence of cinema art lies in the creativity of the director and the artist: everything is based on composition. To make a picture the director must compose the separate filmed fragments, disordered and disjointed, into a single whole and juxtapose these separate fragments into a more advantageous, integral and rhythmical sequence, just as a child constructs a whole word or phrase from separate scattered blocks of letters.' He termed this process 'montage', and it formed the basis of the so-called 'Kuleshov effect' when, with his pupils, Kuleshov demonstrated the different meanings an audience would attribute to the same shot when it was placed in different sequences.

Sergei Eisenstein* went further, proclaiming montage to be the basis of cinema art. But his idea of a 'montage of attractions' was not one of building bricks but of objects in collision, producing an explosion that would arouse the viewer. In its more sophisticated form this became known as 'intellectual montage', the foundation for the 'intellectual cinema' exemplified by his film *Oktyabr'/October* (1927). Eisenstein went on to examine ways of incorporating sound, and later also colour, into his montage system, investigating the possibility of establishing common denominators for audiovisual montage. Dziga Vertov* also believed that montage represented the essence of cinema and he too experimented with sound, although his principal concerns were to create a new sense of cinematic space and time through the use of montage. It was in Soviet cinema that the notion of montage was most extensively examined and promoted, yet the early practitioners of the Soviet montage school of film-making would have been the first to acknowledge their debt to what they termed 'Americanism', acclaiming D. W. Griffith as the pioneering exponent of montage and *The Birth of a Nation* (1915) and *Intolerance* (1916) as paradigms of the techniques involved. RT

SOVIET STATE CINEMA ORGANISATIONS

Russian cinema became the first nationalised cinema in the world by decree on 27 August 1919, but it was not until 1922 that the first state production and distribution organisation, Goskino, was established. Starved of funds, it did not produce the goods and in January 1925 it was replaced by Sovkino. This was also short of funds and made commercially-oriented films in order to compete with the imports that dominated the market and make money for further production. At a party conference in 1928, Sovkino was severely criticised for putting 'cash before class', and it was in turn replaced in 1930 by a more centralised body, Soyuzkino, shortly afterwards headed by Boris Shumyatsky* with his vision of a 'cinema for the millions'. The increasing importance of cinema as a propaganda weapon at a time of great economic, social and political upheaval – the period of forced collectivisation and rapid industrialisation and urbanisation – led to a further reorganisation in 1934 when Soyuzkino gave way to GUKF, which was directly under the control of the Council of People's Commissars. It was at this time that the studio system which survived until the 1980s was established, with Mosfilm in Moscow, Lenfilm in Leningrad, and so on, and central studios for documentaries (TsSDF) and children's films (Soyuzdetfilm). GUKF itself survived the Great Terror, even if the individuals who peopled it did not, and in 1946 it was replaced by a Ministry of Cinematography, which in turn survived until 1954, when it was subsumed into the Ministry of Culture. In 1963 responsibility for cinema was again devolved, to Goskino, the State Cinema Committee, which, like GUKF, was directly responsible to what was now the Council of Ministers. Goskino was dissolved after the collapse of the Soviet Union in 1991 and post-Soviet cinema then faced the shock of privatisation. RT

SOVIET UNION (FORMER)

Cinema first came to Russia in May 1896 as a music-hall turn when the Lumière brothers' Cinematograph was demonstrated between two acts of an operetta performance in St Petersburg and gained immediate popular success. In the early years itinerant tradesmen travelled from town to town with a selection of short films imported from France. Cinema's novelty attracted audiences. The writer Maxim Gorky saw the new invention at the Nizhny Novgorod annual fair in 1896 and was one of the first to realise its potential, describing it as 'the kingdom of the shadows ... so unusual, so original and so complex'. In the same year the first newsreel filming in Russia took place – of the coronation of Tsar Nicholas II. The itinerant tradespeople gradually built up an audience for the new medium, so that by 1903 the first permanent cinemas were being opened in Moscow and St Petersburg, while Pathé and Gaumont opened offices in Moscow to cope with the increased demand.

Initially cinemas were installed in what had previously been shops or private apartments, and it was only gradually that Russian cinemas acquired the later conventional shape of the long auditorium. The early films depended very much on the novelty value of the moving picture, but as audiences slowly became more sophisticated the films became longer and more complex. By 1907–8 the filmgoing public was large enough, and sufficiently demanding, to warrant the production of the first Russian feature films, based on events from Russia's turbulent history, Drankov's (uncompleted) *Boris Godunov* and *Sten'ka Razin*. These were followed by a series of adaptations from the Russian classics: Pushkin's *Pikovaya dama/The Queen of Spades* (1910) and *Yevgeni Onegin/Eugene Onegin* (1911), Tolstoy's *Zhivoi trup/The Living Corpse* and *Kreitserova sonata/The Kreutzer Sonata* (both 1911) and works by Chekhov, Gogol and Dostoyevsky. In 1912, two years after Tolstoy's death, Yakov Protazanov* made a film, using both newsreel footage and staged action, entitled *Ukhod velikogo startsa/The Departure of a Grand Old Man*. Its ending showed Tolstoy being led into heaven hand-in-hand with an angel. The Orthodox Church regarded this as blasphemous and the film was not released in Russia. Indeed the Church exercised considerable censorship over cinema, of which it generally disapproved as morally reprehensible and even degenerate, at least in part because the foyers of some cinemas in the larger cities were frequented by prostitutes. The tsar also viewed cinema with some disdain. In 1913, despite allowing his family to be filmed with some frequency, he was to describe cinema as 'an empty, totally useless, and even harmful form of entertainment. ... It is complete rubbish and no importance whatsoever should be attached to such stupidities.' Because of its demotic appeal and its concentration in the towns and cities of the Empire, cinema appeared to threaten the old order – spiritual, political and aesthetic – and that is why it first appealed to artistic iconoclasts such as the Futurists, above all the poet Vladimir Mayakovsky, who was later to script and act in a number of films.

Despite – or perhaps to some extent because of – the prevailing climate of disapproval, audiences for the 'forbidden fruit' of film grew rapidly until, on the eve of World War I, the audience for cinema outstripped that for all other forms of urban entertainment put together.

The war increased the desire for escapism and boosted audiences even further, but it also hindered the import of films and caused an explosion in Russian film production, dominated by Alexander Khanzhonkov*, Pavel Thiemann and Reinhardt, and Iosif Yermolev, and bringing the names of Protazanov and Yevgeni Bauer* in particular to the fore. Bauer's films were heavily influenced by the tenets of Russian literary Symbolism, exploring themes at the margins of society and of life and death. Indeed it was almost *de rigueur* for pre-Revolutionary films to have an unhappy ending, following the tradition of Russian melodrama. The *kheppi end*, as it became known, was added purely for export. The war years also produced the first home-grown stars of the Russian cinema – Vera Kholodnaya*, who was to die in the influenza epidemic in 1918, and Ivan Mosjoukine*, who emigrated after the Revolution.

The tsarist government was slow to realise the propaganda potential of film. At first, as elsewhere in Europe, all filming at the front was banned; later it was placed in the hands of a veterans' charity, the Skobelev Committee. Some propaganda shorts were made, but on the whole the potential of Russian cinema for war propaganda remained unrealised. After the February Revolution of 1917 the Provisional government set up the first government newsreel, *Svobodnaya Rossiya* ('Free Russia'), but very few newsreels were released and they were not widely distributed.

When the Bolsheviks seized power in October 1917, cinema was not an urgent priority for them: survival was. Their coup did, however, frighten a significant number of film producers, artists and entrepreneurs into leaving the cities of northern Russia and fleeing to the Crimea, still held by White forces in the ensuing Civil War, and many later emigrated altogether, to France, Germany or Hollywood. The Civil War itself helped the Bolsheviks to realise that, if they were to survive, they needed an effective propaganda weapon to win over the hearts and minds of a hostile population and to maintain morale in the ranks of the Red Army. They chose cinema: as Lenin* remarked, in contrast to Nicholas II, 'Of all the arts, for us cinema is the most important.' As a silent visual medium it could appeal to the more than three-quarters of the population who were illiterate and to an audience who spoke more than a hundred different languages and had different cultural standards; as a portable medium it could be transported to wherever it was most useful. Moving pictures had a dynamism and simplicity lacking in the other media available at the time and therefore appealed to everybody, especially the all-important population of the rural areas (including regions populated by ethnic minorities) who had mostly never seen a film before. For them cinema was to be the technological wonder that presaged mechanisation and industrialisation and demonstrated the progressive nature of the new government. That was the theory, but the reality at first was somewhat different. During the Civil War agit-films* were used in a network of agit-trains and ships to maintain morale and propagandise the population of areas newly captured from White forces. At the same time, in August 1919, the government issued a decree nationalising all cinema property. This was more a gesture than a reality: many of those active in pre-Revolutionary cinema had fled the country, taking their expertise, and in some cases their portable property, with them. After years of wartime neglect the cinema network was in poor repair and lines of production and distribution had broken down. Above all, there was a chronic shortage of materials and equipment, and an attempt at importation from the US proved abortive.

The end of the Civil War in March 1921 led to the introduction of the relatively liberal New Economic Policy, designed to release enterprise to bring Russian production up to 1913 levels. A variety of mainly regionally-based official organisations began to compete for business against the first centralised state cinema organisation, Goskino, established in 1922 but never adequately funded. At the end of 1924, against a barrage of complaints about its failings, Goskino was replaced by Sovkino, which subsumed some of the other organisations and was granted an all-important monopoly over import and export. The middle to late 1920s are associated in the Western mind with the 'golden age' of Soviet silent cinema and with such giant figures of the avant-garde as Sergei Eisenstein*, Lev Kuleshov*, Vsevolod Pudovkin* and Dziga Vertov*. But their works, especially the documentaries of Vertov and his Cine-Eye group, were neither widely distributed nor widely seen. These film-makers were determined to create a new perception of reality through identifying the essence of cinema specificity in the theory and practice of montage*. But montage, at least as they practised it, tested popular audiences who preferred to be entertained, so that the diet of the average Soviet cinemagoer in this period differed little from that of audiences in most advanced countries in Europe or North America. Chaplin, Keaton and, above all, Mary Pickford and Douglas Fairbanks were as popular in the USSR as elsewhere in Europe. Even films by lesser directors that attempted to highlight contemporary social problems, such as Abram Room's* *Tret'ya Meshchanskaya/Bed and Sofa/Third Meshchanskaya Street* (1927), failed to stimulate widespread audience interest even when they provoked a critical scandal. The most popular Soviet films were those that imitated Hollywood melodrama, made by men like Protazanov, one of the few survivors from the pre-Revolutionary era.

The tenth anniversary of the Revolution in 1927 was a time for taking stock. Cinema's production levels, like those of other branches of industry, had risen to match 1913 levels but film had still scarcely penetrated beyond the urbanised areas of the Soviet Union. The anniversary produced a range of celebratory avant-garde films (such as Eisenstein's *Oktyabr'/October*, Vertov's *Odinnadtsatyi/The Eleventh Year*, Esfir Shub's* *Padenie dinastii Romanovykh/The Fall of the Romanov Dynasty* or Pudovkin's *Konets Sankt-Peterburga/The End of St Petersburg*) that failed to strike a popular chord. In January 1928

226

Anatoli Lunacharsky*, who, as People's Commissar for Enlightenment, had overall political responsibility for cinema, remarked on the
need to bring 'cinema closer to the masses, especially the rural masses'
and observed that 'boring agitation is counter-agitation'. In March
1928 the Party held its first conference on cinema and demanded a
complete reorganisation, criticising Sovkino for emphasising 'cash
rather than class', and calling for 'a cinema that is intelligible to the
millions'. The task of creating this cinema was eventually entrusted to
an Old Bolshevik, Boris Shumyatsky*, who became head of the recently formed Soyuzkino in October 1930. He called it a 'cinema for
the millions', a cinema that would be both ideologically effective and
entertaining.

The 'cultural revolution' that accompanied the rapid industrialisation and forced collectivisation of the first Five Year Plan period
from 1928 to 1932 was characterised by a brutal cultural iconoclasm in
the name of 'proletarian culture'. In a desperate attempt to forge the
new Soviet citizen, all perceived forms of bourgeois influence were
ruthlessly attacked and rooted out. This campaign in cinema coincided with the advent of sound, for which the Soviet Union was ill
equipped and poorly prepared, being unable to choose at first between
optical and mechanical sound systems. Striving to achieve self-
sufficiency in the production of the necessary film stock and equipment, to expand the cinema network through the new collective farms
into the countryside, to establish cinema studios in the national republics, and to provide that extended network with suitable films,
proved more than the protagonists of proletarian cultural hegemony
had bargained for, and in April 1932 the Party decided to call a halt to
partisan campaigning and abolished all proletarian cultural organisations in cinema and elsewhere.

This was but a prelude to the proclamation of the official cultural
doctrine of Socialist Realism* at the First Congress of Soviet Writers
in August 1934: its tenets were adopted by the Congress of Workers in
Soviet Cinema in January 1935, a month after the assassination of the
Leningrad Party chief, Sergei Kirov, had unleashed the first purges of
the Great Terror. But the brave proclamations 'for a great cinema art'
were belied by increasing difficulties. The transition to sound was
more prolonged and wasteful than had been anticipated and the advent of sound had complicated the spread of cinema to the national republics. Film production was still grossly old-fashioned and inefficient
compared to that of the West, and the rapid political changes associated with the Great Terror were making it more difficult for film-
makers to complete politically acceptable films, and more hazardous
to embark on the film-making process in the first instance. Soviet cinema had been bedevilled since its inception by recurrent 'screenplay
crises' since, despite official exhortations, writers continued to regard
scriptwriting as an inferior activity to 'real' writing. Their disdain was
reinforced by the insecurity engendered by the purges.

In an effort to overcome this crisis, Shumyatsky led a delegation to the West in the summer of 1935: they visited Paris, New York, Hollywood and London (and the rest of the delegation also went to Babelsberg, by then the powerhouse of the Nazi film industry) and returned to produce a draft proposal for a studio complex in the Crimea to be known as 'Cine-City' or, more popularly, 'the Soviet Hollywood'. The project was, however, too grandiose and proved to be a fatal albatross around Shumyatsky's neck: he fell victim to the purges in January 1938, when he was arrested, denounced as a 'fascist cur' and subsequently shot. Many lesser-known colleagues – directors, scriptwriters and actors – were banished to the Gulag or perished in the purges too. But Shumyatsky's legacy – the notion of a cinema that was both entertaining and ideologically effective – shaped Soviet sound cinema, and his ghost was to haunt it until its demise.

In 1936 what had hitherto been referred to as 'film factories' became 'film studios', as part of Shumyatsky's 'Hollywoodisation' process, and film directors were increasingly obliged to involve themselves in the training of new generations of film-makers. At the height of his troubles over *Bezhin lug/Bezhin Meadow*, for instance, Eisenstein was made a professor at VGIK*. A workshop system was introduced which ensured that old and young worked in tandem and a continuity of ideas and practices was assured. This led initially to a higher technical and artistic quality in Soviet films, but in the longer term to timidity and stagnation. But it did ensure a familiar style with which audiences felt increasingly comfortable, as for instance in Grigori Alexandrov's* series of superficially escapist musical comedies, which also represented one of the few examples of films in which the heroic role model was played by a woman. Greater contact with reality was, however, also maintained through a series of overtly anti-fascist films, of which Eisenstein's *Aleksandr Nevskii/Alexander Nevsky* (1938) is probably the most widely known example.

When Nazi Germany attacked the USSR in June 1941, cinema was again mobilised to maintain and boost morale, at first through newsreel footage and a series of short 'fighting film albums', and later through a number of costume pictures recalling significant episodes from Russian history, such as the war against Napoleon. The greatest of these historical epics, Eisenstein's *Ivan Groznyi/Ivan the Terrible* (1943–6), was also from the official point of view the most disturbing, and the second part was banned until 1958. The war created a sense of solidarity against a common enemy and the peace that eventually followed built upon this foundation to create the period of high Stalinist culture [> STALIN] that marked the apotheosis of the personality cult, in which the heroicised depiction of the war itself played a central role, as in Mikhail Chiaureli's* *Klyatva/The Vow* (1946) and *Padenie Berlina/The Fall of Berlin* (1949). The centrality of cinema to the creation of this culture was underlined by the establishment of a separate Ministry of Cinematography in 1946 and by a further wave of purges unleashed by Zhdanov, who by this time was effectively Stalin's cultural commissar. Ironically, severe 'screenplay crises' in these years

228

necessitated the release of around fifty 'war booty' films retrieved from Babelsberg by the invading Red Army in 1945. At the height of the Cold War, Nazi propaganda films such as *Ohm Krüger/Uncle Krüger* (released as *Tranzvaal' v ogne/The Transvaal in Flames*), *Mein Leben für Irland/My Life for Ireland* (released as *Shkola nenavisti/ School for Hatred*) or *Titanic* (released as *Gibel' Titanika/The Loss of the Titanic*) filled a significant gap in the film schedules and fed Soviet audiences with the anti-British propaganda that their own cinema in-dustry was unable to provide in sufficient quantity.

After Stalin's death in 1953 and Khrushchev's 'secret speech' in 1956 denouncing the excesses of the personality cult, Soviet cinema turned to less heroic themes and began to examine the downside even of heroism, in war films such as *Letyat zhuravli/The Cranes Are Flying* (1957) and *Ballada o soldate/The Ballad of a Soldier* (1959), for example. This tendency may well have been in part encouraged by greater fa-miliarity with more downbeat, smaller-scale films regularly produced by other socialist countries in Eastern Europe. In 1957 the Union of Filmmakers* of the USSR was established, ostensibly to protect the interests of film-makers but actually to help the authorities control both them and their output. It collaborated in this process with Goskino, the State Committee for Cinematography, set up in 1963.

Although the Brezhnev 'period of stagnation' produced its own more laughable versions of the Stalinist cult films, exaggerating the new leader's historical role in the war and the development of Soviet socialism, the filmgoer's diet moved increasingly towards 'chamber' films dealing with everyday problems (while not, of course, explicitly criticising the system that had created or exacerbated those problems), and mass entertainment pictures. Throughout this period a complex system of censorship and differentiated categories of release meant that experimental films (such as those of Andrey Tarkovsky* or Sergo Paradzhanov*) continued to be made in state studios, but were usually given only limited release. In peripheral republics film-makers achieved a more substantial degree of freedom, albeit still limited: in Georgia and Latvia, in particular, this was reflected, for example, in the work of film-makers such as Tengiz Abuladze*, Irakli Kvirikadze* or Jūris Podnieks*. Nevertheless, many films, such as Alexander Askoldov's* *Komissar/The Commissar*, Alexei German's* *Moi drug Ivan Lapshin/ My Friend Ivan Lapshin*, or the works of Kira Muratova* were shelved for years because of their theme, content or treatment, or all three. The leading foreign films were often available for viewing by film-makers, but not at this stage by audiences, although from the late 1970s onwards popular international films were increasingly imported for mass consumption, among them *My Fair Lady* and *Crocodile Dundee*.

With the advent of *glasnost** and *perestroika*, following the appoint-ment of Mikhail Gorbachev as Communist Party General Secretary in 1985, Soviet cinema entered its death throes. In 1986, in an act un-precedented in Soviet history, the Fifth Congress of the Union voted in a new and radical board headed by Elem Klimov*, which really did aim to protect the interests of film-makers against political and other forms of interference. The Conflict Commission that the Union then established unshelved many banned films from the Brezhnev period and, when released, a number of them attracted vast audiences, the best example being Abuladze's *Monanieba/Repentance*, which was also widely distributed in the West. Film-makers were now able to address hitherto taboo subjects such as the Stalinist labour camps (Marina Goldovskaya's *Vlast' solovetskaya/Solovki Power*, 1988), sex and social problems (Vasili Pichul's* *Malen'kaya Vera/Little Vera*, 1987), ecological disaster, drugs, prostitution or AIDS.

The disintegration of the USSR after the abortive coup of August 1991 and the increasingly hectic pace of the transition to a market economy undermined the unique position that Soviet cinema had held in the Soviet state: the two institutions disappeared together. Audiences feverishly demanding the hitherto largely forbidden earthly delights of consumerist societies further West, and above all America, undermined the market even for domestic popular films. Specialist films continue to be made, increasingly with money invested by Western companies or the *nouveaux riches* of the new Russian mafias, but in mainstream production 'Soviet Hollywood' – as in the 1920s – has failed to keep pace with its American mentor, quite simply because the real Hollywood does Hollywood films better. If Soviet cinema has by now disappeared, Russian cinema is in danger of following in its footsteps in the looming chaos of transition to shadowy notions of capitalism and democracy. A seminal chapter in the history of European and world cinema has come to an end. RT

[> MEZHRABPOM, RUSSIAN AND SOVIET FILM PRESS, SOVIET STATE CINEMA ORGANISATIONS]

STAIKOV, Ljudmil   Sofia 1937

Bulgarian director and writer. Upon graduating in 1962 from the Sofia Academy of Dramatic Art (VITIS), Staikov worked as an actor and stage director in Burgas before joining Bulgarian television in 1965 as a director of short films and televised stage plays. His modern style and prolific output paved the way for the success of his first feature film at Boyana* Studios: *Obič/Affection* (1972). A youth theme dealing with the painful side of the generation gap, it shared First Prize at the 1973 Moscow film festival. Appointed artistic manager of the Mladost (Youth) film unit at Boyana Studios, where he specialised in historical chronicles in a thriller context – *Dopălnenie kăm zakona za zaštita na dăržavata/Amendment to the Defence of State Act* (1976) and *Iljuzija/Illusion* (1980) – Staikov crowned these state-supported achievements with the three-part epic *Han Asparuh/Khan Asparukh* (1981), the cornerstone production for the 1,300th anniversary of the founding of the Bulgarian state and the most expensive production in Bulgarian film

230

history. It was re-edited later into an abridged English-synchronised version for world distribution, titled *681 – Veličieto na hana/681 AD – The Glory of Khan* (1983). In 1987, Staikov was appointed head of the Bulgarian Cinematography Corporation, a position he held until 1991. Despite official duties in the Ministry of Culture, he still found time to direct his heavily nationalistic *Vreme na nasilie/Time of Violence* (1988), about a clash in a village between Turks and Bulgars during Ottoman rule. RH

SPASSOV, Radoslav   Kovacevitza 1943

Bulgarian cameraman. Spassov graduated in cinematography from Moscow's VGIK* in 1972. He regularly worked with Bulgaria's best-known directors, such as Djulgerov*, Staikov*, Valcanov* and Zahariev*, and contributed to the creation of the definitive visual style which came to be known as Bulgaria's 'poetic realism.'* Spassov shot Georgi Djulgerov's debut, *Izpit/The Test* (1971, an episode of *Colourful World*), and subsequently Djulgerov's acclaimed features, *I dojde deniat. . ./And the Day Came. . .* (1973), *Mera spored mera/ Measure for Measure* (1982) and *Cernata ljastovitza/The Black Swallow* (1995). He worked on favourite Bulgarian village classics by Eduard Zahariev (*Mazki vremena/Manly Times*, 1977) and Rangel Valcanov (*Lacenite obuvki na neznajnija voin/The Unknown Soldier's Patent Leather Shoes*, 1979). Spassov also shot one of the best-known and most popular Bulgarian films, Ljudmil Staikov's adaptation of Anton Donchev's novel, *Vreme na nasilie/Time of Violence* (1988). In the post-1989 period Spassov has been acting as a chairman of the Copyrights' Association 'Filmautor' and on the board of Boyana* Film. Spassov made his directorial debut with *Sirna nedelya/Day of Forgiveness* (1993) which he also wrote and produced. DI

STALIN, Joseph V.   Gori, Georgia [Russian
Empire] 1879 – Moscow 1953

Soviet dictator. Like many political leaders of his epoch, Stalin enjoyed watching films. Initially he saw cinema as a substitute for vodka, in terms of both leisure time and state revenue, but, like Lenin* (whom he succeeded in 1924), he soon realised the importance of cinema for Soviet propaganda and this led him to intervene increasingly in the production process, influencing the final release versions of, for instance, Sergei Eisenstein's* *Staroe i novoe/The Old and the New* (1929), *Aleksandr Nevskii/Alexander Nevsky* (1938) and *Ivan Groznyi/ Ivan the Terrible* (1943–6), and suggesting projects like Alexander Dovzhenko's* *Shchors* (1939). The terror he unleashed on the population at large made film-makers adhere to 'Socialist Realism'* rather than actual realism and Khrushchev argued that Stalin's view of the

Soviet countryside after collectivisation was entirely shaped by propaganda films, showing him what film-makers thought he wanted to see. Soviet film in this period had to be 'intelligible to the millions' and experimental notions like montage* were excoriated. Under the guidance of Boris Shumyatsky*, Soviet film-makers were encouraged to make films with a simple plot construction and a straightforward notion of good and evil, hero(ine) and villain(ess). The musical comedy genre, pioneered in the USSR by Grigori Alexandrov*, was particularly popular both with officialdom and with audiences. These films entertained the masses in the new collectivised farms and the rapidly industrialising towns and cities, while propagating the ideology of common sacrifice for the common future. Film played a central part in the propagation of the personality cult, ordinary heroes being paralleled by glorified icons from a heroicised past. The process of deification of the leader figure can be seen, for instance, in Eisenstein's *Aleksandr Nevskii* and in numerous films based on the events of the Revolution and the ensuing Civil War, but it reached its cinematic apotheosis with Mikhail Chiaureli's* *Padenie Berlina/The Fall of Berlin* (1949), presented by the Mosfilm studio to Stalin on his seventieth birthday in 1949. RT

STALINISM AND THE 1950s IN EAST EUROPEAN FILM

The quasi-iconic status of Stalin's image is used in films such as the animated *The Death of Stalinism in Bohemia* (1990, Jan Švankmajer*) or *Europa, Europa* (1993, Agnieszka Holland). Stalin, the real person, appears mostly in Soviet-made films – glorified in the earlier ones (e.g. *Klyatva/The Vow*, 1946, *Padenie Berlina/The Fall of Berlin*, 1949, both directed by Mikhail Chiaureli*) and vilified in the later ones (*Piry Valtasara, ili noch so Stalinym/The Feasts of Balthazar or a Night with Stalin*, 1989, d. Yuri Kara). Stalin is also portrayed in American-made films direct by East Europeans, such as *The Inner Circle* (1991, d. Andrei Konchalovsky*), or *Stalin* (1993, d. Ivan Passer*). Other Soviet films prefer to deal with the oppressive spirit of Stalinism – like Tarkovsky's* *Zerkalo/The Mirror* (1974) or Abuladze's* *Monanieba/Pokayanie/Repentance* (1984). For Eastern Europe the period of Stalinism falls within the time frame of the late 1940s to the mid-1950s and coincides with the first years of state socialism. It is considered the darkest period in the newer history of these countries, associated with brutal repressions, staged trials, unexplained disappearances, forced labour camps, the cult of personality, and an overall moral crisis. It is no wonder that many of the films which chose to focus on this gloomy and compromising period were censored although the predominant trend in East European film-making has been to offer indirect allegories rather than engage in a direct indictment of the regime. *Czlowiek z Marmuru/Man of Marble* (1976, d. Andrzej Wajda*), for example, includes a mock documentary about the protagonist, a model worker whose glorification is an epitome of the propaganda spirit of the 1950s. Janusz Zaorski's* *Matka królów/Mother of Kings* (1983) chronicles the fates of several brothers, each one of whom is affected in some way by the gloomy political situation. The whole nightmarish story of Ryszard Bugajski's* *Przesluchanie/The Interrogation* (1982) where the protagonist is kept in jail for years without it ever becoming clear what the charges against her are, is an allegory for the brutal Stalinist police state. Andrzej Lipicki's *W zawieszeniu/Suspended* (1987) tells another depressing story from his period, in which the protagonist who escapes custody is forced into voluntary confinement and has to hide for years in his wife's basement. In Hungarian cinema, the 1950s have naturally been the subject of intense attention by filmmakers. The best films about the period again offer psychological explorations of the ways Stalinism affected the state of mind of ordinary people. Such are Pál Gabór's *Angi Vera* (1978), a great study of conformism, or Marta Mészarós's* personal coming-of-age-under-Stalinism *Diary Trilogy* (*Napló gyermekeimnek/Diary for My Children*, 1982, *Napló szerelmeimnek/Diary for My Loves*, 1987, *Napló apámnak, anyámnak/Diary for My Father and Mother*, 1990). The subtle *Love* (1979, d. Károly Makk*) depicts Stalinism by showing its repercussions on the fragile old protagonist whose son is jailed. Péter Gárdos's *Azamárköhögés/Whooping Cough* (1986) is another sensitive exploration of the 1956 events through the eyes of children. Péter Bacsó's* satirical mockery of totalitarianism, *A Tanú/The Witness* (1969) and his study of deported intellectuals, *Te rongyos élet/Oh, Bloody Life!* (1983), are set in the 1950s and directly indict the anti-intellectual and anti-individualist premises of the system. In Balkan cinema, the topic of the totalitarian years has been tackled in a variety of films. Makavejev's* *W. R. – Misterije organizma/W. R. – Mysteries of the Organism* (1971) is built on scattered references to Stalinism but also to other forms of repression. Recent Bulgarian films *Kladenetzat/ The Well* (1992, d. D. Bodzakov) and *Sezonat na kanarcetata/The Canary Season* (1993, d. Ergeni Mikhailov) chronicle the deprivation and humiliation of individuals in the 1950s. The absurd demands of class-conscious behaviour are explored in Rajko Grlić's* *Samo jednom se ljubi/You Love Only Once* (1981). Due to the Stalin–Tito split, the Yugoslav cinematic explorations of the period have looked into Tito's personality cult, like Goran Marković's *Tito i ja/Tito and I* (1992). Macedonian Stole Popov's *Srecna Nova '49/Happy New '49* (1986) explores this same period. The Cannes-winner *When Father Was Away on Business* (1985, d. Emir Kusturica*) is set in the 1950s and deals with the historical moment when politics is so overwhelming that its repercussions are felt in every single aspect of one's personal life. DI

ŠTIGLIC, France   Kranj, Slovenia 1919 – Ljubljana 1993

Slovene director. When Slovenia was looking for someone to direct its first feature film after World War II, Štiglic – a former law student, Tito partisan, cultural promoter and war correspondent turned film critic – was a perfect choice. *Na svoji zemlji/On Our Own Land* (1948) combines the spirit of resistance with a surprisingly accomplished narration [>YUGOSLAV 'PARTISAN FILMS']. Štiglic always knew how to tell stories, whether it was a search for paradise by two children in the company of a black American soldier (*Dolina miru/The Valley of Peace*, 1956, Best Actor award for John Kitzmiller at the 1957 Cannes festival), or the journey through hell of a young Jewish girl (*Deveti krug/The Ninth Circle*, 1960, Oscar nomination for Best Foreign Film). Evoking the eternal battle between good and evil in human nature, Štiglic's films create sublime moments that transcend their historical context. Such was the case with *Balada o trobenti in oblaku/Ballad of a Trumpet and a Cloud* (1961), based on a short story by Slovene writer Ciril Kosmač, in which an episode from the war was transformed into a timeless tragedy filmed with a light modernist touch. In the 1970s Štiglic 'discovered' the north-eastern region of Slovenia called Prekmurje, where he shot three films. As the title of one of them, *Povest o dobrih ljudeh/The Story of Good People* (1975), suggests, he seemed to have discovered a place where the forces of good had won out. SP

Bib: Vladimir Koch, Rapa Šuklje *et al.*, *France Štiglic* (1983).

Other Films Include: *Trst/Trieste* (1950); *Svet na Kajžarju/Life in Kajžar* (1952); *Volčja nok/The Night of the Wolf/One Dreadful Night* (1955); *Viza na zloto/The Visa of Evil* (1959); *Tistega lepega dne/That Fine Day* (1962); *Ne joči, Peter/Peter, Don't Cry* (1964); *Amandus* (1966); *Pastirci/Shepherds* (1973); *Praznovanje pomladi/Return of Spring/Call of Spring* (1978); *Veselo gostüvanje/Happy Marriage* (1984).

STRAUCH [SHTRAUKH], Maxim M.   Moscow 1900–74

Soviet actor. Strauch's early career is closely associated with that of Sergei Eisenstein*, who was a childhood friend. They worked together in the Proletkult Theatre and Strauch played the police spy in *Stachka/The Strike* (1925) and acted as Eisenstein's assistant on his next three films, including *Staroe i novoe/The Old and the New* (1929). Strauch later became one of the first to play the role of Lenin on stage and screen, in such films as Sergei Yutkevich's* *Chelovek s ruzh'ëm/The Man with a Gun* (1938), where he appeared alongside Mikhail Gelovani*; *Rasskazy o Lenine/Tales of Lenin* (1958); and *Lenin v Pol'she/Lenin in Poland* (1966). He also appeared in Mikhail Kalatozov's* *Zagovor obrechënnykh/Conspiracy of the Damned* (1950) and Mikhail Romm's* *Ubiistvo na ulitse Dante/Murder on Dante Street* (1956). He was twice awarded a State Prize for his stage work with the Mayakovsky Theatre. RT

STUHR, Jerzy Cracow 1947

Polish actor. The 'discovery' of the 1970s, Stuhr had established a successful theatre career before achieving acclaim for his comic roles in Felix Falk's* *Wodzirej/Top Dog* (1978) and Krzysztof Kieślowski's* *Amator/Camera Buff* (1979) and *Three Colours: White* (1995). Stuhr's portrayal of small-time hustlers and amoral careerists who make up the small cogs in the great Communist Party wheel, established him as one of the leading actors of the 'cinema of moral unrest'. In the 1990s Stuhr established himself as a high-profile Polish *auteur* after he made several highly acclaimed films for which he functioned as a writer, director and lead actor – *Spis cudzoloznic/List of Lovers* (1995), the multiple award-winning *Historie milosne/Love Stories* (1997), in which he played five different middle-aged men faced with difficult choices, and *Tydzien z zycia mezczyzny/A Week in the Life of a Man* (1999). In the 1990s he also served as rector of the Cracow theatre and film academy. AW

SURIKOVA, Alla I. Kiev, Ukraine [USSR] 1940

Russian director. Surikova graduated in philology from Kiev State University. In 1972 she completed the Higher Courses for Directors in the workshop of Georgi Danelia*. She made a number of films in the 1970s, many for television, but gained an international reputation with her *Chelovek s bul'vara Kaputsinov/The Man from the Boulevard des Capucines* (1987). In this comic melodrama Mr Fest arrives in the Wild West with a film projector, and uses his film shows to compete for customers with the local barman. Among her successes in the 1990s are the musical comedy, *Choknutye/Cranks* (1991), and *Moskovskie kanikuly/Moscow Holidays* (1995), in which an Italian lady, Luciana, arrives in crime-ridden Moscow to bury her dead poodle. With *Deti ponedel'nika/Monday's Children* (1997) Surikova made a light-hearted comedy about the difficulties of everyday life in contemporary Russia. *Khochu v tiur'mu/I Want to Go to Prison* (1998) is a comedy with patriotic overtones: Sergei Lyamkin has to face the law for a fraud which he has not committed. Instead, he decides to hide from prosecution in a Dutch jail, but before long he is driven back to his native land by homesickness. Surikova is a very talented and skilful director of the light comic genre, though her popularity does not quite compare with that of Alexander Rogozhkin*. BB

ŠVANKMAJER, Jan
Prague 1934

Czech director of animated films, visual and ceramic artist. Educated at the School of Applied Art and the Academy of Performing Arts (Puppetry Department), Švankmajer worked with the Black Theatre of Prague and the Laterna Magika theatre before making his first puppet film (*Poslední trik pana Schwarcewalldea a pana Edgara/The Last Trick of Mr Schwarzwalld and Mr Edgar,* 1964). While he made a number of important films in the 1960s, including the live-action and Kafkaesque *Byt/The Flat* and *Zahrada/The Garden* (both 1968), it was not until the retrospective of his work at the 1983 Annecy Animation Festival in France that he made an international impact. A committed surrealist (he joined the Prague group in 1970), his aggressive, even sadistic, work with its emphasis on texture, juxtaposition and montage is best characterised by *Možnosti dialogu/Dimensions of Dialogue* (1982), in which opposing heads confront and devour each other in destructive interplay. In 1987 he made his first feature, *Něco z Alenky/Alice*, adapted from Lewis Carroll, following this with *Lekce Faust/Faust* (1994), based on an unproduced play written for the Laterna Magika. PH

Bib: Peter Hames (ed.), *Dark Alchemy: The Films of Jan Švankmajer* (1995).

Other Films Include: *J. S. Bach: Fantasia g-moll/J. S. Bach: Fantasy in G-minor, Spiel mit Steinen/Play With Stones* (1965, Aust.); *Rakvičkárna/Punch and Judy, Et cetera* (1966); *Historia naturae (suita)* (1967); *Picknick mit Weissmann/Picnic with Weissmann* (1968, Aust.); *Tichý týden v domě/A Quiet Week in a House* (1969); *Kostnice/The Ossuary, Don Šajn/Don Juan* (1970); *Žvahlav/Jabberwocky* (1971); *Leonardův deník/Leonardo's Diary* (1972); *Otrantský zámek/The Castle of Otranto* (1973–9); *Zánik domu Usherů/The Fall of the House of Usher* (1980); *Do pivnice/Do sklepa/Down to the Cellar, Kyvadlo, jáma a naděje/The Pendulum, the Pit and Hope* (1983); *Mužné hry/Virile Games* (1988); *Tma–Světlo–Tma/Darkness–Light–Darkness* (1989); *Konec stalinismu v Čechách/The Death of Stalinism in Bohemia* (1990, UK); *Jídlo/Food* (1992); *Spiklenci slasti/Conspirators of Pleasure* (1996); *Jan Švankmajer: Alchemist of the Surreal* (1998).

SVĚRÁK, Jan
Zatec, Czechoslovakia 1965

Czech director. Son of screenwriter and actor Zdeněk Svěrák*. Studied at FAMU* where he made two well-received shorts in the mock-documentary genre. Svěrák's debut feature, *Obecná škola/Elementary School* (1991), a tongue-in-cheek bittersweet comedy in the best tradition of the Czech New Wave*, received an Oscar nomination. His second film *Jizda/The Ride* (1994), a light-hearted and exuberant road movie which Svěrák made for the mere sum of US $30,000, won at Karlovy Vary* and was a huge box-office success in the Czech Republic. Svěrák's next film, *Akumulator 1/Accumulator 1* (1994), an anti-technological sci-fi satire budgeted as US $2 million was the most expensive Czech film ever but also a blockbuster at the box-office. In 1996, Svěrák directed and co-produced what was to be his biggest hit, *Kolja/Kolya* (1996). The script was written by his father who also starred in the film. Set in the eve of the velvet revolution, the film told the poignant story of the gradual bonding of a deserted Russian boy and an ageing, Russian-hating, Czech loner. The film won numerous international awards, including a Golden Globe, and Academy Award for best foreign language film in 1997. Within a decade after his graduation, Svěrák had established himself as one of the most versatile directors, a leading figure of the younger generation of Czech filmmaking (which also includes Vladimir Michalek, Petr Václav, Petr Zelenka and Slovak, Martin Sulík) and as a film-maker with considerable business skill. DI

SVĚRÁK, Zdeněk – see SMOLJAK, Ladislav

SZABÓ, István   Budapest 1938

Hungarian director. The best-known and most successful of the second postwar generation of Hungarian film-makers, Szabó graduated from the Academy of Theatre and Film Art in 1961. He was one of the founders of the Balázs Béla Stúdió*, where he made several remarkable short films. His first feature, *Álmodozások kora/The Age of Daydreaming* (1964), showed the influence of the French New Wave, and especially of François Truffaut. In his second film, *Apa/Father* (1966), he created a distinctive subjective style, successfully adapting the lyricism of the New Wave to the interest in historical analysis which prevailed in Hungarian cinema at the time. In the 1970s his style became highly abstract and often symbolic, while the city of Budapest was a thematic source for both his feature and short films. In the 1980s Szabó made an important career shift, leaving behind his lyrical-abstract style, anchored in melancholic reminiscences of a near-obsolete Hungarian middle-class mentality. Instead, he embarked on a series of films focusing on issues of personal identity in Eastern Europe, couched in a form accessible to an international audience. The first film of the series, *Mephisto* (1981), was a major international success – winning the 1982 Academy Award for Best Foreign Film – though subsequent films of the decade were less successful in both critical and box-office terms. In his most recent film, *Édes Emma, drága Böbe/Sweet Emma, Dear Böbe* (1992), Szabó returned to Hungarian social reality, with a story about the struggle of two elementary school teachers for material and moral survival after the collapse of a

237

(communist) social system that had provided them with basic security. He continues to direct in Europe and North America. KAB

Other Films Include: *Szerelmesfilm/Love Film* (1970); *Tüzoltó utca 25/25 Fireman's Street* (1973); *Budapesti mesék/Budapest Tales* (1976); *Bizalom/Confidence, Der Grüne Vogel/The Green Birds* (1979, Ger.); *Redl Ezredes/Colonel Redl* (1985, Hung./Ger./Aust.); *Hanussen* (1988, Hung./Ger.); *Meeting Venus* (1991, UK); *Offenbach titkai/Offenbach's Secrets* (1996, Ger./Hung.); *Taste of Sunshine* (1999, Aust./Can./Ger./ Hung.).

SZŐTS, István   Vályaszentgyőrgy 1912

Hungarian director, the first important representative of *auteur* cinema in Hungary. Szőts started his film-making career in 1940 and two years later directed *Emberek a havason/Men on the Mountains*, which won first prize at the Venice Biennale and was Hungarian cinema's first international success. Szőts' film was very different from the mainstream popular comedies and melodramas that had dominated Hungarian film production since the early 1930s. Deploying a narrative style resembling the Hungarian folk tale, *Emberek a havason* depicted with ethnographic authenticity the arduous life of the people living on the high mountains of Transylvania*. Not only was this a unique stylistic initiative in Hungarian cinema, it was also a revelation for Italian cinema since it dovetailed with the neo-realism that was soon to emerge in Italy. Immediately after the war, in 1945, Szőts published a manifesto setting out how Hungarian film production should be reorganised. This is a fervent defence of art cinema and of the cultural-educative function of film. Szőts directed one more feature film in the 1940s, *Ének a búzamezőkről/Song of the Cornfields* (1947), which, unlike his first film, was made in an expressionist style. Though approved by the censors, the film was banned just before its planned release because of the religious nature of the story. Szőts made short films during the 1950s. He emigrated to Austria during the 1956 revolution, where he has made several shorts on art and other cultural topics. KAB

238

T

TADIĆ, Zoran
Zagreb, Croatia 1941

Yugoslav director, scriptwriter and critic of Croatian origin. The title of Tadić's film debut, *Hitch...*, *Hitch...*, *Hitchcock* (1969), is indicative of his film taste. In his film journalism Tadić promoted the cause of thrillers, B-movies and *auteur* cinema. In a national cinema with no tradition of this kind, he was obliged to shoot documentaries before he could make his feature film debut, at the age of forty. But in the 1980s he directed almost a film per year, most of them with the same team: writer Pavao Pavličić, cinematographer Goran Trbuljak, actor Fabijan Šovagović. Like Polish director Krzysztof Kieślowski*, Tadić proved that the dark suburbs of communist capitals can make perfect surroundings for modern *films noir*. His 1997 film, *Treca zena/The Third Woman* was based on Carol Reed's *The Third Man*, with the setting transposed to 1991 Zagreb. SP

Other Films Include: *Ritam zločina/The Rhythm of Crime* (1981); *Treči ključ/ The Third Key* (1983); *San o ruži/Dream of a Rose* (1986); *Osudjeni/ The Condemned* (1987); *Čovjek koji je volio sprovode/The Man who Loved Funerals* (1989); *Orao/Eagle* (1990).

TARKOVSKY, Andrey A.
Zavrazhye, Russia [USSR] 1932 – Paris, France 1986

Russian Soviet director and theorist. Son of the poet Arseni Tarkovsky, Andrey first studied Arabic, then worked as a geologist, and finally graduated from VGIK*, where he had been a pupil of Mikhail Romm*, in 1961. At VGIK he made a short television film, *Segodnya uvol'neniya ne budet/There Will Be No Leave Today* (1959), and for his graduation diploma a children's film entitled *Katok i skripka/The Steamroller and the Violin* (1961). His first feature, *Ivanovo detstvo/Ivan's Childhood* (1962), dealt with the relationship between the generations in World War II, mixing footage of the grim realities of war with dream sequences of a more tranquil past; it won the Grand Prix at the Venice film festival. But it was his next film, the epic *Andrei Rublëv* (1966, released 1971), which won the FIPRESCI Prize at Cannes, that brought him international fame, partly because it was suppressed in its complete form. The film, about the fifteenth-century icon painter, dealt with the problem of the artist's relationship with his environment and confronted the issue of artistic freedom, a dangerous notion in the USSR at that time. *Andrei Rublëv* was given only a limited home release and cut for distribution abroad. Tarkovsky's next film was the science-fiction epic *Solyaris/Solaris*

(1972), which marked a significant shift towards the more metaphysical obsessions of his later work. He then shot two deeply personal and somewhat obscure films, which were partly autobiographical, *Zerkalo/ The Mirror* (1974) and *Stalker* (1979), both characterised by a sense of longing and a search for meaning. Subsequently he worked abroad, making *Vremya puteshestviya/Tempo di viaggio/A Time for Voyaging* (1982) and *Nostalghia* (1983) in Italy. When *Nostalghia* was shown at Cannes the Soviet representatives, led by Sergei Bondarchuk*, successfully prevented it winning the Palme D'Or and instead it was joint winner of a Special Jury Prize. Tarkovsky's treatment by his compatriots was one factor impelling him to the exile he dreaded, and his last film, *Offret/Zhertvoprinoshenie/The Sacrifice* (1986), was shot in Sweden. During his final illness from cancer there were moves towards a reconciliation, but he died in Paris, still an exile. Tarkovsky was very much a film-maker's film-maker, rejecting Eisensteinian notions of montage and believing instead that cinema represented what he called 'sculpted time'. Some of his writings have been published in English as *Sculpting in Time: Reflections on the Cinema* (1986) and *Time within Time: the Diaries* (1991). RT

Bib: Vida Johnson and Graham Petrie, *The Films of Andrei Tarkovsky: A Visual Fugue* (1994).

TARR, Béla   Pécs 1955

Hungarian director. Tarr was only twenty-two when he made one of the most successful of the documentary-fiction [> DOCUMENTARY (HUNGARY)] films with his *Családi tűzfészek/Family Nest* (1979). It was only after completing this film that he started his studies at the Hungarian Academy of Theatre and Film Art. Since then he has made four feature films, moving steadily away from his generic starting point. His third film, *Panelkapcsolat/Prefabricated People* (1982), used professional actors whose style, as in many examples of Italian neo-realism, was intended to look non-professional, although the storyboard still followed the conventions of the documentary-fiction genre. In his next film he adopted a highly stylised setting and improvised dialogue (though by professional actors). In *Kárhozat/ Damnation* (1988) Tarr used black-and-white film stock and highly literary dialogue to achieve a mode of sophisticated abstraction. His most recent film (in production in 1993) is based on the novel *Sátántangó (Satan-Tango)* by László Krasznahorkai and reputedly runs for more than six hours. KAB

Other Films Include: *Szabadgyalog/The Outsider* (1980); *Őszi Almanach/Autumn Almanac* (1985); *Satantango* (1994).

240

TATOS, Alexandru

Romanian director and occasional scriptwriter whose subtle films show individuals as cogs in history. Tatos began as a playwright, then graduated as a stage director at the Bucharest Theatre and Film School and worked in theatre, often in collaboration with television. Following the major television series *Un August în flăcări/August in Flames* (1973), co-directed with Dan Piţa*, Tatos' first feature *Mere roşii/Red Apples* (l976) was a drama about a solitary young surgeon's conflict with authority in a provincial town, told with wit and sarcasm. The engineer Radu in *Casa dintre cîmpuri/The House Among the Fields* (1979) also isolates himself through his professional commitment. Tatos regarded *Secvenţe/Sequences* (1982), which he also wrote, as his best film and a personal statement: 'reality' is the film crew, and fiction the film-within-the-film concerning torturer and victim. Tatos found that his own scripts were often unfilmable, and he was forced to adapt others' work. In *Întunecare/ Gathering Clouds* (1985), influenced by Billy Wilder's *Sunset Boulevard*, a man is victim of his egotism, surrounded by complex and powerful women. The distinctive strands are all visible in his last film, *Cine are dreptate?/Who is Right?* (1990), about the solitude and loves of a district lawyer. Always a frail man, Tatos died at the height of his career a few weeks after the December 1989 revolution. MM

Bib: Cristina Corciovescu, 'Alexandru Tatos', *Moveast* (1992).

TEPTSOV, Oleg P.

Russian director. In 1979 Teptsov graduated from the Leningrad Conservatoire, where he had studied oboe. In 1986 he completed the Higher Courses for Directors organised by Goskino, the State Cinema Committee, in the workshop of Emil Lotianu. His first feature film, *Gospodin oformitel'/Mr Designer* (1987), is scripted by the poet Yuri Arabov, from the Soviet writer Alexander Grin's story 'The Grey Car', and contains music by the avant-garde composer, Sergei Kurekhin. Set in St Petersburg at the beginning of the twentieth century, it tells the story of a mannequin which comes to life and destroys its artist creator. Teptsov's artistic boldness is also apparent in his second film, *Posvyashchennyi/The Initiate* (1989), also from an Arabov script and with Kurekhin's music, in which the angel of destruction gives the hero the frightening power to judge and execute people at will. In the early 1990s he co-directed two documentaries with Sergei Vinogradov, *Krasnaya armiya/The Red Army* (1991) and *Pokhorony Lenina/Lenin's Funeral* (1993). JG

THEMERSON, Franciszka
Warsaw 1907 –
and
London 1988

THEMERSON, Stefan
Płock 1910 – London 1988

Polish film-makers and artists who lived in Paris from 1938 and London from 1942. The Themersons' masterpiece, *Europa* (1932), which gave a dramatic, lyrical and abstract form to the social protest of Anatol Stern's futurist poem, was hailed as the first Polish avant-garde film. They were founder-members in 1935 of SAF, the world's first film-makers' cooperative (others were Aleksander Ford* and Wanda Jakubowska*), created its journal *f.a.* ('Artistic Film') and forged links with France and Britain (including with John Grierson).

Constructivist abstraction rubs shoulders with Dadaist humour in the Themersons' work. They invented an apparatus for making 'photograms in motion', scratched and painted on film, and fused animation and photomontage with live action. Apart from stills and photograms, *Przygoda Człowieka Poczciwego/The Adventure of a Good Citizen* (1937) was the only one of their five Polish films to survive the war. It uses free narrative to subvert conventional notions of culture/nature, abstraction/realism and content/form, and was influential on Polish postwar film, not least Roman Polanski's* *Dwaj Ludzie z Szafą/Two Men and a Wardrobe* (1958). *The Eye & the Ear* (1944–5, UK), their culminating 'music to picture essay', typifies their lifelong interest in unexpected meaning arising from translation. *Calling Mr Smith* (1943, UK) was a propaganda film for the exiled Polish government, which, like their early commissioned films, transcended its brief and became a poetic technical experiment. The Themersons scripted, directed, shot and edited their films in partnership. Subsequently they followed independent careers, Franciszka as artist, Stefan as writer, but co-founded a publishing house, Gaberbocchus Press (1948). Their last illustrated book, *The Urge to Create Visions* (1983), which includes Stefan's prophetic 1928 piece on 'radio with images', is a manifesto of their vision of cinema as an open medium. IH

Bib: *Pix*, vol. 1 (1993–4).

TISSE, Eduard K.
Liban, Latvia [Russian Empire] 1897 –
Moscow 1961

Latvian-born Soviet cameraman. Tisse worked at the front in both World War I and the Russian Civil War, during which he made a number of agit-films*. He is best known for his association with Sergei Eisenstein*, working on all his films, including the abortive Mexican project. After Eisenstein's death Tisse collaborated with Grigori Alexandrov* on *Vstrecha na El'be/Meeting on the Elbe* (1949) and *Kompozitor Glinka/The Composer Glinka* (1952). Regarded as one of the leading Soviet cameramen, Tisse taught at the state film school in Moscow, later VGIK*, from 1921. RT

TODOROVSKY, Petr   Bobrinets, Ukraine [USSR] 1925

Russian director and scriptwriter. After serving at the front during World War II, Todorovsky entered the cinematography faculty of VGIK* in 1949, studying in the workshop of Boris Volchek and graduating in 1954. He worked as a cinematographer on a number of films, notably *Vesna na Zarechnoi ulitse/Spring in Zarechnaya Street* (1956), directed by Felix Mironer and Marlen Khutsiev* and Khutsiev's *Dva Fedora/The Two Fyodors* (1959). He had an acting part in Khutsiev's *Byl mesyats mai/It Was the Month of May* (1970), and has written the music and the songs for a number of films, including most of his own. Todorovsky's first feature film as a director, *Vernost'/Fidelity* (1965) is the story of young people who went straight from school to fight in World War II. He had a big success with *Lyubimaya zhenshchina mekhanika Gavrilova/The Beloved Woman of the Engineer Gavrilov* (1981), scripted by Sergei Bodrov*, in which the enduringly popular actress, Lyudmila Gurchenko plays a woman who turns up at the registry office only to find that her fiancé is not there. It was followed by *Voenno-polevoi roman/A Military Field Romance* (1983) in which the paths of a couple who had met and parted during the war cross again years later. *Interdevochka/Intergirl* (1989), the story of a Leningrad hard currency prostitute who marries a Swede and escapes abroad, only to find herself missing the USSR, tackled a subject that would have been completely taboo only a few years earlier. Forty million Russians saw it in its first year of release. Todorovsky followed it with two films set in the immediate postwar years. *Ankor, eshche ankor!/Encore, Another Encore!* (1992) follows the lives and loves of the inhabitants of a garrison town, and won both the Grand Prix at the Sochi *Kinotavr*, post-Soviet Russia's leading film festival, and the Nike for best film of the year. The darker and more ambitious *Kakaya chudnaya igra/What a Wonderful Game* (1995) shows early 1950s' students taking too many risks and falling into the clutches of the secret police. In 1998 Todorovsky made *Retro vtroem/Ménage à trois*, styled as a remake of Abram Room's* famous 1920s' triangle drama, *Bed and Sofa*. But the change in social conditions is too huge for the film to be able to enter into a serious debate with Room, and the film is best viewed as a lyrical comedy of contemporary Moscow, graced by charming performances by its stars Yelena Yakovleva, Yevgeni Sidikhin and Sergei Makovetsky*. Todorovsky was made Honoured Artist of the Russian Federation in 1985. He is the father of the director and scriptwriter, Valeri Todorovsky*. JG

TODOROVSKY, Valeri P.   Odessa, Ukraine [USSR] 1962

Russian director, producer and scriptwriter. Todorovsky is the son of the well-known director, Petr Todorovsky*. He graduated from VGIK* in 1984 as a scriptwriter and has written a number of screenplays and directed several features. *Lyubov'/Love* (1991) focuses on the difficulties in the relationships between two students and their girlfriends. *Podmoskovny vechera/Katya Ismailova* (1994) is a modern version of Nikolai Leskov's nineteenth-century story, 'A Lady Macbeth of the Mtsensk District', about a bored wife who has a passionate affair with a carpenter. Together, they kill her husband and mother-in-law. Todorovsky's film provides a cold, detached view of the events, using only a minimal amount of the plot of the story. He avoids psychological insights into the characters and neglects the motivation for their actions; the characters do not develop. It is a film which would fit more within *film noir* than within the mainstream of Russian cinema. Todorovsky's latest film, *Strana glukhikh/The Land of the Deaf* (1998) deals with love and the dream of happiness: Rita dreams of simple happiness with her boyfriend Alesha, who is being pursued by the Russian mafia since he has lost their money gambling. YaYa is a deaf girl, who dreams of taking Rita with her into the happy land of the deaf. The two women get involved with the mafia in order to earn enough money to realise their respective dreams. They survive a shoot-out of rival gangs, during which Rita too becomes deaf: the dream of the journey to the land of the deaf comes true for her. Todorovsky usually portrays a world that is devoid of love; where there is love, it is either an erotic obsession, as for Katya, or prey to financial considerations, as for Alesha and Rita. BB

TÖRÖCSIK, Mari   Pely, Hungary 1935

Hungarian actress. Töröcsik is one of the finest and most versatile actresses of Hungarian cinema. Although outwardly plain, her screen presence carries a refined and supreme sensibility. She started her career in 1957 at the Hungarian National Theatre. Her first role in cinema was in Zoltán Fábri's* love story *Körhinta/Merry-go-round* (1955) where she played a village Juliet. She also had the lead in Fábri's adaptation of Dezső Kosztolányi's novel, *Édes Anna/Anna* (1958). In Miklós Jancsó's* *Szerelmem, Elektra/Elektreia* (1974) Töröcsik paired with György Cserhalmi* for an impressive performance. She also played the leads in films by Pál Sándor* and Attila Janisch. Töröcsik is the favourite choice of Hungarian directors for a variety of supporting roles. She was chosen for crucial secondary parts by Márta Mészáros* and Károly Makk*, and by Péter Gárdos for his sensitive exploration of the 1956 events, *Szamárköhögés/Whooping Cough* (1986). Married to director Gyula Maár, Töröcsik was cast by him in a number of roles focusing on mid-life crisis. Töröcsik's international appearances are mostly in supporting roles, most notably in Costa-Gravas's *Music Box* (1990). DI

TRANSYLVANIA

Central European province now part of modern Romania (but historically disputed territory with Hungary), given mythical status in film as the homeland of the hero of Bram Stoker's novel *Dracula* (1897), much adapted in European – as well as American – cinema: over 160 versions are recorded, among which the most famous are: F. W. Murnau's *Nosferatu, eine Symphonie des Grauens/Nosferatu the Vampire* (1922, Ger.), Terence Fisher's *Dracula* (1958, UK) and *Dracula, Prince of Darkness* (1965, UK), and Werner Herzog's *Nosferatu – Phantom der Nacht/Nosferatu the Vampyre* (1979, Ger.). Transylvanian Romanians, however, view Dracula, based on the medieval Romanian prince Vlad Tepeş, as a national hero and resent his bloodthirsty image in European film culture. *Vlad Tepeş/Vlad the Impaler* or *The True Life of Dracula* (1980, d. Dimitru Fernoagă) presents the Romanian version. Transylvania is a semi-mythic cultural heartland for both the Hungarian and the Romanian nations, and is regularly used as the backdrop for nationalist Romanian historical epics such as *Dacii/The Dacians* (1966). The earliest Romanian and Hungarian documentaries recorded Transylvanian peasant life and scenery, notably Paul Călinescu's *Tara Moţilor/Land of the Motzi* (1938) and *Emberek a havason/Men on the Mountains* (1942, by the Hungarian director István Szőts*); and the first Romanian Western mildly parodied hardy peasant virtues in *Profetul, aurel şi ardelenii/The Prophet, the Gold and the Transylvanians* (1977). Until recently, Romanian and Hungarian film-makers have been unable to examine seriously the complex interweaving of diverse national cultures in the region, since the political passions are too strong (in Hungary the subject was taboo during the communist period), and the large Hungarian, Romany and other Transylvanian minorities are poorly represented in Romanian film. A brief postwar balance of power in the region, however, allowed a Romanian–Hungarian co-production to be made – the romantic comedy *Doua lumi şi o dragoste/Two Worlds and One Love* (1947). MM

TRAUBERG, Leonid Z.   Odessa, Ukraine [Russian Empire] 1902 – Moscow 1990

Soviet director and writer, who began his career by organising a theatre studio in Odessa in 1919 and in 1921 co-founded FEKS with Grigori Kozintsev*, with whom he worked closely until 1945. Their joint works were always suffused with a strong degree of experimentalism, from the early parodies like *Pokhozhdeniya Oktyabriny/The Adventures of Oktyabrina* (1924) and *Mishki protiv Yudenicha/The*

Mishkas versus Yudenich (1925), through *Chërtovo koleso/The Devil's Wheel*, in which the action is played out against a fairground setting, and their version of Gogol's *Shinel'/The Overcoat* (both 1926), to their films depicting the history of the international revolutionary movement. These began with *S. V. D.* (1927), which dealt with the Decembrist uprising of 1825, and *Novyi Vavilon/New Babylon* (1929), centring on a department store during the Paris Commune of 1870. These silent films (*Novyi Vavilon* had a score by Dmitri Shostakovich*) and their first sound film, *Odna/Alone* (1931), prepared the ground for their most famous achievement, the so-called 'Maxim trilogy' which portrayed the revolutionary awakening of its eponymous hero in *Yunost' Maksima/The Youth of Maxim* (1935), *Vozvrashchenie Maksima/The Return of Maxim* (1937) and *Vyborgskaya storona/The Vyborg Side* (1939). Their last collaborative effort was *Prostye lyudi/ Simple People*, made in 1945 but not released until 1956. After this Trauberg's film-making career went into a severe decline but he enjoyed an Indian summer as director of the Higher Courses in Direction in the 1960s and as an author of many books about cinema, operetta and popular culture in the 1970s and 1980s. RT

TRNKA, Jiří
Plzen [then Austria-Hungary] 1912 – Prague 1969

Czech director of animated and puppet films, painter and designer. After working as a designer in Josef Skupa's puppet theatre, Jiří Trnka studied at the Arts and Crafts School in Prague from 1929 to 1935. Active as a graphic artist, cartoonist, painter and book illustrator, he founded his own puppet theatre in 1936. Together with Hermina Týrlova and Břetislav Pojar, he was one of the pioneers of the puppet film and began making his own films in 1946. He established his reputation with the feature-length *Špalíček/The Czech Year* (1947) and *Staré pověsti české/ Old Czech Legends* (1953), based on the book by Alois Jirásek, devoting the late 1950s to his adaptation of Shakespeare's *A Midsummer Night's Dream* (*Sen noci svatojánské*, 1959). At a time of conformity, his invention served to keep artistic traditions alive and, in his later films, he moved to a more visionary level with works such as *Kybernetická babička/Cybernetic Grandmother* (1963) and *Ruka/The Hand* (1965), a striking parable about the role of the artist under totalitarianism. PH

Other Films Include: *Zasadil dědek řepu/Grandfather Planted a Beet* (1945); *Zvířátka a petrovští/The Animals and the Brigands, Perák a SS/The Springer and the SS Man* (1946); *Císařův slavik/The Emperor's Nightingale, Román s basou/Novel with a Contrebass, Arie prérie/Song of the Prairie* (1949); *Čertův mlýn/The Devil's Mill* (1950); *Osudy dobrého vojáka Švejka/The Good Soldier Švejk* (1954); *Vášeň/Passion* (1961); *Archanděl Gabriel a paní Husa/Archangel Gabriel and Mother Goose* (1964).

TSYMBAL, Yevgeny V.
Yeisk, Russia [USSR] 1949

Russian director and scriptwriter. Tsymbal studied history at the University of Rostov on Don, where he then worked as a sociologist. He studied on the Higher Courses for Scriptwriters and Directors in Moscow in 1982–4, but he had already begun to work as Mosfilm in 1974, and from 1975 he was assistant to such directors as Andrey Tarkovsky*, Larisa Shepitko*, Nikita Mikhalkov* and Eldar Ryazanov*, before making the short film, *Zashchitnik Sedov/Defence Counsel Sedov*, in 1988. Shot in black-and-white, and seamlessly incorporating archival footage, the film offers an astonishingly acute picture of the Stalinist 1930s in its tale of the vicissitudes of a lawyer hired to defend four men unjustly condemned to death for sabotage. It achieved great success at international festivals, and won the Best Short Film award at BAFTA in 1989. Tsymbal returned to the Stalinist period with his next film, *Povest' nepogashennoy luny/The Tale of the Unextinguished Moon* (1990), adapted from the short story by Boris Pilnyak about the death of the Soviet Commissar for War, Mikhail Frunze, after an operation in 1925, a fate widely interpreted as Stalin's surgical murder of a potential rival. In the 1990s Tsymbal made two documentaries about the actor and director Alexander Kaidanovsky*, a contribution to the television series *Chtoby pomnili* [Lest We Forget], 1996, and *Sny Stalkera/Stalker's Dreams* (1998), as well as the documentary, *Obyknovennyi bol'shevizm/Ordinary Bolshevism* (1999). JG

U

UHER, Štefan
Prievidza 1930 – Bratislava [now Slovakia] 1993

Slovak director. Štefan Uher graduated from FAMU* in 1955, becoming the leading figure in the first generation of Slovak directors. His early film, *Slnko v sieti/Sunshine in a Net* (1962), was one of the key Slovak films of the 1960s and paved the way for the more open cultural approaches that developed in both Czech and Slovak cinema during the remainder of the decade. Its intricate and associative structure challenged classical narrative, and its use of introspection and metaphor earned an initial ban. It was also the beginning of Uher's collaboration with the leading novelist Alfonz Bednar, which was to extend for a further eight features. In 1966, Uher made his most unusual film when he adapted *Panna zázračnica/The Miraculous Virgin* from the novel by the surrealist writer Dominik Tatarka. His post-1969 films, many made in association with Bednar, avoided the bland entertainments of some of his Czech colleagues but, like most Slovak films, went unnoticed by international critics. *Správca skanzenu/Down to Earth* (1988), again unrecognised, was a profound attack on the distortions of 'normalisation'. PH

Other Films Include: *Organ* (1964); *Tri dcéry/Three Daughters* (1967); *Génius* (1969); *Keby som mal pušku/If I Had a Gun* (1971); *Javor a Juliana/The Maple and Juliana* (1972); *Dolina/The Valley* (1973); *Vel'ká noc a vel'ky deň/Great Night and Great Day* (1974); *Keby som mal dievča/If I Had a Girl* (1976); *Penelopa* (1977); *Zlaté časy/Great Times* (1978); *Kamarátky/Friends* (1979); *Kosenie jastrabej lúky/ Mowing Crane Meadow* (1981); *Pásla kone na betóne/She Grazed Horses on Concrete/Concrete Pastures* (1982); *Šiesta veta/The Sixth Sentence* (1986).

UNION OF FILMMAKERS OF THE RUSSIAN FEDERATION

With the demise of the Soviet Union in 1991, the role of the Union of Filmmakers of the USSR* was taken over by the Union of Filmmakers of the Russian Federation* and by similar unions in the other newly independent republics. The Russian union contained guilds for directors, actors, producers, scriptwriters, cinematographers, designers, composers, critics and others. The union has three-yearly congresses, and between these is run by a board. In recent years the main problem it has had to deal with has been supporting its members both artistically and materially during a period when economic crisis has decimated the number of films being made and kept many of them permanently out of work. At the Third Congress in December 1997 the director Nikita Mikhalkov* replaced Sergei Solovyov*, who had served in the role since April 1994, as chairman of the board and set in motion an audit of the union's activities. He then called an extraordinary Fourth Congress, in May 1998, at which he presented a programme for the reform of the union and the industry. Mikhalkov was scathing about the way the post-Soviet industry had betrayed the Russian viewer, particularly through swamping the distribution system with large numbers of second-rate American films. He planned to increase the revenues available for the making of new Russian films by an aggressive system of licensing video production and television rights. He proposed to revive exhibition by putting a tax on video sales, the revenue from which would be deployed in building and renovating cinemas across the country. Soon after this Russia was hit by yet another economic crisis and at the end of the century production figures remain catastrophically low. JG

UNION OF FILMMAKERS OF THE USSR

The union, which combined directors, scriptwriters, actors and actresses, camera operators, designers, composers, sound engineers, critics and film writers, editors and technicians, was inaugurated at its First Congress in November 1965, though the organisational committee of the union had been set up in 1957. Its explicit aims included promoting the creation of works which 'affirm the principles of communist ideology and help in the formation of good taste'; 'participating in the elaboration of a Marxist-Leninist theory of cinema art'; and 'helping in the ideological and aesthetic education of young people'. The union was to have a congress every five years, and to be administered between congresses by a board, elected at the congress. The board would elect a secretariat and set up creative and practical commissions. The director Lev Kulidzhanov* was elected First Secretary in 1965. Each republic of the Soviet Union had its own Union of Filmmakers. The union set up a complex system of creative commissions and subsections covering such areas as theory and criticism; scriptwriting; feature, documentary, scientific, animated and children's films; acting; television; technical questions; foreign links; work with young people; dubbing foreign films; and distribution. It organised conferences, discussions, showings of films, and seminars to discuss future production. It created cinematic centres known as 'Houses of Cinema' in major cities. It organised the publication of film journals such as *Iskusstvo kino/The Art of Cinema* and the more popular *Sovetskii ekran/Soviet Screen*. In 1971 the union was awarded the Order of Lenin.

But, if this 'official' description of the union's activities suggests an efficiently run industry, the union's main purpose was in fact to collaborate with Goskino, the State Committee for Cinematography, set up in 1963, in the strict ideological control of all aspects of cinema production and distribution. Just how far its secretariat, still headed by Kulidzhanov, failed to defend the true interests of film-makers during the Brezhnev period is evident not only from the number of important films shelved during that period, but also from the proceedings of the revolutionary Fifth Congress of May 1986, one of the first major cultural breakthroughs of the Gorbachev years, which removed most of the union's board, including Kulidzhanov, and at which a new generation of film-makers at last assumed positions of power. The new First Secretary was Elem Klimov*, most of whose earlier films, like those of his new deputy Andrei Smirnov*, had been subject to banning and delay. Other new board members included the directors Vadim Abdrashitov* and Eldar Shengelaya*. The old board and secretariat were accused of failing to influence the creative process in a positive way, and the nineteen decisions taken at the congress revealed the extent of the industry's crisis, whether in its lamentable technical level, in its failure to support young people in making careers in cinema, or in the conformist unprofessionalism of the cinema press. The crucial decision of the congress was the establishment of a Conflict Commission headed by the *Pravda* film critic Andrei Plakhov, charged with viewing all banned films and deciding whether they should be released. The commission reviewed scores of films and the subsequent release of work by directors such as Tengiz Abuladze*, Alexander Askoldov*, Andron Mikhalkov-Konchalovsky*, Kira Muratova* and Alexander Sokurov* altered the picture of Soviet cinema of the Brezhnev years.

At its Sixth Congress, held early, in June 1990, the union elected the Tadjik director, Davlat Khudonazarov, as its new First Secretary, and reorganised itself into a 'Federation of Sovereign National and Territorial Organisations of Filmmakers'. It also introduced a system of guilds for directors, actors, camera operators and other groups, and expressed concern about authors' and artists' rights, about production and distribution. But by now the rapid changes introduced by increased marketing of the industry were making the union an anachronism, and by the time of the demise of the Soviet Union in 1991, its role was greatly diminished. Its activities were taken over in that year by the Union of Filmmakers of the Russian Federation* and by similar unions in the other newly independent republics. J.G.

URSULIAK, Sergei V. 1958

Russian director. Ursuliak graduated as an actor from the Shchukin Theatre School in 1979, and completed the Higher Courses for Directors in the workshop of Vladimir Motyl in 1993. From 1979 to 1991 he acted in the company of the Satirikon Theatre in Moscow. His first feature film, *Russkii regtaim/Russian Ragtime* (1992), explored the fascination of the young generation of the 1970s with American music, which Ursuliak refrains from interpreting as a form of anti-Soviet protest. *Letnie lyudi/Summer Folk* (1995) is an adaptation of Gorky's play, using documentary footage to create the temporal setting of his film. The contemporary characters emerge from the footage and stand to be photographed in front of the theatrical curtain, which drops away to reveal the woods and the summer house where the action will develop. *Sochinenie ko Dnyu Pobedy/Composition for Victory Day* (1998) was made to order for the Gorky Film Studios to mark Victory Day. Three men, who have not seen each other for twenty-five years, meet for the victory parade: the dissident, Morgulis, the Mafioso sports manager, Kilovatov and the committed participant in the parade, Dyakov. Kilovatov is arrested as a result of political intrigue, and the other two hijack a plane to force his release. BB

V

VĂLČANOV, Rangel

Wyczanow (Pol.); Vulchanov; Krivina 1928

Bulgarian director. Bulgaria's best-known director abroad, and the individual most responsible for the rapid postwar development of a new national cinema in Eastern Europe. The poetic, philosophical tone of Vălčanov's first feature film, *Na malkija ostrov/On a Small Island* (1958) heralded a promising awakening in Bulgarian cinema; the film's success was the result of a close collaboration with writer Valeri Petrov*, cameraman Dimo Kolarov, composer Simeon Pironkov, and several of the country's finest actors. The same team then collaborated on *Părvi urok/First Lesson* (1960) and *Slănceto i sjankata/Sun and Shadow* (1962), save that Vălčanov now preferred to work with non-professional as well as professional actors (a method he has employed with astonishing success to the present day).

Despite the international success of the trilogy, Vălčanov and Petrov's style of personal poetic cinema was officially frowned on during the post-'thaw' period, and Vălčanov was thereafter forced to accept scripts approved by the government. Nevertheless, he was able to experiment in various genres and to inject into each film he made from the early 1960s to the late 1970s a challenging moral question. When the domestic release of his Bulgarian–Czechoslovakian co-production *Ezop/Aesop* (1970) was cancelled without explanation, the director decided to stay on in Prague to enjoy the more liberal atmosphere of the Czech New Wave* and make *Tvar pod maskou/Face behind the Mask* (1970) and *Šance/Chance* (1970). He also went to North Africa to shoot the lyrical documentary *Meždu dva brjaga/Journey between Two Shores* (1967), before settling in Sofia again to make the folkloric documentary *Bulgarski ritmi/Bulgarian Rhythms* (1973), along with two commissioned documentary portraits of state artists: *Tvorčeski portret na Konstantin Kocev/Portrait of Artist Konstantin Kotsev* (1973) and *Tvorčeski portret na Ljubomir Pipkov/Portrait of Composer Ljubomir Pipkov* (1974).

After winning the Golden Peacock at the New Delhi film festival for *Lačenite obuvki na neznajnijat voin/The Unknown Soldier's Patent Leather Shoes* (1979), directed from his own screenplay (which had been shelved for fifteen years), Vălčanov was instrumental in launching a Bulgarian film revival. His later feature films – *Posledni žhelania/ Last Wishes* (1983), *Za kăde pătuvate?/Where Are You Going?* (1985), *A sega nakăde?/Where Do We Go from Here?* (1987) – all underscore his continuing search for truth and integrity within a prescribed social structure. After editing a compilation film of short features titled *Razvodi, razvodi/Divorces, Divorces* (1989) – composed of episodes by directors and scriptwriters on marriage, infidelity and divorce in contemporary Bulgarian society – he was prompted to contribute his own personal statement on the matter in a separate feature film: *Nemirnata ptica ljubov/Love is a Wilful Bird* (1990). His latest projects are the Bulgarian–French co-productions, *Mechtata na alkhimika/The Dream of the Alchemist* (1992) and *Fatalna nezhnost/Fatal Tenderness* (1993). RH

VAČKOV, Grigor   Sofia 1931–80

Bulgarian actor. An eminent stage and screen actor, Grigor Vačkov first appeared in films in a minor role in Peter Donev's *Bednata ulica/Poor Man's Street* (1960). He is best known as an interpreter of dramatist-screenwriter Jordan Radičkov's* tragic heroes: the recalcitrant peasant in Hristo Hristov's* *Posledno ljato/The Last Summer* (1972–4) and the defiant tree-dweller in the monologue play *Januari/January*. RH

VANČURA, Vladislav   Háj u Opavy [then Austria-Hungary] 1891 – Prague 1942

Czech novelist and director. Originally a doctor, and a lifelong communist, Vančura was one of the leading novelists of the inter-war years. Unlike that of Jaroslav Hašek and Karel Čapek, his work is not known in translation and his inventive and experimental use of language is culturally specific. Although successful in traditional literary fields, he wrote many unrealised film scripts. His first film, *Před maturitou/Before the Finals* (1932), co-directed by Svatopluk Innemann, impressed through its delicate and lyrical observation of life at a boys' school. He was very much at the centre of Czech intellectual life, his collaborators on *Na sluneční straně/On the Sunnyside* (1933) including the surrealist poet Vitězslav Nezval, the linguist Roman Jakobson and the architect Bedřich Feuerstein, while *Marijka nevěrnice/Faithless Marijka* (1934) bought together novelists Karel Nový and Ivan Olbracht and composer Bohuslav Martinů. Vančura was dedicated to the notion of a film art independent of commercial demands, and his use of anti-psychological acting, symbolism and unconventional camera effects marked out ambitions that could never be fully realised. In 1942, he was one of the intellectuals executed by the Nazis in response to the assassination of the Reichsprotektor, Reinhard Heydrich. A number of his novels have subsequently been filmed, including *Marketa Lazarová* (1965–7, František Vláčil*), *Rozmarné léto/Capricious Summer* (1967, Jiří Menzel*), *Luk královny Dorotky/The Bow of Queen Dorothy* (1970, Jan Schmidt), *Konec starých časů/The End of Old Times* (1989, Menzel), and *Útěk do Budína/The Flight into Budin* (1992, Ivan Balada). PH

252

Other Films as Director Include: *Burza práce/Labour Exchange* [short] (1933); *Láska a lidé/Love and People, Naši furianti/Our Defiant Ones* [both co-d. Václav Kubásek] (1937).

VASILIEV 'BROTHERS': Georgi N. Vologda, Russia 1899 – Moscow 1946
and

Sergei D. Moscow 1900–59

Soviet directors and scriptwriters. Georgi and Sergei Vasiliev shared the same surname but were not actually brothers. Georgi worked from 1924 as an editor for the Goskino studio, cutting foreign films for Soviet distribution. Sergei held a similar job in the Moscow office of Sevzapkino. After the two studios merged the 'brothers' began to work together and became pupils of Sergei Eisenstein*. Their first film was the documentary *Podvig vo l'dakh/Exploit on the Ice* (1928), a film about the Polar expedition of the Italian explorer Nobile (a subject taken up again in Mikhail Kalatozov's* *Krasnaya palatka/The Red Tent*, 1970). The Vasilievs' first feature was *Spyashchaya krasavitsa/ The Sleeping Beauty* (1930), from a script by Grigori Alexandrov*. Their most famous film, however, was *Chapayev* (1934), set in the Civil War in which they both participated: it was one of the most popular Soviet films of the 1930s, a seminal contribution to the Civil War genre, and it was held up by the authorities as the model Socialist Realist* film. They made two more films about the Civil War – *Volochaevskie dni/Volochayev Days* (1938) and *Oborona Tsaritsyna/ The Defence of Tsaritsyn* (1942) – and their last collaborative work was *Front/The Front* (1943). RT

VÁVRA, Otakar Hradec Králové [then Austria-Hungary] 1911

Czech director. Vávra originally studied architecture and made his way into the film industry via publicity work. After a number of experimental films, he moved to features in the late 1930s. His 1938 film, *Cech panén kutnohorských/The Guild of the Kutna Hora Maidens*, won the Golden Lion at Venice but was banned by the Nazis during the occupation. For reasons of both conviction and strategy, Vávra found himself drawn to literary subjects and a conventional academic style that allowed him to survive the vicissitudes of different regimes. He was active in the preparation of plans for the nationalisation of the film industry, and a key figure in the creation of FAMU*, the Prague Film School. In 1970, Vávra was dismissed from FAMU when one of the students, Vlastimil Venclík, made the film *Nezvaný host/The Uninvited Guest*, seen as having a rather obvious political reference.

Vávra soon reinstated himself with an expensive wartime trilogy, *Dny zrady/Days of Treason* (1973), *Sokolovo* (1974) and *Osvobození Prahy/The Liberation of Prague* (1976). The first was a responsible drama-documentary about Munich, the last about the Soviet liberation of 1945. As he later put it, it didn't tell lies but neither did it tell all of the truth. His subsequent films drew directly on his interest in Czech literature and history. PH

Other Films Include: *Světlo proniká tmou/The Light Penetrates the Dark* [short] (1931); *Listopad/November* [short] (1935); *Filosofská historie/A Philosophical Story*, *Panenství/Virginity* (1937); *Humoreska/Humoresque* (1939); *Dívka v modrém/The Girl in Blue* (1940); *Turbína/The Turbine* (1941); *Rozina sebranec/Rosina the Foundling* (1945); *Cesta k barikádám/The Way to the Barricades* (1946); *Krakatit* (1948); *Němá barikáda/The Silent Barricade* (1949); *Jan Hus* (1955); *Jan Žižka* (1956); *Proti všem/Against All* (1957); *Občan Brych/Citizen Brych* (1958); *První parta/First Rescue Party* (1959); *Zlatá reneta/The Golden Rennet* (1965); *Romance pro křídlovku/Romance for Trumpet* (1966); *Kladivo na čarodějnice/Witchhammer* (1969); *Příběh lásky a cti/A Meeting with Love and Honour* (1977); *Putování Jana Amose/The Wanderings of Jan Amos* (1983); *Oldřich a Božena/Oldřich and Božena* (1984); *Veronika* (1985); *Evropa tančila valčík/Europe Danced the Waltz* (1989).

VEROIU, Mircea Tirgu Jiu 1941

Romanian director and occasional scriptwriter and actor, who places visual imagery above narrative development. Initially a sports teacher, Veroiu attended film school in Bucharest under Victor Iliu*, and achieved immediate fame co-directing and scripting, with Dan Piţa*, *Nuntă de piatră/Stone Wedding* (1972) and *Duhul aurului/Lust for Gold* (1973), taken from classic short stories. *Fefeleaga* – Veroiu's section of *Stone Wedding* – has an austere style reminiscent of Bresson in its ritualistic treatment of characters and landscape. His first solo feature, the thriller *Şapte zile/Seven Days* (1973), as well as the science-fiction film *Hyperion* (1975), can be seen as pretexts for a display of visual imagery. Since then Veroiu has generally worked with cameraman Calin Ghibu. The elegant historical drama *Dincolo de Pod/Beyond the Bridge* (1975) shows the consummation of his style, though it is perhaps weighed down by its literary theme and precise period reconstruction. *Între oglinzi paralele/Between Opposite Mirrors* (1978) uses glass and mirrors as exquisite metaphors within a politically orthodox storyline. *Să mori rănit din dragoste de viaţă/To Die from Love of Life* (1983) is almost pure *film noir*. As in the Chekhovian and sensual *Adela* (1984), the story is tied to male friendship – one of Veroiu's preferred themes. *Adela* won the main award at a San Remo retrospective in 1985. MM

Other Films as Director Include: *Somnul insulei/The Island is Asleep* (1994); *At the Orient's Gate* (1995); *Femeia in rosu* (1997).

Bib: Manuela Cernat, 'Romania – Focus on Mircea Veroiu', *International Film Guide* (1987).

VERTOV, Dziga   Denis A. Kaufman; Białystok, Poland
                          [Russian Empire] 1896 – Moscow 1954

Soviet director and theorist. Vertov studied psycho-neurology in Petrograd in 1917 but, after the Revolution, was offered a film job by an old friend. He soon became head of the Moscow Cinema Committee's newsreel section and started to experiment with the camera, using his scientific knowledge to gain experience of the effects on audiences of different cinematic techniques. In 1918 he began producing his *Kinonedelya* ('Cine-Week') newsreel series and in 1919 formed the Cine-Eye (*Kino-Glaz*) group, whose guiding spirit he was to remain. During the Civil War Vertov continued to shoot newsreel footage while working on the agit-trains and this was subsequently used in his first full-length films, *Godovshchina revolyutsii/The Anniversary of the Revolution* (1918) and *Istoriya Grazhdanskoi voiny/ The History of the Civil War* (1922). The Cine-Eye theory of documentary film-making was first publicly proclaimed in the August 1922 manifesto 'We: A Version of a Manifesto', and developed the following year in 'The Cine-Eyes: A Revolution'. These manifestos announced that 'the future of cinema lies in the rejection of its present' and argued that 'the cinema eye is more perfect than the human eye' and therefore that cinema was capable of creating a more perfect reality than reality itself, partly through imaginative camerawork but mainly through montage. Yet at the same time Vertov also set out to portray 'life caught unawares'. Fiction film, in the Cine-Eyes' view, evaded the responsibilities of documentary film and was therefore denounced as unreal, dishonest and fundamentally counter-revolutionary. Vertov set out to realise this new reality in his next newsreel series, called *Kinopravda/Cine-Truth*, in a play on the title of the Party newspaper. Working with his brother Mikhail Kaufman* (a third brother, Boris, emigrated to France, where he worked with Jean Vigo*, and then went to Hollywood) and his wife Yelizaveta Svilova, Vertov also produced a number of stunning full-length documentaries intended to portray Soviet 'life caught unawares' – *Shagai, Sovet!/Forward, Soviet!* and *Shestaya chast' mira/A Sixth Part of the World* (both 1926), *Odinnadtsatyi/The Eleventh Year* (1928), and the best known of them, *Chelovek s kinoapparatom/The Man with the Movie Camera* (1929) – as well as a series of innovative films extending the use of montage to sound: *Entuziazm/Enthusiasm*, also known as *Simfoniya Donbassa/The Donbass Symphony* (1930), *Tri pesni o Lenine/Three*

Songs about Lenin (1934), which won a prize at the Venice film festival, and *Kolybel'naya/The Lullaby* (1937), which was re-edited without his permission to enhance the role of Stalin. He found it increasingly difficult to get work as official interest moved towards popular fiction films and he ended his career working on the regular Soviet newsreel *Novosti dnya* ('News of the Day').

Vertov's theory of documentary film suffered from a fundamental contradiction that he never resolved between the desire to show 'life caught unawares' and the urge to reformulate that life through the mechanical 'Cine-Eye' of the camera. The virulence of his attacks on fiction film-makers, notably Sergei Eisenstein*, made him enemies and he never adequately responded to their critiques of his own position. His films challenged conventional narrative patterns and demanded considerable effort on the part of audiences unfamiliar with his methods. They were not widely shown and therefore never became conventionally acceptable. Vertov's attempts to create a new cinematic non-linear narrative form led him to experiments that were vulnerable, in the increasingly rigid artistic climate of the 1930s, to accusations of Formalism, and a brilliant career was thus prematurely eclipsed. RT

Bib: Annette Michelson (ed.), *Kino-Eye: The Writings of Dziga Vertov* (1984).

VGIK (Vsesoyuznyi gosudarstvennyi institut kinematografii/All-Union State Cinema Institute)

Soviet film school, the most important school of film-making, cinema history and criticism in the USSR. Founded in 1919 by Vladimir Gardin*, Lev Kuleshov* and others as the State Film School, it was reorganised in 1925 as the State *Technicum* for Cinema (GTK). In 1930, as part of the general centralisation of cinema institutions, it became the State Institute for Cinema (GIK) and, in 1934, VGIK. Almost all the leading figures in Soviet cinema have taught at VGIK, including the following who all have entries in this volume: Nikolai Batalov, Sergei Bondarchuk, Alexander Dovzhenko, Sergei Eisenstein, Sergei Gerasimov, Marlen Khutsiev, Grigori Kozintsev, Lev Kuleshov, Vsevolod Pudovkin, Mikhail Romm and Sergei Yutkevich. The majority of those staffing Soviet film studios also passed through the institution. In the 1960s, VGIK came to be seen as a bastion of the old order and of the 'period of stagnation', and rival 'Higher Directors' Workshops' were established, although they never threatened VGIK's hegemony. Institutes for the study of cinema history and theory were, however, more effectively decentralised, and research in these areas benefited from these changes from the 1970s onwards. RT

VLÁČIL, František   Český Těšín 1924 – Prague 1999

Czech director. Vláčil, who originally studied philosophy and art history, began his film career in documentary, moving to features with his poetic parable *Holubice/The White Dove* (1960), which won several international awards. He is best known for his remarkable trilogy of historical films, *Ďáblova past/The Devil's Trap* (1961), *Marketa Lazarová* (1965–7) and *Údoli včel/Valley of the Bees* (1967). All are deliberate attempts to resurrect the psychology of a past age and deal with the tragic outcomes of cultural and ideological conflict. His post-1969 work continued to show his dramatic and poetic talents and his frequently bleak vision, while retaining a commitment to historical themes. The visionary and barbaric qualities of *Marketa Lazarová* now mark it as one of the key Czech films of the 1960s, and it was singled out for revival at the 1992 Karlovy Vary* Festival. PH

Other Films Include: *Adelheid* (1969); *Dým bramborové natě/Smoke on the Potato Fields* (1976); *Stíny horkého léta/Shadows of a Hot Summer* (1977); *Koncert na konci léta/Concert at the End of Summer* (1979); *Hadí jed/Serpent's Poison* (1981); *Pasáček z doliny/The Little Shepherd Boy* (1983); *Stín kapradiny/The Shadow of the Fern* (1984); *Mág/The Magus* (1987).

VORKAPICH, Slavko   Dobrinjci, Serbia 1894 –
Mijas 1976

Serbian-American editor and theoretician; also director. After studying painting in Belgrade, Budapest and Paris, Vorkapich moved to Hollywood in 1921. He began collaborating with different art directors, and co-directed one of the earliest American avant-garde experiments, *The Life and Death of 9413 – a Hollywood Extra* (1927, with Robert Florey). His speciality soon became creative editing and special effects, in such films as W. S. Van Dyke's *Manhattan Melodrama* (1934), George Cukor's *David Copperfield* (1935), Frank Capra's *Mr Smith Goes to Washington* (1939) and many others. His courses at the University of Southern California, New York's MOMA and the Belgrade Film Academy were based on a specific view of *gestalt* perception theory. He considered film as an autonomous medium, a visual composition in time, capable of liberating fragments of visible dynamic energy from reality and of producing new meanings through the process of creative editing. He published articles but his theory was never systematically developed in book form, so his work is mostly available from the transcription of his lectures. SP

257

VOSKOVEC, Jiří
and
WERICH, Jan

Sázava Budy [then Austria-Hungary]
1905 – Pear Blisson, US 1981

Prague [then Austria-Hungary]
1905 – Prague 1980

Czech actors, writers and producers. Voskovec and Werich were one of the major Czech comic influences of the twentieth century, extending beyond their origins in theatre to influence the whole arena of Czech culture. Principally associated with Osvobozené divadlo (The Liberated Theatre), they worked on no less than twenty-five original productions between 1927 and 1938. Musical satires and parodies, the plays featured Voskovec and Werich made up as clowns, whatever their costume, with key improvised interludes. Their 'pure humour and semantic clowning' (Roman Jakobson) was combined with a similar talent for physical comedy.

A year after their 1930 appearance in Paramount's all-star revue, *Paramount on Parade*, they made their first feature film, *Pudr a benzin/Greasepaint and Gasoline* (1931), which is an invaluable record of their theatrical work. In *Pudr a benzin* and *Peníze nebo život/Your Money or Your Life* (1932), both directed by their stage director, Jindřich Honzl, the influence of American crazy comedy is most in evidence. *Peníze nebo život* has some notable sequences, including an elaborate routine on a sinking raft and a climactic battle with criminals in a museum that looks forward to the Marx Brothers. Their later films, *Hej rup!/Heave Ho!* (1934) and *Svět patří nám/The World Belongs to Us* (1937), both directed by Martin Frič*, have more orthodox and tightly constructed scripts and parallel the increasing political commitment of their theatrical work. *Hej rup!* deals with the destruction of a corrupt capitalist at the hands of a workers' collective, while in *Svět patří nám* Voskovec and Werich defeat a Hitler-like demagogue and his big business supporters with the help of the workers. Voskovec and Werich spent the war years in the US and briefly continued their partnership in Czechoslovakia in 1946–7. Voskovec subsequently settled in the US where, as George Voskovec, he became a successful stage and screen actor, while Werich remained in Prague. At the height of Stalinism, Werich appeared in Frič's film adaptation of a Voskovec and Werich play, *Císařův pekař – Pekařův císař/The Emperor's Baker – The Baker's Emperor* (1951), and in 1963 he played a key role in Vojtěch Jasný's* 'new wave' film *Až přijde kocour/That Cat*. Their work was a major influence on other directors of the Czech New Wave* such as Miloš Forman* and Jiří Menzel*. PH

258

W

WAGENSTEIN, Angel Plovdiv 1922

Bulgarian scriptwriter. The author of more than thirty internationally recognised screenplays for feature films, television films, documentaries and animated cartoons. Upon graduating in 1950 from Moscow's VGIK*, Angel Wagenstein collaborated with Socialist Realist* dramatist Orlin Vassilev on the screen version of the latter's play, *Trevoga/ Alarm* (1951), directed by documentarist Zahari Žan-dov*; it marked the beginning of modern Bulgarian cinema. Žandov then collaborated with Wagenstein again on the young scriptwriter's diploma work, *Septemvrici/Septembrists* (1954), on a revolutionary theme. While studying in Moscow, Wagenstein had made the acquaintance of director Konrad Wolf, and they collaborated on *Zvezdi/Sterne/Stars* (1959), a Bulgarian–East German co-production that ranks as a milestone in both national cinemas. *Zvezdi*, a love story praised as an example of Bulgarian 'poetic realism'*, dealt with the tragic fate of a Jewish girl about to be transported to Auschwitz and her relationship with a young German soldier torn by his conscience.

Wagenstein's major talent as an award-winning film-writer is his ability to sketch vulnerable and warmly human characters. One example is his script for Ivan Ničev's *Zvezdi v kossite, sălzi v očite/ Stars in Her Hair, Tears in Her Eyes* (1977), a nostalgic story about a wandering troupe of actors set at the turn of the century during the period of the Bulgarian National Revival. His feel for the significance of the historical moment also singled him out from other scriptwriters in the treatment of revolutionary and anti-fascist themes. His *Dopălnenie kăm zakona za zaštita na dăržavata/Amendment to the Defence of State Act* (1976), directed by Ljudmil Staikov*, found room for flesh-and-blood portraits of well-known political personalities during the troubled 1920s. And his script for Rangel Vălčanov's* *Ezop/ Aesop* (1970), a Bulgarian–Czechoslovak co-production, was a profound political allegory about the possibility of 'socialism with a human face' as propagated by Alexander Dubček; the film was banned in both Czechoslovakia and Bulgaria.

In addition, Wagenstein wrote the script for Konrad Wolf's *Goya* (1971), an East German production shot in 70mm. And he collaborated with Wolf again on a new interpretation of Saint-Exupéry's adult fairy tale *Le Petit prince* in *Der kleine Prinz/The Little Prince* (1966), produced for East German television. His *Sled kraja na sveta/After the End of the World* (1999, d. Ivan Nitchev), set in a mixed ethnic neighbourhood explores the unique ethnic tapestry of the Balkans. RH

WAJDA, Andrzej

Polish director. A world-class director, Wajda has dominated Polish cinema for over forty years. He was a resistance fighter in World War II and a Fine Art student before studying film at Łódź*. His debut feature, *Pokolenie/A Generation* (1954), is the first of a trilogy which includes *Kanał/Canal* (1956) and *Popiół i Diament/Ashes and Diamonds* (1958), and looks at the Polish experience of war in a bleak, unromantic light. The trilogy launched the 'Polish School' and introduced Wajda to international audiences. His subsequent films varied in theme: contemporary and social issues in *Niewinni Czarodzieje/ Innocent Sorcerers* (1960), about the disillusionment and cynicism of modern youth; an examination of the death of actor Zbyszek Cybulski* and of the nature of illusion and reality in the film world in *Wszystko na Sprzedaz/Everything for Sale* (1968). He also made several adaptations of Polish literature, including Żeromski's *Popioły/ Ashes* (1965) and Wyspiański's *Wesele/The Wedding* (1972).

In the early 1970s Wajda formed his own film unit, the 'X' unit. There he gathered a group of young film-makers, including Agnieszka Holland* and Ryszard Bugajski*, and used his international status to push through politically 'difficult' projects. In 1976 he finally gained permission to film a project dating from 1961, *Człowiek z Marmuru/ Man of Marble*. This daring exposé of the Stalinist propaganda machine of Poland's recent past paved the way for the 'cinema of moral unrest'. Powerful and uncompromising, both *Człowiek z Marmuru* and its sequel, *Człowiek z Żelaza/Man of Iron* (1981), played an important role in documenting and supporting the changing public consciousness of the Solidarity years. Somewhat protected from political retribution by his international standing, Wajda worked partly outside Poland during the martial law period. Although he remained resident in Warsaw, he shot *Danton* (1982) in France with Gérard Depardieu as Danton and the great Wojtek Pszoniak as Robespierre, and *Eine Liebe in Deutschland/A Love in Germany* (1983), starring Hanna Schygulla, in Germany.

With the changes of the late 1980s Wajda became a parliamentary senator. He continued film-making, however, returning to war themes in *Korczak/Dr Korczak* (1990) and *Pierścionek z Orłem w Koronie/The Ring with a Crowned Eagle* (1993). In 1991 Wajda was awarded a Felix* for his achievements as a film-maker and his contribution to the creation of a new cultural and political climate in Poland. In 1994 Wajda worked on *Nastasja* (1994) a Polish–Japanese co-production based on a book by Dostoevsky. In his subsequent work he continued his earlier interest in topics such as the Holocaust (with *Wielki tydzien/Holy Week* (1995), based on a story by Jerzy Andrzejewski and set during the Warsaw Ghetto uprising), contemporary social issues (with *Panna Nikt/Miss Nobody* (1996), based on the popular novel by Tomek Tryzna, critically exploring the new post-communist realities), and with adaptations of classical literary works (with *Pan Tadeusz/ Master Tadeusz*, 1999 based on a poem by Adam Mickiewicz). AW

Bib: Andrzej Wajda, *Double Vision: My Life in Film* (1990); Boleslaw Michalek, *The Cinema of Andrzej Wajda* (1973); Janina Falkowska, *The Political Films of Andrzej Wajda* (1996); Gerard Pangon, *Andrzej Wajda* (1997).

Other Films Include: *Lotna* (1959); *Samson, Sibirska Ledi Magbet/ Siberian Lady Macbeth/Fury is a Woman* (1961, Yug.); *L'Amour à vingt ans/Love at Twenty* [ep] (1962, Fr.); *The Gates to Paradise/Vrata Raja* (1967); *Polowanie na Muchy/Hunting Flies* (1969); *Krajobraz Po Bitwie/Landscape After Battle* (1970); *Ziemia Obiecana/Promised Land* (1974); *Bez Znieczulenia/Rough Treatment* (1978); *Panny z Wilka/Les Demoiselles de Wilko/The Young Ladies of Wilko, Dyrygent/The Conductor* (1979); *Kronika Wypadków Miłosnych/A Chronicle of Amorous Incidents* (1985); *Les Possédés/The Possessed* (1987, Fr.).

WEISS, Jiří Prague [then Austria-Hungary] 1913

Czech director. Jiří Weiss originally studied law, then worked as a journalist before making his first film *Lidé na slunci/People in the Sun* (1935), which won an award at Venice. He worked consistently in documentary until World War II, moving to Britain to work for the Crown Film Unit, where his films included *Before the Raid* (1943). Besides writing a novel in English, *The Lost Revolution*, he made his fiction film debut with the medium-length *Who Killed Jack Robins?* and *John Smith Wakes Up* (both 1940). Weiss became one of Czechoslovakia's leading postwar directors with films such as *Uloupená hranice/The Stolen Frontier* (1947), about the Munich crisis, achieving international recognition with *Vlčí jáma/The Wolf Trap* (1957) and *Romeo, Julie a tma/Romeo, Juliet and Darkness* (1960), both noted for their psychological depth and dramatic visual style. Weiss left Czechoslovakia after the Soviet invasion, but returned to film his own script, *Martha und Ich/Martha and I* (1990), starring Marianne Sägebrecht and Michel Piccoli, a deeply felt portrait of pre-war Czechoslovakia and one of his best films. PH

Other Films Include: *Dejte nám křídla/Give Us Wings* [short] (1936); *Píseň o smutné zemi/Song of a Sad Country* [short] (1937); *Cesta ze stínu/Journey from the Shadows* [short] (1938); *The Rape of Czechoslovakia* [short] (1939, UK); *Vstanou noví bojovníci/New Heroes Will Arise* (1950); *Můj přítel Fabián/My Friend the Gypsy* (1953, rel. 1955); *Taková láska/Appassionata/That Kind of Love* (1959); *Zbabělec/ The Coward* (1961); *Zlaté kapradí/The Golden Fern* (1963); *Třicet jedna ve stínu/90° in the Shade* (1965); *Vražda po našem/Murder, Czech Style* (1966); *Spravedlnost pro Selvina/Justice for Selwyn* [TV] (1968).

WERICH, Jan – see VOSKOVEC, Jiří

WÓJCIK, Jerzy

Nowy Sacz, Poland 1930

Polish cinematographer. Wójcik started his work in cinema as camera operator on the set of Wajda's* *Kanal/Canal* (1957), and eventually worked as DP on two important early Wajda features – the classic, *Popiól i diament/Ashes and Diamonds* (1958), an internationally recognised cinematographic masterpiece of black-and-white camerawork, and on the Holocaust drama, *Samson* (1961). Wójcik is the man who is largely responsible for the epic feel of some of the Polish superproductions of the 1960s and for the cinematic image acquired by a number of Polish literary classics in their cinematic metamorphosis. He worked on Jerzy Hoffman's* historical epic *Potop/The Deluge* (1974), an adaptation of Henryk Sienkiewicz's 1886 novel, on Jerzy Kawalerowicz's* *Matka Joanna od aniolow/Mother Joan of the Angels* (1961), an adaptation of Jaroslaw Iwaszkiewicz's story, and later on Kawalerowicz's *Faraon/Pharaoh* (1966), an adaptation of Boleslaw Prus's 1897 novel. In his earlier period Wójcik worked closely with Andrzej Munk's* on his World War II dramas, *Eroica/Heroism* (1957) and *Czlowiek na torze/Man on the Tracks* (1957). He also shot features by directors Kazimierz Kutz*, Janusz Morgenstern, and most frequently with Stanislaw Rózewicz. DI

WOMEN IN EASTERN EUROPEAN CINEMA

Despite all the policies designed to ensure gender equality under state socialism, women have traditionally been restricted from taking the leading role in film-making and have had fewer chances to direct. But women have, nevertheless, actively participated in the film-making process in various capacities – as screenwriters, DPs, set and costume designers, actresses and film critics. In their work women directors from Eastern Europe have managed to address all major feminist concerns – restricted opportunities, abusive relationships, single motherhood, the glass ceiling. It is not only female directors who have focused on women, however. Some of the finest portrayals of women in East European cinema have come from male directors – in Hungary, for example, in films such as Karoly Makk's* *Szerelem/Love* (1971) and *Egymásra nézve/Another Way* (1982), Péter Gothár's *Ajándék ez a nap/A Priceless Day* (1979), or Jánosz Rózsa's *Vasárnapi szülök/ Sunday Daughters* (1980). Hungarian Márta Mészarós* is probably the most productive and deservedly best-known figures among the East European women film-makers. Mészarós's filmography includes over twenty titles, and she has worked in France, Canada, and for international co-productions as well as in Hungary. Her films deal exclusively with the problems of women. Her work encompasses a wide range of issues affecting women of various generations – motherhood, abortion, adoption, love, lovelessness, marriage, communal confinement, the generation gap and victimisation. It also includes fine explorations of eroticism and women's sexuality, nurturing friendships, loneliness and ageing. Thus Mészáros has quite naturally been classified as a feminist – a classification she herself refutes. Other active women directors from Hungary are Lívia Gyarmathy, a director of a number of films focusing on inter-ethnic relations, and Judit Elek, director of *Mária-nap/Maria's Day* (1983) whose more recent work has been devoted to exploring anti-Semitism (*Tutajosok/The Raft*, 1989; *Mondani a mondhatatlant: Elie Wiesel üzenete/To Speak the Unspeakable: The Message of Elie Wiesel*, 1996), and Ildikó Enyédi whose 1989 *Az én XX. századom/My Twentieth Century* is a stylish feminist discourse in black-and-white about the intersections of history and personal fate. Enyédi's 1994 *Büvös vadász/Magic Hunter* and 1997 *Tamás és Juli/Tamas and Juli* (1997) confirmed her reputation as an original and innovative figure in European film-making. Ildikó Szabó (*Gyerekgyilkosságok/Child Murders*, 1993) and Ibolya Fekete (*Bolse Vita*, 1996) enjoy deserved international acclaim for their work.

The major female figure in Czech cinema is Vera Chytilová*. Her best feature film is the experimental Dadaist *Sedmikrásky/Daisies*, 1966. Other works which reveal an uneven career include *Hra o jablko/Apple Game* (1976), *Panelstory* (1979), *Kalamita/Calamity* (1981), *Faunovo prilis pozdní odpoledne/The Very Late Afternoon of a Faun* (1983). Screenwriter Esther Krumbachová is one of the most important figures of the Czech New Wave*, having scripted such surrealist features as Jan Nemec's* *O slavnosti a hostech/Report on the Party and the Guests* (1966) and *Mucedníci lásky/Martyrs of Love* (1966).

Most notable women in Polish film-making include Holocaust survivor Wanda Jakubowska* who made a personal film about the death camps, *Ostatni etap/The Last Stage* (1948). The interest in Jakubowska has been recently revived and her work featured at many international film festivals in the 1990s. Barbara Sass-Dort*, director of *Bez milosci/Without Love* (1980), *Debiutantka/The Debutante* (1982), *Dziewczeta z Nowolipek/The Girls of Nowolipki* (1985) and Magdalena Lazarkiewicz, director of *Prezez dotyk/By Touch* (1985) have displayed a continuous commitment to making films about women, and their works are quite interesting within the 1980s East European sociopolitical context. Agnieszka Holland's* early work presents some very interesting portraits of women (e.g. *Kobieta samotna/A Lonely Women*, 1981) but she does not exhibit a special preference for women's issues although she created fine female portraits in *Bittere Ernte/Angry Harvest* (1985, Ger.) and *Washington Square* (1997, US). The work of Dorota Kedzierzawska including *Diably, diably/Devils, Devils* (1991), *Wrony/Crows* (1995), and *Nic/Nothing* (1998) has garnered considerable international acclaim. Like Mészáros, Bulgarian

263

Binka Zeljazkova* was educated at VGIK* and then went back to Bulgaria to make a long succession of films, many of which deal with the problems of women. Her best works are the absurdist *Privarzaniat Balon/The Attached Balloon* (1967) and the innovative *Poslednata duma/The Last Word* (1973) which features a group of female political prisoners in fascist Bulgaria of the 1940s. Roumiana Petkova started an active career in cinema committed to the problems of women (*Otrazheniya/Reflections*, 1985); her work in the 1990s focused on ethnic minorities (*Gori, gori oganche/Burn, Burn, Little Flame*, 1994; *Mezhdinen sviat/A World In-Between*, 1995). Women working as directors in East European cinema are Malvina Ursianu and Elisabeta Bostan* in Romania, Anisa Markajani in Albania and Gordana Boškov and Mirjana Vukomanovic in Serbia. DI

Y

YIDDISH CINEMA IN POLAND

At the beginning of the twentieth century Poland was home to over three and a half million Jews. There was a thriving Yiddish and Hebrew cultural tradition, particularly in the theatre. The first forays into film were made as early as 1908 by the Sila Company, which filmed Yiddish plays. It was not until the 1930s, however, and the arrival of Polish-born Joseph Green from America, that Yiddish cinema really established itself in Poland.

Green saw an opportunity to make films cheaply in Poland for the American-Jewish market. He founded Green-Film, the Polish arm of his company, in 1936. His first production introduced American-Jewish comedienne Molly Picon in the musical comedy *Yidl Mit Fidl/Yiddle with a Fiddle* (1937), an international success. Green operated in true movie-mogul fashion, with publicity splashes and American 'stars'. Under his guidance, Yiddish cinema began to play a prominent role on the Polish film scene, and his films were distributed throughout Europe. It was not unusual for mainstream directors to make Yiddish films. Aleksander Ford* shot *Chalutzim/Sabra* in 1934 with actors from the famous Habimah theatre in Palestine, and it was popular comedy director Michal Waszyński who made the true Yiddish classic, *The Dybbuk* (1937). Most of Joseph Green's productions survived the war because he took the negatives to America in 1939. When comedians Shimon Dzigan and Israel Schumacher made a semi-documentary in 1949 – *Unzere Kinder/Our Children* – the new Polish government banned the film and the film-makers emigrated to Israel. More recently, with the demise of communism, Yiddish cinema is being re-explored in Poland, and a selection of titles was screened at the 1990 Festival of Culture in Cracow. AW

Bib: Judith Goldberg, *Laughter Through Tears* (1983).

YUGOSLAV 'BLACK WAVE'

Radical Yugoslav films of the late 1960s/early 1970s. The 1960s saw the first great political and economic liberalisation in postwar Yugoslavia. At the same time, film-makers used their newly acquired knowledge of neo-realism and the French New Wave in order to reject the unwritten rules of 'real socialism' (Socialist Realism*) – imitation of life, combined with patriotic education. They turned 'naughty', and suddenly the dark side of the new society emerged on the screen: corruption and hypocrisy, and the narrow-mindedness and boorishness of the ruling class. Two 1967 Živojin Pavlović* films (*Budjenje pacova/Awakening of the Rats* and *Kad budem mrtav i beo/When I Am Dead and White*) are representative of this movement. No more heroes: the lack of any individual perspective can be seen as a kind of desperate cry. Together with those of Dušan Makavejev*, Aleksandar Petrović*, Želimir Žilnik and Bata Čengić, they form a core of twenty to thirty films which were labelled 'Black Wave' (or 'Black Film'). The term was first used pejoratively by the communist authorities in order to censor and even ban some of the films. Much later, 'Black Wave' became a positive critical notion embraced by oppositional film culture. SP

YUGOSLAV 'PARTISAN FILMS'

Yugoslav genre, designating World War II action films. The appeal of the first postwar films in Yugoslavia derived from the fact that they knew how to combine the triumphalism of the official postwar posture with a certain naïvety of narration. Examples include Nikola Popović's *Živjeće ovaj narod/This Nation Will Live!* (1947) and France Štiglic's* *Na svoji zemlji/On Our Own Land* (1948). Emphasis was put on psychology and emotions. As the films evolved, much of this dimension was lost and replaced with pure, Western-like action, and the 'partisan' genre was born. The schema was simple: every big battle from the rich history of Yugoslavia's World War II experience deserved a monument – and a movie. Veljko Bulajić's* *Kozara* (1962) and *Bitka na Neretvi/Battle on the River Neretva* (1969) are two examples of such historic battles used as a pretext to stage a confrontation between bad Nazi soldiers and good partisans in action. As the good guys usually won, the genre was extremely popular with the audience, and some actors – such as Ljubiša Samardžić and Bata Živojinović – achieved stardom through it. The 1970s were the golden age of these commercially successful but aesthetically simple films that were often turned into even more successful television series. Such was the case with two Aleksandar Djordjević films about the resistance movement in Belgrade, *Otpisani/Written Off* (1974) and *Povratak otpisanih/The Return of the Written Off* (1976).

Two factors made 1980 the final year for this genre: Tito died, and Živojin Pavlović* shot *Na svidenje v naslednji vojni/Farewell Until the Next War*. If the death of Tito symbolically closed the period of partisan triumphs, Pavlović's film was a clinical diagnosis of the death of the genre itself. SP

YUGOSLAV PRAGUE GROUP

The term refers to the work of a group of Yugoslav directors who were all educated at FAMU* in Prague. It includes directors of different ethnic backgrounds including Croatian, Rajko Grlić* and Lordan Zafranović*, Serbian, Srdjan Karanović*, Goran Marković and Goran Paskaljević*, and the somewhat younger Bosnian, Emir Kusturica*. The work of the group is characterised by interest in plots combining humorous and dramatic elements and by the subtle characterisation of the protagonists. They also display meticulous attention to visual style and detail, working with highly skilled cameramen, from veteran Tomislav Pinter to Vilko Filać. The directors in the Prague Group started with an explicit interest in contemporary topics but later on made films on a wider range of subjects. The violent legacy of the Ustasa regime is revisited in Zafranović's *Okupacija u 26 slika/Occupation in 26 Scenes* (1977) while the limits of patriarchy are challenged in Karanović's *Virdzina/Virginia* (1991), both visually remarkable films. The newer history of Yugoslavia and particularly the early Tito years are explored in Grlić's *Samo jednom se ljubi/You Love Only Once* (1981), Kusturica's *Otac na sluzbenom putu/When Father Was Away on Business* (1985), and Marković's *Tito i ja/Tito and I* (1992), all of which approach history through the personal experiences of the protagonists. *Petrijin Venac/Petria's Wealth* (1980, Karanović) is the story of a peasant woman, while other contemporary works combined social drama and satire, like *Čuvar plaže u zimskom periodu/Beach Guard in Winter* (1976, Paskaljević), *Variola vera* (1981, Marković), and *U raljama života/In the Jaws of Life* (1984, Grlić). The violent and tragic disintegration of Yugoslavia led to the creation of acclaimed films like *Underground* (Kusturica, 1995) and *Bure baruta/Powder Keg* (Paskaljević, 1998). In the 1990s some of the members of the Prague Group emigrated and now live and work abroad. Grlić teaches at Ohio University, Zafranović is in the Czech Republic, Paskaljević and Kusturica are in France. DI

YUGOSLAVIA (former)

A film tradition in Yugoslavia existed before the actual birth of the state (the kingdom of Serbs, Croats and Slovenes was named 'Yugoslavia' in 1929) and will certainly outlast it: the death of the Socialist Federal Republic of Yugoslavia came in 1991 with the proclaimed independence of several states, including Slovenia, Croatia, Bosnia–Herzegovina and Macedonia. However, since Yugoslavia was a country in the time-span covered by most of the following material, it will be referred to here as such.

The first film screenings on the territory of the future Yugoslavia took place only six months after the Lumière brothers' first screening in Paris: the films of the Lumière Cinematograph were shown in Belgrade on 6 June 1896. Most of the early travelling operators were foreign – and it was they who filmed the first footage shot in these regions. Some sixty metres of views of the port of Šibenik (Croatia), shot in 1903 by the Polish operator Stanislaw Noworyta, are considered to be the first known film ever shot in Yugoslavia. National pioneers also emerged in the first two decades of the century: Karol Grosmann* in Slovenia and Milton Manaki* in Macedonia. Svetozar Botorić, the owner of several Belgrade hotels and the film theatre Paris, started to produce short documentaries in collaboration with the French company Pathé. This collaboration also produced the first feature-length film shot in Serbia (and Yugoslavia): *Život i dela besmrtnog vožda Karadjordja/The Life and Work of the Immortal Leader Karadjordje*. This biographical portrait of the Serbian leader who fought against the Turks and founded the dynasty of Karadjordjević was shot in 1910 and distributed in 1911 under the title *Karadjordje*. Čiča Ilija Stanojević, the leading actor, was credited as a director. Several film companies were established in the 1920s and 1930s whose main field of interest was documentary, but we can hardly speak of regular film production before 1945. Al Popović's *S verom u boga/In God We Trust* (1934), a fresco about the sufferings of the Serbian people in World War I, Janko Ravnik's *V kraljestvu zlatoroga/In the Kingdom of the Goldhorn* (1931), a *Heimat*-like glorification of the Slovene Alps, and some 'fantastic' parodies by Croat Oktavijan Miletić (*Faust*, 1931, *Nocturno*, 1938) are the most noteworthy films of the prewar period.

All organised film production ceased with the onset of World War II, with the exception of the company Hrvatski Slikopis ('Croatian Image-writing') in the pro-Nazi independent state of Croatia. At the same time, Tito's partisans began to document their battles on film. In 1943, his military headquarters (then in Bosnia) issued a 'decree for documenting partisan battles' and formed the first official team of film cameramen, but most of their footage was destroyed. On 13 December 1944, Tito signed the first official act of the new state administration, establishing a film section. This act is considered the formal beginning of cinematography in socialist Yugoslavia. The Yugoslav communist

267

authorities took seriously Lenin's* dictum about film as 'the most important art'. Film became elevated to a cultural and national resource and was consequently allocated significant funds. The National Film Company (DFJ) was created in 1945 and the government's Committee for Cinematography formed in 1946. By 1947 the process of nationalisation was complete, and film became a state art. Film companies were then founded in every republic: Triglav Film in Ljubljana, Jadran* Film in Zagreb, Avala Film and Zvezda Film in Belgrade. Belgrade also opened a Kinoteka (film archive) in 1949 and a Film Academy in 1950.

The first postwar Yugoslav feature was Vjekoslav Afrić's *Slavica* (1947). Like most early postwar films, it was a barely disguised eulogy of the Resistance and the triumphalist spirit. National reconstruction became an overriding theme – even obsession – as titles like *Živjeće ovaj narod/This Nation Will Live!* (Nikola Popović, 1947) or *Na svoji zemlji/On Our Own Land* (1948, France Štiglic*) suggest. However, it is possible that the popular appeal of these films derived less from their historical relevance than from the authenticity of their characters and a certain naïvety of narration. It would be unfair to label all films from this period as state propaganda. On the one hand, the centralised administration of film ended in 1951, following the introduction of the concept of 'self-management' into most economic, social and political structures, including film production and distribution. The founding of the famous 'workers' councils' also had its cinematic equivalent in the creation of associations of producers enjoying creative and financial autonomy. On the other hand, some directors were quite successful in carving out their own niches even in the 1950s. At least two figures stand out in this regard: Branko Bauer* and France Štiglic. Both were capable of directing nuanced emotional scenes, usually with a strong children's presence, as in Bauer's *Ne okreći se, sine/Don't Turn Back, Son* (1956) and Štiglic's *Dolina miru/The Valley of Peace* (1956). Their careers flourished, and were crowned by the 1956 Cannes festival Best Actor award for John Kitzmiller in *Dolina miru* and a 1960 Oscar nomination for Bauer's *Deveti krug/The Ninth Circle*.

The first (and only) Oscar for Yugoslav film came much later from a completely different genre: animation. The Zagreb School of Animation* was founded in the 1950s by Dušan Vukotić, who later won an Oscar for *Surogat/The Substitute* in 1962. Although there was never really a scholarly institution, this movement of animators (including Nedeljko Dragić, Borivoj Dovniković, Joško Marušić and many others) set new standards, both in animation experiment and socially critical content, proving that Disney-like cartoons were not exhaustive of the genre's possibilities.

In the late 1950s and early 1960s, Yugoslavia was producing around fifteen films per year and the first signs of different themes began to appear. The films of Bauer and Štiglic revealed a significant shift towards the problems of modern life. Adaptations of famous literary titles were also adopted as a way to circumvent the proclaimed values of Socialist Realism*. Forms of 'poetic licence' allowed some film-makers to develop more complex stories with less transparent messages (Štiglic's existentialist drama *Balada o trobenti in oblaku/Ballad of a Trumpet and a Cloud* from 1961 is one example). Serbian director Puriša Djordjević also introduced his lyrical and oneiric style into films about the partisan war, with his trilogy *Devojka/Girl* (1965), *San/Dream* (1966) and *Jutro/Morning* (1967). Slowly, films became more critical, while subjects were chosen from hitherto untouched territory, such as the failures of the social welfare system or corruption within the communist leadership (Bauer's *Samo ljudi/Traces*, 1957, and *Licem u lice/Face to Face*, 1963).

This trend led directly to a strong movement of socially conscious directors, who formed a kind of Yugoslav new wave known as the 'Black Wave'*, which flourished in the late 1960s. Živojin Pavlović* was the leading figure of this movement (*Budjenje pacova/Awakening of the Rats, Kad budem mrtav i beo/When I Am Dead and White*, both 1967), which also included Dušan Makavejev*, Aleksandar Petrović*, Želimir Žilnik and others. The movement was closely linked to the liberalisation of the country in the 1960s; one can detect evidence of a less rigid Marxist ideology in Žilnik's *Rani radovi/Early Works* and of a more permissive regime in Makavejev's *W.R. – Misterije organizma/W. R. – Mysteries of the Organism*. At the same time, the 'freedom' of the movement was limited. Most of the works were censored in one way or another; they were either officially banned or their distribution was impeded, while some of the film-makers were forced to work abroad. The 1960s were also the years of powerful individual cinematic stylistics. Slovene directors Boštjan Hladnik and Matjaž Klopčič* were strongly influenced by the French New Wave, and Croat Zvonimir Berković 'composed' his first film, *Rondo*, in 1966. These films were not as strongly attached to themes of everyday life as the 'Black Wave' films, but they shared a common atmosphere of despair.

The 1970s in Yugoslavia were marked by both an expansion of social welfare (financed by foreign loans) and increased repression, as the regime became dominated by hard-line communists. One of the ways to escape the tensions created by these contradictory forces was to produce popular mainstream films. Two main popular genres emerged. The first is the so-called 'newly composed Serbian comedy', named by analogy with a popular Serbian musical genre called 'newly composed music', an amalgam of folk songs and pop. This genre is based on simple situations and character comedy, and includes work by directors such as Zoran Čalić, Milan Jelić and Miča Milošević. The second genre is that of the 'partisan films'*, Western-like movies using World War II battles as a pretext for action (Hajrudin Krvavac, Aleksandar Djordjević). Such was the popularity of these genres that more than thirty films were produced annually during this period. The 'newly composed Serbian comedy' succeeded in combining a traditional comedy of errors with the 'new primitivism' of vulgar jokes and ambiguous sexual messages, based on clichés of betrayed

269

husbands, lusty girls-next-door and voyeuristic grandfathers. The comedies of the 1950s – those of František Čap*, for example – used teenagers to address adults, and therefore possessed a certain innocence. The 1970s took away all the charm and turned the genre into adult cinema for teenagers, on the edge of soft-core pornography.

A breakthrough in Yugoslav cinema came at the end of the 1970s, when the first generation of Yugoslav students returned from Prague's film school FAMU*; they were henceforth referred to as the 'Prague School'. Most famous among them is Emir Kusturica*, whose films have won accolades at almost every international festival in the last decade: *Sječaš li se Dolly Bell?/Do You Remember Dolly Bell?* (1981 Venice), *Otac na službenom putu/When Father Was Away on Business* (1985 Cannes), *Dom za vešanje/Time of the Gypsies* (1989 Cannes), *Arizona Dream* (1993 Berlin). Other 'Prague School' directors made their mark: Goran Paskaljević combined popular comedy with a human touch (*Čuvar plaže u zimskom periodu/The Beach Guard in Winter*, 1976; *Pas, koji je voleo vozove/The Dog That Loved Trains*, 1977); Goran Marković has moved with great elegance over the whole generic range (from social melodrama in *Specijalno vaspitanje/Special Education*, 1977, to the disaster movie *Variola Vera*, 1982, and the psycho-thriller *Déjà vu*, 1987); Srdjan Karanović chose a more melancholic point of view, whether depicting the elderly (*Zemaljski dani teku/The Fleeing of Earthly Days*, 1979) or the difficulties of rural life (*Petrijin venac/Petrija's Wreath*, 1980); Rajko Grlić revisited the territory of World War II partisans in a brilliant melodrama, *Samo jednom se ljubi/You Only Love Once/The Melody Haunts My Reverie*, 1981; Lordan Zafranović also returned to this topic in order to examine different wartime positions, from partisans and Uštaše traitors to the broken aristocracy of Dubrovnik (*Okupacija u 26 slika/Occupation in 26 Images*, 1979). Beyond their differences, the 'Prague School' generation can be seen to share a belief in simple, everyday stories (as opposed to epics and historical dramas), pinpointing the same problems as the 'Black Wave' films of the 1970s but with more humour and a gentler sarcasm.

Another generation of independent film-makers with recognisable individual styles and a respect for the classical film tradition emerged in the 1980s: the Slovene Karpo Godina*, the Croat Zoran Tadič*, the Serbs Miloš Radivojević and Slodoban Šijan* and the Macedonian Stole Popov. These film-makers have been supported by a young generation of film critics gathered around magazines such as *Ekran** in Ljubljana, *Filmska kultura* in Zagreb, *Sineast* in Sarajevo and *Filmograf* in Belgrade.

Although the directors of the 1980s have not been as commercially successful at home as some of their 'partisan' predecessors, they can be credited with making Yugoslav cinema known throughout the world. Kusturica, Godina, Šijan, Marković and Paskaljević have been regular guests at international festivals. A huge retrospective of Yugoslav cinema at the Pompidou Centre in Paris in 1985 represented a culmi-

270

nation of their achievement. From today's point of view, this retro-spective can be seen as a requiem for Yugoslav film. The economic difficulties of the 1980s drastically reduced the number of films produced, and the increasingly intractable political problems began to be reflected in the politics of national cinema too. Acrimonious debates at the national film festival in Pula* were perhaps symptomatic of the imminent collapse of the country as a whole. SP

The 1990s have seen not only the breakdown of Yugoslavia as a political unit, but also a radical change in the economic system of each of the new states. Conditions for film financing have drastically changed: once fully subsidised by the ministries of culture, film production is now subject to the laws of the market. Films from former Yugoslavia have enjoyed wide international acclaim in the 1990s – Milcho Manchevski's *Pred dozdot/Before the Rain* (1994) and Emir Kusturica's *Black Cat, White Cat* (1998) received awards at Venice, and Cannes celebrated Kusturica's *Underground* (1995). Yugoslavia's break-up* which led to a significant exodus of members of the intelligentsia, attracted the attention of a large number of film-makers, both from within the country and internationally. Over 250 films (feature or documentary) were devoted to the Balkan conflict, making the Yugoslav break-up the event that inspired most Eastern European-related cinematic works in post-communist times. Since the break-up, the cinemas of the newly independent countries have evolved separately, entering festivals and contenders for the Academy Awards on their own, and developing their respective national film funds, film institutes, and national film festivals. Political factors make it necessary to trace the film cultures of the former Yugoslav republics by giving special recognition to their specific cinematic traditions, and to the respective directors.

Bosnia. The first feature films were made in Bosnia after World War II. Toma Janić made a crime film for adolescents, *Crni biseri/Black Pearls* (1958), and two dramas on topics from everyday life – *Rana jesen/Early Fall* (1962) and *Glineni golub/The Clay Pigeon* (1966). Hajrudin Krvavac directed a number of epic partisan action adventures including *Vrtlog/Vortex* (1964,) *Diverzanti/Saboteurs* (1967), *Most/Bridge* (1969), and the well-known *Valter brani Sarajevo/Walter Defends Sarajevo* (1972). A high-profile figure in the Bosnian film industry, Bato Cengić came to prominence with his sarcastic takes on ill-fated socialist endeavours in *Uloga moje porodice u svetskoj revoluciji/The Role of My Family in the World Revolution* (1971) and *Slike iz života udarnika/Scenes from the Life of a Shockworker* (1972). Both films were censored and for over a decade Cengić had only limited chances to work in film. In 1990 he won an award at the Pula* film festival for his adaptation of Branko Copić's novel, *Gluvi barut/Silent Gunpowder* (1990), considered a premonition of the troubles in Bosnia. Nenad Dizdarević's sensitive take on children, *Magarece godine/The Awkward Age* (1994) was distributed during the war. Of all 'Bosnian' directors, Emir Kusturica has enjoyed most international acclaim. Ironically, however, he is also the one who decided to leave Sarajevo and renounce his Bosnian roots for the sake of maintaining his Yugoslavian identity. This move was interpreted negatively by the public in Bosnia and the director no longer enjoys the high esteem of audiences in his native land. Kusturica's works made during his Sarajevo period include the coming-of-age story, *Sjećas li se Dolly Bell?/Do You Remember Dolly Bell?* (1981), and the Cannes-winning, *Otac na službenom putu/When Father Was Away on Business* (1985) and *Dom za vešanje/Time of the Gypsies* (1989). In his early films Kusturica collaborated with Sarajevan screenwriter and poet, Abdullah Sidran who later started working with Ademir Kenović. American-educated Kenović had made a debut with the TV drama *Ovo malo duse/A Little Bit of Soul* (1986). Before the war he made the melodramatic *Kudyz* (1989), and during the war he started SaGA and worked on documentaries. Eventually he became the first director to make a feature film in the new Bosnian state – his *Savršeni krug/Perfect Circle* (1996) won the main award at the Tokyo film festival. The siege of Sarajevo brought the city to the attention of film-makers. Parallel with the destruction of the city, Sarajevo was perpetually revived in the films chronicling its proud survival. This is particularly visible in the numerous documentaries that Sarajevans shot about themselves. The works of the members of the Sarajevo Group of Authors (SaGA)* and many other film-makers chronicled the agony and the strength of their city on a day-to-day basis and created an impressive record of visual testimonies. Some of the most active film-makers during the war were Kenović, Pjer Zalica, Mirza Idrizović, Haris Prolić, and Benjamin Filipović. Since 1995 Sarajevo re-established itself as a lively cultural centre with its own film festival and a grant scheme for young film-makers whose production is showcased annually.

Croatia. The beginnings of cinema in Croatia are linked to the name of pioneer, Josip Karaman who made six films early in the century. Other film pioneers were Maksimilian Paspa and Josip Halla. The first film studio started around 1917 and released several feature and documentary films. After World War II, some of the first films to be made in Croatia were directed by Branko Marijanović – the war films, *Zastava/Checkpoint* (1947), *Opsada/Siege* (1956), and the musical comedy, *Ciguli miguli/Fiddle Diddle* (1952). Croatian film classics, Fedor Hanzeković and cameraman, Oktavijan Miletić, adapted Simo Matavulji's novel *Bakonia fra brne/Brother Bakonja Brno* (1951) which tells the story of a Franciscan monk in Herzegovina. Vatroslav Mimica, well known for his works in animation, also acted as feature director and made the melodrama, *U oluki/Within the storm* (1952) and *Jubilej gospodina Ikla/Mr Ikla's Anniversary* (1955). In the 1950s the Jadran* film studio was built near Zagreb. Prolific director Branko Bauer* directed, among others, *Ne okreci se sine/Do Not Turn Around* (1956) and *Cetri saputnik/The Fourth Companion* (1967), Krsto Papić directed a number of dramas, comedies, and literary adaptations, best known of which is *Lisice/Foxes* (1969). Born in Montenegro in 1921, the regime's favourite Veljko Bulajić* worked mostly in Croatia. He made the historical epic, *Sarajevski Atentat/The Day That Shook the World* (1975), set in the crucial days of 1914 which led to the beginning of World War I. The middle generation of Croatian directors includes Vanca Kljaković, Fadil Hadzic, Krešo Golik, Ante Babaja, Zvonimir Berković and Zoran Tadić who directed a number of crime films. Croatian members of the Yugoslav Prague Group* are Rajko Grlić* and Lordan Zafranović*, who were both preoccupied with history and ethics, and both creators of impressive and finely crafted dramas. Members of the younger generation of Croatian directors include Branko Schmidt with *Djuka Begovic/Evil Blood* (1991) and *Vukovar se vraca kuci/Vukovar Returns Home* (1994), Vinko Brešan with *Kako je poeeo rat na mom otoku/How the War Started on My Little Island* (1996), Davor Zmegac with *Zlatne godine/Golden Years* (1993), and Jakov Sedlar with *Gospa* (1995).

Montenegro. The pioneer of Montenegrin cinema was Velimir-Velja Stojanović who worked in documentary and features in close collaboration with cameraman and director, Ratko Djurović. Together they made *Lažni car/The False King* (1955) and the comedy, *Zle pare/Evil Money* (1956). Zdravko Velimirović directed *Dan četrnaesti/The Fourteenth Day* (1960) and the adaptation of Meša Selimović's *Derviš i smrt/The Dervish and the Death* (1974). Other directors from the region include Boško Boskovic, Milo Djukanović and Živko Nikolić, whose beautiful mountain landscapes are the backdrop for stories about proud female protagonists who clash with patriarchal traditions, such as *Bestije/The Beasts* (1977), *Luka's Jovina/ Jovana Lukina* (1979), *Ćudo nevideno/Miracle Unseen* (1981), and *Lepota poroka/The Beauty of Sin* (1986). The leading Montenegrin production company is Lovčen film.

Serbia. Film production in Serbia evolved around several companies, best-known of which was Avala film. Directors Dušan Makavejev* and Aleksandar Petrovic* are well-known in the West. Veteran Puriša Djordjevic directed over fifty features. The middle generation of Serbian directors include Milos Radivojević, Jovan Aćin (*Bal na vodi/Hey, Babu Riba*, 1986), Slobodan Šijan*, Branko Baletić (*Balkan Express*, 1983), Zdravko Sotra, Dragan Krešoja, Boro Drasković (*Zivot e lep/Life Is Beautiful*, 1985, based on Aleksander Tišma's novel and Yugoslav break-up drama, *Vukovar – jedna priča/ Vukovar: Poste Restante*, 1994), Gordana Boškov, 'Black Wave's'* Živojn Pavlović* and Želimir Žilnik*, Prague Groups's* Goran Marković (*Specijalno Vaspitanie/Special Education*, 1977, *Variola Vera*, 1982), Srdjan Karanović* and Goran Paskaljević*, and the noteworthy screenwriters Dušan Kovacević* and Gordan Mihić. Best known among the younger generation of Serbian film-makers are Srdjan Dragojević*, Gorcin Stojanović (*Premeditated Murder*, 1996 and *Strsljen/Hornet*, 1998), Oleg Novković (*Kazi zasto me ostavi/Why Did You Leave Me?*, 1994) and Mirjana Vukomanović (*Tre letuja*

273

dana/Three Summer Days, 1997). After the break-up of Yugoslavia there was a proliferation of smaller production companies. Radio-TV-Serbia (RTS) is involved in financing a number of productions, another well-known company is the Belgrade-based Komuna film. Popular comedian, Ljubiša Samardzić turned producer and runs one of the most active production companies, Cinema Dizajn. Many of the films critical to the nationalist regime of Milosevic have been produced by the independent company, Studio B'92. Belgrade is the location of the Yugoslav Film Institute and the site of the annual FEST* which takes place in February and of the Festival of Auteur Films. A number of small festivals take place in smaller cities across Serbia.

Slovenia has a strong cinematic tradition as of early in this century. The first Slovene film was made by Karol Grossman* in 1905. The most prolific film pioneer was Metod Badjura who, together with his wife Milka, produced numerous ethnographic documentaries featuring life in the beautiful Triglav mountains. The first feature film in Slovenia was set in these same mountains – *V kraljestvu zlatoroga/In the Realm of the Golden Horn* (1931), directed by Janko Ravni. France Štiglic* made some classic films in close collaboration with writer Ciril Kosmac. Czech-born Fratisek Čap* is perceived as the other leading Slovenian film-maker. Jože Gale established himself internationally with a series of acclaimed children's films. Other directors belonging to this generation are Vojko Duletić, Milan Ljubić, Bojan Stupica, Jože Babić, Jane Kavcić and Igor Pretnar. Boštjan Hladnik's and Matijaš Klopcić's* work is considered to have represented the equivalent of a *nouvelle vague* in Slovene cinema, and includes a number of documentaries and features. Karpo Godina* who worked as a cameraman on a number of Yugoslavian masterpieces is considered to be the most original Slovenian director with his haunting *Splav Meduze/The Raft of Medusa* (1980), as well as *Rdeci boogie/Red Boogie* (1982) and *Abyssinia* (1998). Another leading member of the newer generation of directors is Franći Slak who made *Eva* (1983) and *Ko zaprem oci/When I Close My Eyes* (1993). After declaring independence from Yugoslavia in 1991, Slovenia's film industry evolves around the Slovenian Film Fund. An internationally acclaimed film about the Ljubljana rock-group Laibach, *Prerokbe Ognija/Predictions of Fire* (1994), was made by Slovenian-based American, Michael Benson.

Macedonia. The pioneers of cinema in Macedonia were the brothers Manaki* – Yanaki and Milton, as well as Blagoja Drinkov who made a number of short films throughout the 1930s. In 1952, Vojslav Nanović shot *Frosina*, which is believed to be the first Macedonian feature. Serbian-born, Žika Mitrović revisited in his films some of the most important Macedonian historical events, like the kidnapping of an American missionary in *Miss Stone* (1958), the failed conspiracy of 1903 in *Solunskite Atentatori/The Assassins of Salonika* (1961), and the war drama, *Do pobedata i po nea/Till Victory and Beyond* (1966) starring Bulgarian, Nevena Kokanova*. Trajče Popov made *Make-donska krvava svatba/Macedonian Blood Wedding* (1967) based

274

on the folk-play of Vojdan Ćernodrinski. Ljubisa Georgievski's war drama, *Pod isto Nebo/Under the Same Sky* (1964) was realised with the participation of Miomir Stamenković. Georgievski also made *Republikata vo plamen/The Republic in Flames* (1969) about the Illinden uprising, the legend-based, *Cenata na gradot/The Price of the City* (1970), and *Planinata na gnevot/The Mountain of Wrath* (1977). Other milestones of Macedonian cinema are Dimitrije Osmanli's village drama, *Zed/Thirst* (1971) and Kiril Cenevski's controversial take on the Greek civil war, *Crno Seme/Black Seed* (1971). One of the most active figures in Macedonian cinema today is Stole Popov (1950) who first came into the spotlight with his Gypsy documentary *Dae* (1979), and has since completed several features – *Ćrveniot konj/The Red Horse* (1981), *Srećna Nova '49/Happy New '49* (1986), *Tetoviranje/Tattoo* (1991), and *Gypsy Magic* (1997). Other directors belonging to this generation are Boris Damovski, Aleksandar Popovski and Darko Mitrevski. Antonio Mitrićeski* made the interethnic love story, *Preku ezeru/Across the Lake* (1998). The most acclaimed young Macedonian director is Milcho Mančevski*, director of Venice festival-winning *Pred dozdot/Before the Rain* (1994), a beautiful and poetic tale which serves as a powerful indictment of ethnic rivalries. The main film production company in the region was and remains Vardar Film. DI

YUGOSLAVIA'S BREAK-UP IN FILM

Yugoslavia's break-up attracted the attention of a large number of film-makers, both from within the country and internationally. The body of film productions about the conflict in the Balkans was, in its nature, a truly international project. Over 250 feature and documentary films were made, and one can claim that the Yugoslav break-up was the event that inspired most cinematic works in post-communist times.

The global trend that turns all feature film-making into a multinational enterprise is clearly visible in the case of the features that look at aspects of the Yugoslav break-up. The early conflict of the Croatian break-up was featured in Serbian, Boro Drašković's *Vukovar: Poste Restante* (1994) and in Croatian, Vinko Brešan's *Kako je poeeo rat na mom otoku/How the War Started on My Little Island* (1996). At least thirty-five international feature films were made in response to the Bosnian war. The films were telling different stories. The most ambitious ones were tackling the complex history of the Balkans, like Emir Kusturica's* Cannes-winner, *Underground* (1995, Fr./Ger./Hung.) which offered a controversial take on the history of Yugoslavia since 1941, or Theo Angelopoulos's *To vlemma tou Odyssea/Ulysses' Gaze* (1995, Gr./Fr./It.) which told the story of a weary Greek expatriate travelling through the Balkans in search of lost memories of harmonious coexistence. Numerous films explored the difficult choices in taking sides in the ethnic conflict, like Srdjan Dragojević's* acclaimed *Lepa sela lepo gore/Pretty Village, Pretty Flame* (1996, Yug.) and Milcho Manchevski's Venice-winner, *Pred dozdot/Before the Rain* (1994, Mac./Fr./UK). Many films focused on Sarajevo. Ademir Kenović's *Savrseni krug/Perfect Circle* (1997, Bosnia/Fr.) explored the fate of displaced children; Michael Winterbottom's *Welcome to Sarajevo* (1997, UK/US) looked at the moral issues facing journalists covering the siege, as did *Territorio Comanche/Comanche Territory* (1997, Sp./Ger./Fr./Arg. Gerado Herrero). The Italian *Il carniere/Gamebag* (1997, Maurizio Zaccaro) told the story of two hunters caught in the middle of the siege. Other films focused on the psychological stagnation of people in Belgrade, like Gorćin Stojanović's *Ubistvo s predumisljajem/Premeditated Murder* (1995), Želimir Žilnik's* *Dupe od Mramora/Marble Ass* (1995), and Goran Paskaljević's* *Bure baruta/Powder Keg* (1998). The experiences of displacement that many people from former Yugoslavia lived through were the subject of various works which looked at diasporas in the making, like Zoran Solomun's *Müde Weggefähren/Tired Companions* (1997), set in Germany, Gregor Nicholas's *Broken English* (1996), set in New Zealand, and Goran Paskaljević's *Tudja Amerika/Someone Else's America* (1995), set in the US.

In documentaries, of which there are over 200, the Balkan crisis attracted the attention of internationally renowned film-makers, such as French veterans, Chris Marker who made the thirty-minute long, *Le 20 heures dans les camps/Prime Time in the Camps* (1993) and Marcel Ophuls who made the four-hour-long post-modern documentary collage *Veillées d'armes: Histoire du journalisme en temps de guerre/The Troubles We Have Seen: A History of Journalism in Wartime* (1994). The best-known documentary is the international Western TV co-production in four parts *Yugoslavia: Death of a Nation* (1995) which used a large variety of documentary sources and featured interviews with most of the main political figures in the conflict. Documentaries were made by well-known public intellectuals whose usual domain is the written word, like French, Bernard-Henri Lévy with *Bosna!* (1994) and Canadian, Michael Ignatieff with *Blood and Belonging, Part I: The Road to Nowhere* (1993). *Truth under Siege* (1995, Natalie Borgers and Leslie Asako Gladsjo, Fr./US) tackled the workings of independent media across former Yugoslavia. Some displaced Yugoslav directors returned from exile to make films, like Serb Radovan Tadić who came from France to shoot *Les vivants et les morts de Sarajevo/Living and Dead in Sarajevo* (1993), while some other Yugoslav directors had to go into exile to complete their films, like Croatian, Lordan Zafranović* who finished his *Decline of the Century* (1995) only after leaving for the Czech Republic in 1992. Critical voices from within Yugoslavia came up with specific mock-documentaries which mixed fact and fiction and used re-enactment, such as the hilarious production of Studio B 92, Želimir Žilnik's *Tito Among the Serbs for a Second Time* (1993). The topic of the largest number of films was Sarajevo.

Death in Sarajevo (1995, Haris Prolić) was one of over seventy shorts which explored the city's ordeal. While being systematically destroyed, the city was perpetually revived in the works of the Sarajevo Group of Authors (SaGA)* who chronicled the agony and the proud survival of the city on a day-to-day basis. Films were made also by many foreign documentary-makers like British, *Urbicide: A Sarajevo Diary* (1993, Dom Rotheroe) or the Australian, *Exile to Sarajevo* (1996, Tahir Cambis). DI

Bib: James Gow, Richard Paterson and Alison Preston, *Bosnia by Television* (1996).

YUTKEVICH, Sergei I.   St Petersburg 1904 – Moscow 1985

Soviet director and writer, who graduated from Meyerhold's theatre workshop and, with Sergei Eisenstein*, produced a number of stage shows for Foregger's studio, before joining the 'Blue Blouse' travelling theatre troupe. He was co-founder, with Leonid Trauberg* and Grigori Kozintsev*, of FEKS in 1922. His first involvement in cinema was with the eccentric comedy *Daësh' radio!/Give Us Radio!* (1924). His first features attempted to combine FEKS circus techniques with a degree of social comment, as in *Kruzheva/Lace* (1928) and *Chërnyi parus/The Black Sail* (1929), while *Zlatye gory/The Golden Hills* (1931) developed individual characters and marked a transition culminating in Yutkevich's first sound film, *Vstrechnyi/Counterplan* (1932), made with Fridrikh Ermler*. He went on to direct a number of historical biographical films, such as *Yakov Sverdlov* (1940), *Przewalski* (1952) and *Skanderbeg* (1954), but he is probably most remembered for a series of films about Lenin, from *Chelovek s ruzh'ëm/The Man with a Gun* (1938) – starring Maxim Strauch* and Mikhail Gelovani* as Lenin and Stalin respectively – through *Rasskazy o Lenine/Tales of Lenin* (1958) and *Lenin v Pol'she/Lenin in Poland* (1966), to *Lenin v Parizhe/Lenin in Paris* (1981). At the same time Yutkevich continued to stage plays, including the works of Mayakovsky and Blok. In 1962 he directed an animated film version of Mayakovsky's *Banya/The Bathhouse*. He chaired the commission that oversaw the publication of Eisenstein's writings, wrote a number of articles and books on cinema, including the main Soviet cinema encyclopedias, and taught at VGIK* from 1929. RT

Z

ZAGREB SCHOOL OF ANIMATION

Yugoslav animation movement attached to the 'Studio for animation' of the Croatian film production company Zagreb Film. The name was suggested in the late 1950s by French critics Georges Sadoul and André Martin to describe a coherent movement that began to attract festival audiences around the world. Although they did not constitute an institution as such, the animators shared a certain philosophy: experiment and abstract animation were combined with themes of alienation and dehumanisation. The films of Nedeljko Dragić – such as *Idu dani/The Days Are Passing* (1969), *Tup-tup* (1972) and *Dnevnik/Diary* (1974) – show most clearly the harmony between the simplicity of the drawings and the complexity of the message. Another film-maker of great expressive power is Vladimir Kristl (*Don Kihot/Don Quixote*, 1961), who left Croatia in 1962 to work in Germany (*Prometheus*, 1966). The achievements of the Zagreb school were reflected in an Oscar for Dušan Vukotić's *Surogat/The Substitute* in 1962 and the organisation of the first World Festival of Animation in Zagreb in 1970 (one of four major international animation festivals). Among other animators of the school are Vatroslav Mimica, Borivoj Dovniković, Nedeljko Dragić, Pavao Štalter, Zdenko Gašparović and Joško Marušić. SP

Bib: Ron Holloway, *Z is for Zagreb* (1972).

ZAFRANOVIĆ,Lordan
Maslinica, Yugoslavia (now Croatia) 1944

Yugoslav director of Croatian origin, now in the Czech Republic. Zafranović studied at FAMU* and was a member of the Yugoslav Prague Group. His films challenge the deepest foundations of nationalism and question the justification of historical violence. His masterpiece *Okupacija u 26 slika/Occupation in 26 Scenes* (1977), set in Dubrovnik and shot by Karpo Godina*, explored the confrontation of three former friends – a Croat, an Italian, and a Jew – who end up on opposite sides after the fascist regime is established in Croatia. Zafranović's preoccupation with this most awkward and violent period of Croatian history continued through films such as *Pad Italije/The Fall of Italy* (1981), and *Krv i pepeo Jasenovca/Blood and Ashes of Jasenovac* (1983). The highlights of Zafranović's work during the 1980s were the erotic drama, *Ujed andjela/An Angels' Bite* (1984) and *Vecernja zvona/Evening Bells* (1986), set during World War II. Disapproving of the new Croatian nationalism in the 1990s, Zafranović settled in Prague where he completed his epic documentary *Decline of the Century: The Testament of L. Z.* (1994), a personal treatment of Croatia's history which was found too controversial by the Tudjman regime. In the Czech Republic, Zafranović made the Prague-set contemporary drama, *Ma je pomsta/Vengeance Is Mine* (1995), the story of a man in mid-life crisis who gradually loses control over his personal affairs. DI

Other Films Include: *Kronika jednog zlocina/Chronicle of a Crime* (1973); *Rad zida grad/Labour Builds the City* (1974); *Muke po Mati/Passion According to Matthew* (1974); *Gosti i radnici/Guests and Workers* (1976); *Slobodna interpretacija/Freedom of Interpretation* (1979); *Haloa – praznik kurvi/Haloa – Hookers' Holiday* (1988).

ZAHARIEV, Eduard   Moscow, Russia 1938–96

Bulgarian director. Better known for his satirical comedies, although equally respected as a director of perceptive documentaries. Upon graduating in 1961 from the Budapest Academy of Theatre and Film Art, Zahariev returned to Bulgaria to work in the Documentary Newsreel Film Studio in Sofia. His style of dramatising labour and industry themes won him immediate recognition in the documentary field for *Relsi v nebeto/Rails in the Sky* (1962), *Skok/Leap* (1965), *Sol/Salt* (1965), *Stomana/Steel* (1971), and *BDŽ/Bulgarian State Railways* (1972). But when two of his provocative fiction-documentaries – *Ako ne ide vlak/If the Train Doesn't Arrive* (1967), made in collaboration with satirist scriptwriter Georgi Mišev*, and *Nebeto nad Veleka/The Sky over the Veleka* (1968) – irritated the authorities at the Documentary Studio (*Nebeto na Veleka* was banned shortly after release), he transferred his allegiance to the feature film department at Boyana* Studios. Collaborating again with Mišev, he made two of the most successful comedies in Bulgarian film history: *Prebrojavane na divite zajci/The Hare Census* (1973) and *Vilna zona/Villa Zone* (1974), both starring popular deadpan comic actor Itzhak Finci as a socialist petit bourgeois and both the recipients of major festival awards at, respectively, Locarno and Karlovy Vary*. Zahariev's *Mǎžki vermena/Manly Times* (1977), a stolen-bride mountain tale made in collaboration with writer Nikolai Haitov*, established him as one of Bulgaria's most popular film directors. Zahariev's work in the 1980s was dominated by interest in moral issues and belongs to the wider East European trend of 'cinema of moral concern'. He died during post-production of his last feature, *Zaskasnialo palnolunie/Belated Full Moon* (1997). The film, which deals with the drab realities and the prevailing moral crisis of post-communism, was completed by his crew and presented at the Toronto Film Festival. RH

Other Films Include: *Pochti lyubovna istoriya/Nearly a Love Story* (1979); *Elegia/Elegy* (1982); *Skapa moya, skapi moy/My Darling, My Dear* (1985); *Reservat/Reserve* (1991).

ŽANDOV, Zahari
Ruse, Bulgaria 1911–98

Bulgarian director. The father of the postwar Bulgarian documentary and the director of the breakthrough feature film in Bulgarian cinema. Although over fifty feature films had already been made in Bulgaria before the then documentary film-maker Žandov was assigned to direct *Trevoga/Alarm* (1951), this adaptation of a play by Socialist Realist* dramatist Orlin Vasiliev is generally recognised as the birth of a new national cinematography. One of the older generation of Bulgarian film-makers who learnt their trade before World War II, Žandov first made his mark abroad at international film festivals with humanistic documentaries and short films, for instance *Edin den v Sofia/A Day in Sofia* (1946) and *Hora sred oblacite/Men amid the Clouds* (1947), the latter about weather stations and winner of the First Prize at the Venice festival. Žandov also collaborated with documentarist Joris Ivens as his cameraman on the Bulgarian episode of *Pierwsze Lata/The First Years* (1949), a co-production with several East European countries including the USSR.

Although restricted in its artistic expression by the schematic formula of the personality cult, *Trevoga* possessed a documentary freshness in its portrayal of the anti-fascist struggle in 1944. Žandov had the good fortune to collaborate with talented screenwriter Angel Wagenstein* on both *Trevoga* and *Septemvrijci/Septembrists* (1954), but he was not as fortunate thereafter – until he made *Bojanskijat majstor/Master of Boyana* (1981), the first of a series of historical epics celebrating the 1,300th anniversary of the founding of the Bulgarian state. The film drew its visual strength from the renowned frescoes painted by an unknown artist in Boyana church near Sofia in 1259. RH

ZANUSSI, Krzysztof
Warsaw 1939

Polish director and producer. Zanussi studied physics and philosophy and was active in the amateur film movement before graduating from Łódź* in 1966. His feature debut, *Struktura Kryształu/The Structure of Crystals* (1969), looked at the problems and complexes facing the Polish intelligentsia, and their social marginalisation. It also prefigured themes that would soon typify the 'cinema of moral unrest': decline in moral and cultural values, breakdown of relationships, and the compromises of everyday life. Both *Struktura Kryształu* and *Iluminacja/ Illumination* (1973) were important landmarks in Polish cultural life of the period. In offering a bleak and depressing picture of the individual's prospects in 1970s Poland, Zanussi was speaking to a generation who felt constrained and cut off from the rest of the world. His filmic exploration of philosophical and moral questions proved popular in European and American art-house circles and he established co-production links with Germany, France, America and Britain. This allowed him to continue working throughout the difficult climate of the 1980s, although he remained based in Poland. Using international casts and locations, in films like *Rok Spokojnego Słonca/The Year of the Quiet Sun* (1985), Zanussi looked at the difficult choices faced by individuals in times of war and social crisis.

A strong participant in the restructuring of the cinema industry since 1989, Zanussi heads the successful Tor film unit, acting as producer as well as director. His 1990 feature, *Dotknięcie/The Silent Touch*, stars Max von Sydow as a classical composer and alcoholic Holocaust victim who is coaxed back to creativity by a mysterious young man. Since the 1978 election of Polish Karol Woytila as Pope John Paul II, Zanussi displayed a significant involvement with Catholicism. In 1998 he even adapted for the screen an early play by Woytila, *Brat naszego boga/Our God's Brother*. AW

Other Films Include: *Barwy Ochronne/Camouflage* (1977); *Constans/ The Constant Factor* (1980); *Der Unerreichbare/The Inaccessible* (1982, Ger.); *Stan Posiadania/The State of Possession* (1989); *Cwal/In Full Gallop* (1996).

ZAORSKI, Janusz

Warsaw 1947

Polish director. Zaorski graduated from Łódź* in 1969 and worked in television. He made his first feature, *Uciec Jak Najbliżej/Run Away Nearby* (1972), at the age of twenty-five. The same year, he submitted a script to the Central Office of Cinematography for *Matka Królów/ Mother of Kings* but had to wait until 1980, and the help of Andrzej Wajda's* 'X' unit, to film it. *Matka Królów*, released in 1982, is the epic tale of the life of a Polish woman and her four sons between 1933 and 1956. It is based on a book by Kazimierz Brandys, who was unpopular with the authorities, and perhaps for this reason, as well as the frank portrayal of life under communism, the film was shelved. Zaorski continued to work, however, and in 1986 initiated a ninth Polish film unit, Dom, headed by himself. Dom has made a reasonable transition to privatisation, producing documentaries and features for cinema and the expanding television market. AW

Other Films Include: *Awans/Advance* (1975); *Pokój z Widokiem na Morze/Room with a Sea View* (1977); *Baryton/Baritone* (1985); *Jezioro Bodeńskie/Boden Lake* (1986); *Piłkarski Poker/Football Poker* (1988); *Panny i wdowy/Maidens and Widows* (1990); *Szczesliwego Nowego Jorku/Merry Christmas and a Happy New York* (1997).

ŽELJAZKOVA, Binka
Slivengrad 1923

Bulgarian director. A prominent member of the Bulgarian 'new wave' of the late 1950s and early 1960s. After graduating in 1953 from the Sofia Academy of Dramatic Art (VITIS), Binka Željazkova worked as assistant director on Anton Marinovič's *Rebro Adamovo/Adam's Rib* (1956). With the coming of the 'thaw', she co-directed, with her scriptwriter husband Hristo Ganev, *Partizani (Životăt si teče tiho)/Partisans (Life Flows Quietly by)* (1958, banned for thirty years, released 1988). The pair then 'redeemed' themselves with the authorities with the poetic *A byahme mladi/We Were Young* (1961), directed by Željazkova from a script by Ganev and based on autobiographical experiences in the resistance movement. Her next film, *Privărzanijat balon/The Attached Balloon* (1967), shelved shortly after release and also banned until 1988, was the last high-water mark in Bulgarian cinema before Socialist Realism* was restored at Boyana* Studios. A political fairy tale adapted for the screen by writer Jordan Radičkov* from his own story, it deals with a group of villagers who dream of climbing into a giant balloon and thus, in an allegorical sense, escaping from the bonds of Stalinist ideology. Although her subsequent films were all politically oriented, none was to attain the same political immediacy and stylistic standards set by *Privărzanijat balon*. Nevertheless, her commitment to film at personal risk to her career won her praise and respect as one of the most important film-makers in Eastern Europe. During the 1980s Željazkova grew preoccupied with the gap between the younger consumer-oriented generation and the ageing group of devoted idealist communists, to which she herself belonged. Three films – *Baseynat/The Swimming Pool* (1977), *Golyamoto noshtno kupane/The Big Night Bath* (1980), and *Noshtem po pokrivite/On the Roofs at Night* (1988) – were scripted by Ganev and were well received. In the 1990s Žheljazkova made two impressive socially-committed documentaries tackling the problems of female prisoners. RH

ZEMAN, Karel
Ostroměř [then Austria-Hungary] 1910 –
Prague 1989

Czech director of animated films. In the 1930s, Zeman worked as a poster designer and artist with various advertising agencies in Paris. In 1943 he joined the Baťa Film Studios and, after becoming assistant to Hermína Týrlová, began directing in 1946. He is noted for making perhaps the largest number of feature-length animated films anywhere, including *Cesta do pravěku/A Journey to Primeval Times* (1955), *Vynález zkázy/An Invention for Destruction* (1958), *Baron Prášil/Baron Münchhausen* (1961), and *Bláznova kronika/A Jester's Tale* (1964). With its blend of graphic illustration, special effects and live action, his work recalls the conjuror's world of Georges Méliès*. In

Vynález zkázy, adapted from Jules Verne, and *Baron Prášil*, from Bürger, he based his graphic design on illustrations from the original novels. PH

Other Films Include: *Ukradená vzducholoď/The Stolen Airship* (1966); *Na kometě/On a Comet* (1970); *Pohádky tisíce a jedné noci/Tales of a Thousand and One Nights* (1974); *Čarodějův učeň/The Magician's Apprentice* (1977); *Pohádka o Honzíkovi a Mařence/The Tale of Honzík and Mařenka* (1980).

ZILNIK, Zelimir
Nis, Yugoslavia 1942

Yugoslav director of Serbian origin. Zilnik's highly original works, mostly docudramas, re-enacted documentaries and provocative features, have secured him a unique position within Yugoslavian cinema. Zilnik is a master of subversive film-making. His radical-liberal political orientation and daring explorations of social taboos make him somewhat comparable to Makavejev*, maybe even bolder. Zilnik studied law and entered film-making as maker of amateur documentaries. His critical approach and gritty visuals were first appreciated internationally in the late 1960s. His documentary, *Nezaposleni Ijudi/The Unemployed* (1968) won at Oberhausen, and his experimental feature, *Rani radovi/Early Works* (1969) won the Grand Prix at the Berlin Film Festival. Shot by Karpo Godina* and named after the Hegelian writings of Marx, *Early Works* is considered a prime example of the Yugoslav 'Black Wave'*. At home, Zilnik was subjected to ideological scrutiny. *Early Works* and his subsequent *Sloboda ili strip/Freedom of Cartoons* (1972) were censored and banned, as was his documentary, *Lipanjska gibanja/June Turmoil* (1969), which dealt with the awkward subject of student dissent. In the 1970s Zilnik worked in exile in Germany, making a number of independent leftist documentaries and was once again subjected to censorship, this time by the Germans. Back in Yugoslavia, in the 1980s, Zilnik worked on a number of made-for-television documentaries on a variety of socially-sensitive topics. His black comedy, *Tako se kalio celik/How the Steel was Tempered* (1988) revealed the disastrous state where underground personal economies flourished within state socialism. In the 1990s, Zilnik became an outspoken critic of nationalism and worked on a number of dissident productions realised jointly with Belgrade's Studio B 92. His internationally acclaimed 'mockumentary' *Tito po drugi put medju srbima/Tito among the Serbs for a Second Time* (1993) questions Tito's personality cult. In this film, Zilnik lets a well-known Tito impersonator spend a few hours on the sidewalks of Milosevic's Belgrade wearing the Marshall's uniform and pretending that Tito has come back to life. By subverting the conventions of the documentary genre, Zilnik critically challenges many of the popular myths of Yugoslavia's historical destiny. In this next *Dupe Od Mramora/Marble Ass* (1995), Zilnik attacks Serbian machismo by featuring a male prostitute who claims that by enduring the sometimes excessive passions of his lovers he in fact diverts the violence which otherwise would affect society at large. Zilnik's *Kud plovi ovaj brod/Wanderlust* (1998) critically examines the developments that the Eastern Bloc underwent during the first decade of post-communism through the fates of common people across Central Eastern Europe and the Balkans. DI

Other Films Include: *Zurnal o omladini na selu zimi/Newsreel on Village Youth, in Winter* (1967); *Pioniri maleni, mi samo vojska prava, svakog dana nicemo ko zelena trava/Little Pioneers* (1967); *Crni film/Black Film* (1970); *Zene dolaze/The Women Are Coming* (1971); *Ustanak u jasku/The Uprising in Jazak* (1972); *Öffentliche Hinrichtung/Public Execution* (1975); *Unter Denkmalschutz/Protected Heritage* (1975); *Das Paradies: eine imperialistische Tragikomödie/ Paradise: An Imperialist Tragicomedy* (1976); *Druga generacija/The Second Generation* (1983); *Lijepe zene prolaze kroz grad/Pretty Women Walking through Town* (1986).

Bibliography

Andrew, Geoff, *The 'Three Colours' Trilogy* (London: BFI, 1998)

Attwood, Lynne (ed.), *Red Women on the Silver Screen: Soviet Women and Cinema from the Beginning to the End of the Communist Era* (London: Pandora, 1993)

Avisar, Ilan, *Screening the Holocaust: Cinema's Images of the Unimaginable* (Bloomington: Indiana University Press, 1988)

Beumers, Birgit (ed.), *Russia on Reels: The Russian Idea in Post-Soviet Cinema* (London and New York: Tauris, 1999)

Beumers, Birgit, *Burnt By the Sun* (London and New York: Tauris, 2000)

Biró, Yvette, *Miklós Jancsó* (Paris: Editions Albatros, 1977)

Blazevski, Vladimir (ed.), *Dusan Makavejev: 300 Cuda* (Belgrade: Studenski kulturni centar, 1988)

Bren, Frank, *World Cinema 1: Poland* (London: Flicks Books, 1986)

Brossard, Jean-Pierre, *Aspects Nouveaux du Cinéma bulgare* (Chaux-de-Fonds: Cinédiff, 1986)

Burns, B., *World Cinema: Hungary* (Cranbury, NJ: Farleigh Dickinson UP, 1996)

Christie, Ian and Julian Graffy (eds), *Protazanov and the Continuity of Russian Cinema* (London: BFI/NFT, 1993)

Coates, Paul (ed.), *Lucid Dreams: The Films of Krzysztof Kieślowski* (Trowbridge: Flicks Books, 1999)

Coates, Paul, *The Story of the Lost Reflection: The Alienation of the Image in Western and Polish Cinema* (London: Verso, 1985)

Durgnat, Raymond, *W. R.: Mysteries of the Organism* (London: BFI, 1999)

Esteve, Michel and Yvette Biro, *Krzysztof Kieślowski* (Paris: Lettres Modernes, 1994)

Falkowska, Janina, *The Political Films of Andrzej Wajda: Dialogism in* Man of Marble, Man of Iron, *and* Danton (Providence and Oxford: Berghahn Books, 1996)

Forman, Miloš and Jan Novák, *Turnaround: A Memoir* (New York: Villard Books, 1994)

Garbowski, Christopher, *Krzysztof Kieślowski's Decalogue series: the problem of the protagonists and their self-transcendance* (Boulder, CO: East European Monographs, 1996)

Gencheva, Galina, *Bulgarian Feature Films: An Annotated Filmography: Volume II (1948–1970)*, Bulgarian National Cinema-theque (Sofia: Petar Beron State Publishing House, 1988)

Goulding, Daniel, *Liberated Cinema: The Yugoslav Experience* (Bloomington and Indianapolis: Indiana University Press, 1985)

Goulding, Daniel (ed.), *Post New-Wave Cinema in the Soviet Union and Eastern Europe* (Bloomington: Indiana University Press, 1989)

Goulding, Daniel (ed.), *Five Filmmakers: Tarkovski, Forman, Polanski, Szabó, Makavejev* (Bloomington: Indiana University Press, 1995)

Gow, James, Richard Paterson and Alison Preston (eds), *Bosnia by Television* (London: BFI, 1996)

Grbić, Bogdan, Gabriel Loidot and Rossen Milev (eds), *Die Siebte Kunst auf dem Pulverfass: Balkan-Film* (Graz: Blimp, 1995)

Hames, Peter, *The Czechoslovak New Wave* (Berkeley: University of California Press, 1985)

Hames, Peter (ed.), *Dark Alchemy: The Films of Jan Švankmajer* (Westport, CT: Praeger, 1995)

Harászty, Miklós, *The Velvet Prison* (New York: Noonday Press, 1987)

Holloway, Ronald, *The Bulgarian Cinema* (London and Toronto: Associated University Press, 1986)

Holloway, Ronald, 'Slovenian Film: Slovenian Post-war Cinema, 1945–1985', *Kino: Special Issue* 1985 with Cleveland Cinémathèque, Berlin

Holloway, Ronald, 'Bulgaria: The Cinema of Poetics', in *Post New Wave Cinema in the Soviet Union and Eastern Europe* (Bloomington: Indiana University Press, 1989)

Holloway, Ronald, 'Macedonian Film: A History of Macedonian Cinema, 1905–1996', *Kino: Special Issue* 1996 with Cinémathèque of Macedonia, Berlin

Horton, Andrew and Mikhail Brashinsky, *The Zero Hour: Glasnost and Soviet Cinema in Transition* (Princeton: Princeton University Press, 1992)

Johnson, Vida and Graham Petrie, *The Films of Andrei Tarkovsky: A Visual Fugue* (Bloomington: Indiana University Press, 1994)

Kenez, Peter, *Cinema and Soviet Society, 1917–1953* (Cambridge: Cambridge University Press, 1992)

Kieślowski, Krzysztof and Krzysztof Piesiewicz, *Decalogue: the Ten Commandments*, trans. Phil Cavendish and Suzannah Bluh, Foreword by Stanley Kubrick (London: Faber, 1991)

Lawton, Anna, *Kinoglasnost: Soviet Cinema in our Time* (Cambridge: Cambridge University Press, 1992)

Liehm, Antonin J., *Miloš Forman's Stories* (New York: International Arts and Sciences Press, 1975)

Liehm, M. and A. Liehm, *The Most Important Art: Soviet and East European Film after 1945* (Berkeley: University of California Press, 1977)

Mayne, Judith, *Kino and the Woman Question: Feminism and Soviet Silent Film* (Columbus: Ohio State University Press, 1989)

Michalek, Boleslaw, *The Cinema of Andrzej Wajda* (London: The Tantivy Press, 1973)

Michalek, Boleslaw and Frank Turaj, *Modern Cinema of Poland* (Bloomington: Indiana University Press, 1988)

Murri, Serafino, *Krzysztof Kieślowski* (Milano: Il Castoro, 1997)

O'Grady, Gerald (ed.), *Makavejev Fictionary: The Films of Dusan Makavejev* (Boston/New York: Harvard Film Archive/American Museum of the Moving Picture/Film and the Public, Spring 1995)

Pangon, Gerard, *Andrzej Wajda* (Paris: Editions Mille et une nuits, 1997)

Pangon, Gerard and Vincent Amiel, *Krzysztof Kieślowski* (Paris: Editions Payot & Rivages, 1997)

Passek, Jean-Loup and Zoran Tasic, *Le Cinéma Yugoslave* (Paris: Centre Pompidou, 1986)

Paul, David (ed.), *Politics, Art and Commitment in the East European Cinema* (New York: St. Martin's Press, 1983)

Petrie, Graham, *History Must Answer to Man (The Contemporary Hungarian Cinema)* (Budapest: Corvina Kiadó, 1978)

Petrie, Graham and Ruth Dwyer, *Before the Wall Came Down: Soviet and East European Filmmakers Working in the West* (Lanham, MD: University Press of America, 1990)

Petrie, Graham, *Red Psalm* (Trowbridge: Flicks Books, 1998)

Portuges, Catherine, *Screen Memories: the Hungarian Cinema of Márta Mészáros* (Indianapolis: Indiana University Press, 1993)

Roberts, Graham, *Forward, Soviet! History and Non-fiction Film in the USSR* (London and New York: Tauris, 1999)

Roberts, Graham, *The Man with the Movie Camera* (London and New York: Tauris, 2000)

Skvorecky, Josef, *All the Bright Young Men and Women: A Personal History of the Czech Cinema* (Toronto: Peter Martin Associates, 1971)

Slater, Thomas J., *Miloš Forman: A Bio-bibliography* (New York: Greenwood Press, 1987)

Slater, Thomas J. (ed.), *Handbook of Soviet and East European Films and Filmmakers* (New York: Greenwood Press, 1992)

Stoil, M. J., *Cinema beyond the Danube: the camera and the politics* (New Jersey: Scarecrow Press, 1973)

Stoil, M. J., *Balkan Cinema: Evolution after the Revolution* (Ann Arbor: UMI Research Press, 1982)

Stok, Danusia (ed.), *Kieślowski on Kieślowski* (London: Faber, 1993)

Tarkovsky, Andrei, *Sculpting in Time: Reflections on the Cinema* (London: Bodley Head, 1986)

Tarkovsky, Andrei, *Andrei Rublëv* (London: Faber, 1991)

Tarkovsky, Andrei, *Time within Time: The Diaries 1970–1986* (London: Faber, 1994)

Tarkovski, Andrei, *Collected Screenplays* (London: Faber, 1999)

Taylor, Richard, *The Politics of the Soviet Cinema 1917–1929* (Cambridge: Cambridge University Press, 1979)

Taylor, Richard (ed. and trans.), *S. M. Eisenstein: Selected Works. Volume I: Writings, 1922–34* (London: BFI, 1988)

Taylor, Richard (ed.), *S. M. Eisenstein: Selected Works. Volume IV: Beyond the Stars: The Memoirs of Sergi Eisenstein* (London: BFI, 1995)

Taylor, Richard (ed.), *S. M. Eisenstein: Selected Works. Volume III: Writings, 1934–47* (London: BFI, 1996)

Taylor, Richard, *Film Propaganda: Soviet Russia and Nazi Germany* (2nd revised edn, London and New York: Tauris, 1998)

Taylor, Richard (ed.), *The Eisenstein Reader* (London: BFI, 1998)

Taylor, Richard and Ian Christie (eds), *The Film Factory: Russian and Soviet Cinema in Documents 1896–1939* (London: Routledge, 1988; pbk edn 1994)

Taylor, Richard and Ian Christie (eds), *Inside the Film Factory: New Approaches to Russian and Soviet Cinema* (London: Routledge, 1991)

Taylor, Richard and Michael Glenny (eds), *S. M. Eisenstein: Selected Works. Volume II: Towards a Theory of Montage* (London: BFI, 1991)

Taylor, Richard and Derek Spring (eds), *Stalinism and Soviet Cinema* (London and New York: Routledge, 1993)

Vincenti, Giorgio de (ed.), Yugoslavia: *Il Cinema dell'Autogestione* (Venice: Marsillo, 1982)

Wajda, Andrzej, *Double Vision: My Life in Film* (New York: Henry Holt and Company, 1986)

Wexman, Virginia Wright, *Roman Polanski* (Boston, MA: Twayne, 1985)

Woll, Josephine, *Real Images: Soviet Cinema and the Thaw* (London and New York: Tauris, 2000)

Youngblood, Denise, *Movies for the Masses: Popular Cinema and Soviet Society in the 1920s* (Cambridge: Cambridge University Press, 1992)

Youngblood, Denise, *The Magic Mirror: Moviemaking in Russia 1908–1918* (Madison: University of Wisconsin Press, 1999)

Chapters/articles

Eagle, Herbert, 'Andrzej Wajda: Film Language and the Artist's Truth', in *Cross Currents: A Yearbook of Central European Culture* (Ann Arbor: University of Michigan, 1982), pp. 339–53.

Galik, Mihaly, 'Who Laughs Last. Film and Broadcasting in Hungary', in Peter Boorsma, Annemoon van Hemel and Niki van der Wielen (eds), *Privatization and Culture* (Boston-Dordrecht-London: Kluwer Academic Publishers, 1998), pp. 131–41.

Graffy, Julian, 'Cinema', in Catriona Kelly and David Shepherd (eds), *Russian Cultural Studies* (Oxford: Oxford University Press, 1998), pp. 165–91.

Goban-Klas, Tomasz, 'Politics versus
the Media in Poland; A Game
Without Rules', in Patrick O'Neil
(ed.), *Post-Communism and the
Media in Eastern Europe* (London
and Portland, OR: Frank Cass,
1997), p. 26.
Horton, Andrew, 'The Mouse That
Wanted to F—k a Cow', in Andrew
Horton (ed.),
Comedy/Cinema/Theory (Berkeley:
University of California Press,
1991), pp. 222–39.
Horton, Andrew, ' "Only Crooks Can
Get Ahead": Post-Yugoslav
Cinema/TV/Video in the 1990s', in
Sabrina Petra Ramet and Ljubisa S.
Adamovic (eds), *Beyond
Yugoslavia: Politics, Economics and
Culture in a Shattered Community*
(Boulder, CO: Westview Press,
1995), pp. 413–31.
Iordanova, Dina, 'Kusturica's
Underground (1995): Historical
Allegory or Propaganda', *Historical
Journal of Film, Radio and TV*, vol.
19, no. 1, 1999, pp. 69–86.
Iordanova, Dina, 'Balkan Film
Representations since 1989: The
Quest for Admissibility', *Historical
Journal of Film, Radio and TV*, vol.
18, no. 2, 1998, pp. 263–80.
Iordanova, Dina, 'Canaries and Birds
of Prey: The New Season of
Bulgarian Cinema', in John Bell
(ed.), *Bulgaria in Transition*
(Boulder, CO: Westview Press,
1998), pp. 255–81.
Iordanova, Dina, 'Conceptualizing the
Balkans in Film', *Slavic Review*, vol.
55, no. 4, Winter 1996, pp. 882–91.
Iordanova, Dina, 'Women in New
Balkan Cinema: Surviving on the
Margins', *Film Criticism*, vol. XXI,
no. 2, Winter 1996–7, pp. 24–40.
Iordanova, Dina, 'College Course File:
Eastern European Cinema', *Journal
of Film and Video*, vol. 51, no. 1,
Spring 1999, pp. 56–77.
Makavejev, Dušan, 'Film Censorship in
Yugoslavia', *Film Comment*,
Jul.–Aug. 1975.

Portuges, Catherine, 'Border Crossings:
Recent Trends in East and Central
European Cinema', *Slavic Review*
51, no. 3, Fall 1992,
pp. 531–5.
Portuges, Catherine, 'Hidden Subjects,
Secret Identities. Figuring Jews,
Gypsies, and Gender in 1990s
Cinema of Eastern Europe', in
Gisela Brinkler-Gabler and Sidonie
Smith (eds), *Writing New Identities:
Gender, Nation, and Immigration in
Contemporary Europe*
(Minneapolis, MN: University of
Minnesota Press, 1997), pp.
196–215.
Robinson, Homer, 'Freedom Gained
but Funding Lost', *RFE/RL
Research Report*, vol. 2, no. 2, 8 Jan.
1993, pp. 58–61.
Sparks, Colin, 'Post-Communist Media
in Transition', in John Corner,
Philip Schlesinger and Roger
Silverstone (eds), *Inter-national
Media Research. A Critical Survey*
(London and New York: Routledge,
1997), pp. 96–122.
Terziev, Yanko, 'Bulgarian Cinema:
Landscape after the Battle', *Bul-
garian Quarterly*, 1/1992, pp. 48–60.

Other resources
The documentary *A. Wajda, A Portrait*
(1989, d. E. Lachnit).
Dokumentacija za internu upotrebu.
Prepared by Svetozar Udovicki.
Neoplanta film, 1971. A 1,009
mimeo report containing all important documents pertaining to the
controversy over *W. R. – Mysteries
of the Organism.*
Stanimirova, Neda. *Bulgarski kinorezhi-
siori* (Bulgarian Film Directors).
Sofiq Nauka i izkustvo, 1984, pp.
48–86.
Cineaste, vol. XIX, no. 4, 1992.
Film Criticism, vol. XXI, no. 2, Winter
1996–7.
Journal of Film and Video, vol. 44, nos
1–2, Spring–Summer 1992.

288